The Once and Future
Roman Rite

Related books by Peter Kwasniewski

Resurgent in the Midst of Crisis

Noble Beauty, Transcendent Holiness

Tradition and Sanity

Reclaiming Our Roman Catholic Birthright

The Holy Bread of Eternal Life

Ministers of Christ

True Obedience in the Church

The Road from Hyperpapalism to Catholicism

Related books edited by Peter Kwasniewski

Are Canonizations Infallible?

From Benedict's Peace to Francis's War

Newman on Worship, Reverence, and Ritual

And Rightly So: Selected Letters and Articles of Neil McCaffrey

The Once and Future Roman Rite

Returning to the Traditional Latin Liturgy after
Seventy Years of Exile

Peter A. Kwasniewski

Foreword by Martin Mosebach

TAN Books
Gastonia, North Carolina

Excerpts from the English translation of the *Catechism of the Catholic Church* for use in the United States of America © 1994, United States Catholic Conference, Inc.—Libreria Editrice Vaticana. Used with permission.

Scripture quotations are taken from the Douay Rheims Bible, in the public domain, as well as the American Literary Version of the Bible (based on the American Standard Version), copyright © 2016 Writ Press, Inc. in the United States of America. Used with permission.

Cover design by Michael Schrauzer

Cover image: Frontispiece to a 1629 edition of the *Missale Romanum*, published by Cornelius ab Egmondt in Cologne; print by Simon van de Passe, after design of the Monogrammist DVB; public domain image from the Rijksstudio of the Rijksmuseum in Amsterdam

Library of Congress Control Number: 2022939270

ISBN: 978-1-5051-2662-4
Kindle ISBN: 978-1-5051-2663-1
ePUB ISBN: 978-1-5051-2664-8

Published in the United States by
TAN Books
PO Box 269
Gastonia, NC 28053
www.TANBooks.com

Dedicated to all priests who offer the Holy Sacrifice
in communion with the Church of all times
adhering to the Tradition of all ages
yesterday, today, and forever
sacerdotes in aeternum
pro ecclesia et
pro Deo

✠

Quoniam quae perfecisti destruxerunt: iustus autem quid fecit?

For that which Thou hast perfected, they have destroyed; but what has the just man done?

—Psalm 10:4

The pope is not an absolute monarch whose will is law; rather, he is the guardian of the authentic Tradition and, thereby, the premier guarantor of obedience. . . . His rule is not that of arbitrary power, but that of obedience in faith. That is why, with respect to the Liturgy, he has the task of a gardener, not that of a technician who builds new machines and throws the old ones on the junk-pile.

—Joseph Ratzinger

Contents

Publisher's Note

Since our founding in 1967, TAN Books has published works that preserve and promote the spiritual, theological, and liturgical traditions of Holy Mother Church. Our uncompromising mission is to be the publisher you can trust with your faith and to help people become saints. We have published over one thousand titles on traditional devotions, Church doctrine, Church history, the lives of the saints, catechesis, Sacred Scripture, Thomistic theology, and much more. Yet, of them all, our works on the Holy Sacrifice of the Mass—our greatest treasure—are at the heart of TAN Books.

Everything flows from the Holy Sacrifice of the Mass, most especially the Holy Eucharist, the "font and apex of our faith," as defined by the Second Vatican Council itself. In an age of secularism, relativism, ecclesiastical confusion, and growing disbelief in the Real Presence, Catholics must better grasp the roots of our present liturgical crisis. The following work by Dr. Peter Kwasniewski, *The Once and Future Roman Rite*—his *magnum opus* and the fruit of over twenty-five years of research—sheds light on the beauty of the traditional Latin liturgy as practiced by the Church in an unbroken line from early centuries through Pope Pius V and down to our own time, and shows how distinctly it differs from the new liturgy Pope Paul VI promulgated in 1969.

The aim throughout this work has been to articulate a position that is of maximum consistency with Catholic tradition, history, and teaching and which is intellectually honest, even when it leads to conclusions that run against the grain of current thought. TAN Books, in its loyalty to the Church, only publishes books consistent with Church teaching, and has taken measures to ensure that what is opinion and what is dogma are clearly distinguished and stated as such for the reader's ease. The author herein published is, and intends to be, in all of his works, acts, and writings, a loyal son of the Church, and writes as such. The author holds, as do all Catholics, that the Novus Ordo is a valid Mass, in which the Body and Blood of Christ are confected. The opinions expressed in this book are the author's own and should not be equated with the views of TAN Books.

It is our sincere prayer that those who read this book will find their understanding of the Roman Rite deepened, will fall ever more in love with Christ and His Church through a greater love for the Holy Sacrifice of the Mass, and will grow in holiness and love of God in their daily pursuit of what the Mass points to: union with God forever in heaven.

Foreword

Few things are total and absolute failures. On this earth, what is right and wrong, good and evil, ugly and beautiful rarely tends to appear unalloyed. Usually, contradictions are mixed up with each other; the discussion revolves around an endless "on the one hand—on the other." Therefore, it makes me uneasy that, for the past fifty years, try as I may, there is nothing that I can find to be praised in Paul VI's reform of the Roman rite's Mass as engineered by Archbishop Bugnini, that master of the *tabula rasa*, not to forget the innumerable unauthorized inventors of liturgy throughout the world. To be fully, intellectually honest, I can't think of anything, even though I distrust myself and in principle can accept as possible that in a matter so personally painful, others may be proven right against me.

At the same time, in a certain way, I am also grateful for Paul VI's gigantic disaster. During the grand enterprise of demolition after 1968, which ruined the structure of the Church that had been preserved up till then through so many dangers—as churches and convents emptied, as altars were turned around and guitars made their appearance in the Mass, and as priests, to the extent that they hadn't abandoned their office, wallowed in liturgical inventions—I had distanced myself greatly from any practice of religion. When, a few years later, I had returned, I was astonished, confronted with the work of destruction accomplished in the meantime.

My membership in the Catholic Church derives from my mother, a native of Cologne. Cologne was once quintessentially Catholic and was called "Holy Cologne" because of its twelve Romanesque churches, all of which have the status of a cathedral and which many connoisseurs view as more important than Cologne Cathedral itself. But as usual in the case of such closed milieus, there was no escaping the Church, especially its temporal authority. Everything belonged to the Church, the Church was involved in all affairs of the city—that wasn't always pleasant. Many people kept a skeptical distance from the Church, above all, the men. In this respect, the Church in Cologne had something in common with Latin culture: church was a woman's affair. If they went to Mass at all, many men came at the consecration and left after the Pater Noster. Too much involvement in church matters was perceived as unmanly. The oldish bachelors who rummaged around in the sacristy were called "holy water frogs."

That was the atmosphere in which I grew up. If the liturgical catastrophe hadn't befallen the Church and the world—for the traditional liturgy always kept its focus on the whole world, or at least on its salvation—in the best case, I would far more likely have remained at a benevolent distance from the Church. At least for me, that sad law has been proved once again, that a good thing must first be mortally threatened in order for its true value to be once more recognized. So, the years of my return to the Church were characterized more and more by the effort to get to know better that which had been lost.

Let me be very specific. In Frankfurt, after a long struggle with a hostile bishop, we managed to have a Mass in the traditional rite celebrated once a month and, later, once a week on workdays, in an ugly chapel in a hotel. (The thousand-year-old churches of my native city were, of course, out of the question.) But then we had to learn from scratch how to serve at the altar. The celebrants appointed by the bishop were likewise uncertain. It soon emerged that the laymen themselves had to find out how to celebrate a Mass *rite et recte* in order to assist the priest. Now I myself had to become a "holy water frog" if a regular celebration was to happen. Either I served at the altar or there was no altar server. My inherited notion of what was compatible with the dignity of a grown man had to be forgotten without further ado. But in so doing, my life experienced an almost limitless enrichment!

A short manual for sacristans with detailed instructions for the liturgy called "Müller-Frei" was very helpful. But it was like the Prussian drill regulations transposed to the liturgy. The little book didn't spend any time on the justification and reinforcement of the individual rubrics. Whoever wanted to ridicule the set of rules for the old liturgy as "rubricism" would find rewarding material in "Müller-Frei." One thing became clear to me: the liturgical catastrophe wasn't just the work of presumptuous prelates who threw together with suspicious haste a protestantizing worship service. Rather, it was preceded by a lack of understanding that had grown up over many decades. Even pious priests often couldn't answer questions about liturgical details. But what a joy it was to discover that such answers did exist and that each one opened a more profound insight into the fundamental coherence of the whole!

And I have never ceased to learn. After nearly forty years of involvement with the traditional Latin liturgy, no year passes in which I do not discover something important, the existence of which I had never suspected—all this, after I had returned to the pews and had left serving at the altar to a crowd of young altar boys all of whom are much more competent than I ever was. That is the great error to which Roman prelates succumb when they imagine that they can now suppress the traditional Roman rite. Anyone, from the moment he has obtained a real understanding of this liturgy, will always remain aware of the many defects of the new rite. There is no going back to a time before this perception. But no one should get into a debate over the "validity" of the new rite. It is valid. Precisely because it is valid (at least when celebrated correctly according to the liturgical books), its obscuring of the divine sacrifice is all the more ignominious.

The struggle for the restoration of the Roman Church's traditional liturgy has several aspects: theological, because it involves preserving the character of the Holy Mass as a sacrifice; political, because the hierarchical structure of the Church is thereby upheld; and aesthetic, because the conviction is thereby defended that the religion of the divine Incarnation demands an expression accessible to the senses. It is a spiritual struggle—but if it only involved the strength and weight of the arguments, it should have been won long ago. For in the face of the disaster the liturgists have created, the powerful party of the reform has lost the drive to defend its work. It relies now entirely on foolish legal positivism: "the Church has taken another path; the changes are irreversible; it's simply this way now, one must submit." It does no injustice to the current prefect of the Congregation for Divine Worship to summarize his instructions in this manner.

In this liturgical battle, it's not just a matter of defeating a perverse ideology and theology and so, in the end, of prevailing in the clash of arguments.

The Roman liturgy, which we may call "divine" with the same right as the Orthodox—perhaps we should get used to doing so—connects the natural and the supernatural. Its cause will not endure if it does not experience supernatural confirmation. Saints are such a confirmation. The movement for preserving the traditional rite will succeed only if it produces saints. As I write this, I am terrified, but it's of no use; this insight is nothing other than a spiritual law. In the past, we can absolutely name saintly protectors of the Roman liturgy. At their head is certainly Pope Saint Gregory the Great, who did not at all invent these rites but reverently organized them. His heirs are all those who celebrate the traditional Mass today. We should next remember Saint John Damascene, who fought against the iconoclasm of Constantinople. The twentieth-century reforms not only were accompanied by a new wave of iconoclasm but dared to damage the greatest icon of all: the Holy Sacrifice of the Mass. Saint John Damascene is, in addition, connected with the "Feast of the Triumph of Orthodoxy" celebrated in the Orthodox world on every first Sunday of Lent; this feast can be a model for the Catholic hope for the "restoration of the orthodox liturgy."

During the Reformation in Germany, England, and France, there certainly were martyrs who stood up and suffered not just generally for the Catholic religion but in particular for the liturgy. We have to seek them out in order to call upon their intercession. The fate of the Ruedesheimer vineyard peasants in the late eighteenth century is moving. They resisted the ban on singing Gregorian chant imposed by the "enlightened" bishop of Mainz, and as a result, they were deported and condemned to lengthy imprisonment. Nobody has taken the trouble to pursue their canonization, but one can be sure that their sacrifice was accepted. Also among their number are the priests in German and Russian concentration camps who celebrated the unabbreviated Holy Mass with a couple of smuggled raisins, were betrayed, and had to pay for it with their lives. Then there's the stigmatic Saint Padre Pio, who with the bleeding wounds of Christ became an icon himself and thus made apparent in a unique way the sacrificial character of the Mass. He never celebrated the new Mass, having died shortly before its introduction.

Peter Kwasniewski is not just a bulwark of learning but a man of provocative wit. Thus, he has recently proposed to have the United Nations declare the traditional Roman rite to be part of the world's "intangible cultural heritage."[1] In view of the general cultural destruction by the wars of the twentieth and twenty-first centuries and the often violent reshaping of the entire world by industry and commerce, the concept of the world's cultural heritage is understandable: preserving certain outstanding buildings, landscapes, and traditions at least temporarily from destruction.[2] That which has come down to our threatening present day from the past, which belongs to the traditions of a people and which may also be fruitful in the future, should be removed from the raging torrent of change and the "fury of disappearance" of which the philosopher Hegel spoke. In context, violinmaking in Italian Cremona, Indian Yoga, Cuban Rumba, the Zaouli dance of the Ivory Coast, and the building of Pinisi boats in Indonesia have made this list; doesn't the traditional Catholic liturgy fit in here too? Viewed from a non-Christian perspective, definitely yes! The petition for enrollment in this list would be easy to write. According to the procedure of the United Nations, however, it must be a state which takes an interest in the matter. Would the sovereign state of Vatican City be ready to do this? One sets such value on the magnificent old churches: the basilicas of the first Christian millennium, the Gothic cathedrals, the splendid temples of the Baroque, all of which were built to the smallest details according to the rubrics of the old liturgy; thus, these structures are "built liturgy" and are completely incomprehensible outside of the purpose for which they were made.

At the beginning of the twentieth century, the French state expropriated the country's churches and it seemed that politics influenced by Freemasonry might prohibit the celebration of the Holy Mass in them. The great French novelist Marcel Proust—baptized a Catholic but living as an agnostic—wrote a moving appeal: "La Mort des Cathedrales."[3] If the divine liturgy would be prohibited in the old churches, their architecture would

---

[1]   See Peter Kwasniewski, "The Latin Mass as Intangible Cultural Heritage," *OnePeterFive*, November 24, 2021.

[2]   In fact, at the petitioning of the governments of Greece and Cyprus, UNESCO in 2019 recognized Byzantine chant as part of the intangible cultural heritage of humanity.

[3]   For an English edition with commentary, see Marcel Proust, *Death Comes for the Cathedrals*, trans. John Pepino (Milwaukee, WI: Wiseblood Books, 2021).

be condemned to death as well. He went so far as to demand that the cathedrals be torn down if no more Holy Masses could take place there, since without the liturgy, they would have lost their soul. Connoisseurs travelled to Bayreuth to experience the operas of Wagner, but every Sunday in the cathedrals, a "show" is performed that is far more important than all the operas of Wagner taken together. Oscar Wilde too was enthusiastic for the qualities of the traditional liturgy: it is the only thing that connects the modern age with ancient Greek culture. The many English intellectuals—Agatha Christie was the least among them—who implored Paul VI not to lay hands on the old liturgy argued in a similar vein.[4] What they declared is good and just: indeed, this liturgy gave birth to a major part of European culture. Dante, Cervantes, and Mozart participated in it innumerable times and allowed it to inform their spirit as artists. But more important than Oscar Wilde's pagan antiquity is the amazing continuity with the ancient Jewish temple worship, which lives on in the traditional Roman liturgy and links it to the early history of mankind. Among the many dubious aspects of Paul VI's reform of the Mass was precisely the removal of many Jewish elements from the liturgy. If *anything* deserves the title "world cultural heritage," it is the traditional Roman liturgy.

Yet Kwasniewski's UNESCO proposal is a sardonic joke, not only because he appeals to an entity that is unimaginably removed from any religion, but also because the United Nations nevertheless can muster more understanding for the precious nature of liturgy than the institutions that are charged with protecting it! What this scholar, who has placed his entire life under the sign of the traditional liturgy, knows better than Marcel Proust and Oscar Wilde is that the undeniable beauty and superabundant cultural riches that can be found in the old rites are just external side effects of something that is a mystery for modern aesthetes: the truth. And truth does not need the protection of being housed in a museum but rather demands living witness. The communities dedicated to the old rite have understood this. The pope and his functionaries, on the contrary, with all their arguments (such as they are), don't even seem to approach this reality.

---

[4]   For the declaration and its signatories, see Joseph Shaw, ed., *The Case for Liturgical Restoration* (Brooklyn, NY: Angelico Press, 2019), 213–16.

Thus, for decades now, we have been at cross-purposes. In the conflict over liturgy, the power and the truth stand on different sides. Will the abundance of knowledge, of wisdom, of prayer already brought to bear in favor of the truth of divine liturgy one day tip the scales—will the emptiness of power become obvious? Whoever inclines to pessimism in this regard (for, in principle, so many things argue for that) should ask himself another question: Would he be ready, if the Roman enemies of the traditional liturgy permanently prevail, to acquiesce—to give up the struggle and accept Pope Paul's Novus Ordo? The author of this book has settled this question as it concerns himself; you will find his answer in these pages.

Martin Mosebach
Frankfurt
March 3, 2022

Preface

"The beginning of wisdom is calling things by their proper name."
—Confucius

The heart of the present book is a series of lectures given and articles penned around the time of the fiftieth anniversary (the term "golden" somehow doesn't seem fitting) of the issuance and the going-into-effect of the *Novus Ordo Missae*—that is to say, April 3 and November 30 of the year 1969. As the year 2019 came and went, the anniversaries of these two fateful moments afforded occasions for pondering, for lamentation, for renewed commitment to the great work of restoration. My intention had been to publish a book at the end of 2019, but Divine Providence had other plans for that year—and for the two following as well.

As I continued my liturgical studies, I realized more and more the extent to which the problems routinely identified in the Novus Ordo had been anticipated, both in theory and in practice, for a good many years prior to the work of the committee known as the *Consilium ad exsequendam Constitutionem de sacra Liturgia* ("Consilium" for short) established by Paul VI during the Second Vatican Council. The awareness grew in me that the anniversary book, even if it would focus on the Novus Ordo, needed to look beyond fifty years to the seventy-year "Babylonian captivity" we could symbolically date either from 1948, the year the Pian Commission was established, to 2018, when an unnecessary but courteous permission was first given by the Ecclesia Dei Commission for celebrating the pre-Pacellian Holy Week, *or* from 1951, the year the experimental Easter Vigil was first introduced, to 2021, the year in which it was expected that Rome would give a global wink to those wishing to resume many traditional pre-55 elements. In April of 2021, I wrote the hopeful words: "No express permission is being given, because none is needed for that which is immemorially sacred and great. Catholics of the Latin rite, in small groups, here and there, are returning to the liturgical temple after seventy years of exile."[1]

And then on July 16, 2021 came the motu proprio *Traditionis Custodes* and its accompanying letter, meant to supplant the motu proprio *Summorum Pontificum* and *its* accompanying letter, and on December 18 came the *Responsa ad Dubia* of the Congregation for Divine Worship. I compared *TC* and the *Responsa* to the atom bombs dropped on Hiroshima and Nagasaki.[2] A war to reduce all traditional Catholics to ideological compliance had commenced. In a flash, the entire landscape changed.

What has changed, however, is not exactly what the pope or the curia might have thought would change. Under the influence of old-school ultramontanism, the fumes of which still linger in the gas tanks of the upper hierarchy, it would have been assumed that once the "grand experiment" of "two forms" of the Roman rite running side by side had been declared a failure, all Catholics would rally round the successor of Peter and his trusty curial band. In reality, the reactions of bishops have been decidedly varied, ranging from lockstep compliance to generous dispensations to Carthusian silence, and what is more, laity and lower clergy have been stirred to a white-hot zeal by what nearly the entire world, including the culturally unsympathetic, interpreted as a gratuitous declaration of war being carried out with a punctilious legalism and a heartless rigidity that reeks of hypocrisy when emanating from the prophets of sheep-scented peripherality, Abrahamic dialogue, and limitless mercy to sinners. In short, the traditionalist movement was given its biggest internal boost and greatest advertising campaign in history, with more Catholics becoming aware of the issues at stake than ever before, with evidence of more widespread curiosity, sympathy, and support, and a rekindling of the fervor that characterized the (then much smaller) traditionalist movement in the most difficult period it faced, circa 1969 to 1984.

What does the present book purport to accomplish? In these pages, I demonstrate that there is, in fact, only one Roman rite—and it is not the

---

[1] "Ending Seventy Years of Liturgical Exile: The Return of the Pre-55 Holy Week," *New Liturgical Movement* [*NLM*], April 19, 2021.
[2] See my article "A Supreme Moment of Decision, Courtesy of 'Divine Worship,'" *OnePeterFive*, December 18, 2021.

Novus Ordo, or rather, the Novus Ordo is no true part of it but some other rite entirely. I argue that we have a grave obligation to restore the traditional Latin Mass as the proper and normative Eucharistic rite of the Church of Rome, the *lex orandi* definitively codified by Saint Pius V and received intact by all his successors until the tempestuous twentieth century. In chapter 2, which could be called the core of the work—originally presented as a lecture entitled "Beyond 'Smells and Bells': Why We Need the Objective Content of the *Usus Antiquior*"—I argue that the *Novus Ordo Missae* constitutes a rupture with fundamental elements of all liturgies of apostolic derivation, and that, as a consequence, it violates the Church's solemn obligation to receive, cherish, guard, and pass on the fruits of liturgical development. Since this development is, in fact, a major way in which the Holy Spirit leads the Church into the "fullness of truth" over the ages, as Christ promised, so great a "sin against the Holy Spirit" (as it were) cannot fail to have enormous negative consequences, as indeed the past five decades have verified. Nor is it possible to bridge the abyss between old and new by applying cosmetics or the drapery of elegant clothing, because the problem is on the order of a genetic mutation or damage to internal organs. The profound and permanent solution is to maintain continuity with the living liturgical tradition found in the *usus antiquior*.

Thus expressed, the thesis is hardly novel: I would be a bad traditionalist if I were not following in the footsteps of many predecessors! Decades ago, the German liturgist Klaus Gamber said the new rite could not be called the *ritus Romanus* but had to be called the *ritus modernus*. Michael Davies argued much the same, as did the priests Bryan Houghton, Roger-Thomas Calmel, Raymond Dulac, and Anthony Cekada, among others. One might mention in the same breath the *Short Critical Study*, better known as the "Ottaviani Intervention." Joseph Ratzinger diplomatically chose a different way of speaking but said many things in his pre-papal years that come very close to Gamber's formulation.[3]

---

[3] It was Cardinal Ratzinger's writings that first awakened my sense of wonder at the mystery of the liturgy, my desire to understand what has happened to it in our era, and my zeal for recovering what has been lost. He set me on a path that began with the "true intentions of Vatican II," went on to the Reform of the Reform, stopped briefly at "mutual enrichment" of the "two forms," and ultimately wound its way to an unqualified traditionalism (or restorationism, if you prefer). Of course, in that last leg of the journey, I left Ratzinger behind;

Given that my thesis is by no means unfamiliar, the present book's value consists in furnishing the reader with a convincing, up-to-date presentation of fundamental reasons why traditionalists believe there has been a severe and abidingly harmful rupture in the Latin-rite liturgy of the Catholic Church and why, in response, we advocate an unqualified return to the full tradition. In order to make my case, I show the following:

- that tradition is normative for the Church and for *everyone* in the Church—not excluding, but on the contrary especially for, the pope;
- that it is legitimate to speak of "organic development" in the liturgy, and that we can articulate the laws of said development;
- that with these tools we can distinguish growth from corruption, as Newman did for Christian doctrine (*lex credendi*), and thus protect a divinely-willed tradition (the *lex orandi*) from the tinkering tendencies of antiquarianism and modernism;
- that there are prominent identifying traits to the Roman rite, and indeed to all traditional rites, that are partially or totally absent from the Novus Ordo, thereby estranging it from their company;
- that the liturgical reform as it transpired exhibits traits of nominalism, voluntarism, Protestantism, rationalism, and other distinctly modern errors;
- that the Church is suffering from the influence of a false and dangerous "hyperpapalism" that makes the pope an absolute monarch whose will is law, who may treat the Catholic inheritance as his own possession to modify as he pleases and may compel everyone else to bend to his designs;
- that the defense given of the postconciliar reform by Paul VI proves rather that it should be rejected *tout court*;
- that we ought to recover the Roman rite in its Tridentine plenitude by utilizing editions of liturgical books that do not suffer from the ravages of the ill-considered and temporizing reforms of the mid-1950s and early 1960s;

he seems to have retired at the third station. But I will never cease to be grateful to him for igniting a tremendous enthusiasm in my soul and for accompanying me along the way with his magnificent insights.

- and last but not least, that no special permission is or could ever be required for worshiping God with the Catholic Church's authentic liturgical rites.

Such are the topics covered in this book. The lectures and articles have been extensively revised for their inclusion herein. An appendix contains the full text of three addresses on liturgical reform delivered by Paul VI (commented on in chapter 4), plus a selection of shorter quotations in the same vein. The book ends with the sources of the epigraphs and a select bibliography.

In discussions of this kind, the impression can easily be given that the sole topic of conversation is the Mass. While it is understandable and fitting that the Mass should be the focal point—it is, after all, the central act of worship of the Catholic Church and the "place" where most Catholics "encounter" Christ and His Church—nevertheless the sacred liturgy comprises far more: not only the other six sacramental rites but also the Divine Office, the blessings, the exorcisms, the pontifical rites, and so forth. *All* of these things were changed as dramatically as (and sometimes even more drastically than) the Mass was. The critique in these pages of the *Novus Ordo Missae* is therefore meant to be, *mutatis mutandis*, a critique of all of the new liturgical books issued by Paul VI, for, being products of the same committees driven by the same agendas, they share the same kinds of weaknesses, even as their traditional counterparts, the distillation of over two millennia of prayer (let us not forget the Jewish antecedents), share similar perfections.

The "liturgical establishment" can offer no substantive argument in favor of the Consilium's costly fabrications. Their argument from the start was a fist, at first sheathed in velvet, nowadays naked. Their work consisted of exhuming, redacting, and combining bits and pieces of liturgical history and calling it "restoration." When the work was finished, its enforcers spoke dishonestly about how it maintained continuity with the past, how nothing of importance had been lost, how all that was valuable had been retained—and, what is more, improved![4] Did they expect their colossal imposture to remain

---

4   For numerous examples of such claims and a data-driven refutation, see Matthew Hazell, "'All the Elements of the Roman Rite'? Mythbusting, Part II," *NLM*, October 1, 2021. See also my articles "'O, What a Tangled Web...': Thirty-Three Falsehoods in the CDW's *Responsa*

forever undetected? Nothing escapes the watchful eye of Christ; those who seek to manipulate His Church will be brought to justice.

The responsibility for the rupture from tradition rests squarely on the shoulders of those who intended the new thing, designed it, and executed it. More than fifty years after the novel rites were formally introduced, we're like fish swimming in contaminated waters we ourselves did not pollute. Slowly, step by step, the faults have to be undone, one missal, one priest, one altar, one Mass at a time. Paul VI thought he could abolish the traditional Mass with a stroke of the papal pen. Time has proved the vanity of his ambition. All over the world, in every country, the Mass of the Ages is rising again. Ironically, it is the untamable rapid-fire internet that has powered the spread of a movement to restore a tradition that long predates the technology of the printing press, let alone electric or electronic machinery. In this convergence of the very old and the very new, there is both pathos and humor. The divine, the sacred, the holy, cannot be buried, cannot be banished, cannot be bartered away. The voice of the Church at prayer cannot be silenced. It will, in due time, reemerge, erupt anew, wherever it may have been suppressed. We are just beginning to see the Catholic renaissance, even while the rest of the modern Western world rushes at a mad pace to populate the circles of hell.

Catholics in search of tradition have for many decades now favored a return to the 1962 *Missale Romanum* and its related liturgical books, prior to the landslide of change that followed the Council. Yet these liturgical books fall squarely *within* a period of accelerating mutation that already bit hard into the substance of the Tridentine inheritance: the new Easter Vigil of 1951, the new Holy Week of 1955, the new code of rubrics of 1960, and so forth. All of these were interim projects preparing for the "total reconstruction" or *instauratio magna* (to use a phrase from the philosopher Francis Bacon) that took place in the decade following *Sacrosanctum Concilium* of 1963. In a period of chaos, the Missal of 1962 has been a "rock of stability," as Michael Davies once called it, but it is also an island on which one cannot camp out permanently.

---

ad Dubia," OnePeterFive, January 5, 2022, and "The Outrageous Propaganda of Archbishop Roche," *Rorate Caeli,* January 22, 2022.

When, exactly, did a chaste love of gentle reform became an unbridled passion for novelty? Some put the blame on Pius X for his major modifications to the course of psalms prayed by the Roman Church from the earliest centuries. Others would single out Pius XII for throwing his weight behind a commission of liturgical reform that gave Annibale Bugnini his first Vatican position and gave the world a mutilated Holy Week, its quondam grandeur shattered by incoherence. Still others point the finger at John XXIII for his modification of the Roman Canon and for his naïveté in summoning an ecumenical council crowded with blinking bishops and progressive propagandists. Most, however, would squarely name Paul VI the destroyer par excellence who could not rest until he had seen the inheritance of millennia dismantled and rebuilt in modern fashion. Do we not see, all along, a papal predilection to overreach, to indulge a monarchical Petrine power of *remaking* the Church's worship, when, as most of papal history shows, the popes have rather been its grateful recipients, vigilant defenders, and reverent adorners? Should not the popes, above all, see themselves as servants of the great patrimony that has been handed down to them, rather than judges of its supposed defects and manufacturers of its latest model? Is it too much to ask that they be "guardians of tradition"?

The true believers in the "advances and successes" of the liturgical reform are mostly rather elderly now. They have been sitting on top of the ecclesiastical world for so long that they have found it hard to pay attention to traditionalists or to believe they pose a threat. Progressives more attentive to the deterioration of their party's hegemony, like Massimo Faggioli, Andrea Grillo, Anthony Ruff, Austin Ivereigh, and, of course, Arthur Roche, can't make up their minds between smug denial and white-knuckled panic. All of the serious scholarship is on the traditionalist side, and the case for the reform is weaker by the day, whether assessed by its operating principles or judged by its actual fruits. There is no longer any serious scholarship backing the reform (on the contrary, many of its guiding axioms have been overturned by better scholarship), but its adherents will be the last to recognize that void. Look at how the last living supporters of the Novus Ordo ignore the painstaking work of such scholars as Laszlo Dobszay, Lauren Pristas, Dom Alcuin Reid, and Michael Fiedrowicz, while peppering their own discourse with roughly equal parts of nostalgic bromides from the '60s and the stale "certainties" of the late Liturgical Movement that have about as much scientific currency as mesmerism and phlogiston. Such are the heedless habits of despots on the eve of their overthrow.

In the months that have followed *Traditionis Custodes*, we have seen many well-intentioned people sending personal letters, open letters, and petitions to the pope and to Vatican officials, begging them, with many a "please" and "thank you," to "let us keep the Mass" and so forth. Far be it from me to say that such initiatives can bring about no good; I don't disapprove of anyone signing them. Perhaps I've just been disappointed too many times by the lack of any response to over two dozen earlier petitions on the most serious matters, some of them signed by *hundreds of thousands* of people, directed to the pope, which all led to exactly nothing[5]—or, more likely, which only confirmed for the pope and his circle the dangerous existence of a growing "traditionalist, fundamentalist, integralist" (etc.) movement that has to be crushed before it infiltrates and steers the Church toward a deep continuity with its preconciliar teaching and way of life!

Forget about petitions. What we need most of all is priest after priest after priest who will refuse, under any circumstances whatsoever—including threats, banishments, or penalties—to give up the Latin Mass, the *Rituale*, the Breviary, and so forth; who will continue to be the heroes that the laity need and that Our Lord deserves and rewards; who will understand that in a time of crisis, in a state of war, one does whatever can and may be done, leaving the rest to God; who will experience the riches of God's providence in the laity who rush to their support, so that, giving and receiving natural and supernatural goods, the members sustain one another, as Saint Paul so often urges. That was how the tradition was saved in the '70s, and it will be no different in our times. Will it be messy and ugly? Sure it will. But there is great glory in defending what is true, right, and sacred against its perverse and petty persecutors.

There are a few things that this book will not do. It will not present a formal history and analysis of the *usus antiquior*; for this, I recommend

---

[5] See *Defending the Faith against Present Heresies*, ed. John R. T. Lamont and Claudio Pierantoni (Waterloo, ON: Arouca Press, 2020), 323–31.

PREFACE xxvii

Michael Fiedrowicz's *The Traditional Mass: History, Form, and Theology of the Classical Roman Rite* (Angelico Press, 2020). It will not mount a full-scale defense of the all-around superiority of our ancient rites; for that, you should check out my book *Reclaiming Our Roman Catholic Birthright: The Genius and Timeliness of the Traditional Latin Mass* (Angelico Press, 2020), and other books of mine in the same vein.[6] It will not tell the history of the traditionalist movement; for that, American readers may wish to pick up a copy of Stuart Chessman's *Faith of Our Fathers: A Brief History of Catholic Traditionalism in the United States, from* Triumph *to* Traditionis Custodes (Angelico Press, 2022). It will not offer a detailed analysis of *Traditionis Custodes*, or defend the rights and duties of laity and the lower clergy against the illegitimate commands or prohibitions of their superiors; on these points, I recommend *From Benedict's Peace to Francis's War: Catholics Respond to the Motu Proprio* Traditionis Custodes *on the Latin Mass* (Angelico Press, 2021) and my tract *True Obedience in the Church: A Guide to Discernment in Challenging Times* (Sophia Institute Press, 2021). The aforementioned books, together with the one you have in your hands, would make a strong core library on the whys and wherefores of Roman Catholic liturgical traditionalism.

No one who understands Catholic theology and the history of the Roman liturgy and who strives for intellectual honesty can accept the Novus Ordo as a true, organic expression of Rome's liturgical prayer. There is only one Roman rite; there can be and will be only one Roman rite. The sole expression of the *lex orandi* of the *ritus Romanus* is the traditional Latin liturgy of the Church of Rome. All else is vanity and vexation of spirit. Whatever egregious errors and breathtaking blunders drove us into our modern Babylonian captivity, we who love the Church and her Tradition must "keep calm and carry on," cherishing, defending, and promoting the precious inheritance we, all unworthy, have received.

Peter A. Kwasniewski
March 12, 2022
Feast of Saint Gregory the Great

---

6   See the bibliography.

Abrahamus Bloemaert inuentor et huius fol. Cum Priuil. Cæs. incisor. Cum priuileg. Suc Cæsareæ Maiestatis nec non Regis Christianissimi.

S. AUGUSTINUS. in Psal. 98. S. HIERONYMUS. epist. ad Heliodorum ep. 2. S. GREGORIUS. apud Pendam Hist. in vita eius. S. AMBROSIUS. de iis qui myst init. Ca. 9.

ILLUST. ET EXCELL. PRINCIPI AC DÑO. D. GUNDACKERO DUCI IN SILESIA, OPPAVIÆ CARNOVIÆ TESSINI ET MAIORIS GLOGOVIÆ, PRINCIPI A Liechtenstein, et Nicolspurg, Comiti Rietpergæ, Domino in Moravico, Cremsovio, Ostra, et Wilsersdorff, Sacræ Cæs. Maj. intimo Consiliario, &c Cæsareæ, Principi ac Domino suo gratiosissimo. Abrahamus Blommaert dedicat et conservat Aº 1629.

Abbreviations and Conventions

NLM	*New Liturgical Movement*
DOL	*Documents on the Liturgy 1963–1979*
SC	*Sacrosanctum Concilium*
ST	*Summa Theologiae*
TLM	Traditional Latin Mass

To avoid the ungainly sprawl of hyperlinks in the notes, online articles have been referred to simply by author, title, website, and date.

Psalms are referenced by their Septuagint/Vulgate numbering.

This book often mentions the years 1955 and 1969. In each of those years, a major document was issued: the decree *Maxima Redemptionis Nostrae Mysteria* of the Sacred Congregation of Rites (November 16, 1955), establishing a "restored" Holy Week; and the apostolic constitution *Missale Romanum* (April 3, 1969), promulgating the *Novus Ordo Missae*, which was to go into effect on November 30 of 1969. Some writers use "1956" and "1970" as their points of reference because the Pacellian Holy Week went into effect in 1956 and the first full edition of Paul VI's "*Missale Romanum*" was promulgated on March 26, 1970, via the Decree of the Sacred Congregation for Divine Worship *Celebrationes Eucharistiae*. In fact, upon close examination, the rolling-out of the new Mass was exceedingly clumsy and confusing, with four versions of the *General Instruction* between April 6, 1969 and March 27, 1975 (not including *ad hoc* corrections) as well as multiple versions and corrections to the new missal (see *DOL* 202–13), not to mention the tardy appearance of vernacular editions of the same.

As the Church is a society not of spirits but of men, creatures composed of soul and body, who express all truths under images and signs, carrying in their bodies an ineffable form of their soul, in the Church this whole celestial complex of confession, prayer, and praise, spoken in a sacred language, modulated by a supernatural rhythm, is also produced by the external signs, rites, and ceremonies that are the body of the Liturgy. . . . Let us not be afraid to say that the Liturgy contains every beauty of sentiment, melody, and form, not only equal to, but infinitely superior to anything that could be compared to it, except the Holy Books of Scripture.

—Dom Prosper Guéranger

The Catholic Church alone is beautiful. . . . The celebrant, deacon, and subdeacon, acolytes with lights, the incense, and the chanting—all combine to one end, one act of worship. You feel it *is* really a worshipping; every sense, eyes, ears, smell, are made to know that worship is going on. The laity on the floor saying their beads, or making their acts; the choir singing out the *Kyrie*; and the priests and his assistants bowing low, and saying the *Confiteor* to each other. This is worship, and it is far above reason.

—John Henry Newman

Of the many evils that have been visited on the Church since the Second Vatican Council, the most grievous by far is the destruction of the traditional liturgy and the devotional life that used to accompany it. If the liturgy had not been touched, the doctrinal anarchy and the subservience to modern mores that entered the Church with Pope Paul VI would have had slight effect on the ordinary faithful. It is more than anything the loss of the Mass on which centuries of devotion were nurtured that has turned the modern Church into a wasteland and crippled it as a spiritual force.

—Henry Sire

1

Tradition as Ultimate Norm

E very time a Christian liturgy is celebrated, various prayers, hymns, and readings must be said or sung, and actions both practical and symbolic must be performed by various people. The event will most likely also involve manipulable objects, furnishings, and special clothing.

If we were to limit ourselves to this thirty-thousand-foot view, most Christian liturgies have a lot in common. You have a minister leading it, a few persons in supporting roles, the Bible, and some bread and wine. But as the saying goes, "the devil's in the details," which is a somewhat twisted way of thinking, because God, who is their creator and providential governor, is to be found in the details much more. Unlike papal in-flight press conferences, liturgy does not normally exist at a distance of thirty thousand feet.[1] It is something highly concrete, articulate, and definite; it cannot be

---

[1] A newspaper reports a Catholic saying about the Mass: "Luke 24 introduced to me the Eucharist and made the Mass more powerful to me. . . . In this passage, Jesus comes to the disciples, teaches them through Scripture, which is the Liturgy of the Word, and breaks bread with them, which is the Liturgy of the Eucharist. Then they leave, which is the dismissal, telling people what happened to them. Well, that's the Mass!" ("St. Paul VI's 'Missale Romanum' Turns 50," *National Catholic Register*, April 3, 2019). That's what it's been reduced to: a sketchbook caricature. In contrast, one who turns the pages of the preconciliar *comic book* for kids, *Know Your Mass* (Catechetical Guild, 1954, republished by Angelus Press), will find a more accurate, complete, and profound catechesis on the Mass than what would be found in any of our flashy adult catechetical programs. Continuity between traditional and modern rites has to be assessed at the level of *specifics*, not at the level of generalities. One can (more or less) line up the *parts* of the old and new Mass and say: "Look, not so much difference after all!" But the immense difference is not at the level of (e.g.) "having readings from the Bible"; at so general a level, there are barely even distinct *rites*, since every rite does basically the same kinds of things—chants Propers, reads readings, has litanies or petitions, has an anaphora, the Lord's Prayer, etc. Rather, the difference will be seen with (e.g.) *which* Sunday Epistles and Gospels are read, and on what arrangement, and for what reasons.

1

generic or vague, but it must commit itself to this or that particular path, each step of the way. The urgent question then arises: How ought Christian liturgy to be celebrated? Do we make it up as we go along? Do we hire someone to make it up for us? Do we assemble a committee and ask them to prepare drafts and vote on them? Or can we find it complete somewhere and gratefully take it up so that instead of wasting our energy on reinventing the wheel, we can devote ourselves to making the most prayerful and beautiful use of a gift already given?

Catholics once had a compelling answer to the question: "How is liturgy to be celebrated?" The answer was as rich as it was simple: *tradition*. We receive our liturgy from apostolic tradition developed over centuries of faithful practice. Because the Apostles were united around Christ in the cenacle, our rites of worship will always have certain features in common; because the Apostles were scattered throughout the world and planted local churches everywhere they went, our rites will also be diverse—as diverse as Greek and Latin, Coptic and Slavic, Ambrosian, Roman, Mozarabic. But the fundamental intuition or instinct of a Catholic is always to look for tradition so that we can be confident that *what* we are doing and *how* we are doing it rests, as much as possible, on precedent—the precedent of thousands of saints, countless churches and chapels of Christendom, untold armies of priests, monks, nuns, and layfolk. Every one of the twenty-one ecumenical councils of the Catholic Church was solemnized with a liturgy that was already regarded, by the council fathers, as traditional—be it the early Greek liturgy of the Council of Nicaea or the Tridentine rite at the Second Vatican Council.

Against this unanimous practice of two thousand years of apostolic-sacramental Christianity, Eastern and Western, it is no minor problem that today the answer to the same question "How is liturgy to be celebrated?" has become vexed, divisive, explosive. It has become thus for one and only one reason: the normativity of tradition has been repudiated. Those who refuse to be guided by it have fallen into an arbitrariness from which there is no escape, except by still further arbitrary decisions and actions. It is time to rethink our basic question from the ground up.

All of the chapters of this book will contribute to the enterprise. This chapter will establish two principles: broadly speaking, the constitutive role of tradition in Catholicism; more particularly, the importance of holding fast to traditions that have long been practiced and handed down, even if they are not part of the deposit of faith. My thesis is twofold. First, ecclesiastical traditions, especially in regard to the "externals" of liturgy in its development over time, must be honored and preserved because they are intimately connected with the content and right practice of religion. Second, after a period of over half a century in which this relationship has been loosened or denied, an increasing number of Catholics are encountering "revived" traditions for the first time and experiencing them as right and just, given the truths we believe and the mysteries we venerate. The success of this revival at a time of sharp decline in religious practice offers experimental proof that the so-called "externals" defended by lovers of tradition continue to be and will always be an efficacious path to union with God.[2]

Stand firm and hold to the traditions

It would once have caused no raising of eyebrows to state that Catholicism is inherently a religion of tradition. This was one of the main objections raised against it by Protestants, who, having settled on the unscriptural doctrine of *sola scriptura*, discovered unsurprisingly that much of what the Catholic Church taught and practiced could not be found *verbatim* in the

---

[2] It is sometimes objected against traditionalists that their analysis of the Church crisis is based solely on the developed Western world (especially Europe and the USA) and that they fail to take into account the situation in South America, Africa, and Asia, where the Church—with the Novus Ordo—is growing and even, in some places, flourishing. In response, I would say, first, that traditionalists are well aware of the world situation, as can be seen, for example, in the work of the International Federation *Una Voce* and *Paix Liturgique*. Second, the Church in the developing parts of the world should not be romanticized; it too suffers from a host of evils analogous to those afflicting the modern West (these being largely visited upon them by liberal democratic politicians and financiers), evils to which Catholic tradition offers singularly apt and urgent remedies. Third, most of the Catholic world was originally evangelized by traditional Catholics (at a time when they were the only kind in existence), and wherever Catholic tradition survives or is reintroduced today, good fruits abound. See my article "Did the Reformed Liturgical Rites Cause a Boom in Missionary Lands?" *NLM*, July 6, 2020; cf. Joseph Shaw, ed., *The Case for Liturgical Restoration: Una Voce Studies on the Traditional Latin Mass* (Brooklyn, NY: Angelico Press, 2019), esp. chs. 25–34 on "The Ancient Mass and Evangelization."

Bible. Yet this discovery should not have startled followers of the Apostle
Paul, who wrote to the Corinthians: "I commend you because you remember me in everything and maintain the traditions even as I have delivered
them to you" (1 Cor 11:2), and to the Thessalonians: "So then, brethren,
stand firm and hold to the traditions which you were taught by us, either
by word of mouth or by letter" (2 Thess 2:15).

The Church Fathers drive home this point with their customary vehe-
mence. In his treatise *On the Holy Spirit*, published in 375, Saint Basil the
Great writes: "Of the dogmas and proclamations that are guarded in the
Church, we hold some from the teaching of the Scriptures, and others we
have received in mystery as the teachings of the tradition of the Apostles.
Both hold the same power with respect to true religion. No one would deny
these points, at least no one who has even a little experience of ecclesiastical
institutions. For if we attempt to reject non-scriptural [*agraphos*] customs
as insignificant, we would, unaware, lose the very vital parts of the Gospel,
and even more, we would establish the proclamation merely in name."[3]

Saint Basil provides examples of things Christians hold by tradition,
some of which may be surprising to modern readers:

> For instance—I will mention the first and most common—who
> has learned through the Scriptures that those who hope in the
> name of our Lord Jesus Christ are marked with the sign of the
> cross? What sort of scriptural text teaches us to turn to the East for
> prayer? Which saint has left us a scriptural account of the words
> of the *epiclesis* at the manifestation of the bread of the Eucharist
> and the cup of blessing? We are not satisfied with the [Eucharis-
> tic] words that the Apostle or the Gospel mentions, but we add
> other words before and after theirs, since we have received non-
> scriptural teaching that these words have great power in regard to
> the mystery. We bless the water of baptism and the oil of chrism
> in addition to the very one who is to be baptized. By what Scrip-
> tures? Is it not by the secret and mystical tradition? But why? What
> scriptural authority teaches the anointing itself of oil? Where does

---

[3]   Saint Basil, *On the Holy Spirit*, 27:66, trans. Stephen Hildebrand (Yonkers, NY: St. Vladimir's Seminary Press, 2011), 104.

a man being immersed three times come from? How much of the baptismal ritual is for the renunciation of Satan and his angels, and what scriptural text does it come from? Does it not come from this secret and unspoken teaching, which our fathers guarded with a simple and unprying silence, since they were well taught that the solemnity of the mysteries is preserved by silence? Such matters must not be seen by the uninitiated, and how is it appropriate that this teaching be published abroad in writing?[4]

Another Church Father, Saint Vincent of Lérins, around the year 434, has this to say in his great treatise *Commonitory for the Antiquity and Universality of the Catholic Faith Against the Profane Novelties of All Heresies* (now that's a title Hilaire Belloc would have been proud of):

Keep the deposit. What is the deposit? That which has been entrusted to you, not that which you have yourself devised: a matter not of cleverness, but of learning; not of private adoption, but of public tradition; a matter brought to you, not put forth by you, wherein you are bound to be not an author but a keeper, not a teacher but a disciple, not a leader but a follower. *Keep the deposit.* Preserve the talent of Catholic Faith inviolate, unadulterate. That which has been entrusted to you, let it continue in your possession, let it be handed on by you. You have received gold; give gold in turn. Do not substitute one thing for another. Do not for gold impudently substitute lead or brass. Give real gold, not counterfeit.[5]

Such quotations can be multiplied indefinitely. The Church Fathers see Christianity as a social and hierarchical religion in which certain men—the Apostles and their successors—have been entrusted with dogmas, liturgical practices, and moral judgments that are intended to be passed on faithfully from one generation to the next.

---

4   Saint Basil, 104–5.
5   Saint Vincent of Lérins, *Commonitorium*, ch. 22, n. 53, trans. C. A. Heurtley, in *Nicene and Post-Nicene Fathers*, Second Series, vol. 11, ed. Philip Schaff and Henry Wace (Buffalo, NY: Christian Literature Publishing Co., 1894), rev. and ed. for New Advent by Kevin Knight.

A deposit in words and symbols

This is a key point: the truth and way of life revealed by God, *in its totality*, was first deposited in *tradition*—that is, in the minds of the men whom God had chosen as His confidants; only subsequently was *some* of it placed in writing, at the discretion of the ones to whom the deposit had been given.[6] We have to get away from any notion of a Bible, a catechism, or a *Summa* falling from the sky into the hands of prophets or Apostles. Revelation was a definite spiritual light that God planted in the minds of His instruments, entrusting them with the task of explaining it in their spoken words and putting some portion of it into writing for the benefit of distant or future audiences. But it is clear that it would have been impossible to put *all* of it into writing: Saint John tells us in chapter 21 of his Gospel: "There are also many other things which Jesus did; which, if they were written every one, the world itself, I think, would not be able to contain the books that should be written." Neither the Apostles nor the Church Fathers felt that they should or could put into writing all that belonged to the mystery of life in Christ. The Church preserves in her maternal heart some memories that are too deep for words, and some realities that find their expression in signs and symbols rather than in written language.

For example, Christians worshiped *ad orientem*, or facing eastwards, for centuries before anyone thought to give an explanation in writing of why they did so, and even such explanations exist only because here or there a Church Father such as Saint Basil the Great decided to mention the custom in passing while arguing in defense of a different dogma. The fact is that worship *ad orientem* is not a doctrine, though it has doctrinal foundations and implications; it is not a statement or assertion or text that we can

---

[6]   I say this because the Apostles were given the Lord's teaching prior to its being written down (see Fr. Chad Ripperger, *Topics on Tradition* [n.p.: Sensus Traditionis Press, 2013], 5). Orestes Brownson has an excellent statement of this, the Catholic view: "Catholicity teaches that the whole revelation was made to the church, irrespective of written documents. . . . The depository of the revelation is not the Holy Scriptures, plus tradition. The divine traditions cover the whole revelation, and not merely that portion of it not found in the Holy Scriptures; and it is because the church has the whole faith in these divine traditions, which, by supernatural assistance, she faithfully keeps and transmits, and infallibly interprets, that she can establish the rule of Scriptural interpretation" ("Newman's Development of Christian Doctrine," *Brownson's Quarterly Review* 3.3 [July 1846]).

analyze.[7] It is a bodily posture, an action we perform, a wordless attitude we take with our entire being. It is, in that sense, pre-doctrinal, pre-verbal, pre-conceptual; and that is part of the reason why it is so fundamental. The first things human beings take in after birth and during infancy are not subject-predicate compositions but simple sensible images; language and thought grow in us slowly, but the face of our mother leaning over us in love is there from the start—immediate, palpable, dominating, and determinative. The fundamental symbols of the liturgy are like this: they train us before we know we are being shaped by them; they determine our thoughts before we think them; they impress the truth on our eyes, ears, and noses, on our hands and knees. The gestures, postures, and objects of Christian worship are for this reason no less important than the texts of the liturgy; indeed, in many ways, they are more important. For instance, a Mass in which the faithful kneel for long periods of silence will more strongly affirm the hidden, mysterious, and awe-inspiring presence of God than a Mass at which silence and kneeling are less prominent or even absent. A Mass with incense will have immediately a more elevated sacred character than a Mass without incense.[8] "Let my prayer be directed as incense in thy sight; the

---

[7] This is a major part of the weakness of modern Catholic apologetics, which fixates on doctrinal propositions but neglects their predoctrinal foundations, liturgical context, and doxological purpose. One might say that apologists try to have the *lex credendi* independently of the *lex orandi*. A Catholic apologist may have the entire *Summa* memorized, but if he is not praying in continuity with the way Saint Thomas did, he is very likely not to believe and live the same religion Saint Thomas believed and lived. Writing to Edward Pusey, John Henry Newman describes the difference his conversion made to his relationship with the Fathers of the Church: "I recollect well what an outcast I seemed to myself, when I took down from the shelves of my library the volumes of St. Athanasius or St. Basil, and set myself to study them; and how, on the contrary, when at length I was brought into Catholic communion, I kissed them with delight, with a feeling that in them I had more than all that I had lost; and, as though I were directly addressing the glorious saints, who bequeathed them to the Church, how I said to the inanimate pages, 'You are now mine, and I am now yours, beyond any mistake'" (*A Letter Addressed to the Rev. E. B. Pusey, D.D. on Occasion of his Eirenicon*, §1). This is how it is with the traditional liturgy; through it, one can say to Catholic tradition of all the centuries: "You are now mine, and I am now yours, beyond any mistake." With the Novus Ordo, this is impossible in principle.

[8] When King Solomon is telling Hiram king of Tyre about his desire to build the Temple, he practically equates worship with the offering of incense: "The house which I desire to build, is great: for our God is great above all gods. Who then can be able to build him a worthy house? if heaven, and the heavens of heavens cannot contain him: who am I that I should be able to build him a house? but to this end only, that incense may be burnt before him" (2 Chron. 2:5–6).

lifting up of my hands, as evening sacrifice" (Ps 140:2; cf. Rev 8:3–4). The Offertory of the Mass for Corpus Christi adapts Leviticus 21:6 to the ministers of the New Covenant: *Sacerdotes Domini incensum et panes offerunt Deo: et ideo sancti erunt Deo suo, et non polluent nomen ejus, alleluia*, "The priests of the Lord offer incense and loaves to God: and therefore they shall be holy to their God, and shall not defile His Name, alleluia." So much is communicated by the sweet billowing smoke, the deliberate motion of hands, the angle of the head, the direction of a gaze, the elevation of a chalice![9] We have to take seriously the panoply of non-verbal manifestations of tradition, since these things, too, have been handed down to us by our forefathers, and they carry the truth of the Gospel along with them.

Different kinds of tradition

The word "tradition" comes from *trans* and *dare*, a handing-across of something. For something to be traditional, it must be established by due authority and then handed on and nurtured by others. One of the best twentieth-century textbooks, the *Manuale Theologiae Dogmaticae* of Jean-Marie Hervé, distinguishes four kinds: dominical, divino-apostolic, humano-apostolic, and ecclesiastical. "Dominical tradition" is that which was established by Christ Himself, such as the indissolubility of marriage and the need for fasting. "Divino-apostolic tradition" comprises that which the Holy Spirit inspired the Apostles to introduce as part of the Church's constitution, such as the ordination of deacons and the initial determinations of liturgy that would develop, over time, into the families of Eastern and Western rites; "humano-apostolic" refers, in contrast, to that which they themselves deemed fitting to institute as Christ's representatives, such as determinate periods when Christians should practice fasting and abstinence. Lastly, "ecclesiastical tradition" refers to everything that the Church has instituted or adopted after the time of the Apostles (e.g., the exact duration of the seasons of Advent and Lent, the octaves of Christmas, Easter, and Pentecost, the Rogation Days, and the vestments to be worn by the clergy at the altar).[10]

---

[9] See Romano Guardini, *Sacred Signs*, trans. Grace Branham (St. Louis: Pio Decimo Press, 1955; repr. Os Justi Press, 2015).

[10] See Ripperger, *Topics on Tradition*, 6–10. Saint Leo the Great attributes the Ember Days to the Apostles.

All four types of tradition have this in common: they are started by an authority (Christ, the Holy Spirit, the Apostles, the Church) and then continuously handed down, preserved, and fostered. The Deposit of the Faith, the sum total of dominical and divino-apostolic tradition, admits of no change; it is fully established upon its promulgation, which is complete by the time of the last Apostle's death. Humano-apostolic tradition had only a certain window in which it could be established; after Saint John's death, it cannot be modified, only discarded. Ecclesiastical tradition is the most complex category.

The first two categories, dominical and divino-apostolic, may be called Tradition with a capital *T*: in their origin and in their content, they are divine and, like God, immutable. The last two categories, humano-apostolic and ecclesiastical, may be called human rather than divine, but with the important qualification that they come into existence under divine guidance and possess a measure of divine authority. Although ecclesiastical traditions develop and change, the consistent practice of the Catholic Church over the centuries—it would be no exaggeration to call it a rule or a principle—has been to carry along with her whatever is already part of her life, and the more so, the more universally it permeates the body of the faithful.[11] Two corollaries follow. First, the longer the tradition, the more certain it is to be true, fitting, and beneficial. Second, new practices are to be admitted only when they refine, crystallize, amplify, or otherwise enhance traditions already in place. Well-established and long-enduring practices are known as customs; these function as laws, enjoying normative standing and binding force within a community. When a custom is so old and/or widespread that no one recalls its introduction (often enough, there will be no precise knowledge of who introduced it, or where and when), it is called immemorial; it is thereby also venerable.

---

[11] The significance of this principle is apparent when we consider that the *Missale Romanum* of Pius V, promulgated in 1570, was little different from missals already in use for many centuries and subsequently remained in universal use throughout the Roman Catholic Church for four hundred years. Its abolition, therefore, was a particularly egregious example of contempt for ecclesiastical tradition. Indeed, it would be difficult to conceive of a more temerarious and *uncatholic* act than this arrogant dismissal of the accumulated wealth of centuries of public worship and personal piety.

The great veneration in which the Church holds her traditions comes
through in the following words of the Council of Trent, praising the
Roman Canon:

> Since it is fitting that holy things be administered in a holy man-
> ner, and of all things this sacrifice is the most holy, the Catholic
> Church, to the end that it might be worthily and reverently offered
> and received, instituted many centuries ago the holy canon, which
> is so free from error that it contains nothing that does not in the
> highest degree savor of a certain holiness and piety and raise up to
> God the minds of those who offer. For it consists partly of the very
> words of the Lord, partly of the traditions of the Apostles, and also
> of pious regulations of holy pontiffs.[12]

In this quotation, we hear all the spheres of tradition referred to: dominical ("the very words of the Lord"), divino- and humano-apostolic ("the
traditions of the Apostles"), and ecclesiastical ("pious regulations of holy
pontiffs"). The Council of Trent holds up for our admiration and adherence the most perfect illustration of the rightness of the Church's age-old
practice of worship—namely, the central and definitive liturgical text of
the Eucharistic sacrifice in all Western rites, complete since the year 604. It
should give us considerable pause that this very prayer was not only modified but rendered optional in the liturgical reforms of the 1960s, whose
protagonists viewed the Canon with disdain.[13]

Confusion about essentials and incidentals

Acknowledging with Hervé that there are different kinds of tradition in
the Church and that not all of them enjoy the same authority or immutability, Catholics should nevertheless value the *whole* of their tradition at
every level, because all of its elements taken together constitute the beautiful and subtle tapestry of the Faith. It is therefore not only misleading

---

[12] Council of Trent, Sess. 22, ch. 4.
[13] As we will discuss in detail in chapters 8 and 9.

but dangerous to make too sharp a distinction between what is "essential," "substantive," or "primary" and what is "accidental," "incidental," or "secondary."[14]

Consider the following statement: "All that matters at Mass is that Jesus is present; everything else is secondary." Or, more succinctly, "the Mass is the Mass." Undoubtedly it matters a great deal that Jesus is present, for otherwise we are eating no more than ordinary food. But the liturgy has a greater purpose than putting on a meal for us, and even Our Lord's presence has a greater scope and purpose than sacramental Communion. The Mass is the solemn, public, formal act of adoration, thanksgiving, and supplication offered by Christ the High Priest to the Father, and by His entire Mystical Body in union with Him. It is the foremost act of the virtue of religion, by which we offer to God a sacrifice of praise worthy of His glory. It is the chief expression of the theological virtues of faith, hope, and charity. It is the irruption of the kingdom of heaven into our earthly time and space. It is the nuptial feast of the King of Kings. It is the recapitulation of the entire created universe in its Alpha and Omega. Because it is all these things, the Church down through the ages has spared no effort and no expense to augment the beauty and elevate the solemnity of her liturgical rites. As John Paul II rightly said: "Like the woman who anointed Jesus in Bethany, the Church has feared no 'extravagance,' devoting the best of her resources to expressing her wonder and adoration before the unsurpassable gift of the Eucharist."[15] So while it may be true that the only things *necessary* for a valid Mass in the Roman rite are wheaten bread and wine from grapes, a priest, and the words of consecration, to see this as *sufficient* for the offering of the Holy Sacrifice of the Mass would betray a reductive, minimalist, and parsimonious view of things. Glorifying God and sanctifying our souls cannot be divorced from the *fittingness* of the worship we offer Him.

---

[14] The term "accidental" as I will be using it comes from Greek philosophy: in contrast with substance, which is the permanent underlying reality, accidents are those characteristics that have their existence only *in* a substance, qualifying or quantifying or otherwise modifying it. Examples of substance are man, horse, rosebush, oak tree, iron, gold; examples of accident are white, yellow, hot, cold, five-foot, seven-foot, double, half, sitting, standing. These things have no extramental existence by themselves, but only in connection with substances.

[15] Encyclical *Ecclesia de Eucharistia*, §48.

We could make an analogy: dominical tradition is like the soul, divino-apostolic tradition is like the body, and the remaining two (humano-apostolic and ecclesiastical) are like the clothing worn over the body. All three come together to "make the man." Someone might say that a person's clothing isn't important because it's not a part of his nature or essence. The prince of philosophers, Aristotle, classifies clothing as one of the categories of accident. The essential thing (it might be said) is to be who and what you are, a human being, a person; what you are *wearing* is purely incidental. The fallacy of this reasoning consists in substituting a metaphysical consideration for a moral and psychological one. Our clothing is metaphysically extrinsic to us, but for all that, we are not nudists: our clothing *is* an extension of our humanity, a manifestation of our personality. We need not go so far as to say "the clothing *makes* the man," but without a doubt it *presents* the man, typifies him, readies him for one task and not another, and also disguises or hides or shields him.[16] As John Senior has written, in words that apply not just to monks but to everyone: "In the moral and spiritual order, we become what we wear as much as what we wear becomes us—and it is the same with how we eat and what we do. . . . The habits of the monks, the bells, the ordered life, the 'conversation,' the music, gardens, prayer, hard work and walls—all these accidental and incidental forms conformed the moral and spiritual life of Christians to the love of Mary and her Son."[17]

In like manner, the essence of the Church's liturgy is simple: it is contained in the temple of the Heart of Jesus Christ, our Eternal High Priest, where perfect worship of the Father in the Spirit resides. But the "clothing" of that worship is of decisive importance to *us*, who interact with Our Lord through His visible Body, the Church, and through her visible rites. How these rites are structured, performed, and participated in will inevitably influence our understanding of the mysteries of the Faith and our ability to live them

---

[16] This point is an application of the larger truth that cultures (including subcultures) manifest themselves in appearance, clothing, behavior, language, and other traits. Subcultures defined by styles of music—classical, jazz, heavy metal, rap, country, reggae—offer clear examples of this truth.

[17] John Senior, *The Restoration of Christian Culture* (Norfolk, VA: IHS Press, 2008), 130–31.

out. The clothing draped over the body of our prayers is, if anything, of far greater importance than any clothing a human being puts on.

One can see how weak and problematic is the distinction so often drawn between primary and secondary elements in the liturgy by considering some other examples from ordinary life. Is a person's sex—male or female—primary or secondary? Human nature as such—that is, abstractly considered—is neither masculine nor feminine, but only a fool could think that masculinity or femininity is not of enormous importance to *how* this or that person is human, how his or her humanity is experienced, lived, and shared. Is the language in which a person happens to be reared, and through which he learns not only to speak but to *think*, a matter of secondary and incidental importance, just because he might have spoken a different one? On the contrary, we know that language can open up or limit the very possibilities of thought.[18] The same can be said about the broader culture into which a child happens to be born, and from which the child will gain higher or lower aspirations, wider or narrower horizons. Is culture, then, primary or secondary in the constitution of a human person? Again, does it make no real difference whether someone is tall or short? Aristotle notes that a small person can be pretty but not beautiful.[19] In like manner, a Eucharistic liturgy, to be beautiful, has to have a certain magnitude, scope, density, and weight; otherwise the best it can achieve is prettiness. In general, the cumulative force of the so-called "secondary" is so great that the "primary" cannot exist, be expressed, ring out, or resonate without it. Saint Basil captures well the vanity of pursuing an essence independent of its qualities: "Do not let us seek for any nature devoid of qualities by the condition of its existence but let us know that all the phenomena with which we see it clothed regard the condition of its existence and complete its essence. Try to take away by reason each of the qualities which it possesses, and you will arrive at nothing. Take away black, white, weight, density, the

---

[18] Christianity developed in a Greco-Roman milieu in which philosophy had achieved a remarkable conquest of the conceptual territory necessary for theological formulations. Later missionary work discovered that some primitive tribes use languages in which the Christian Creed cannot even be formulated.

[19] Cf. *Nicomachean Ethics*, Bk. 4, ch. 3, 1123b7.

qualities which concern taste, in one word all that which we see in it, and the substance vanishes."[20]

For this reason we must reject the clumsy and superficial manner in which this distinction between substance and accident has been wielded to dismantle and reconfigure the Roman liturgy in a manner that violates its genealogy, its culture, its physiognomy, its language, its beauty, its "personality."

What we say and how we say it

Let me offer another illustration. Consider the relationship between what we say and how we say it. *What* we say is the conceptual content we wish to communicate to another; *how* we say it includes diction, elocution, and emotion—that is, choice of words, clarity of pronunciation, and tone of voice. Take Hamlet's famous soliloquy:

> To be, or not to be: that is the question:
> Whether 'tis nobler in the mind to suffer
> The slings and arrows of outrageous fortune,
> Or to take arms against a sea of troubles,
> And by opposing end them? To die: to sleep;
> No more; and by a sleep to say we end
> The heart-ache and the thousand natural shocks
> That flesh is heir to, 'tis a consummation
> Devoutly to be wish'd.

Now, what if we attempted to rewrite this great speech in the style of a modern-day textbook?

> The question for him was whether to continue to exist or not—whether it was better to put up with the difficulties of a scarcely bearable situation, or to resist the numerous troubles that afflict a person, and so put an end to them through opposition. He thought of the prospect of dying: how simple it would be, like sleeping. And

[20] Basil of Caesarea, *Hexaemeron*, Hom. I, n. 8, trans. Blomfield Jackson, in *Nicene and Post-Nicene Fathers*, Second Series, vol. 8, ed. Philip Schaff and Henry Wace (Buffalo, NY: Christian Literature Publishing Co., 1895), rev. and ed. for New Advent by Kevin Knight.

with that sleep we can stop the many pains and miseries human beings have to endure. It's an end we would all greatly hope for.[21]

Dreadful, isn't it? No one would pay money to go to a theatre and listen to it. But the real poetry of Shakespeare has drawn audiences for over four hundred years and continues to do so even in our day, when Elizabethan English is difficult for many to understand in full. The audience is not going to the play simply to get the "bottom line," which they know they can find more easily on Wikipedia. They are going for a complex experience of story and characterization, acting and suffering, audible and visible beauty. The meaning of the play is found in the irreducible totality of these things.

Or if we compare a page in any great romantic poet with the screenplay of one of today's forgettable Hollywood films, we can see immediately that even if both are dealing with the same reality—say, *eros*, or erotic love, which, though marred by sin, is still part of God's creation—the way they express it is so vastly different that they might as well be talking about different realities. The poet elevates his theme with beautiful language, giving it an almost spiritual glow; the moviemaker sullies and debases his theme with gratuitous images inciting lust and corrupting the imagination. The one makes *eros* somehow better than itself; the other evacuates from it whatever rudiments of unselfish love might be there. Regrettably, we encounter the same contrast when comparing an eloquent translation of the Bible, such as the King James Version, with a tone-deaf translation like the New American Bible, by which countless ears in the United States have been under assault for decades.[22] If human beings were pure intellects, we could exchange between ourselves concepts without words, but in reality, we are embodied intellects, or, with greater Thomistic realism, intellectualized

---

[21] I found the raw materials of this rewrite at www.nosweatshakespeare.com/quotes/soliloquies/hamlet-to-be-or-not-to-be, accessed February 26, 2020. The webpage has subsequently changed but its content is in the same spirit.
[22] Dr. Anthony Esolen says the New American Bible is written not in English but in Nabbish, a language spoken by no existing race of creatures. See "A Bumping Boxcar Language," *First Things*, June 2011. He has returned to the NAB's vices many times, most recently in his *In the Beginning Was the Word: An Annotated Reading of the Prologue of John* (Brooklyn, NY: Angelico Press, 2021).

bodies, and so the meaning we intend to convey includes the manner of conveyance. Here, the body and its clothing are, in a way, inseparable.

There is a certain naïveté in saying "dogma is one thing, how you express it is another," as if the words we use to articulate Christian doctrine, the external forms, are like a bunch of interchangeable T-shirts that can be cycled through *ad libitum* because they all "do the job."[23] But we have seen that this is a false metaphor. In the realm of dogma, too, the *way* something is said is intimately connected with *what* is being said. A dogmatic formulation arrived at by a Church council or a pope is, in its concrete particularity, the manifestation of the truth to which the Church has arrived by dint of study, debate, and prayer, and which she authoritatively imposes on the faithful. The truth to be held is not a concept beyond the formula but the concept-*in*-the-formula. It is, in short, a miniature likeness of the Word-made-flesh. It is not as if our authoritative formulas, such as the Apostles' Creed or the Niceno-Constantinopolitan Creed, are groping for something adequate but never quite reaching it. The Creed is perfectly true in every line and need never be changed. There are, to be sure, additional truths we can add—that is why our creeds get longer over time. But what was already there is not altered or discarded.

To give a liturgical application: It is not a matter of indifference whether we say "Lord, I am not worthy to receive you, but only say the word and I shall be healed," as English-speaking Catholics did for forty years at the Novus Ordo, or "Lord, I am not worthy that you should enter under my roof, but only say the word and my soul shall be healed," as Catholics have said since 2011, when a new and more accurate translation came into effect. It is not a matter of indifference whether we say it once in English or three times in Latin. It is not "six or one-half-dozen" whether we receive Communion standing and in the hand or kneeling and on the tongue, or whether the Holy Sacrifice is offered facing eastwards and outwards to the Sun of Justice or inwards to the congregation. These are not "the same

---

[23] The most famous statement of this position is in John XXIII's opening speech at Vatican II: "What is needed is that this certain and immutable doctrine, to which the faithful owe obedience, be studied afresh and reformulated in contemporary terms. For this deposit of faith, or truths which are contained in our time-honored teaching is one thing; the manner in which these truths are set forth (with their meaning preserved intact) is something else."

thing said in different ways." They are, at best, similar things said in various ways; sometimes, alas, they are contrary things being said in contrary ways.

We were "made for more"—and that includes tradition

Separating substance from accident, the essential from the incidental, the concept from the expression, the meaning from the manner, is not so simple after all. Indeed, I am aware of only one instance where, by divine power, substance is separated from accident: namely, in the miracle of transubstantiation. In every other case, substance and accident are together, at times even tightly bound, the way skin color is in the skin, or hair, which is not alive, is nonetheless rooted in the scalp or the face of a man—and we should take this lesson to heart when considering the value and weight of humano-apostolic and ecclesiastical traditions.[24] For it is just these traditions—including some that go back to the apostolic age, as Saint Basil reminded us with his mention of worship facing eastwards (*ad orientem*)—that have fared badly in the past fifty years. We have seen a wholesale discarding, almost a Stalinist purge, of traditions, to which the precise term "memoricide," the murder of memory, might be justly applied.

There is, however, a divine irony in our current situation. Younger generations are encountering the traditional Roman liturgy in its beauty and power as if it were something new rather than something already around and taken for granted. This unforeseen glow of newness on the aged face of religion[25] often produces a feeling of excitement, wonder, delight. It

---

[24] In other words, we run the risk of injuring or disfiguring a substance when we modify its accidents. Only God can flawlessly perform this operation, and He does it for one special reason: to feed us with Himself. The laws of nature are suspended but once. The rest of the time, we are obliged to live by them and respect them as God's decrees. There is, moreover, the particular problem of not being able to know with certainty which details in the practice of our religion are of divine or divinely-inspired institution. For example, in the Middle Ages, the exact phrasing of the consecration of the chalice, including the words *mysterium fidei*, was attributed to Our Lord or the Apostles, and even the most rigorous scholarship has not been able to detect a particular moment in history when the words *mysterium fidei* were added for the first time; all we can say, recognizing the woeful incompleteness of our ancient records, is that thus-and-such is the first extant manuscript containing these words. Is it not far safer—indeed, an obligation of reverence for the most sacred things—to preserve the formula as it exists in the earliest written records we possess of the Roman Canon? See chapter 9.

[25] Could we fancifully turn this around and say: a noble golden shine of antiquity coming to rest on what had been the Church's unremarkable modern countenance? (I have Aristotle in

is provocative and challenging. It nourishes faith like the fabled "super-foods" sold in the health-food markets. Generations born after the Council can encounter things like Latin, Gregorian chant, polyphony, *ad orientem*, Gothic chalices, or brocade vestments *for the first time* and have the reaction: "*This* is the way things ought to be!" They are, one might say, experimentally verifying the reasons why the Holy Spirit inspired the Church to adopt these practices and works of art in the first place.[26] The reappearance of elements of Catholic tradition that many had considered dead and buried has something of the magical quality of a time-lapse film that shows plants rapidly growing from seed to maturity to fruit. Younger folk have the privilege of receiving all at once, as if descending fully-formed from the heavenly Jerusalem, a heritage that actually took centuries to reach perfection.

Youth are always being told by well-meaning new evangelizers: "You were MADE FOR MORE." This is the contemporary version of Saint Augustine's oft-quoted line: "Thou hast made us for Thyself, O Lord, and our hearts are restless until they rest in Thee." To be sure, this MORE refers to God Himself, but it also refers to all that God has lavished upon His people in the history of the Church, gifts through which we can find (and find rest in) His beauty and holiness. He came to bring not only the bare necessities but a rich banquet. Catholics of the Latin rite can find this God-given abundance in the traditional Roman rite of the Mass, the ancient Divine Office, rites of the sacraments, blessings and processions, and a multitude of devotions. How welcome is the feast, the more starved we are of sacredness and thirsty for transcendence! The Catholic liturgy of the centuries is the fertile offspring of the dew of the Holy Spirit, as if the words of Isaac's blessing upon Jacob were fulfilled in Christ's blessing of His Church: "May God give thee the dew of heaven, and of the fatness of the earth, abundance of corn and wine" (Gen 27:28). The story of Israel gives us a clue: "When

---

mind, who says that pleasure completes activity "like the bloom on the faces of young men": *Nicomachean Ethics* 10.4.)

[26] On the fittingness of Latin and Gregorian chant for Roman Catholic worship, see the unsurpassed treatment by Michael Fiedrowicz, *The Traditional Mass: History, Form, and Theology of the Classical Roman Rite*, trans. Rose Pfeifer (Brooklyn, NY: Angelico Press, 2020), ch. 8: "Sacred Language," 153–89; cf. my lecture "Gregorian Chant: Perfect Music for the Sacred Liturgy," *Rorate Caeli*, February 1, 2020.

the dew fell in the night upon the camp, the manna also fell with it" (Num 11:9), as if to say: Where the Holy Spirit acts within the body of the faithful, there we will find the nourishment God has provided for us. We may then say with the prophet Job: "My root is opened beside the waters, and dew shall continue in my harvest" (Job 29:19).[27]

The fearful and fascinating

An ever-growing mountain of data suggests that young people are abandoning Christianity in droves. This cuts across all denominational lines. Recent studies like the Shell-Jugendstudie show that church isn't one of the places young people are likely to be found as a rule. What exactly is the problem?

There are, as usual, a variety of theories, but I think we should take very seriously the argument of Dom Karl Wallner, a monk of Heiligenkreuz Abbey with decades of experience in youth ministry. In a lecture entitled "The Profanation of the Sacred and the Sacralisation of the Profane," Wallner claims that

> the experience of the sacred is more fundamental than the notion of the divine. This means that religiosity is based in the first place on letting oneself be touched by the existence of something that transcends the everyday, through a sort of purity and majesty, something that compels respect, something unexpected. It is only based on this experience that a man seeks the origin of this sentiment in God. . . . The necessity of being affected by what one feels is "sacred," even to the point that it makes our hair stand on end, is fundamental for man—for man is predestined for the sacred.[28]

Based on this insight, he came to see the fundamental problem of modern Catholic worship as its lack of a palpable *feel* of, or encounter with, the sacred: "If we do not cultivate the sacred and the dignified in our churches,

---

[27] Or as the RSV translation has it: "My roots spread out to the waters, with the dew all night on my branches."

[28] Given as an address at the International Academy held August 31, 2016, at Aigen; Aelredus Rievallensis, trans., "Dom Karl Wallner: The Profanation of the Sacred and the Sacralisation of the Profane," *Canticum Salomonis* weblog, January 10, 2018.

if we forget the *tremendum* and *fascinans*, then we can expect that human psychology will go looking elsewhere to fill the need to tremble before something majestic. If we degrade our liturgical ceremonies to the level of simple mundane ceremonies, if we banalise them, we should not be surprised to see people going elsewhere to satisfy their innate desire for sacred places, sacred symbols, sacred texts, and persons to venerate."[29] It was precisely the movement of desacralization in the name of modernization—with "modernity" conceived of in rationalistic, utilitarian terms, crowding out the sensuous, the poetic, the intuitive, and the mystical dimensions of Catholicism—that characterized the liturgical and ecclesial reforms of the 1960s!

Why were these reforms doomed to failure? One major reason is the domination of verbiage from beginning to end—verbiage locked, moreover, in the Zeitgeist of the 1960s and 1970s. In an attempt to be "with it," the Novus Ordo cemented itself into the period of its appearance, losing timeless and perennial features of Catholic worship. Conjure up in your mind's eye the way Mass is done at a typical parish church in the USA. The vestments, vessels, hymn choices, and architecture are far too often fossilized fads from the Boomer generation's coming of age. How many young adults would want to have *anything* to do with that? How many people in general wish to be inundated with words: in the opening rite and its hollow pleasantries (including unliturgical "Good mornings"[30]), in several recited readings, in a rambling homily, in an anemic and sentimental "Prayer of the Faithful," in a Eucharistic Prayer and Communion rite entirely said out loud, and in closing remarks

---

[29] Rievallensis, trans., "Dom Karl Wallner." *Tremendum* means terrible, awe-inspiring, fearful; *fascinans* means absorbing, spellbinding, gripping. The pair of words was applied as a description of the sacred by Rudolf Otto. Wallner offers illustrations of ersatz religious practices in which people try to find or make meaning for themselves and come into contact with something "separate" from the everyday, such as pilgrimages to famous people's tombs, obsessive devotion to sports, the cult of "star" personalities, the dramaturgy of films and rock festivals, zealous dedication to political movements, or superstitious practices. I cannot recommend his lecture too highly, as it contains precious insights into the course of the past half-century and the prospects and dangers of the present moment. In particular, all who are involved in youth ministry should read it carefully.

[30] See "De-ritualization" in Thomas Day, *Why Catholics Can't Sing*, rev. ed. (New York: Crossroad, 2013), 38–54. For more on the problem of verbosity and the loss of integral chant and silence, see Peter Kwasniewski, *Noble Beauty, Transcendent Holiness: Why the Modern Age Needs the Mass of Ages* (Kettering, OH: Angelico Press, 2017), ch. 10, "The Peace of Low Mass and the Glory of High Mass."

and further announcements about parish activities? How can the peace of Christ permeate souls when there is wall-to-wall noise and chatter? This is hardly a recipe for attracting converts and reverts.[31] The so-called "nones"— that is, those who profess no religion—would rather fast with Zen silence or take mind-altering drugs than surfeit on an all-you-can-eat buffet of words. And who can blame them?

Witnesses of the unexpected

While the world of modern worship, as cutting-edge as disposable razors, continues to bleed its population, newspapers, magazines, social media, and blogs regularly feature testimonies from Catholics young and old about how their encounter with the traditional liturgy was a dramatic moment of discovery, an unexpected "shock of the beautiful," a theophany, that drew them powerfully to Christ and His Church.

As a writer on liturgy, I frequently hear from people who want to share their experiences with me. Sometimes they say the traditional Latin Mass has taught them for the first time how to *pray* rather than merely saying prayers. That was true for me too: I could never understand the idea of *lectio divina*, praying with the Bible, until I went to the traditional Mass and discovered that it is meditating on, indeed *mediating* the Bible from start to finish:

> From Psalm 50 at the Asperges and Psalm 42 at the foot of the altar, to the Gradual and the Alleluia or Tract between readings, to Psalms 140 and 25 during the Offertory, to Psalm 115 at the priest's Communion, to the Prologue of John at the end of Mass, and verses from Psalms 17, 84, 101, 123, and others woven in here and there, with allusions to other books as well, the *usus antiquior*

---

[31] Judging from contacts with Catholics over the decades, accounts read in books or online, and anecdotes shared with me by others, I would hazard to say that few of those who come into the Catholic Church today were motivated to do so by the Novus Ordo liturgy in its 1970s guise. They enter and remain either *in spite of* the liturgy or because they know nothing whatsoever about what liturgy is supposed to be or because they have encountered the Novus Ordo done in a nobler manner that corresponds to their expectations. What the Consilium gave us, in Paul VI's preferred *modus celebrandi*, has no attractive power whatsoever. See chapter 4.

practices an "immersive" approach to Scripture that is sorely lacking in its replacement. The ancient liturgy is teaching the priest and the people how to *pray* God's Word, how to understand its fulfillment and reality in the present moment. It is a crash course in *lectio divina.* The liturgy is showing us that the Word is for the sake of worship, and worship for the sake of one-flesh communion with God Incarnate.[32]

Let us have a look at four testimonies—chosen from and representative of the large number I have collected—on the spiritual efficacy of the traditional liturgy.[33] The first:

It has now been five months since I started attending the Latin Mass every Sunday. I have to say it has completely and utterly taken over my heart in ways I would have never expected. I have tried to remain open and compassionate towards both expressions of the Mass, but as I journey I am finding that the TLM holds a beauty and truth that are simply missing elsewhere. I find it fascinating that it has been suddenly revealed to me like this. I had attended the Novus Ordo very faithfully, daily, for a very long time. It is like a veil has been lifted from my eyes and I am utterly head-over-heels in love.

A similar report from someone else:

We now attend the TLM as our ordinary Mass. It was a little overwhelming at first but after a couple of months it became more normal for us. Both my wife and I were astounded that even though at the beginning we had no idea what was going on, we still prayed more at Mass in the first month of TLM liturgies than in the last 10 years of Novus Ordo liturgies combined (or at least it felt like that!).

---

[32] Peter Kwasniewski, *Reclaiming Our Roman Catholic Birthright: The Genius and Timeliness of the Traditional Latin Mass* (Brooklyn, NY: Angelico Press, 2020), 163. Nothing could be more profoundly un-Protestant and anti-Protestant than this feature of the old Catholic liturgy. Cf. Peter Kwasniewski, *Resurgent in the Midst of Crisis: Sacred Liturgy, the Traditional Latin Mass, and Renewal in the Church* (Kettering, OH: Angelico Press, 2014), 33–46 and 124–38.
[33] Additional examples may be found in chapter 1 of *Noble Beauty.*

From an alumnus of the Franciscan University of Steubenville:

> I can honestly say that I have never been more confident, excited, and utterly confused about our faith since I walked into my first Latin Mass this spring. Where has this been all my life?!? Why on earth would anyone change it?!? Why wasn't this available at Franciscan University?!? It was like being starved and suddenly falling upon a feast, or completely desiccated and then mercifully carried out into the rain. *Finally*, in spite of and in the midst of my anguish and confusion, Catholicism makes sense. I feel like I've finally come home.[34]

A fourth example:

> I am 38 years old and have spent my entire life in the Novus Ordo Mass. I was very lukewarm until about four years ago when Our Lady brought me into relationship with her Son through the Rosary. . . . I finally attended the TLM for the first time last month and I was so overcome by the solemnity and beauty of the Mass that I was reduced to tears.

She is just one of so many people who have reacted thus—and not, obviously, from nostalgia (a thirty-eight-year-old isn't old enough for that, unless one takes "nostalgia" in the rarefied philosophical meaning given to it by Wojtyła and Ratzinger[35]). In company with the Desert Fathers, we ought to dwell on the significance of tears. In my twenty-five years of directing sacred music for the Novus Ordo, only a couple of times did I see someone go away from Mass in tears because the liturgy had so moved them. But it happens rather often at a High Mass that middle-aged and older people will have tears in their eyes because of the "solemnity and beauty" they experienced. This is common knowledge among musicians, probably because we are most likely to be accosted by these people afterwards. Tears like this are a sign of being moved in the depths, beyond

---

[34] This alumnus had attended Steubenville before the TLM began to be offered regularly on campus.
[35] See Peter Kwasniewski, "'What Is Most Deeply Human': Two Contrasting Approaches to Nostalgia," *NLM*, December 30, 2013.

the noise of opinions and preconceptions. They are the sign of an interior release and restoration, both a coming to oneself and a going out of oneself. They are the very opposite of something put on for show or grimly willed because it is good for you, like the taking of cod-liver oil. Even though the same person is not likely to have this reaction repeatedly, especially as he or she becomes more accustomed to attending the traditional Mass, the simple fact that this form of Mass prompts such reactions is already highly significant in light of Wallner's points.

As if to sum up all such reactions, Dom Alcuin Reid says, speaking of the traditional liturgy:

> Its demands bring forth a response in us. We find that the restraint and beauty of the ritual, the silence in which we find space to pray interiorly, the music which does not attempt to imitate the world or soothe the emotions but which challenges us and facilitates worship of the divine, indeed we find the overall ritual experience of the numinous and of the sacred, to be uplifting and nourishing.[36]

The splendor of the truth

"Wait a minute," a skeptic interjects at this point. "Isn't all this just a kind of aestheticism? Aren't you people getting preoccupied with superficial things and forgetting what *really* matters—that Jesus is present in the Eucharist, and that I have faith and love in my heart?"[37]

That, to be sure, is a common objection raised against our insistence on the primacy of tradition. It can be refuted if we return to the relationship

---

[36] See Alcuin Reid, "On the Tenth Anniversary of *Summorum Pontificum*, We Can Safely Say the Doomsayers Are Wrong," *Catholic Herald* [UK ed.], July 7, 2017.

[37] Thus, to give a real example, popular apologist Dave Armstrong states, concerning the manner of receiving Communion: "Reverence, solemnity, and piety, according to Holy Scripture and Holy Mother Church, are heart and soul matters. It is what is on the inside that counts, and will determine our outward behavior and demeanor and disposition" (www.patheos.com/blogs/davearmstrong/2020/03/communion-in-the-hand-reactionaries-vs-st-cyril.html). Oddly, he doesn't note the obvious point that the Church gradually replaced communion in the hand with communion in the mouth *because* her faith was seeking the most suitable outward comportment; nor does he grant that causality works in the opposite direction—namely, one's behavior, demeanor, and disposition influence "what is on the inside." There will be far fewer casual, unbelieving, and sinful communions with a ritual that makes the believer more conscious of taking part in a significant religious act.

of substance and accident. For it is not merely the case that substance and accident always go together and that, outside of the Holy Eucharist, we never get one apart from the other. More to the point, we perceive substance *through* its accidents; the liturgy addresses us as incarnate beings, not as free-floating intellects or vibrating rods of emotion, and we need to respond with our whole being, not just some favorite part of ourselves. Accidents are precisely what give us access to substance, purchase on it, insight into it, awareness of its depths. Concerning the power of intellect to "read the interiors of things" on the basis of what is taken in through the senses, Saint Thomas Aquinas writes: "*within* the accidents lies hidden the substantial nature of the thing; *within* words lie hidden the meanings of words; *within* likenesses and symbols lies hidden the symbolized truth; and effects lie hidden in causes, and vice versa."[38] The non-essential opens on to the essential, as a smile or a scowl, laughter or tears, open onto the heart, or as the ocean receding off to the horizon opens onto the infinity of its Maker. The greatest works of art have just this quality to them: as we gaze at the immediate contours and colors of a portrait by Vermeer or Rembrandt, our mind is borne beyond it to a reality greater than anything an artist could ever paint: the intensity of life, the light of the soul.

Beauty happens, so to speak, when there is a *clarity* about what the *thing itself is*. When someone is attracted to the traditional liturgy for its sights and sounds, it is not because he is stuck on these things but because these things coalesce around the reality, the Sacrifice of the Cross, and make it stand forth with a satisfying clarity. The surface qualities (or "accidents") so harmonize with the nature of the mystery that the result is the *splendor* of the *truth*. For men as body-soul composites, for Christians as disciples of the Word-made-flesh, there must be *both* elements: the truth *and* the splendor. *Confessio et pulchritudo in conspectu ejus; sanctimonia et magnificentia in sanctificatione ejus.* "Praise and beauty are before Him: holiness and majesty in His sanctuary" (Ps 95:6). Dom Gerard Calvet offers the perfect commentary:

> One enters the Church by two doors: the door of the intelligence
> and the door of beauty. The narrow door . . . is that of intelligence;

---

[38] *Summa theologiae* [ST] II-II, qu. 8, art. 1.

it is open to intellectuals and scholars. The wider door is that of beauty. The Church in her impenetrable mystery . . . has need of an earthly epiphany accessible to all: this is the majesty of her temples, the splendour of her liturgy and the sweetness of her chants.

Take a group of Japanese tourists visiting Notre Dame Cathedral in Paris. They look at the height of the stained-glass windows, the harmony of the proportions. Suppose that at that moment, sacred ministers dressed in orphried velvet copes enter in procession for solemn Vespers. The visitors watch in silence; they are entranced: beauty has opened its doors to them. Now the *Summa Theologiae* of St. Thomas Aquinas and Notre Dame in Paris are products of the same era. They say the same thing. But who among the visitors has read the *Summa* of St. Thomas? The same phenomenon is found at all levels. The tourists who visit the Acropolis in Athens are confronted with a civilisation of beauty. But who among them can understand Aristotle?

And so it is with the beauty of the liturgy. More than anything else it deserves to be called the splendour of the truth. It opens to the small and the great alike the treasures of its magnificence: the beauty of psalmody, sacred chants and texts, candles, harmony of movement and dignity of bearing. With sovereign art the liturgy exercises a truly seductive influence on souls, whom it touches directly, even before the spirit perceives its influence.[39]

For this very reason—that the externals are meant to tell us something about the reality to which they are in service, and draw us toward it—we must take care that they harmonize, that the outward aspect does not openly or subtly contradict the inward. It would be unfitting to put a king's robes on a pauper, or a gold ring in a pig's snout: there is discordance between the decoration and the thing decorated. The same holds in the other direction: a king does not wear dirty rags nor his horse a cheap saddle. Putting the king's robes on the king, and bedecking his mount in regal fashion: this is

---

[39] A Benedictine Monk [Dom Gerard Calvet], *Four Benefits of the Liturgy* (Southampton: Saint Austin Press, 1999), 19–20.

dignum et justum. The surface should correspond to the thing's nature and lead us directly into it. This is not to be "caught up in" the externals but to be caught up *by* the externals into the inner meaning.[40] Coventry Patmore condenses the insight into a stanza:

> Would Wisdom for herself be woo'd,
> And wake the foolish from his dream
> She must be glad as well as good,
> And must not only be, but seem.[41]

It is *through* humano-apostolic and ecclesiastical tradition, as "accidents," that we have access to dominical and divino-apostolic tradition, the "substance." The wealth of more changeable and, if you will, superficial features gives us access to the wealth of the unchangeable deposit, purchase on it, insight into it, awareness of its depths. What we encounter through ecclesiastical traditions is the divine truth in its incomprehensible majesty— and we have no other way, short of direct divine inspiration, to encounter it. This is why the love of liturgical tradition is not a passing whim or a fixation on externals but a normal and necessary path to the very heart of the matter—the Sacred Heart of Our Lord and the wisdom and love He has willed to entrust to His Church. We are integrally sanctified along this path, which both humbles our intellects with dependency on sensible, contingent, and inherited things and ennobles our senses by making them escorts into transcendent truth.

Giving all that is best to the Beloved

It is worth mentioning a marvelous but somewhat unknown spiritual author from seventeenth-century France, Mother Mectilde of the Blessed

---

[40] Dr. Glenn Arbery's argument on behalf of good oral rhetoric may be applied to liturgy as a mode of rhetoric: "Cunning orators have long been criticized for making false ideas of good seem more attractive than real good. In *Paradise Lost*, Milton writes that the devil Belial 'could make the worse appear/The better reason, to perplex and dash/Maturest counsels.' If someone on the wrong side can be so effective, is it enough to be on the right side? Hardly. It's necessary that the better reason appear as better, in its true lineaments and beauty, and that what is good appear as good through the mastery of the same arts also available to the subtlest of enemies. Our future depends on it" ("O Oratory!," *President's Bulletin*, February 22, 2018).

[41] *The Angel in the House*, Bk. I, canto X, opening lines.

Sacrament (1614–1698), foundress of the Benedictines of Perpetual Adoration. On one occasion, when the Blessed Sacrament was to be brought into the chapel of one of her religious houses for the first time, Mother Mectilde freely expressed her shock at the lack of care taken in the decoration of altars and sanctuaries by the Jansenists of her time:

> Jesus Christ, Our Lord, was supposed to make His entrance into His house. The next day, the feast of All Saints, she said, as if all in amazement: "What inconceivable goodness in Our Lord, to want to dwell with us! Oh! How great a day is tomorrow, a great feast for us! Let all that is most beautiful, most magnificent, be brought, so that I may adorn the altar with it. I am truly astonished that from every part of the world is not brought all that is most rich and rare to put upon the altar. What! When kings make their entry into their towns and kingdoms, every sort of pomp is prepared to receive them. And what! My God will come to dwell among some poor little wretches and paltry creatures, and no one thinks about this? It is amazing. I cannot bear it, and I do not know how to be astounded enough at these Jansenists who do not want to adorn their altars.[42]

Mother Mectilde has the good, natural, correct reaction of any lover when thinking of the honor due to the beloved, and feeling with zeal that the beloved deserves all we can give, the best we can give, from top to bottom, inside and out.

Recall the reactions quoted earlier—the lady who wrote: "I was so overcome by the solemnity and beauty of the Mass that I was reduced to tears"; the family man who confessed: "I am finding that the TLM holds a beauty and truth that are simply missing elsewhere. . . . It is like a veil

---

[42] *The Mystery of Incomprehensible Love: The Eucharistic Message of Mother Mectilde of the Blessed Sacrament* (Brooklyn, NY: Angelico Press, 2020), 101. We should realize that the Jansenists were rationalists in the liturgy: they wanted simplification, abbreviation, vernacularization, reduction of feasts, reintroduction of long-surpassed early practices, and so forth—all of which tendencies would recur in the late phase of the Liturgical Movement that yielded the Novus Ordo. See Kwasniewski, *Noble Beauty*, 115–33; Kwasniewski, *Reclaiming Our Birthright*, 48–53; "Does Pius VI's *Auctorem Fidei* Support Paul VI's Novus Ordo?," in my book *The Road from Hyperpapalism to Catholicism: Rethinking the Papacy in a Time of Ecclesial Disintegration* (Waterloo, ON: Arouca Press, 2022), vol. 1, ch. 9.

has been lifted from my eyes and I am utterly head-over-heels in love"; the Franciscan alumnus who sighed: "I feel like I've finally come home"; the husband and wife who were "astounded" at how the ancient Mass elicited their prayer; the scholar who noted: "Its demands bring forth a response in us." Please note that such reactions are *not* in response to the Real Presence of Christ, which is there in any form of the Mass. They are reactions to a *concentrated constellation of ecclesiastical traditions* that was handed down for centuries and indecorously scrapped in the postconciliar reinvention of our corporate self-image. Traditional liturgy has the power to induce in us appropriate attitudes when we are assisting at the Holy Sacrifice, privileged to be in the flesh-and-blood presence of Our Lord: humility, reverential fear, devotion, contrition, self-abandonment, tranquil joy. Without these, how can we be those "true adorers" who "adore the Father in spirit and in truth" (cf. Jn 4:23–24)? How will the Church find healing from her interior chaos, or be able to offer to the world a sure salvation?

Enthusiastic proponents of a "New Evangelization" need to adjust their ears to a new message: what we need most in the Catholic Church today is not more accommodation to the tastes and tactics of the secular world but a rekindling of the fire, light, and warmth that made the *Old* Evangelization successful and glorious.[43] "He who has an ear, let him hear what the Spirit says to the churches" (Rev 2:17). The revival of tradition is an extraordinary grace, given in response to the alarming amnesia of identity, the crisis of fidelity and even of identity through which the Catholic Church is passing in our times. To use a medical metaphor, it is as if the recrudescence of modernist cancer is being met with the cellular regeneration of tradition.

In the end, Catholics will be traditional, or they will not be at all. This realization brings both comfort in the midst of trial and a sense of growing responsibility: tradition is not something that automatically prevails in us, without our effort, as neither does orthodoxy or good morals. Just as we have to school ourselves in Catholic doctrine and labor against our fallen

---

[43] See Claire Chretien, "US Bishops ask young Catholics why they stayed in Church. They respond it's the Latin Mass," *LifeSiteNews*, June 13, 2019. The number of such testimonies is so numerous now that one could easily compile several anthologies. See, to get a taste, David Dashiell, ed., *Ever Ancient, Ever New: Why Younger Generations are Embracing Traditional Catholicism* (Gastonia, NC: TAN Books, 2022).

human nature with asceticism and conscious aspiration to virtue, so too we need to learn (or re-learn) our traditions in all their amplitude and richness, or they will evaporate under the scorching winds of late modernity. A contemporary writer, Lewis Hyde, coined the phrase "the labor of gratitude": truly taking possession of a heritage means being aware of its value, being grateful to God for it, laboring to get to know it better, and working to ensure that it remains alive and well—that it will, in spite of every obstacle, be passed on to the future. We must make our own the sentiment of the Psalmist: "My lot has fallen happily to me: my inheritance is precious to me" (Ps 15:6). Saint Augustine once wrote: "God who created you without you, will not save you without you." Happily, we do not have to *create* ecclesiastical traditions, but we *are* asked by God to save them with His help. These traditions deserve environmental protection far more than any endangered animal or plant species has ever deserved it.

Surely, Saint Paul is interceding for us, and continues to admonish us from his apostolic throne in glory: "Brethren, stand firm and hold to the traditions." God has truly given us of the dew of heaven, the fat of the earth, an abundance of corn and wine. He desires the tears of our longing for Him, which He provokes in the midst of His Temple, by the piercing beauty and awesome reverence of our traditional worship. He has turned the bread of our sorrow into the manna of angels; the natural water that keeps us alive He has transformed into the wine of His blood, which bestows eternal life in the beatific vision. To the happy couple at the wedding feast of Cana, and therefore to all of us who have been invited, with His mother, to the nuptials of the Lamb, we can surely apply these words of the Psalmist: "They shall be inebriated with the plenty of thy house; and thou shalt make them drink of the torrent of thy pleasure" (Ps 35:9).

It is in the Liturgy that the Spirit which inspired the Sacred Scriptures still speaks; the Liturgy is tradition itself in its highest degree of power and solemnity.

—Dom Prosper Guéranger

We must keep, and continue with the greatest respect, a Tradition handed down from century to century, a Tradition full of meaning (as everybody must admit), a Tradition, finally, which just because of its mysterious inspiration by the Holy Ghost, escapes all human calculations.

—Herman Schmidt (1961)

By the "profane novelties of words" we here refer to new chants, new histories, new readings and orations, and other such novelties which were not part of our forefathers' worship. . . . The Apostle urges us to avoid these profane novelties of words because "in determining matters anew, there ought to be some clear advantage in view, so as to justify departing from a rule of law which has seemed fair since time immemorial" (*CICiv*, Dig. 1.4.2 pr.). "Novelties should not be introduced without cause because change is dangerous and rightly blamed for opening the door to [further] novelty" (distinction 11, Quis nesciat). And "novelty adopted in church ritual is the mother of temerity, the sister of superstition, and the daughter of levity," according to Saint Bernard in his Epistle to the Canons of Lyon.

—Radulph of Rivo (d. 1403)

2

The Laws of Organic Development and the Rupture of 1969

Of the questions one can ask about the liturgy, three of the most elementary are: Where did it come from? Why is it the way it is? And what difference does it make?

One sometimes meets traditional Catholics who think of the classical Roman rite as something that was instituted by Christ in detail, either at the Last Supper or during the forty days after His resurrection, in a more leisurely version of the Latin Mass training camps offered in the wake of *Summorum Pontificum*. Some might be disappointed to know that this is not at all the way things happened historically. But as I hope to show, it would have been as unfitting for the liturgy to be instituted in detail from the very start as it would have been for Our Lord to hand over to the Apostles the *Summa theologiae* or Ludwig Ott's *Fundamentals of Catholic Dogma*. The reasons are very similar to the ones given by Saint Augustine when he praises the meandering path taken by the seventy-three inspired books of Scripture, written over many centuries by many individuals with different styles and points of emphasis, but altogether making up a single God-given volume that converges on Christ.

We know from Scripture that Our Lord instituted the liturgy of the New Covenant and that it was in a process of growth even during the lives of the Apostles, who continued to attend Jewish services for as long as their presence was tolerated, while meeting privately for the "breaking of the bread." The records of history—for example, the various missals, lectionaries, and chant books we possess—show a gradual development in the Church's public worship, especially after she gained her freedom with the Edict of Milan in 313, which allowed her to resituate the liturgy in spacious Roman basilicas. In both Eastern and Western rites, each century bears the fruit of new prayers, new feasts, new ceremonies, but *always* building upon what came before, in a process best understood as elaborating and extending further the preexisting content. This, I believe, is the most basic meaning of "organic" development: whatever comes later on arises, as if naturally, out of what is already there.[1]

Of course, human free will is involved, and the free play of contingent historical events. We are not automatons who act in a predetermined way, nor is the history of the Church like a train running on pre-set tracks. There was no intrinsic necessity that Saint Stephen be the first martyr, or that the cultus of Saint Lawrence have such prominence in the Roman Church, or that the Roman rite would be taken up by Charlemagne in Gaul and later delivered back across the alps with Gallican embellishments such as the Palm Sunday procession.[2] More broadly speaking, neither was it necessary that all Christians worship in the same way: this is why we have many families of orthodox liturgical rites, be they Roman, Ambrosian, Mozarabic, Coptic, Chaldean, Byzantine, Slavic, or Syro-Malabar.

How liturgical development is to be understood and evaluated is the fundamental issue behind every liturgical debate or divergence, not only in our day, but, arguably, in the entire history of the Church. Thus, understanding how liturgy develops presents us with a challenge not unlike the one faced by John Henry Newman in writing his *Essay on the Development of Christian Doctrine.* How do we distinguish good developments from bad

---

[1]   The Second Vatican Council appeals to just this concept: "There must be no innovations unless the good of the Church genuinely and certainly requires them; and care must be taken that any new forms adopted should in some way grow organically from forms already existing" (Constitution on the Sacred Liturgy *Sacrosanctum Concilium* [SC], §23). Never was a conciliar text more violated in the event. To date, the definitive study on the concept is Dom Alcuin Reid's *The Organic Development of the Liturgy*, 2nd ed. (San Francisco: Ignatius Press, 2005). I should note, however, that I disagree with Reid over the defensibility of Pius XII's Holy Week. See chapters 7 and 12.

[2]   See Michael Fiedrowicz's excellent historical summary in *The Traditional Mass: History, Form, and Theology of the Classical Roman Rite*, trans. Rose Pfeifer (Brooklyn, NY: Angelico Press, 2020), 17–24.

ones, otherwise known as corruptions?[3] What is the relationship between unchanging essential elements and incidental changeable elements? Could it be legitimate to view "the divine liturgy" as coming down to us from heaven, something we simply ought to receive, analogous to divine revelation? Or is Christian liturgy in a state of perpetual evolution? Can we harmonize the two views by seeing liturgy as teleological—that is, moving over time toward some perfection or fullness of form that, in fact, it achieves at a certain point? And if this is true, can we identify that point? What would be our criteria for doing so?

In his foreword to Alcuin Reid's book *The Organic Development of the Liturgy*, Joseph Cardinal Ratzinger wrote the following:

> Growth is not possible unless the liturgy's identity is preserved. . . . Proper development is possible only if careful attention is paid to the inner structural logic of this "organism": just as a gardener cares for a living plant as it develops, with due attention to the power of growth and life within the plant, and the rules it obeys, so the Church ought to give reverent care to the liturgy through the ages, distinguishing actions that are helpful and healing from those that are violent and destructive. If that is how things are, then we must try to ascertain the inner structure of a rite, and the rules by which its life is governed, in order thus to find the right way to preserve its vital force in changing times, to strengthen and renew it.[4]

If such criteria can be articulated, they will furnish sound guidance for many other debated points, such as how (and how much) solemnity should be present in liturgical celebrations, whether eastward orientation and the Latin language ought to be retained, what kind of music, vestments, and architecture are to be employed, how the faithful should comport themselves for Holy Communion, and so forth.

---

[3] See "Claude de Vert's Simple, Literal, and Historical Explanation of the Ceremonies of the Mass: A Watershed of the Catholic Enlightenment," *Canticum Salomonis*, May 6, 2019.
[4] Reid, *Organic Development*, 9–10.

The Vincentian distinction: *profectus* and *permutatio*

The fifth-century Church Father Saint Vincent of Lérins explains how Christian doctrine may legitimately develop over time. Vincent is not interested in merely describing change, as a sociologist would do; rather, he proposes a theological account of what kind of change is possible and desirable within Christianity:

> The growth of religion in the soul must be analogous to the growth of the body, which, though in process of years it is developed and attains its full size, yet remains still the same. There is a wide difference between the flower of youth and the maturity of age; yet they who were once young are still the same, now that they have become old, insomuch that though the stature and outward form of the individual are changed, yet his nature is one and the same, his person is one and the same. An infant's limbs are small, a young man's large, yet the infant and the young man are the same. Men when full grown have the same number of joints that they had when children; and if there be any to which maturer age has given birth these were already present in embryo, so that nothing new is produced in them when old which was not already latent in them when children.
>
> This, then, is undoubtedly the true and legitimate rule of progress, this the established and most beautiful order of growth, that mature age ever develops in the man those parts and forms which the wisdom of the Creator had already framed beforehand in the infant. Whereas, if the human form were changed into some shape belonging to another species, or at any rate, if the number of its limbs were increased or diminished, the result would be that the whole body would become either a wreck or a monster, or, at the least, would be impaired and enfeebled.
>
> In like manner, it behooves Christian doctrine to follow the same laws of growth [*profectus*], so as to be consolidated by years, enlarged by time, refined by age, and yet, withal, to continue uncorrupted and unadulterated, complete and perfect in all the

measurement of its parts, and, so to speak, in all its proper members and senses, admitting no mutation [*permutatio*], no waste of its distinctive property, no variation in its limits.[5]

A similar point was made by Cardinal Alfons Maria Stickler (1910–2007), a great canonist and a proponent of the traditional liturgy. He writes that the Church "was not founded by Christ as an institution already rigidly and irrevocably constituted, but as a living organism, which—like the [human] body, which is an image of the Church—would have to have a development, passing from the embryonic state, in which all of the essential characteristics of her being were present in seminal form, to a process of growth, according to external circumstances and a necessary adaptation to them, and also—not least of all—following the positive action of human free will."[6] This analogy to a living bodily organism has often been applied to the liturgy as well, which grows to full maturity by a process of articulation and expansion, like an oak tree from an acorn.

However, can't we question this analogy because it would imply eventual decrepitude? Indeed, this is what the liturgical reformers of the mid-twentieth century actually thought: that the Roman liturgy had become aged, wizened, ossified, fossilized. It had stopped developing and had turned into a "museum piece." That is why, in their view, it had ceased to attract or edify modern people.[7]

---

[5] Saint Vincent of Lérins, *Commonitorium*, ch. 23, nn. 55–56, trans. C. A. Heurtley, in *Nicene and Post-Nicene Fathers*, Second Series, vol. 11, ed. Philip Schaff and Henry Wace (Buffalo, NY: Christian Literature Publishing Co., 1894), rev. and ed. for New Advent by Kevin Knight.

[6] Cited by Roberto de Mattei, "Defending 'True Devotion to the Chair of St. Peter': A Response to Professor Douglas Farrow," *Catholic Family News* weblog, December 17, 2018.

[7] Admitting that such claims were exaggerated—there were many positive signs in the period between World War I and World War II: conversions, abundant vocations, large family sizes, and excellent Catholic writing in all major languages—nevertheless there was undeniably a growing disaffiliation of continental Europeans from Catholicism, and a dip was already seen in the relevant statistics prior to Vatican II. The awareness of a new need for outreach explains the surface plausibility of John XXIII's rationale for convening Vatican II. As everyone knows, however, the decline in all areas rapidly accelerated in the Western world after the Council. It has, at very least, obviously failed to achieve the goals for which it was convened.

But Saint Vincent's analogy is not meant to imply a one-for-one cor-
respondence to the laws that govern biology, especially under the reign of
original sin and its punishment, death. If man had not fallen, he would
still have grown from infancy to full stature, but then he would have
remained in the prime of health until summoned by God directly into
heaven. Similarly, the Church's doctrine, or rather, the expression of her
doctrine, develops to maturity, but it does not ever decline into sickness,
old age, or senility.[8] Her liturgy likewise develops under the guidance of
Divine Providence, under the breath of the Holy Spirit, the Lord and the
giver of *life*, making present anew the mysteries of the glorified Christ who
has conquered death and lives forever. As a consequence, *this* liturgy, in
its broad lines and beloved details, grows from strength to strength, from
glory to glory, until it reaches a stature that may be considered its mature
form, like that of a thirty-three-year-old man.[9] The archetype of liturgical
development, as of all other realities, is Our Lord Jesus Christ Himself. *Et
Jesus proficiebat sapientia, et aetate, et gratia apud Deum et homines*: "And
Jesus advanced in wisdom, and age, and grace with God and men" (Lk
2:52). Note that, according to Saint Luke, Our Lord advances, *proficiebat*;
He does not retreat or surrender, collapse or corrupt. As King David says,
speaking in the person of the anointed king to come: "For thou wilt not
leave my soul to Sheol; neither wilt thou suffer thy holy one to see corruption" (Ps 15:10).

---

[8] This is what happens, rather, to heresy and schism, as we can see with Protestants and the
Old Catholics. The Indian Cardinal Ivan Dias, representing the Vatican at the Fourteenth
Lambeth Conference in 2008, said these striking words: "Much is spoken today of diseases
like Alzheimer's and Parkinson's. By analogy, their symptoms can, at times, be found even in
our own Christian communities. For example, when we live myopically in the fleeting present, oblivious of our past heritage and apostolic traditions, we could well be suffering from
spiritual Alzheimer's. And when we behave in a disorderly manner, going whimsically our
own way without any coordination with the head or the other members of our community, it
could be ecclesial Parkinson's." See Hilary White, "Anglican Communion Suffering Spiritual
Alzheimer's and Ecclesial Parkinson's: Vatican Observer," *LifeSiteNews*, July 24, 2008.
[9] The great passage in chapter 4 of Saint Paul's Epistle to the Ephesians can thus be seen in a
fresh light. Christ ascending on high gave gifts to men: some He made apostles, some prophets, some evangelists, some pastors and doctors—and why? "For the perfecting of the saints,
for the work of the ministry, for the building up of the body of Christ: until we all meet in the
unity of faith and of the knowledge of the Son of God, unto a perfect man, unto the measure
of the age of the fullness of Christ" (Eph 4:12–13).

Our Lord chose to enter the world not as one already full-grown and glorified but as one who would begin with our smallness, accept our growth, suffer our death, be buried, rise again from the grave, and ascend into heaven with His luminous wounds. The liturgy of the Church, patterned after Christ's life, will also begin small, grow up to maturity ("unto the measure of the age of the fullness of Christ"), and then experience a kind of death. But this is not a death *in the realm of history*, as if the liturgy, after achieving its prime, might then decline and become corrupted. In the life of a human being, there are many dramatic changes from conception to birth, infancy to childhood, adolescence to full adulthood, but after that point, the most significant change is bodily death. Hence, just as doctrine progresses from conception as a revealed truth through its full maturity expressed as dogma and never ceases to be true, so too does the liturgy progress in such a way that it achieves and retains its perfection of form—"Thou shalt bring them in, and plant them in the mountain of Thy inheritance, in Thy most firm habitation which Thou hast made, O Lord; Thy sanctuary, O Lord, which Thy hands have established" (Ex 15:17)— and after this, it will "die," so to speak, at the end of time, when Christ returns in glory, and all symbolic rites will give way to the light of God fully manifested. As Saint John says of his vision of heaven in the Apocalypse: "I saw no temple therein. For the Lord God Almighty is the temple thereof, and the Lamb. And the city hath no need of the sun, nor of the moon, to shine in it. For the glory of God hath enlightened it, and the Lamb is the lamp thereof" (Rev 21:22–23).[10] And even so, the earthly liturgy will not so much be abolished as it will be absorbed into the heavenly liturgy. Like the Old Law, it will not be canceled out but fulfilled, brought to completion. If the liturgy could speak up for itself, it, too, could boldly say the Messiah's words: "Thou wilt not leave my soul to Sheol; neither wilt thou suffer thy holy one to see corruption."[11]

---

[10] One may fittingly see the "sun" here as representing the Eucharist and the "moon" the other sacraments and sacramentals that prepare for it or derive from it.

[11] In its magnitude, the Pauline liturgical reform was wrong *in principle*, because it assumes that the liturgy could, so to speak, "die" at some point *during* history and had in fact died and needed to be revived or replaced. Such a radical intervention is more like replacing someone with his clone than performing cosmetic surgery for skin blemishes.

The Vincentian canon: doctrine and liturgy

Saint Vincent of Lérins is famous also for the so-called "Vincentian canon"—that is, a rule by which orthodox doctrine can be distinguished from heresy so that we may distinguish the Catholic Faith from counterfeits. The canon reads thus: "In the Catholic Church itself, all possible care must be taken that we hold that faith which has been believed everywhere, always, by all. For that is truly and in the strictest sense Catholic, which, as the name itself and the reason of the thing declare, comprehends all universally. This rule we shall observe if we follow universality, antiquity, consent."[12]

As satisfying and impressive as it sounds—*ubique, semper, et ab omnibus*—this rule is not altogether easy to apply, and much ink has been spilled over its strengths and weaknesses, and the subtlety that must be brought to bear in its application.[13] Nevertheless, it epitomizes the conservatism of the Church Fathers as a whole and may be said, without exaggeration, to reflect the mind of the Church herself, since we find the same canon or paraphrases of it invoked as an authoritative principle down through the centuries.

The Vincentian canon was formulated in regard to doctrine, but it can and should be applied to liturgy as well, in keeping with the axiom *lex orandi, lex credendi*—that is, the way we pray reveals and confirms what we believe. Since we know that liturgy develops historically, even as doctrine does, we have to make the same distinction between change or mutation of essence (*permutatio*) and development in terms of enrichment, expansion, and new insight (*profectus*).[14] As the great admirer of Saint Vincent, John Henry Newman, put it: "A true development . . . may be described as one which is conservative of the course of antecedent developments being really those antecedents and something besides them: it is an addition which illustrates, not obscures, corroborates, not corrects, the body of thought from which it proceeds; and this is its characteristic as contrasted with a corruption."[15]

---

[12] Saint Vincent of Lérins, *Commonitorium*, ch. 2, n. 6.

[13] See Thomas G. Guarino, *Vincent of Lérins and the Development of Doctrine* (Grand Rapids, MI: Baker Academic, 2013).

[14] Inspired by Vincent, we might almost speak of a formula: age * universality = venerableness.

[15] John Henry Newman, *Essay on the Development of Christian Doctrine*, ch. 5, §6, n. 1 (London: Longmans, Green, and Co., 1909), 200.

New liturgical seasons, feasts, processions, and devotions introduced in the course of time are comparable to the dogmatic definitions that adorn the history of the Church. The dogmas are not new, but their formulation is; the celebration of the sacred mysteries is not new, but the particular shape of the calendar, the texts and rituals through which they are celebrated, emerge in time. But once liturgical rites *have* emerged, they are the privileged means by which the faith of the Church is expressed and lived; they cannot be swapped out at whim, or modified past recognition, any more than the canons and decrees of the Council of Trent can be contradicted or retired into oblivion. This is the principle of theological and liturgical conservatism: the Church holds on tightly to that which the Holy Spirit brings to birth in her.

Thus, we have to think of the "liturgical Vincentian canon" like this: What we find in all apostolic liturgical rites as they develop over time is that which must be recognized as being, whether explicitly or implicitly, "always, everywhere, and by all." Some few elements are explicit from the start, such as the use of bread and wine as matter for the Eucharist. Other elements emerge in the course of centuries but are subsequently taken up by all, everywhere, and retained from that point onwards—that is, they are treated with the same reverential respect as the original elements. A long list of such elements could be made, but here I shall confine myself to eight particularly important ones.

1. All traditional liturgies, East and West, celebrate the sacred mysteries with the priest and the people facing eastwards, or in the common phrase, *ad orientem.* As we saw in the last chapter, Saint Basil the Great, one of the Cappadocian Fathers and a preeminent patristic authority, identifies this practice as a custom handed down from the Apostles; Saint John Damascene, a towering figure in Greek theology, defends it with the witness of both Testaments.[16]

---

[16] See Uwe Michael Lang, *Turning Towards the Lord: Orientation in Liturgical Prayer* (San Francisco: Ignatius Press, 2008), and the definitive study by Stefan Heid, *Altar und Kirche: Prinzipien christlicher Liturgie* (Regensburg: Schnell und Steiner, 2019). There are a few cases historically where a liturgy might seem as if it were celebrated *versus populum* due to the unusual geographical location or layout of the church building, but in these cases the east happened to be on the side of the nave where the laity gathered, and therefore, by offering the liturgy eastwards, one would incidentally be saying it towards the people; yet the de-

2. All traditional liturgies, East and West, use an ancient and fixed anaphora (that is, Eucharistic Prayer), or, if they have more than one (as in the Eastern rites), specify which anaphora is to be used for which days or seasons of the liturgical year.

3. All traditional liturgies, East and West, employ an elaborate offertory by which the sacrificial finality of the bread and wine is clearly signified. In the Byzantine rite, this happens in part before the public start of the liturgy, as the priest prepares the prosphora; in the Western rites, such as the Roman and the Ambrosian, the offertory finds its place before the commencement of the anaphora.[17]

4. All traditional liturgies, East and West, treat the most Blessed Sacrament with the utmost veneration. Only the clergy handle the consecrated offerings. The clergy place the Lord directly into the mouths of the laity. Particles are carefully gathered up and consumed. Lavish signs of adoration are never absent. Vessels and fingers are thoroughly cleansed.[18]

5. All traditional liturgies, East and West, are hierarchically structured: the roles of bishop, priest, deacon, subdeacon, lector, acolyte, and so forth are clearly delineated. Only men serve in these roles, since they are all modes of exercising Christ's royal priesthood in the flesh. The faithful in

---

termining factor was the east, not the congregation. Different architectural and ministerial configurations can be found, but the orientation eastward is a common thread. Even so, the ancient basilicas were not designed so that the people could "see what was going on" at the altar; often enough, not only was the altar on an elevated platform beneath a ciborium (or baldachin), but thick curtains hanging around the ciborium were drawn closed during the anaphora, with an effect similar to that of the iconostasis in the East. See Shawn Tribe, "The Altar and Its Canopy: The Ciborium Magnum or Baldachin," *Liturgical Arts Journal*, January 25, 2018 and "The Form of the Altar and the Liturgical Movement," *Liturgical Arts Journal*, January 14, 2022. At any rate, an accidental *versus populum* is very different from an insistence that the liturgy *must* be said "towards the people," an anthropocentric posture that undermines theocentric divine worship.

[17] See the detailed series by Gregory DiPippo, which simultaneously demonstrates the universality of the offertory in all developed Western rites but also refutes the charges made against it by the reformers (both Protestant and modernist Catholic): "The Theology of the Offertory," at *NLM*, part 1, "A Response to a Recent Article Quoted on *PrayTell*," February 24, 2014; part 2, "The Offertory and Priesthood in the Liturgy," February 28, 2014; part 3, "A Different Theology?," March 8, 2014; part 4, "An Ecumenical Problem," March 28, 2014; part 5, "What the Offertory Really Means," May 9, 2014; part 6, "Prolepsis in the Offertory," June 26, 2014. Part 7 consists of many smaller articles on the various Western regional uses in religious and monastic orders, in medieval England, France, Spain, and Germany.

[18] On all these points, see my book *Holy Bread of Eternal Life: Restoring Eucharistic Reverence in an Age of Impiety* (Manchester, NH: Sophia Institute Press, 2020).

attendance also have their role, which is not to be confused with that of any of the ministers. Moreover, multiple layers of liturgical action may be taking place simultaneously, with ministers saying prayers or doing actions not intended to be heard or seen by the congregation, while the people and the choir are singing, and/or silently participating in various ways.[19]

6. Following on the last point, all traditional liturgies, East and West, make expressive use of church buildings in which the sanctuary, representing the Holy of Holies and the Church Triumphant, is clearly separated from the nave, representing this world and the Church Militant. Only certain individuals, correctly vested, may minister in the sanctuary during the liturgy. Christian theology is thus articulated in the architecture itself, especially through the use of barriers, doors, and images of saints.

7. All traditional liturgies, East and West, chant liturgical texts according to age-old melodies that grew up with those texts as their "musical clothing"—in the West, this would be primarily Gregorian plainchant. Moreover, fixed orations (either chanted or spoken) and proper antiphons are appointed for nearly every day of the Church's year; when a votive Mass is chosen, its content is nonetheless articulated in full. These antiphons and orations cover, with total honesty and integrity, the whole of Christian doctrine and belief, not sweeping any uncomfortable matters under the carpet. In this way the liturgy will speak often of human frailty, sinfulness, concupiscence, our need for divine grace in order to be saved, the danger of damnation, our need to resist demons and infidels, our calling to convert pagans, the evil of heresy and schism, the good of fasting, abstinence, and chastity, the primacy of heavenly and spiritual goods over temporal and earthly ones, the kingship of Christ over states and societies, and other such themes—all of which are prominent in the traditional Roman missal. Lectionaries follow the same rules: an annual (one-year) lectionary contains long-established readings, meant to be chanted, chosen for their liturgical suitability, and fearlessly addressing the paradox of weak and wandering mortals called to asceticism and divinization.

---

[19] On the foregoing, see my book *Ministers of Christ: Recovering the Roles of Clergy and Laity in an Age of Confusion* (Manchester, NH: Crisis Publications, 2021).

8. All traditional liturgies, East and West, are conducted in an elevated linguistic mode, whether that involves the use of a stylized hieratic language such as Byzantine Greek, Christian Latin, or Church Slavonic, or the use of florid imagery and unusual phraseology, as one finds in vernacular forms of Eastern rites. In either case, ritualized and numerologically significant repetition is a key component.[20]

And, as a sort of meta-principle, all of the foregoing elements are seen and treated as *requirements*—not options left up to the pastoral discretion or momentary choice of a celebrant or anyone else. In authentic Christian worship, one *must* offer the holy sacrifice facing liturgical east; one *must* use a fixed anaphora; one *must* carry out an oblative offertory and signify unambiguously one's intention to offer the divine victim; one *must* handle, consume, and distribute the Blessed Sacrament with utmost veneration, observing ontological distinctions between clergy and non-clergy and between men and women; one *must* respect the mutual parallelism of liturgy, theology, and architecture; and one *must* say or sing the antiphons, orations, and readings dictated by the rite, which together constitute a mature and rich expression of dogma and devotion.

We can therefore say with utmost confidence that if there was any Eucharistic liturgy that did *not* embody all eight of these elements—or that need not embody any one of them—it would stand in violation of the Vincentian canon and would not be a Eucharistic liturgy in the full and proper sense of the term. It would be a prayer service or paraliturgy with a consecration inserted into it. Any rite that departs from what has come to be practiced always, everywhere, and by all could only be an inexcusable and unforgivable rupture with tradition. No hermeneutic of continuity could ever repair this breach, for it would be a breach caused not by subjective "interpretations" (as the word "hermeneutic" implies) but by objective omissions, defects, aberrations, and vices. Neither could a copious bestowal of "smells and bells" overcome the problem, because the problem pertains not to artistic externals only but to the internal constitution of the rite in its texts, ceremonies, and rubrics. At best, smells and bells could only hide

---

[20] See my lecture "Poets, Lovers, Children, Madmen—and Worshipers: Why We Repeat Ourselves in the Liturgy," *Rorate Caeli*, February 19, 2019.

the deepest problems, even as new-fallen snow might temporarily cover the ugliness of an urban industrial zone.

The Novus Ordo disregards and transgresses the Vincentian canon

Let us now run through the eight elements mentioned to see how the Novus Ordo stacks up against fully-developed Catholic tradition.

1. It is no longer a jealously guarded secret that the rubrics of the Novus Ordo permit, indeed seem to assume, worship facing eastwards (*ad orientem*) instead of facing the people (*versus populum*).[21] However, the implementation of the Novus Ordo by the bishops *and popes* of the past fifty years has relentlessly favored *versus populum*, to the extent that both Paul VI in March 1965 and Francis in July 2016 have virtually equated the reformed liturgy with the *versus populum* stance.[22] A universal restoration of *ad orientem* in the Novus Ordo is as likely as a restoration of the Papal States or the Holy Inquisition. And even if it is done *ad orientem*, the Novus Ordo still allows for either posture in spite of their contrary significations, which amounts to a form of relativism, and leaves the decision in the priest's hands, which is a form of voluntarism. Speaking more broadly, the Novus Ordo encapsulates the errors of modern philosophy: in its prejudice against the universal anthropological language of symbols, its inescapable optionitis, its monotonous verbosity aimed at immediate comprehension, its rubrical sparseness and vagueness, and the veritable Tower of Babel created by vernacular missals, it shows itself to be characterized by nominalism, voluntarism, rationalism, and relativism.[23]

It is also worthy of note that Martin Luther was an early proponent of *versus populum* celebration, which fit in with his non-sacrificial notion of the Mass: "Let all the vestments, the altar, the candles be, until they get

---

[21] See my article "The Normativity of *Ad Orientem* Worship According to the Ordinary Form's Rubrics," *NLM*, November 23, 2015.

[22] Thus, too, Cardinal Cupich attempted to ban *ad orientem* in the archdiocese of Chicago as of December 2021—a move that implies a poor understanding of liturgical rubrics, legislation, history, and tradition.

[23] Together these -isms summarize the entire arc of modern philosophy, with its root in Ockham, its blossom in Descartes, its fruit in Nietzsche, and its decay in Derrida or Rorty (or pick any relativist/reductionist).

used up, or we decide to change them. And if somebody wants to do things differently, let him do it. But for the real Mass among true Christians, the altar should not remain in its current form and the priest should always face the people—as we can undoubtedly assume Christ did during the Last Supper. Well, all this will come to pass in time."[24]

2. The Novus Ordo offers a smorgasbord of newly-composed Eucharistic Prayers from which the celebrant chooses *ad libitum*. The Roman Rite's traditional anaphora, the Roman Canon, need never be used at all, and omitting the crown jewel of the Latin liturgy is standard practice.

3. Against the backdrop of a highly-developed and long-received offertory rite, the Novus Ordo represents the first liturgy in the Church's history that repudiates an oblative offertory, replacing it with a supper-oriented "presentation of gifts," based on the Jewish *berakah*, which does not unambiguously signify that the Mass is a true and proper sacrifice in propitiation for sins and for the good estate of the living and of the dead, offered to the Most Holy Trinity by the Son of God according to His human nature. It is again worthy of note that Luther, when designing his own Order of Mass for his followers, omitted the Roman Offertory, which he called "that complete abomination into the service of which all that precedes in the Mass has been forced, whence it is called Offertorium, and on account of which nearly everything sounds and reeks of oblation."[25] Thomas Cranmer held and acted upon similar sentiments.[26] As "the fruit of an elaboration that

---

[24] From the 1526 document *Deutsche Messe und Ordnung des Gottesdienstes*. Luther's claim about the Last Supper is fallacious: see Fiedrowicz, *Traditional Mass*, 143.

[25] See Martin Luther, *Formula missae et communionis pro ecclesia Wittembergensis* (1523), in *Works of Martin Luther*, vol. 6 (Philadelphia: Muhlenberg Press, 1932), 88. A description of Luther's plan for Mass and his reasoning about what to keep and what to reject is found in F. A. Gasquet and E. Bishop, *Edward VI and the Book of Common Prayer* (London: John Hodges, 1891), 220–24. It is disturbing to see just how many of Luther's exact steps were followed by the architects of the Novus Ordo. Such observations confirm Ratzinger's observation that after Vatican II, liturgists are more inclined to agree with Luther than with Trent. See "The Theology of the Liturgy," in *Theology of the Liturgy: The Sacramental Foundation of Christian Existence* (*Collected Works of Joseph Ratzinger*, vol. 11), ed. Michael J. Miller (San Francisco: Ignatius Press, 2014), 541–57; cf. 207–17. See also Michael Davies, *Pope Paul's New Mass* (Kansas City, MO: Angelus Press, 2009), 329–47.

[26] As Gasquet and Bishop write: "It will therefore appear that the ancient ritual oblation, with the whole of which the idea of sacrifice was so intimately associated, was swept away. This was certainly in accord with Cranmer's known opinions. . . . To understand the full import of the novelty it must be borne in mind that this ritual oblation had a place in all

the Holy Spirit has aroused, guided, and sanctioned," writes Michel-Louis Guérard des Lauriers, the Offertory "constitutes a sacred treasure which it would be a sacrilege to allow to be violated."[27]

4. In the Novus Ordo, the rite's explicit rubrics do not safeguard the Blessed Sacrament: ritual actions that offer to Our Eucharistic Lord the highest veneration we can give and which He is due were intentionally removed. This has resulted in the *Sanctissimum* often being treated with haphazard veneration as the rubrics do not demand more; most expressions of respect and adoration depend on the private religiosity of the clergy and people. The rubrics and ceremonies in this regard are utterly inadequate, which is why devout priests end up importing old practices into the new Mass. Because its architects were working under the influence of mid-twentieth-century theories of Christ's presence in the congregation and in the liturgy as a whole—truths that deserve recognition, but *not* at the expense of the unique personal and substantial presence of Our Lord in the Holy Eucharist—the resulting Novus Ordo may be called the first "non-Eucharistic-centric" liturgy, in the sense of a liturgy that is not manifestly centered on the Real Presence of Christ under the species of bread and wine.

5. The Novus Ordo is stubbornly horizontal in its manner of practice: the hierarchical offices are either canceled out or confused, the distinction between clergy and laity is blurred, the roles of men and women are mingled in a way only conceivable after the Sexual Revolution,[28] and instead of the verticality of simultaneous action directed to God, there is linear, modular, sequential liturgy in service of audience-oriented rationalism.

6. The Novus Ordo has a disintegrating or corrosive effect on ecclesiastical architecture and all other aesthetic elements of the liturgy. The symbolism of separation and articulation inside the church building is not respected by the rite or its rubrics. The Novus Ordo has never been able to produce great church buildings and vestments; its combination of

---

liturgies [of Christendom]" (*Edward VI*, 196). Cf. Michael Davies, *Cranmer's Godly Order: The Destruction of Catholicism through Liturgical Change*, rev. ed. (Fort Collins, CO: Roman Catholic Books, 1995).

[27] Cited in Fiedrowicz, *Traditional Mass*, 261n30.

[28] See Kwasniewski, *Ministers of Christ*.

antiquarianism and modernism is fatal to church design and decoration. Any decent church built in the past fifty years, and any beautiful vestment produced, has been modeled off of art created for the classical Roman rite. Newly built but traditionally-styled churches and vestments are in a state of tension with the rites performed in them, since every recognizably Catholic style, from the Romanesque to the Gothic to the Baroque, was designed solely and specifically with the celebration of the traditional Latin rites in mind. Like an infertile hybrid of two different species, the Novus Ordo lacks the fecundating cultural power of its natural-born parent. Artists and architects will always need to go beyond its confines if they wish to produce great work appropriate for the sacred liturgy.[29]

7. The Novus Ordo *can* be sung with chant, but Paul VI made his intention very clear in 1969: Gregorian chant should be given up for the sake of vernacular verbal comprehension.[30] Hence, the new liturgy's normative mode is text spoken aloud in a declamatory manner for didactic aims; chant is a little-used option, and indeed feels ill-suited to the reformed liturgy, as twenty-five years of experience directing choirs taught me firsthand. Apart from simple dialogues, the chant is contemplative music offered up to God, while the reformed rite calls for music "of the people, by the people, for the people." Moreover, the central texts of the Novus Ordo Mass—the Ordinary, the Propers, the Commons—lack the fixity and stability they have in the classical rite, and the multi-year lectionary, constructed entirely *de novo*, vastly increases the quantity of readings, without concern for their Eucharistic placement, while at the same time removing many readings that used to be present, including some that put before us the more challenging truths of the Faith, which we, as fallen human beings, need to hear as much as we

---

[29] One may see a confirmation of this judgment in the text of the "Agatha Christie petition" signed by many great figures of England's cultural life, protesting the loss of the traditional Latin Mass: see Joseph Shaw, ed., *The Case for Liturgical Restoration: Una Voce Studies on the Traditional Latin Mass* (Brooklyn, NY: Angelico Press, 2019), 213–16; cf. Martin Mosebach, "Liturgy is Art," in *The Heresy of Formlessness: The Roman Liturgy and Its Enemy*, rev. ed. (Brooklyn, NY: Angelico Press, 2018), 67–80.

[30] See chapter 4. Paul VI expected the vernacular for parish situations while simultaneously encouraging monastic communities to retain their Latin chant: see the apostolic letter *Sacrificium Laudis* of 1966, translated by Fr. Thomas Crean, OP, at https://lms.org.uk/sacrificium_laudis. There is so little serious support for Latin chant that the Vatican's website provides no vernacular version of this apostolic letter apart from the Italian.

do the more consoling truths. The orations of the Novus Ordo are notoriously dumbed down and edited for political correctness: they rarely use military imagery, for example, and go out of their way to avoid talking of human weakness, pressing dangers, trials and adversities, the captivity of sin, wounds caused by sin, offending God's majesty, remorse, reparation, penance, enemies of Christ and of the Cross, God's rights over men and nations, the merits of saints, miracles, apparitions, and the four last things. The orations of the old rite abundantly speak of such things, while the new rite deliberately and systematically avoids them, as its own designers admitted, and as many subsequent scholars have exposed.[31] The new rite carried over only 13 percent of the orations of the old missal unaltered, while discarding or heavily editing the remainder, or taking up older prayers and rewriting them to make them palatable to a modern mentality.[32] When I first learned about this, I nearly fell off my chair. Inasmuch as the Mass is the most perfect expression of our holy Faith and its truths, this comparison of texts brought home to me how different is the religion[33] expressed in and presented by the new Mass from the religion expressed in and presented by the old Mass. They overlap to some degree, but they are not the same. The *lex orandi* is the *lex credendi*, so if you make enough changes to the one, you will inevitably change the other.

8. The Novus Ordo in its *editio typica* and its vernacular versions is bereft of an elevated linguistic mode. This judgment includes the New American Bible as well as the 2011 ICEL revision of the Mass, which, although an improvement compared with its predecessor, is still dry, flat-footed, and

---

[31] See Lauren Pristas, "The Orations of the Vatican II Missal: Policies for Revision," *Communio* 30 (Winter 2003): 621–53, which contains a translation of and commentary on Antoine Dumas's 1971 eye-opening essay "The Orations of the New Roman Missal." An abundance of examples may be found in Pristas's groundbreaking book *The Collects of the Roman Missals: A Comparative Study of the Sundays in Proper Seasons Before and After the Second Vatican Council* (London/New York: Bloomsbury T&T Clark, 2013).

[32] Fr. Anthony Cekada, a pioneer in comparative research, first estimated a figure of 17 percent; but Matthew Hazell has now demonstrated the figure to be only 13 percent. For texts, charts, and analysis, see Hazell, "All the Elements of the Roman Rite?"

[33] "Religion" here is being used in the older scholastic sense, according to which it names a virtue—indeed, the highest moral virtue by which we give honor to God *through* external words, actions, and signs.

bereft of eloquence. In keeping with our age's impatient utilitarianism, repeated words and acts have been pared down to a minimum.

So many and such great deviations from the common liturgical heritage of orthodox Christians prompts the question: What was going through the heads of the reformers of the 1960s? On what basis did they act with such disregard or even contempt for that which, only a few years earlier, everyone would have hailed at the Church's most precious possession? The reformers went about their work as if the liturgy were nothing but temporary man-made expedients, having no inherent value or weight such that we ought to privilege the elegantly sprawling structures of the past over our own efficient steel-and-glass blocks. They must therefore have also assumed the neoscholastic reduction of liturgy to the form and matter of the sacrament.[34] The liturgical modernist or modern liturgist thinks that the historical development of liturgy is not included in the scope of Divine Providence or the Holy Spirit's work of leading the Church into the fullness of truth; it is not a teleological process that culminates in maturity.[35] It was never anything other than pure convention, something thrown together by a group of people at a particular time—nothing but "the work of human hands," assembled by a committee of experts and animated by a pope's command. Needless to say, that is not how liturgy was *ever* viewed and handled before the mid-twentieth century. Listen to the assurance with which a Jesuit author wrote, in 1950, of the Latin Mass: "The ritual setting of that central act is guaranteed. . . . It is the Spirit of God Himself who has moved throughout the centuries of our history and fashioned for us this liturgy,

---

[34] The Divine Office has the Psalter as its necessary core, which makes it vulnerable to manipulation by those who proudly believe themselves capable of devising a superior *cursus psalmorum* and who hold the structure and remaining components in disdain. The blessings (as given, e.g., in the *Rituale Romanum*) are even more vulnerable to the worst excesses of constructivism, since they have neither sacramental form and matter nor the Psalter to hold them in place. We will look more closely at neoscholastic reductionism in chapter 5.

[35] Or worse: he attributes to the Holy Spirit the wholesale cancellation and reordering of the Church's worship and even her doctrine and morality. John Rao mordantly notes the irony of the appeal frequently made by postconciliar ideologues to the Third Person of the Blessed Trinity: "All of their man-centered activities were defended by them with reference to the obvious guidance of a Holy Spirit whom I was said to despise, a Holy Spirit who had suddenly and inexplicably exchanged His friendship with Catholic Tradition for a Shiva-like passion for its annihilation." *Love in the Ruins: Modern Catholics in Search of the Ancient Faith*, ed. Anne M. Larson (Kansas City, MO: Angelus Press, 2009), 102.

which therefore bears the weight not only of our beliefs but of that Christian history itself. . . . Our Western Mass enshrines and brings to us alive, as it were, the passage of Christ through the lands where our own civilisation, our own ways of thought and expression, were fostered and matured."[36]

Formulating laws of organic development

Can we gather together our conclusions thus far and formulate them as "laws"? Yes, we may, and we will add the visual aid of DIAGRAM 1.

The background to this diagram is Our Lord's promise: *Cum autem venerit ille Spiritus veritatis, docebit vos omnem veritatem,* "when He, the Spirit of Truth, is come, he will teach you all truth" (Jn 16:13).[37] This promise includes the fullness of liturgy. One would expect, if the Church is truly governed by the Spirit of God, that her liturgy would, in its large lines and accepted forms, mature and become more perfect over time. Would it not then follow that the rate of change will slow down and the Spirit's work will gradually shift from inspiring new prayers to preserving the prayers already inspired? A liturgical rite will grow in perfection until it reaches a certain maturity, and then will cease to develop in any but incidental or minor ways.

The diagram uses two lines to illustrate this inverse relationship. The descending line represents the creation of liturgical forms, while the ascending line represents the preservation of existing liturgical forms. As the former action tapers, the latter action dominates, until that verse from Ezekiel is fulfilled in the Church's sacred liturgy: "Your renown went forth among the nations because of your beauty, for it was perfect through the splendor that I had bestowed on you, declares the Lord God" (Ezek 16:14).[38] The

---

[36] Fr. John Coventry, *The Breaking of Bread: A Short History of the Mass* (New York: Sheed & Ward, 1950), 3. Coventry also says the same about the various Eastern rites.

[37] Saint Thomas Aquinas (*ST* II-II, qu. 1, art. 9, sed contra) cites this verse as evidence for the indefectibility of the Church: "The universal Church cannot err, since she is governed by the Holy Ghost, Who is the Spirit of truth: for such was Our Lord's promise to His disciples (Jn 16:13): 'When He, the Spirit of truth, is come, He will teach you all truth.'" Again, *ST* III, qu. 83, art. 5, sc: "The custom of the Church stands for these things: and the Church cannot err, since she is taught by the Holy Ghost."

[38] This entire chapter of Ezekiel, especially verses 8 to 26, can be taken as a description of a three-stage historical drama: first, the calling of Israel and the old covenant; second, the coming of Christ and the new covenant, which inaugurated a period of maturation and royal

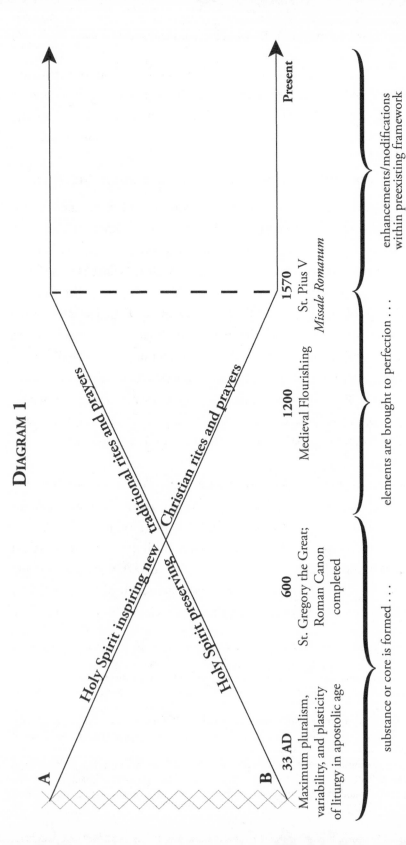

DIAGRAM 1

A

Holy Spirit inspiring new traditional rites and prayers

Christian rites and prayers

Holy Spirit preserving

B

33 AD
Maximum pluralism, variability, and plasticity of liturgy in apostolic age

600
St. Gregory the Great; Roman Canon completed

1200
Medieval Flourishing

1570
St. Pius V
Missale Romanum

Present

substance or core is formed . . . .

elements are brought to perfection . . . .

enhancements/modifications within preexisting framework

descending line reminds us of the descent of the dove on the Messiah, or the tongues of fire on Pentecost announcing a new dispensation. There will never be another dispensation: that of Christ, given to the world by the power of His Spirit, is definitive.[39] Hence, one can never expect a time, after the age of the Apostles, in which either *new* Christian sacraments *or* fundamentally new rites will come into existence. The ascending line, in contrast, reminds us of the Ascension and the Assumption, exemplars of our final destiny in the unchanging bliss of heaven. As liturgy unfolds over time, it becomes, more and more evidently, the unchanging image of the eschatological banquet. In the stately words of Newman:

> When the last Apostle had been taken to his throne above, and the oracle of inspiration was for ever closed, when the faithful were left to that ordinary government which was intended to supersede the special season of miraculous action, then arose before their eyes in its normal shape and its full proportions that majestic Temple, of which the plans had been drawn out from the first by our Lord Himself amid His elect Disciples. Then was it that the Hierarchy came out in visible glory, and sat down on their ordained seats in the congregation of the faithful. Then followed in due course the holy periodical assemblies [the Councils], and the solemn rites of worship and the honour of sacred places, and the decoration of material structures; one appointment after another, realizing in act and deed the great idea which had been imparted to the Church since the day of Pentecost.[40]

---

splendor; third, the apostasy of the twentieth century when churchmen went whoring after secular values, created "colorful shrines" to the gods of the world, and made a religion out of humanism, burning incense to "images of men." To these values, gods, and images, churchmen sacrificed the Church's sons and daughters, in the outward exodus of the baptized who left the Church and the internal exodus of the faithful who have ceased to believe or even to know the Catholic Faith.

[39] Fr. Carlo Balić: "This Spirit of the Seven Gifts Who dwells in us, not as in the midst of ruins, but as in a temple (1 Cor 3:16–17; 6:19), is the Spirit of Pentecost; He is the Spirit of Truth (Jn 14:17) whose special mission consists in revealing to the world the full substance of Christ and all the wonders the Son of God had kept hidden or had not completely and clearly revealed." Cited in Roberto de Mattei, *Love for the Papacy and Filial Resistance to the Pope in the History of the Church* (Brooklyn, NY: Angelico Press, 2019), 119.

[40] John Henry Newman, *Sermons Preached on Various Occasions* (London: Longmans, Green, and Co., 1908), Sermon 11, "Order, the Witness and Instrument of Unity," p. 192.

LAW #1. *There is true development in regard to liturgical rites.* They are not handed down from heaven in their perfection, nor absolutely fixed and frozen.[41] As in general with dogma and morals, so with the liturgy, the Lord bestows on human beings the dignity of being true causes of the articulation of doctrine, the application of laws, and the enrichment of public worship.

LAW #2. *Authentic development begins from and remains faithful to what the Lord entrusted to the Apostles.* The "deposit of faith" contains all the principles of sacred doctrine, such that nothing enunciated later in the ecumenical councils or in the papal magisterium may contradict it. In like manner, the Apostles as they spread out to the four corners of the earth took with them the seeds or principles of the liturgical rites that subsequently flourished as the major rites of the Church. There is no liturgical rite that does not belong to a definite apostolic tradition extended continuously over time. As Joseph Ratzinger says:

> The individual rites have a relation to the places where Christianity originated and the apostles preached: they are anchored in the time and place of the event of divine revelation. Here again, "once for all" and "always" belong together. The Christian faith can never be separated from the soil of sacred events, from the choice made by God, who wanted to speak to us, to become man, to die and rise again, in a particular place and at a particular time. "Always" can only come from "once for all." The Church does not pray in some kind of mythical omnitemporality. She cannot forsake her roots. She recognizes the true utterance of God precisely in the concreteness of its history, in time and place: to these God ties us, and by these we are all tied together. The diachronic aspect, praying with

---

[41] It may be helpful to invoke here a distinction from Saint Thomas: "Just as man has a certain perfection of his nature as soon as he is born, which perfection belongs to the very essence of his species, while there is another perfection which he acquires by growth, so again there is a perfection of charity which belongs to the very essence of charity, namely that man love God above all things and love nothing contrary to God, while there is another perfection of charity, even in this life, to which a man attains by a kind of spiritual growth—for instance, when a man refrains even from lawful things in order to give himself more freely to the service of God" (*ST* II-II, qu. 184, art. 3, ad 3). Analogously, the Christian liturgy even at its birth has the fundamental perfection of being what it is by Christ's institution—namely, the locus of unity in charity; and yet it is meant to grow and does grow by divine favor so that God may be loved and served ever more fully through the acts it posits and the opportunities it affords.

the Fathers and the apostles, is part of what we mean by rite, but it also includes a local aspect, extending from Jerusalem to Antioch, Rome, Alexandria, and Constantinople. Rites are not, therefore, just the products of inculturation, however much they may have incorporated elements from different cultures. They are forms of the apostolic tradition and of its unfolding in the great places of the tradition. . . . They elude control by any individual, local community, or regional Church. Unspontaneity is of their essence. In these rites, I discover that something is approaching me here that I did not produce myself, that I am entering into something greater than myself, which ultimately derives from divine revelation. . . . From this it follows that there can be no question of creating totally new rites.[42]

A rite cannot be fabricated *ex nihilo*. Hence the dictum of Trent anathematizing anyone who would change the received and approved rites into other new ones.[43] It is apparent from this observation that not even a pope has or could have the authority to create a new rite.[44]

LAW #3. *The "truth" into which the Holy Spirit guides the Church includes the development of her liturgy.* Hence, any significant or wholesale rejection of elements that have come to be practiced and accepted over a long period of time in the Church is, in a certain sense, a sin against the Holy Spirit, and any attempt to recast a rite from the ground up cannot but reflect a false theology of the Church and of the Trinity.[45] This is all the more apparent if we recall that the liturgy is the locus of divine revelation given by the

---

[42]   *Spirit of the Liturgy*, trans. John Saward (San Francisco: Ignatius Press, 2000), 163ff.; in the commemorative edition that contains Guardini as well, 177ff.; in vol. 11 of the *Collected Works*, 101ff.

[43]   I will discuss this canon below.

[44]   See chapters 3 and 8 for further discussion.

[45]   To the objection "How can you say this about work endorsed by popes?" I reply: we are not privy to what certain popes were *thinking* or *intending* when they overthrew centuries of tradition, but we know very well *what they did*, and the harm it has caused in ever-widening waves. Were they aware that they were resisting the work of God, the *opus Dei*, the outward signs of the inward dwelling of the Holy Spirit in the Church? How could they *not* have been aware? And if they were emboldened by the ambiance of ultramontanism—the pope can do no wrong; his will is divine law, exempted from error, exempted from imprudence, etc.—or by the swaggering of *aggiornamento*, can we not say that they *should* have known better? The pope is not, after all, Johnny from the local parish, who may not know (and perhaps has no duty to know) much about theology, Scripture, canon law, or liturgy.

Father, the extension through time and space of the incarnation of the·Son, and the outpouring of the Spirit in the prayer of the Bride of Christ.

LAW #4. *As the liturgy develops, it becomes fuller and more perfect,* both as an expression of the mysteries of faith and as a vehicle for inculcating appropriate virtues in the faithful and for eliciting from them the acts of faith, hope, and charity that are demanded by these mysteries. Hence, just as the creeds of the Church grow in their fullness until they reach a certain perfection (see DIAGRAM 2), so too, the liturgical rites of the Church grow over time until they reach a perfection of text, music, ceremony, and kindred signs that are fitting both to expressing the mysteries and to impressing them upon the faithful. The Holy Spirit takes countermeasures, so to speak, against the decrease of the connatural apostolic knowledge of divine truth (one thinks of Saint Paul's "there must be heresies"[46]) by ensconcing certain doctrinal propositions and liturgical rites across history as concrete parameters for faith and worship, like the inescapable givenness of Christ's physical Body during His earthly life, or the continued presence of His Mystical Body on earth. Just as God revealed to Moses the exact pattern of the tabernacle he was to build,[47] so too the Son of God fulfilled all the prophetic types in offering His own sacrifice as the perfection of worship—nothing was left to chance; every detail was deliberate and controlled.[48] In like manner, this exactitude and fulfillment is perpetuated in a new sacramental mode that has its external reflection in a progressive fixity and comprehensiveness of liturgical form.[49]

---

[46] 1 Cor 11:19. See Cardinal Charles Journet on "the privileges of the Apostles as founders of the Church," in *The Theology of the Church*, trans. Victor Szczurek (San Francisco: Ignatius Press, 2004), 116–22, 156–57.

[47] See Ex 25:40; 26:30; Num 8:4. In 1 Chron 28:19, we read that "all these things [*viz.*, the plan of the temple Solomon was to build] came to me written by the hand of the Lord that I might understand all the works of the pattern."

[48] See Saint Thomas, *ST* II-II, qq. 101–3 on the ceremonial precepts of the law, and *ST* III, q. 83, on the rite of Mass. Few have grasped the interplay of the Old and New Testaments as well as the Angelic Doctor, as we can see in his liturgical texts for the Office of Corpus Christi.

[49] Roberto Spataro points out the fittingness of reciting an inflexible creed, the Niceno-Constantinopolitan, in the midst of what had grown into an inflexible Eucharistic sacrifice: "The articles of the faith are professed in the context of a liturgical act that deserves to be called traditional in the noblest sense of the term—a thing slowly forged that, beginning in the dawn of apostolic liturgy, has reached the full splendor of its perfection." *In Praise of the Tridentine Mass and of Latin, Language of the Church*, trans. Zachary Thomas (Brooklyn, NY: Angelico Press, 2019), 79.

DIAGRAM 2

Apostles' Creed	Nicene Creed	Niceno-Constantinopolitan Creed
I believe in God, the Father Almighty, Creator of Heaven and earth, and in Jesus Christ, His only Son Our Lord, Who was conceived by the Holy Spirit, born of the Virgin Mary, suffered under Pontius Pilate, was crucified, died, and was buried; He descended into Hell; on the third day He rose again from the dead; He ascended into Heaven, and is seated at the right hand of God, the Father almighty; from thence He shall come to judge the living and the dead. I believe in the Holy Spirit, the holy Catholic Church, the communion of saints, the forgiveness of sins, the resurrection of the body, and life everlasting. Amen.	I believe in one God, the Father all-powerful, maker of all things both seen and unseen. And in one Lord Jesus Christ, the only-begotten Son of God, begotten from the Father, that is from the substance [*ousias*; *substantia*] of the Father, God from God, light from light, true God from true God, begotten not made, consubstantial [*homoousion*; *unius substantiae*] with the Father, through whom all things came to be, both those in heaven and those on earth; for us men and for our salvation he came down and was incarnate, was made man, suffered and rose up on the third day, went up into the heavens, is coming to judge the living and the dead. And in the Holy Spirit.	I believe in one God, the Father almighty, maker of heaven and earth, of all things visible and invisible; and in one Lord Jesus Christ, the Only-Begotten Son of God, born of the Father before all ages, God from God, Light from Light, true God from true God, begotten, not made, consubstantial [*homoousion*; *consubstantialem*] with the Father, through whom all things were made. Who for us men and for our salvation came down from heaven, and by the Holy Spirit was incarnate of the Virgin Mary, and became man. For our sake He was crucified under Pontius Pilate, suffered death, and was buried, and rose again on the third day in accordance with the Scriptures, and ascended into heaven, is seated at the right hand of the Father. And He will come again in glory to judge the living and the dead, of whose kingdom there will be no end. And in the Holy Spirit, the Lord and giver of life, who proceeds from the Father and the Son, who with the Father and the Son is adored and glorified, who has spoken through the prophets. I believe in one, holy, catholic and apostolic Church. I confess one Baptism for the forgiveness of sins. And I look forward to the resurrection of the dead and the life of the world to come. Amen.

There are three corollaries to this fourth law.

COROLLARY 1. The rate of liturgical change *decreases* over time, as the rite achieves the plenitude intended for it by Divine Providence.

COROLLARY 2. One should expect a rite, after a certain point, to be relatively permanent and immobile, so that it is a compliment rather than a criticism to say of it that "it has hardly changed for four hundred years," as we can say of the Roman Missal in the period from 1570 to ca. 1950.

COROLLARY 3. The clergy offering and the faithful assisting at a particular rite will *understand it to be appropriate* that the rite should be permanent and immobile. It is not merely that liturgies tend toward stability and constancy; it is that this process of stabilization and permanence is seen to be desirable and fitting for the life of the Church. It is seen as a blessing from the Lord, who, having raised up century after century of saints to enhance and enrich the liturgy, now seals it with His sovereign blessing, imparting to it a share in His own immutability and eternity. This attitude is given sublime expression in the Church's book of prayer, the Psalms: "Generation and generation . . .shall publish the memory of the abundance of thy sweetness. . . . Thy kingdom is a kingdom of all ages: and thy dominion endureth throughout all generations" (Ps 144). The philosopher Émile-Auguste Chartier wrote: "It does not surprise me that the Church dreads change of even the slightest sort. Long experience has shown her that true peace of soul presupposes unhesitating prayer on the lips, and this in turn means that things are always said in the same way."[50] The poet Paul Claudel echoed him:

> Men of small and superficial spiritual understanding, heretics, and modernists, are forever itching to get their hands on things, to change everything, to radically reorder everything. The Church for her part remains attached to the unchanging order of her doctrine and her ceremonies, seeing, in the words of Genesis, that these things are not only good but very good. In her psalms and hymns,

---

[50] Cited in Dom Gerard Calvet, *The Sacred Liturgy* (London: The Saint Austin Press, 1999), 66. Someone once asked an Armenian-rite priest: "Don't you ever get tired of celebrating the same liturgy every day?" He replied: "Do you get tired of seeing your mother each day? Would you want a different mother?"

in every morning's Mass, in the great poem of the liturgy—at once both a dramatic action and a chorus, which stretches out through the whole year—the souls of the faithful, thirsting for love and for beauty, constantly find the living satisfaction of their desire, as also their fathers did before them.[51]

Such a mentality was once universal, even taken for granted among Christians, in the West and in the East. Yet Eastern institutions have maintained it, while Western ones have abandoned it.[52] In the words of Fr. Richard Cipolla:

> The Orthodox believe that the Liturgy of St. John Chrysostom and the Liturgy of St. Basil are God-given. And I would dare to say that the same is true for the Traditional Roman Mass. It is God-given. It developed in the womb of the Church like a pearl in an oyster. It has nothing to do with committees or consilia appointed to invent a new form of Mass that has relevance only to those who wrote the texts, whether on a napkin in Trastevere or in an office in the Vatican. The irrelevancy of the Catholic Church in this post-modern age is in great part due to the irrelevancy of a liturgy invented in the modern age and now already obsolete in the post-modern age of freedom defined by the naked self.[53]

LAW #5. *To the extent that a liturgy is perfected, its changes will be proportionately incidental or accidental.* Thus, in the first half of the first millennium, something as basic as the Eucharistic prayers of the Mass were still in process of growth; in the second half of the first millennium, the core of the Gregorian chant corpus was built up; in the first half of the second millennium, the rites of Holy Week achieved their full ceremonial splendor; in the second half of the second millennium (until the liturgical reform),

---

[51] Cited in Calvet, *The Sacred Liturgy*, 68.

[52] Perhaps the most profound demonstration in our times of the inherent bond between church renewal and constancy in tradition is offered by the Coptic Church in Egypt. See Daniel Fanous, *A Silent Patriarch: Kyrillos VI, Life and Legacy* (Yonkers, NY: St. Vladimir's Seminary Press, 2019) and Mark Gruber, *Journey Back to Eden: My Life and Times among the Desert Fathers* (Maryknoll, NY: Orbis Books, 2002).

[53] Fr. Richard Cipolla, "Sermon for the Fifth Sunday after Pentecost: The Western Civilization is Daughter of the Catholic Church," *Rorate Caeli*, July 10, 2017.

growth tended to concern only additions or modifications of feasts in the liturgical calendar.

It is not difficult to find human parallels to these laws of liturgical development. Think of the invention of the gasoline-powered engine: it went through many types and phases, cycles of trial and error, much variation from place to place, but over time the better designs prevailed, and for many decades now, we have known how to build efficient engines. Variations at this point are tiny and would be grasped only by specialists. For that matter, any artifact stabilizes over time once its design is optimal for its purpose. The literary form known as the sonnet was brought to perfection by Shakespeare and his contemporaries; it has remained constant to this day, and continues to be used by serious poets. Let me offer another comparison. The Greek heroic age lasted about 250 years; Homer left an account of it in two epics that cannot be surpassed for beauty or sublimity. Ever after, the Greeks revered and preserved his singular achievement. They quoted Homer for centuries to come, recognizing that he was their foundational poet and that they were indebted to him for their national identity. They did not chafe at the bonds of inferiority or push toward a forced originality but rejoiced in having received the sort of gift that no nation can demand or even expect. The same is true of other towering poets: Italians will never have another Dante, nor Englishmen another Shakespeare. A wise people cherishes its greatest poets and derives its own voice from them. Here, the act of preserving is not a sign of weakness but a sign of strength of discernment. In its inherent artistry and the totality of the culture that surrounds it and lives by it, the traditional Latin Mass is a far greater treasure for Roman Catholics than Homer, Dante, or Shakespeare for their countrymen.

I am reminded of a fine statement by the musicologist Alfred Einstein: "It was in the piano concerto that Mozart said the last word in respect to the fusion of the concertante and symphonic elements—a fusion resulting in a higher unity beyond which no progress was possible, because perfection is imperfectible."[54] Others may try to equal Mozart's concertos; no one

---

[54] Alfred Einstein, *Mozart: His Character, His Work*, trans. A. Mendel and N. Broder (New York: Oxford University Press, 1945), 288.

will ever exceed them. Obviously one does not measure liturgy by the categories of efficiency or aesthetic beauty or any other single category alone, although each would be pertinent in its own way. The point is rather that when liturgy in its texts, ceremonies, music, vestments, and so forth attains a certain fullness of doctrine and richness of expression, it has arrived at its *telos* or goal. After this, changes will concern minor or peripheral matters, such as the introduction of new feasts.

Catholic liturgy as the work of the Holy Spirit

If the "Eucharistic sacrifice is the font and apex of the Christian life,"[55] and the Holy Spirit is "the Lord and giver of life,"[56] it follows that the Holy Spirit is "the Lord and giver of the Eucharistic sacrifice"—and, by extension, of the sacramental and liturgical worship of the Church in its entirety. The Church Father Saint Gregory Nazianzen makes an interesting observation: "To this [transition from the Mosaic law to its abolition] I may compare the case of theology [i.e., Christian revelation], except that the procedure is reversed. For in the former case, the change is made by successive subtractions; here, perfection is reached by additions. For the matter stands thus: The Old Testament proclaimed the Father openly, and the Son more obscurely. The New Testament manifested the Son, and suggested the divinity of the Spirit. Now the Spirit Himself dwells among us, and supplies us with a clearer demonstration of Himself."[57]

What is this "clearer demonstration" of the Spirit? According to Dom Guéranger, it is principally the sacred liturgy, the public prayer of the Church.

It is in the holy Church that this divine Spirit dwells. He came down to her as an impetuous wind, and manifested Himself to her under the expressive symbol of tongues of fire. Ever since that day of Pentecost, He has dwelt in this His favoured bride. He is the principle of everything that is in her. He it is that prompts her prayers, her desires, her canticles of praise, her enthusiasm, and

---

[55]   Dogmatic Constitution on the Church *Lumen Gentium*, §11.
[56]   Niceno-Constantinopolitan Creed.
[57]   Saint Gregory Nazianzen, *Oration* 31, n. 26.

even her mourning. Hence her prayer is as uninterrupted as her existence. Day and night is her voice sounding sweetly in the ear of her divine Spouse, and her words are ever finding a welcome in His Heart. . . .

Let not then the soul, the bride of Christ, that is possessed with a love of prayer, be afraid that her thirst cannot be quenched by these rich streams of the liturgy. . . . Let her come and drink this clear water which springeth up unto life everlasting; for this water flows from the very fountains of her Saviour; and the Spirit of God animates it by His virtue, rendering it sweet and refreshing to the panting stag. . . .

God forbid that we should ever presume to put our human thoughts side by side with those which our Lord Jesus Christ, who is the Wisdom of God, dictates by the Holy Ghost to His well-beloved bride the Church! . . .

This renovative power of the liturgical year, to which we wish to draw the attention of our readers, is a mystery of the Holy Ghost, who unceasingly animates *the work which He has inspired the Church to establish among men*; that thus they might sanctify that time which has been given to them for the worship of their Creator.[58]

Guéranger writes like a romanticizing medievalist, but the view he expresses here was officially endorsed by a pope who tended, if anything, to be sober and scientific in mentality, Pius XII. In his watershed encyclical on the liturgy, *Mediator Dei*, Pius XII pointed out an erroneous tendency found among some avant-garde travelers in the Liturgical Movement "who are bent on the restoration of all the ancient rites and ceremonies indiscriminately":

The liturgy of the early ages is most certainly worthy of all veneration. But ancient usage must not be esteemed more suitable and proper, either in its own right or in its significance for later times and new situations, on the simple ground that it carries the savor

---

[58] Dom Prosper Guéranger, *The Liturgical Year*, vol. 1: *Advent*, trans. Dom Laurence Shepherd (Great Falls, MT: St. Bonaventure Publications, 2000), 1–2, 8, 16, emphasis added.

and aroma of antiquity. The more recent liturgical rites likewise deserve reverence and respect. They, too, owe their inspiration to the Holy Spirit, who assists the Church in every age even to the consummation of the world (cf. Matt 28:20). They are equally the resources used by the majestic Spouse of Jesus Christ to promote and procure the sanctity of man.[59]

This passage is often quoted out of context, as if it amounts to blanket endorsement of any and all "recent liturgical rites." Yet this encyclical was published in 1947, prior to any major changes that would be made to the Roman rite in the years thereafter;[60] the noble Roman rite was still very much intact. The liturgy committee that was to give Bugnini his first post at the Vatican and eventually produce a new Holy Week was yet to come.

Consequently, Pius's mention of "more recent liturgical rites" refers to everything medieval and Baroque—that is, everything *subsequent* to that ancient period of which the Liturgical Movement tended to be enamored. The pope is insisting on two key points: first, the fact that something is more ancient does not *ipso facto* make it better; second, the historical development of the liturgy is not an accident God permits, much less an interference He tolerates, but a plan He positively wills—a plan guided by the Holy Spirit and utilized by the Head of the Church, Our Lord Jesus Christ, to sanctify the members of His Mystical Body. By the time we reach the pontificate of Pius XII, this collective body of liturgy—which was simultaneously ancient, medieval, and Baroque, as an organic reality that had passed through all of these periods and had acquired elements from each of them—was already highly stabilized and consistent for four hundred years, with only minor changes occurring in those four centuries, as now a new feast, now a new cut of vestment or musical style, appeared on the scene. The liturgy in its diachronic *totality*—a treasure of great perfection and

---

[59] *Mediator Dei*, §61. For further commentary, see Peter Kwasniewski, *Reclaiming Our Roman Catholic Birthright: The Genius and Timeliness of the Traditional Latin Mass* (Brooklyn, NY: Angelico Press, 2020), 122–23, 140–41, and esp. 149–60; Kwasniewski, *Noble Beauty, Transcendent Holiness: Why the Modern Age Needs the Mass of Ages* (Kettering, OH: Angelico Press, 2017), 123–27.

[60] Thus, prior also to Pius XII's own inscrutable defacement of the Roman rite in the radical changes made to the Holy Week liturgies. See chapter 12.

beauty, a living reality born of the Holy Ghost in the womb of the bridal Church—was lovingly kept and handed down by the ordering of Divine Providence, which no pope dared disturb or oppose.

If Pius XII is correct to say that medieval and Baroque developments "owe their inspiration to the Holy Spirit, who assists the Church in every age," it follows that no one may *repudiate* what the liturgy has been for long stretches of the Church's history without sinning against the Holy Spirit.[61] Papal authority cannot be legitimately exercised to the detriment or the destruction of that which the Holy Spirit has raised up; such an exercise would be an abuse of office. Rather, what the Spirit has given us remains in its totality not only sacred and great but a permanent model and measure.

Indeed, this passage from *Mediator Dei* reads rather like a commentary on the famous Canon 13 of the Seventh Session of the Council of Trent: "If anyone says that the received and approved rites of the Catholic Church that are customarily used in the solemn administration of the sacraments can be looked down on, or that ministers can without sin omit them according to their own whim, or that any pastor of churches whatsoever can change them into other new ones, let him be anathema."[62]

---

[61] As the prophet Elijah might comment: either God was asleep for four hundred years (or eight hundred or twelve hundred) and forgot to guide the Church's liturgy in accordance with the needs of the Christian people (cf. 1 Kg 18:27) *or* He was fully awake and knew exactly what He was doing. Since we know the Almighty is not Baal, we hold the latter view, not the former.

[62] "Si quis dixerit, receptos et approbatos Ecclesiae catholicae ritus in sollemni sacramentorum administratione adhiberi consuetos aut contemni, aut sine peccato a ministris pro libito omitti, aut in *novos* alios per quemcumque ecclesiarum pastorem mutari posse: anathema sit." As will be shown in chapter 4, Paul VI frequently spoke of the "new liturgy," "new rite," "new Mass," etc.; so by his own admission he was changing "received and approved rites . . . customarily used in the solemn administration of the sacraments" into "other new ones." While Canon 13 was originally framed in response to a tract from Cologne written by Bucer claiming that any pastor has the power to prolong or abbreviate the sacramental forms (and in this sense would certainly apply to the extemporized "Eucharistic prayers" popular in the 1960s and beyond), it testifies to a universal truth about the reverence with which "received and approved rites" must be held by pious and religiously observant Catholics. Cardinals Ottaviani and Bacci may have had Canon 13 in view when asserting that "the 'canons' of the rite [of Mass] definitively fixed at that time [viz., with *Quo Primum* of 1570] erected an insurmountable barrier against any heresy which might attack the integrity of the Mystery." *The Ottaviani Intervention: Short Critical Study of the New Order of Mass*, trans. Anthony Cekada (West Chester, OH: Philothea Press, 2010), 35. A defender of the Novus Ordo could argue that the anathema does not rule out a pope inventing a new rite (though there might be other things in divine law that would call his right to do so into question—thus Suárez,

The seventh canon of the twenty-second Session of Trent is also highly pertinent. This canon states: "If anyone says that the ceremonies, vestments, and outward signs which the Catholic Church uses in the celebration of Masses are incentives to impiety rather than offices of piety; let him be anathema."[63]

When the Council pointedly says "which the Catholic Church uses," we are given to understand that *all* of the liturgical ceremonies, vestments, and external signs received from tradition are offices of piety and *not* incentives to impiety. Thus, the view later popular with twentieth-century reformers—that aspects of the classical Roman rite are to be considered corruptions of authentic liturgy and detrimental to the spiritual life of the faithful—is anathematized ahead of time. As Fr. Engelbert Recktenwald says: "The assumption of decreasing dignity over the years implies the denial of the continual action of the Holy Spirit in the Church, and thus of a Spirit-driven progress in general."[64]

In the same spirit, the *Roman Catechism* published in 1566, three years after the Council of Trent was concluded, says this about the Mass: "The Sacrifice is celebrated with many solemn rites and ceremonies, none of which should be deemed useless or superfluous. On the contrary, all of them tend to display the majesty of this august Sacrifice and to excite the

who maintains that the pope is not legally bound by this canon, acknowledges limits to the pope's moral authority to change rites), but merely excludes his *changing* an existing rite *into* a new one. On this view, however, Paul VI's act in attempting to *replace* the old rite with a new rite was *ultra vires* in a way that introducing a new rite as an alternative alongside the old rite might not have been. For a broader discussion see Peter Kwasniewski, "The Pope's Boundedness to Tradition as a Legislative Limit," in Kwasniewski, ed., *From Benedict's Peace to Francis's War: Catholics Respond to the Motu Proprio Traditionis Custodes on the Latin Mass* (Brooklyn, NY: Angelico Press, 2021), 222–47.

[63] "Si quis dixerit, ceremonias, vestes et externa signa, quibus in missarum celebratione Ecclesia Catholica utitur, irritabula impietatis esse magis quam officia pietatis: anathema sit." On the surface, this canon would seem to require saying that the Novus Ordo must be an "office of piety" and not an "incentive to impiety." However, first, it does not follow that the Novus Ordo fosters piety *as much as* the traditional rite, or that it avoids occasions of impiety as well as the traditional rite does. Second, this canon should not be taken out of context by forgetting that the error to which it is responding is that of the Protestants who rejected aspects of the traditional Latin rites—as did the the liturgical reformers of the twentieth century. See Peter Kwasniewski, *The Road from Hyperpapalism to Catholicism: Rethinking the Papacy in a Time of Ecclesial Disintegration* (Waterloo, ON: Arouca Press, 2022), vol. 1, ch. 9.
[64] Cited in Fiedrowicz, *Traditional Mass*, 210n46.

faithful, when beholding these saving mysteries, to contemplate the divine things which lie concealed in the Eucharistic Sacrifice."[65]

Two hundred and twenty years after this *Catechism*—that is, in the year 1786—a curious diocesan synod of Jansenist leanings met in the town of Pistoia, Italy, held at the height of the so-called Enlightenment. The synod passed many proposals for simplifying Church praxis, including the abolition of indulgences, feast days, and processions, and the vernacularization of the liturgy. In 1794, the tempest-tossed Pope Pius VI caught his breath for a moment between the French Revolution and Napoleon Bonaparte's accession to issue a papal bull called *Auctorem Fidei*, which condemned many propositions of the Synod of Pistoia, among them the following, which we should hear against the backdrop of Trent and its *Catechism*:

> The proposition of the synod by which it shows itself eager to remove the cause through which, in part, there has been induced a forgetfulness of the principles relating to the order of the liturgy, "by recalling it (the liturgy) to a greater simplicity of rites, by expressing it in the vernacular language, by uttering it in a loud voice"; as if the present order of the liturgy, received and approved by the Church, had emanated in some part from forgetfulness of the principles by which it should be regulated,—[is hereby judged] rash, offensive to pious ears, insulting to the Church, [and] favorable to the charges of heretics against it.[66]

The claim of Pistoia that the Catholic Church had effectively forgotten the true principles of the liturgy is precisely the claim that was to be made by liturgists in the twentieth century both before and after the Second Vatican Council. That our worship should be "recalled" to its humbler and simpler origins, placed in the people's language, and uttered in a loud voice throughout are three of the most characteristic aspects of the *Novus Ordo Missae*.[67]

---

[65] "Habet autem hoc sacrificium multos, eosque maxime insignes ac solemnes ritus, quorum nullus supervacaneus aut inanis existimandus est; verum omnes eo spectant, ut et tanti sacrificii maiestas magis eluceat, et salutaribus mysteriis intuendis ad rerum divinarum, quae in eo sacrificio occultae sunt, con- templationem fideles excitentur."

[66] *Auctorem Fidei*, §33.

[67] For an explanation of why Pius VI's *Auctorem Fidei* as well as Gregory XVI's *Quo Grav-*

Immediately after the section quoted above from *Mediator Dei*, which emphasized the value of the "more recent liturgical rites," Pius XII describes the efforts of some liturgists to rid the Church of medieval and Baroque "accretions," and condemns them with the following words: "This way of acting bids fair to revive the exaggerated and senseless antiquarianism to which the illegal Synod of Pistoia gave rise. . . . [P]erverse designs and ventures of this sort tend to paralyze and weaken that process of sanctification by which the sacred liturgy directs the sons of adoption to their Heavenly Father for their souls' salvation."[68]

Paul VI's reformism deserves condemnation no less than Pistoia's, because both violate the fundamental truth expressed by (*inter alia*) Saint Gregory Nazianzen, Dom Guéranger, and Pius XII: from Pentecost until the end of time, the Church is the province of the Holy Spirit—and the Church's most perfect action and expression is the sacred liturgy.[69]

Sinning against the Holy Spirit

In light of the foregoing, we are in a position to circle back for a moment to the claim, in Law #3, that liturgical reform of a certain magnitude would constitute a sin against the Holy Spirit.

Did we become orphans after Constantine, after the Middle Ages, or after the Council of Trent? In the Gospel for the Vigil of Pentecost,[70] Jesus assured us He would not let that happen to us: "I will not leave you orphans: I will come to you" (Jn 14:18). If this is not to be a mere pious platitude, it must actually *mean* something—namely, that the Spirit never abandons the Church, and that He *really does* bless her with gifts at each

---

iora and Pius XII's *Mediator Dei* support the traditionalist position and not the conservative defense of any and all papally-promulgated Church liturgical laws (whatever their premises or content may be), see "Does Pius VI's *Auctorem Fidei* Support Paul VI's Novus Ordo?," in Kwasniewski, *The Road from Hyperpapalism*, vol. 1, ch. 9. In his monograph *The Synod of Pistoia and Vatican II: Jansenism and the Struggle for Catholic Reform* (New York: Oxford University Press, 2020), Shaun Blanchard details—and celebrates—the parallels between Pistoia and Vatican II.

[68] *Mediator Dei*, §64.

[69] For a further development of this idea and practical implications for the clergy, see my tract *True Obedience in the Church: A Guide to Discernment in Challenging Times* (Manchester, NH: Sophia Institute Press, 2021), 23–33.

[70] In the *usus antiquior*.

stage of her pilgrimage, as befits the Bride of Christ on earth. These gifts are a cumulative inheritance: their effects linger in time even as they echo in eternity. Each age inherits the gifts of the saints who have gone before. "The fortuitous majorities that may form here or there in the Church do not decide their and our path: they, the saints, are the true, the normative majority by which we orient ourselves."[71] We dishonor Our Lord Jesus Christ and His Holy Spirit if we consider some later age to be so different, so new, so chaotic, so abounding in unique genius that it must start afresh, cutting the ropes that bind it to the past, rejecting or pushing away the gifts of tradition, in a bid to "modernize"—which is to say, to make orphans or strangers of Catholics within their own household. Indeed, such an approach is the only one that could not possibly be a gift of the Holy Spirit.

Let's say, for the sake of argument, that the twentieth-century reformers believed in the providential guidance of the liturgy as to its conceptual content but had reached the conclusion that Latin had become an insuperable barrier to participation. The liturgy was correct in what it said but not correct in how it delivered it.[72] In that case, would they not have sought merely to translate the *existing* liturgy into an appropriate register of the vernacular? Yet 2,147 bishops and superiors at the Second Vatican Council disagreed by voting, in fact, to *retain* the use of Latin while allowing a certain place to be allotted to modern languages. Or let's say the reformers felt that some ferias or feast days in the missal would benefit from additional Scripture readings. They would then have proposed appropriate readings for those days, leaving the rest of the missal intact. But no. Their postconciliar actions betray their dissent from the very *content* of the old liturgy: its prayers of preparation, its antiphons and readings, its orations, its offertory and canon, its ceremonies, gestures, postures, its language and music, its very orientation. From the 1950s through the 1970s, literally *nothing* was left untouched—and the changes were usually on a large scale, such as the wholesale rewriting of the rites of the Mass, of baptism, priestly ordination,

---

[71] Joseph Ratzinger, *Called to Communion: Understanding the Church Today*, trans. Adrian Walker (San Francisco: Ignatius Press, 1996), 154. He adds: "Majority in the Church can never exist only synchronically but in essence is always purely diachronic, because the saints of all times are alive and because they are the true Church."

[72] See chapter 1 on problems with the attempt to make a clean separation between what is said and how it is said.

extreme unction, the dedication of a Church, the consecration of virgins, the blessing of holy water, *everything*. This was not a revision but a rejection; not a reform but a revolution.[73] It is disturbingly reminiscent of the ancient Gnostics' denial that Jesus Christ has already come in the flesh.[74]

In virtue of the ironclad axiom *lex orandi, lex credendi*, such a rejection means a rejection of the doctrine and spirituality the traditional Roman liturgy incarnates. It is, in other words, not primarily a deviation from rites but a deviation from the perennial theology of the Faith embodied in the rites—a form of infidelity or, dare I say, even apostasy. A rejection of the rites implies a rejection of what they signify and symbolize. Archbishop Piero Marini, who as a young man was Annibale Bugnini's personal secretary as well as part-time secretary of the Consilium itself (along with the undersecretaries Carlo Braga and Gottardo Pasqualetti), writes concerning the Consilium: "They met in public to begin one of the greatest liturgical reforms in the history of the Western church. Unlike the reform after Trent, it was all the greater because it also dealt with doctrine."[75] Fr. John F. Baldovin, SJ, a scholarly advocate of the liturgical reform (and therefore immune to the accusation of rad trad hyperbole), calmly affirms its magnitude again and again in his work *Reforming the Liturgy: A Response to the Critics*:[76]

---

[73] See Wolfram Schrems, "The Council's Constitution on the Liturgy: Reform or Revolution?," *Rorate Caeli*, May 3, 2018; cf. the discussion of "Nietzschean Catholicism" in chapter 11. The question is often asked: Why did nearly all of the bishops, who had voted for something else, meekly go along with Paul VI's increasingly radical liturgical reforms instead of voicing their objections and refusing to comply? The answer may be given in one word: hyperpapalism. The pope is to be revered as Christ on earth and his word is law. *No matter what*. It is for the same reason that nearly all of the bishops during the reign of Pope Francis have remained silent in the face of his dangerous ambiguities and outright errors, to say nothing of the many-sided corruption to which he has been linked.

[74] The substitution of a Jewish meal blessing for a proper Offertory rite is, in this regard, highly suggestive, since the defining trait of post-Christian rabbinical Judaism is its explicit denial that the Christ has come in the flesh. For a discussion of the influence of Gnosticism on the liturgical reform, see "Gnosticism, Liturgical Change, and Catholic Life" in my book *Tradition and Sanity: Conversations and Dialogues of a Postconciliar Exile* (Brooklyn, NY: Angelico Press, 2018), 99–116.

[75] Archbp. Piero Marini, *A Challenging Reform: Realizing the Vision of the Liturgical Renewal 1963–1975* (Collegeville, MN: Liturgical Press, 2007), 46.

[76] John F. Baldovin, *Reforming the Liturgy: A Response to the Critics* (Collegeville, MN: Liturgical Press, 2008). Page numbers in parentheses.

One certainly cannot deny the radical nature of a reform that swept away the use of a common language and simplified the liturgy to the extent that the Missal of Paul VI did. (43)

One can agree that the reformed rite significantly changed how Catholics understood their worship. The reform was no mere minor adjustment of some of the externals of Catholic piety but a thorough reshaping of the Catholic imagination with regard to the liturgy. (59)

Change was needed; it was needed because the pre-Vatican II liturgy was indeed a relic of a bygone age, a relic that had its reasons—the polemical stance that the Church found itself taking with regard to the Protestant Reformation and then the Enlightenment and then the cultural changes that came with the Industrial Revolution and the upheavals of the nineteenth and early twentieth centuries. It was the cumulative effect of these cultural changes that made a radical reform of the liturgy desirable. (102)

Since the reform was clearly intended to update anachronistic aspects of the Roman liturgy (*SC* 23, 50) it was certainly part of the brief of the reformers that they select and edit prayers to suit the changes in theology and spirituality experienced in the late twentieth century. (125)

Mainly for historical and ecumenical reasons, Paul VI made a somewhat radical decision to change the traditional form of the sacrament [of Confirmation] in his Apostolic Constitution introducing the new rite. (130)

If one compares the Missal of 1962 with the Missal of 1969 or the pre- and post-Vatican II ordination rites, for example, one may conclude that the reform was a radical departure from the organic development of the tradition. (137)

The reformed liturgy does represent a radical shift in Catholic theology and piety. (139)[77]

All this—an injury to which was added the insult of ignoring many
explicit stipulations of the conciliar document *Sacrosanctum Concilium*—
amounts to a belief that the Holy Spirit had long ago ceased to guide the
Church into the fullness of truth in her liturgical worship. This belief, however, cannot but be heretical; asserting it would be blasphemous; and acting
upon it would be sacrilegious.[78]

The "sin against the Holy Spirit" has been discussed at great length
by exegetes. For our purposes, it suffices to note that it is connected, in
any case, with rejecting the evidence of the work of God at hand, such as
Christ's power to drive out demons by the Spirit of God rather than by
collusion with Beelzebub, as His critics maintained—for the latter claim is,
implicitly, a rejection of Christ's entire ministry of making the kingdom of
God present in our midst. Now, the kingdom of God is continually made
present to us in the sacred liturgy. Hence a rejection of liturgy is a rejection
of the kingdom, of its Lord, and of the Spirit of the Lord. We may also say,
with Peter Lombard, that there are six kinds of sin against the Holy Spirit:
despair, presumption, impenitence, obstinacy, fighting against known
truth, and envy of a brother's grace.[79] These too are seen in the liturgical
reform: despair that the faithful could enter fruitfully into the mysteries
celebrated in the traditional rites; presumption in thinking to create rites
superior to those handed down; impenitence in refusing to repent of and
repair the obvious damage caused to the People of God by the scope and
speed of the reform, in spite of decades of bad fruits; obstinacy in resisting

---

[77] Similar confirmation comes from a fellow Jesuit, Fr. Bruce T. Morrill: "Francis's directive
[*Traditionis Custodes*] is about more than simply the ritual of the Roman Mass, for exclusive
performance of the older rites by some Roman Catholics cannot but sustain, to varying degrees, ecclesial and social ideology inconsistent with Vatican II's entire reforming agenda for
the church. . . . The conversion from silent women, men, and children 'attending' . . . Mass to
the assembled baptized people of God celebrating word and sacrament in their socio-cultur-
al context is the seismic shift in Roman Catholicism at stake in Pope Francis's reversal of his
two predecessors' incremental accommodations to archconservative, even reactionary clergy
and laity." "Tradition and the Roman Rite: The Ongoing Struggle," *Doxology* 32.3 (2021), 30,
35–36.
[78] Chapter 7 develops this argument more fully.
[79] *Sentences*, Bk. 2, dist. 43.

the prior and authoritative claims of tradition; fighting against the known truth (*lex credendi*) to which the liturgy (*lex orandi*) gives expression; and lastly, envy of a brother's grace, in the form of envy of the Byzantine tradition leading to unintelligent emulations of and mixtures with it.

Fr. John Parsons soberly notes the effects, on the standing of Church authority and the internal coherence of the Magisterium, of the liturgical reformers' negative evaluation of and rupture from the Latin tradition hitherto promoted and defended by the Church:

> The symbolic repudiation of the tradition of Christendom, as Cardinal Ratzinger has stated, has contributed very greatly to an undermining of confidence in the Church in general. While it may be possible *logically* to believe in a Church that is an infallible guide in doctrines of faith and morals but that, for most of the time since her foundation, has promoted, in Archbishop Bugnini's striking phrase, "lack of understanding, ignorance, and dark night" in the worship of God, it is not possible *psychologically* to carry out a mental juggling act of this sort for very long or on a scale that involves any great number of people. If the *lex orandi* could be so profoundly misguided for so many centuries, what confidence can be placed in the *lex credendi* upheld through these long centuries by the same misguided papacy and ecclesiastical authorities? Here again the adage *lex orandi, lex credendi* rules, but with a new and destructive twist. Either the *damnatio memoriae* of the traditional liturgy must be clearly and publicly revoked, or confidence in the Church's authority will never be recovered.[80]

Wending my way to journey's end

In my life as a Catholic, I have gone through several distinct stages over a long period of time, so I have learned to be patient with those who "don't get it." I didn't "get it" either, although it fills me with joy to see how quickly the younger generations today are reaching conclusions that I resisted for

---

[80] Cited in Fr. Thomas Kocik, *The Reform of the Reform? A Liturgical Debate: Reform or Return* (San Francisco: Ignatius Press, 2003), Appendix V, "A Reform of the Reform?," 226–27.

years. If I were to try to put into words what I was seeking and finding at each stage, here is what I'd say.

In the first stage, which coincided with childhood and adolescence, I was trying to be a good son and a dutiful Catholic. I obeyed my parents in most regards, went to church with them on Sundays and Holy Days, and held a Ten Commandments morality (with some gaps owing to bad formation). The parish church was a typical suburban church, covered with carpet and Extraordinary Ministers. Midway through high school, a friend invited me to attend a charismatic youth group meeting, and I loved it. Thanks to the adult leaders, whom I would describe as "John Paul II Catholics," I discovered in that group three important things: first, that the Catholic Faith proposes itself as *true* and therefore as the truth by which everything else ought to be evaluated (up till then, I'm not sure I had heard this claim!); second, that practicing the Faith did not have to be boring or perfunctory but could be emotionally invigorating and satisfying; third, that those who believe in God, the immortal soul, the sacraments, and prayer are, for the most part, better and happier people who, in turn, make for better and happier friends.

But after spending a couple of years in this group, something started to wear thin about it. I'm not sure I could put my finger on it, but the experience was rather like what happens after a sugar high or puppy love: there was something superficial, inadequate, temporary, insubstantial. It was as if I needed to find the external visible and audible form of the truth of the Catholic Faith that I accepted with my intellect; I needed to find the incarnate Christ, not the abstract word or the fleeting feeling. This is what I began to find at Thomas Aquinas College, initially in the Latin Novus Ordo with chant (what we might call the "Reform of the Reform" approach), where the overwhelming effect was one of *reverence*, of taking serious things seriously. Yet there was always a disturbing problem lurking in the background. Almost anywhere else in the world—especially in the 1990s—the Novus Ordo was celebrated in a totally different way from the way it was done at TAC. What was wrong with everyone else? Why couldn't they see how much better a reverent and beautiful liturgy was? I later came to understand that this is a monumental flaw baked into the

Novus Ordo: the "smells and bells" are only *optional*, at the whim of the people in charge. Consequently, everything depends on the education, good taste, and orthodoxy of the pastor or the celebrant, or whoever is entrusted with decision-making power. Yet such optionitis combined with the current ecclesiastical power structure is a deadly combination: all it takes is one too many complaints to the bishop and boom!, Father *Incensa Multa* is gone, sent scurrying across town or away to the boonies; Father *Plaudite Manibus* comes in with a whirl and destroys, in a matter of weeks, the work of beautification and resacralization that may have taken years to build up. We all know this happens. It shows that a liturgy that treats any of the eight elements mentioned earlier as optional is like a building compromised by a giant crack, because of the principle stated by Saint Thomas in the Five Ways: "What is able not to exist, at some time does not exist." Or, to put it more colloquially: If something can go wrong, it will go wrong.

Later on in college, I began to attend clandestine celebrations of the Tridentine Mass, and here I discovered yet another secret: the presence and meaning and value of *tradition*—of doing what has been done for ages, with the same rites that countless Catholics have known over the centuries, praying in the same words as great saints of the past, entering into the mysteries of Christ in a way that demands a transformation of mind and heart even in the very act of worship. I acquired a daily missal and began following it. I could see very quickly that this liturgy was considerably different: deeper in its theology, more truthful to human nature, more obedient to revelation, more beautiful in its presentation; as a matter of fact, it was more emotionally stirring as well, although in more subtle ways. In short: finding this liturgy and yielding to it was the end of a search on which I did not even know I was embarked. This liturgy embraced all that I had found in each stage of my journey, yet went beyond them all. It was, and has remained, inexhaustible: an infinite vista opening backward to history, forward to eternity, outward to culture, upward to heaven.

Seeking God on our terms or His

Consider for a moment what charismatics and proponents of a "Reform of the Reform" have in common. Both are seeking authenticity, an encounter with reality, with the divine presence, with the grace of the Holy Spirit. The problem is that both are forms of anthropocentrism: we want to find God on *our* terms, not on *His* terms; we want to worship Him in our way, not His way. Be it through excessive emotion or a liturgical rite of our own design, we are bringing God down to our own level, instead of letting Him reach us and take us up to Him along a path He has already provided. The words of Andrew Thompson-Briggs may be applied especially to the Reform of the Reform: "We cannot receive the tradition by standing out-side the tradition, appropriating what we will. That is what tourists do. It is an inorganic approach, a postmodern approach, bound to fail. Rather than grafting ourselves onto the venerable tree, we would be assembling a bundle of sticks. When, in the old poetic world, the young received the tradition, they received it whole from a master."[81]

Like Mary Magdalene at the empty tomb, we are looking here and there and everywhere to find Him, when He is standing right in front of us, in His gentle and glorious—though also veiled and mysterious—objectiv-ity. He is the gardener who has already turned the soil, planted the seeds, tended their growth into an orchard of the finest, most succulent, most nourishing fruit trees—all the rites of Holy Mother Church that enable Him to become, more and more, the gardener, the governor, the intimate guest of our souls. This is what we see in the lives of the great mystics: it is the liturgy that forms and grounds and permeates their interior life, keeping it healthy, strong, balanced, rich, and fruitful, preventing it from veering off into arbitrariness, sentimentality, idiosyncrasy, pride, or van-ity. The interior life of grace, hidden in the soul, is reflected, represented, exemplified, in the exterior physiognomy of the traditional liturgy. It is the mystical life of the indwelling Trinity writ large, translated into the language of ritual, ceremony, and prayer—enacted in the choreography of ministers, brushed upon by words, savored in melodious chant, nestled in thundering silence.

I have argued that the Novus Ordo is not the Roman rite or any kind of traditional rite; neither in its texts nor in its ceremonies does it express the fullness of our Faith. Since the liturgical heritage of the Church *does* represent the work of the Holy Spirit over the ages, inspiring, gathering, augmenting, refining, consolidating, and preserving the treasures of our collective worship as Christ's Mystical Body, we are faced with a serious decision: Do we take the path well-trodden by the saints, each generation demonstrably in continuity with the generations before and the generations to follow, by the common bond of an incorruptible God-breathed inheritance; or do we take a different path—liturgy conformed to ideology, confined to a certain time period? For, as Dom Hugh Somerville Knapman recognizes, the Novus Ordo was intended to be (in the words of Consilium member Joseph Gelineau) a "permanent workshop":

> The progressive element among the reforming liturgists saw the 1969 missal as but a stage—a significant one, mind you—in the new project of reconstituting the liturgy as something that continually adapts to the age in which it is celebrated. As we have seen, the result is that the liturgy generally degenerates into reflecting the age rather than speaking to it and sanctifying it. Or more to the point, radical deformations of the liturgy reflect not the face of Christ but the face of the dominant person or clique that imposes them, and so become vehicles not of worship but of narcissism, the cult of self which is the de facto creed of postmodern western society. . . . We are rootless and thus heartless, replacing self-sacrifice with self-service, with self as the only moral absolute, its inescapable subjectivity and impermanence denying the absolutism it demands for itself. Its secondary absolute, novelty, suffers the same inherent flaw.[82]

I will therefore issue a challenge to my readers. To those who do not already consistently attend the traditional Latin Mass, I will say: *you should attend it*, the sooner the better, because it is the highest glorification of our God, the most perfect expression of our faith, and the most exquisite treasury of our culture. It will take time and effort, and perhaps earn for

---

[82] Hugh Somerville Knapman, "Pursuing a Point," *Dominus Mihi Adjutor*, April 13, 2019. Gelineau's statement is found in his *The Liturgy Today and Tomorrow*, trans. Dinah Livingstone (London: Darton, Longman & Todd, 1978), 11.

you some cold shoulders, but it will reward you thirtyfold, sixtyfold, a hundredfold. To those who are already in love with the traditional Roman rite and committed to it, I say: get to know it *still better*—assist at it more often, use your daily missal, study good books about it, spread the knowledge of it, and support the traditional movement with your prayers and your resources as if your very life and the existence of the Catholic Church depended on it. As time goes on, it is increasingly clear that this *is* a matter of life and death, vitality and extinction.

Why do we need not just more beauty, not just more reverence, but above all, the objective content of the *usus antiquior*? The answer is that God intended us to have it. It was brought forth from the womb of the Church by the Holy Spirit; it was received, practiced, and embellished by innumerable saints as they climbed the ladder of humility to heaven; it was given by Providence with a view to our universal human needs and holy desires; it was, and it remains, a gift of God's immense love, a fitting throne to receive the greatest gift of all, His Son Our Lord Jesus Christ. Like His kingdom and laws, its rubrics are constant and fixed. Like the wisdom of the Gospels, its texts are dogmatically, morally, ascetically, mystically rich. The fine arts, especially music, find themselves at home in it, for they were all born there, in the city God hath founded (cf. Ps 86:5–7). Like the Light that shineth in darkness, which the darkness did not overcome (cf. Jn 1:5), the ceremonies of the *usus antiquior* visibly and powerfully convey the Catholic Faith in its dazzling light of truth and its fearless grappling with the dark. The prayer of tradition unites us with all of our predecessors in the faith, and with all traditional Catholics alive right now, in every country, on every continent, who worship in the same rites, aspiring to the same ideals. Its recovery will be the mainstay of lasting renewal in the Church.

The liturgical reform, in its concrete execution, has moved further and further away from this origin [in the best of the Liturgical Movement]. The result has not been reinvigoration but devastation. . . . [I]n place of the liturgy that had developed, one has put a liturgy that has been made. One has deserted the vital process of growth and becoming in order to substitute a fabrication. One no longer wanted to continue the organic developing and maturing of that which has been living through the centuries, but instead, one replaced it, in the manner of technical production, with a fabrication, the banal product of the moment.

—Joseph Ratzinger

The idea of inventing a new liturgy, even if it had been free from the faults we see in it, is questionable in itself; it is one with no precedent in the history of the Church, whether in the West or in the East. Alterations of language made at various times were never accompanied by a re-creation of the rite. . . . The tradition of the Church in liturgical reform is one that excludes radical reconstruction. That is not merely a matter of precedent but of the powers inherent in the hierarchical office. No pope or patriarch in history has ever considered that he had the power of abolishing the rite of his jurisdiction and replacing it with a new one. No theologian has ever mentioned such a competence among the powers of the pope. Its assumption by Paul VI was an extension of habits of papal authority which, in all other areas, he was only too culpable in abandoning. Previous popes had indeed legislated with a high sense of authority, but they did so conscious that it was an authority at the service of tradition and established teaching.

—Henry Sire

3

Hyperpapalism and Liturgical Mutation

Just over fifty years ago, there occurred one of the most momentous and fateful events in the history of the Catholic Church: the promulgation of the new Order of Mass, or *Novus Ordo Missae*, by Paul VI in his Apostolic Constitution *Missale Romanum* of April 3, 1969. Half a century later, it is fairly common to find conservative clergy saying something like the following: "The reform of the liturgy is not what propelled the post-conciliar crisis in the Church; rather, it was doctrinal and moral relativism that led to liturgical chaos. The liturgy is in shambles because doctrine and morals are in shambles. Put colloquially, don't blame the car, blame the drunk driver. The Novus Ordo and, for that matter, all the reformed rites, the Liturgy of the Hours, what have you—it's all fine *in itself*, and if we approach it with the right attitude and follow 'best practices,' we can have a truly Catholic liturgical life, minus the doctrinal and moral aberrations that we all rightly deplore. We can, in other words, have our cake and eat it too: *Novus* in what we do, *Vetus* in what we believe."

To me this seems like a case of severe naiveté. Joseph Ratzinger famously remarked that "the crisis in the Church that we are experiencing today is to a large extent due to the disintegration of the liturgy."[1] And this latter crisis stems directly from several problematic features of the liturgical reform itself, and the results that emerged from it.

---

[1] Joseph Ratzinger, *Milestones, Memoirs 1927–1977* (San Francisco: Ignatius Press, 1998), 148. Or, in the German original: "Ich bin überzeugt, daß die Kirchenkrise, die wir heute erleben, weitgehend auf dem Zerfall der Liturgie beruht."

The cost of sudden and major change

The simple fact that, after well over a millennium of stability in liturgical form, there were *sudden and major* changes to the liturgy in every aspect transmitted a message: "Even the most important things in Catholicism—the things that seem permanent and rock-solid—can change at a moment's notice, as long as the pope wills it." Yes, the liturgy has always developed slowly and in small ways, but never, in the entire history of Eastern or Western Christianity, has there been anything remotely comparable to the *quantity and quality* of change witnessed in the decade from about 1963 to 1973. This, *in and of itself*, quite independently of whether certain changes were arguably good or bad, had a catastrophically destabilizing effect on the mentality of Catholics. Some left the Church for good, scandalized, demoralized, disillusioned. Others bit their lip and put up with a lot of nonsense. Still others tore off the habit (as it were) and embraced liturgical experimentation, pluralism, and subjectivism with wild abandon. *All* Catholics were profoundly damaged with cumulative and lasting damage, like that of genetic defects passed on to offspring, or of family feuds lasting for generations. Due to its rate and scale of change, the liturgical reform unleashed upheaval, confusion, and anarchy. A fracture or wound was introduced into the Mystical Body that has not only *not* healed but has grown worse with each passing decade.

Our faculty of reason, peering through the lenses of philosophy, psychology, and sociology, tells us that a colossal change to the way Catholics worship could carry one and only one meaning—namely, that what we were doing before was incorrect, flawed, unhealthy, even displeasing to God. This, indeed, is still the position of those who oppose the traditional Latin liturgy: they consider it to be inherently an inferior form of worship and they do not hesitate to say so openly. Admitting the validity of both forms, I think we who love the classical Roman rite owe our opponents the courtesy of total transparency by admitting our position with equal candor: we consider the Novus Ordo to be inherently an inferior form of worship.[2]

---

[2] By "form of worship" I mean the *Gestalt* or totality of the rite as celebrated, in its texts, chants, gestures, and ceremonies, as well as its prerequisites, expectations, associations, and history of use and reception.

I've heard more than a few people say: "We've left the silly season behind us and now, decades later, we're coming to the right balance. The Novus Ordo has been accepted by the vast majority of Catholics and is here to stay, while the evils of the chaotic post-council have been left behind by younger clergy with better theology and training."[3]

This is Pollyanna speaking. *Nothing* can fully flourish in the Body of Christ so long as the predominant liturgy of the Western Church exists in a state of novelty-ridden, archaeologistic, ideological rupture from the Latin tradition as it actually unfolded over the first two millennia of Christianity. It's not about "achieving the right balance"—that's a Newtonian way of speaking. It's about the difference between an organism and a mechanism. It isn't only that a rupture occurred; it is that we are living in a *state* of rupture. It's like the difference between the French Revolution, which took place over a certain number of years in the past, and the liberalism of *laïcité* (laicity, i.e., secularism), which has haunted and harmed us ever since.

Someone might object: If we were to change back to traditional Roman Catholic worship today, would we not be guilty of the same crime, by inflicting sudden and major change on the People of God? Wouldn't this, too, have the effect of upheaval, confusion, and anarchy? My answer is that the two cases are altogether different. I do not deny that the greatness of the inherited Catholic liturgy was in many ways obscured or sidelined prior to the Council, and that the original Liturgical Movement had some legitimate proposals for restoring that greatness, such as privileging the sung Mass over the recited Mass, and encouraging the faithful to sing the Ordinary and responses. Nevertheless, the violence done to the liturgy in the reforms of Pius XII and especially Paul VI marked a transition from health to sickness, riches to poverty. As the authentic Roman liturgy is

---

[3] My critique is more fundamental than the question of "liturgical abuses," but in point of fact, such abuses continue today in large numbers and in a wide distribution across the Catholic world. Many recently documented abuses are presented in John Monaco's article "The 'Other' Abuse Crisis in the Catholic Church that No One is Talking About," *Medium*, February 21, 2019. High-ranking church figures bleat occasional complaints about abuses without taking serious steps to uproot them. See "Crocodile Tears and Hand-Wringing: No GPS Coordinates for the Unicorn," in Peter Kwasniewski, *The Road from Hyperpapalism to Catholicism: Rethinking the Papacy in a Time of Ecclesial Disintegration* (Waterloo, ON: Arouca Press, 2022), vol. 2, ch. 59.

rediscovered and reintroduced, we pass from disease to well-being, from penury to wealth. Both transitions can only be called enormous changes, but one of them fractured and wounded, while the other binds and heals. The traditional movement wishes, in imitation of Christ, to "seek and to save that which was lost" (Lk 19:10). As discomforting and trying as it will be for some, the recovery of Catholic tradition is salutary and inevitable, necessary for the peace of the Church and even, I would say, for her survival.

On what basis do I make such bold claims? I will focus here on three problem areas—the evils of arbitrariness, the fact of watered-down, dumbed-down content, and the dangers of hyperpapalism—and then speak of what we can do to heal the wounded body.

The evils of arbitrariness

All liturgical traditions, as they grew under the influence of the Holy Spirit, acquired fixity of language and ritual. Whatever improvisation may have been a feature of early Christian liturgy rapidly gave way, for obvious theological and pastoral reasons, to definite forms couched in hallowed language, passed down and venerated as the embodiment of apostolic and patristic wisdom. Look at the history of every liturgical rite and see: there is no exception to this rule.[4]

The decision, therefore, to re-introduce a wide latitude and choice of options in the neo-Roman liturgy was a blow aimed directly at the traditional understanding and practice of liturgy, a blow against formal, public, objective, ecclesial prayer, and a confirmation of modern voluntarism and liberalism. In other words, the Novus Ordo did not challenge modern man's hubris but capitulated to his proclivities. It is not just a liturgy designed *for* "modern man," viewed as a sort of exotic object of evangelization, having little in common with his predecessors; it is also a liturgy *from* modernity, permeated with the principles of Modernism that were condemned by Saint Pius X in *Pascendi Dominici Gregis*. These principles include the

---

[4]   See my article "From Extemporaneity to Fixity of Form: The Grace of Liturgical Stability," *NLM*, October 11, 2021; cf. "The Fixity of Liturgical Forms as an Incentive to Prayer and *Lectio Divina*," *NLM*, January 23, 2017.

following: that religion is a matter primarily of individual sentiment, an intuition of the heart, an immanent surge of "need" for the divine; that each age must discover for itself the meaning of religion, which will reflect man's evolution in consciousness; that the idea of fixed and stable doctrines, rules of behavior, and ritual actions cannot be reconciled with the progress of science and philosophy; that the miraculous, the supernatural, and the otherworldly have to be purged or at least deemphasized; that the purpose of Scripture is to elicit new experiences in us of being touched by God, and the purpose of sacraments is to remind ourselves of an ethical worldview and to stir up an awareness of our personal value. These principles are not just different from the principles of Catholicism; they are at odds with them.[5]

How does liturgical voluntarism play out on the ground? On Monday, one can pray Eucharistic Prayer II, because Monday's a busy day; on Tuesday, let's go with Eucharistic Prayer III so that we can mention aloud a couple of optionally commemorated saints; on Wednesday, why not go out on a limb with the avant-garde Eucharistic Prayer IV; and, if one happens to be so inclined, on Thursday we might run with the old Roman Canon, which has a quaint charm of its own. In this way, the reformed liturgy elevates to the level of a principle of public worship the arbitrary will and feelings of the celebrant. I say "arbitrary" in the strict sense: whatever his good or bad reasons may be for choosing this or that option, it still comes *from himself*, and to that extent undermines liturgy as a work of God and of the Church, whose humble minister the priest is called to be. The paradox emerges of a *lex orandi* that binds its user to be unbound from a law of motion and diction; that requires him to be unrequired to act or speak in this or that way; that compels an unbecoming freedom, in a realm wherein the soul and the body should be most obviously subject to their heavenly Master.[6] "This is one of the issues with

---

5   See "Pius X to Francis: From Modernism Expelled to Modernism Enthroned," in Kwasniewski, *The Road from Hyperpapalism*, vol. 2, ch. 62.

6   Lest anyone accuse me of exaggerating the problem, we can read, in a newspaper with a conservative reputation, a perfect expression of the mentality I am critiquing here: "The expanded optional parts of the Mass mentioned in *Missale Romanum* have also allowed for greater pastoral latitude in celebrating the liturgy. Father Samuel Martin . . . told the *Register* that the variations of the anaphora allow him to adapt the liturgy to the needs in his parishes.

dressing up the *Novus Ordo*. It involves prudentially adding in practices and accouterments, and this can be a temptation to pride."[7]

In the Christian East, the days on which different anaphoras are used are set in stone; there is no choice involved. The same practice prevailed in the West: regardless of the particular regional variant of the Latin liturgy one was using, there was always a fixed rule of worship that all believers, clergy and laity alike, received with reverence from tradition. In this way, it mirrored the doctrine of the Faith, which is received from Christ, the Apostles, and the Church—not fabricated or modified to suit the convenience, whims, or theories of any person, place, or age.

Thus, just as we accept from Our Lord Jesus Christ that taking another partner while your spouse is still alive is adultery, and from Saint Paul that adulterers cannot guiltlessly approach the Blessed Sacrament or inherit the kingdom of heaven, so too, we accept that the Sacrifice of the Cross was handed down to us in the mystery of the Holy Eucharist, and that the Apostles are the first priests, ordained to perpetuate this mystery. We have no more reason for reverencing marriage or the gift of human life than we have for reverencing the Eucharist or the Mass of which It is the center; put the other way around, one who thinks of liturgy as a human artifact we can freely tinker with in the workshop will sooner or later treat morality as a social construct we can manipulate at will. In this sense, the principles behind and the mindset of Pope Francis's *Amoris Laetitia* are perfectly consistent with those of Paul VI's *Missale Romanum*, the promotion of

---

'For example, I use Eucharistic Prayer No. 2 during the weekdays,' he said, 'No. 3 for funerals and weddings, and No. 1, the Roman Canon, for weekends. . . .' Despite the variety, Father Martin said, the continuity between the Mass and the Church's rich patrimony of faith and Tradition shines through, especially when he prays the First Eucharistic Prayer, the Canon of the Mass. 'Some people get a charge out of the Canon,' he said. 'They like hearing all those names of the early saints and martyrs of the Church. That's one of the times we retain continuity—these prayers have been said for centuries, and there will be someone else standing at the altar at St. John's or Christ the King praying these same prayers centuries from now.'" *National Catholic Register*, "St. Paul VI's 'Missale Romanum' Turns 50," April 3, 2019. Mark the words: "Get a charge out of"; "that's *one of the times we retain continuity*"—as opposed to all the other times when we don't? One could hardly make such stuff up.

[7]   Matthew R. Menendez, "Youth and the Liturgy," in *Liturgy in the Twenty-First Century: Contemporary Issues and Perspectives*, ed. Alcuin Reid (New York: Bloomsburg, 2016), 168. See my article "Men Must Be Changed by Sacred Things, and Not Sacred Things by Men," *OnePeterFive*, September 15, 2021.

women to ecclesiastical ministries and offices extrapolates from Paul VI's attempted suppression of the traditional Minor Orders, and the abolition of the death penalty harmonizes with the abolition of exorcisms in Paul VI's rite of baptism.[8]

For those who have eyes to see and ears to hear, Divine Providence is placing before us in the past half-century the most dramatic proof ever given in the history of the Church of the truth of the axiom *lex orandi, lex credendi, lex vivendi*. The course of our prayer cannot but affect the course of our doctrine, and the course of our doctrine will necessarily spill over into the realm of behavior. It is not for nothing that the prophets of ancient Israel compared idolatry and the violation of the temple cult to fornication and adultery. Massive change in the *lex orandi* announced to the world the possibility and indeed the probability of massive change in the *lex credendi*, to be followed by massive change in the *lex vivendi*.

Watered-down, dumbed-down content

Notoriously, much of the content of the new missal can only be described as watered-down doctrine, music, and ceremonial, and, in comparison to the old, as lighter fare, like a limited salad bar.

Archbishop Arthur Roche tells us every chance he gets that the "current Mass" boasts a "richer selection of prayers and Scripture readings."[9] True, the missal of Paul VI draws its euchology, or prayer texts, from a

---

[8]   See Peter Kwasniewski, *Ministers of Christ: Recovering the Roles of Clergy and Laity in an Age of Confusion* (Manchester, NH: Crisis Publications, 2021); "What Good is a Changing Catechism? Revisiting the Purpose and Limits of a Book," in Kwasniewski, *The Road from Hyperpapalism*, vol. 2, ch. 40; and my article "The Excision of Exorcisms as a Prelude to Devil-Denial," *OnePeterFive*, June 19, 2017; cf. Thomas Pink, "Vatican II and Crisis in the Theology of Baptism," published at *The Josias* on November 2, 5, and 8, 2018.

[9]   See Cindy Wooden, "Archbishop says most bishops see importance of 'Traditionis Custodes,'" *National Catholic Reporter*, January 21, 2022. Elsewhere, in his article "The Roman Missal of Saint Paul VI: A witness to unchanging faith and uninterrupted tradition" (*Notitiae* 597 [2020]: 248–58), Roche claims, with stunning contempt for truth, that the Novus Ordo retains 90 percent of the texts of the missal of Pius V, although the real figure for the euchology is, as we have seen, only 13 percent. He is merely echoing Pope Francis, who in the letter that accompanied the motu proprio says: "Whoever wishes to celebrate with devotion according to earlier forms of the liturgy can find in the reformed Roman Missal according to Vatican Council II all the elements of the Roman rite," and claims that the Novus Ordo is a rite "in which is preserved the great richness of the Roman liturgical tradition." In my opinion, such statements must rank among the greatest lies ever found in a papal document.

wider variety of sources in ancient manuscripts. Yet people like Roche carefully refrain from noting that the Consilium heavily redacted most of the texts it borrowed, altering their message, and removing material deemed "difficult" or "irrelevant" for "modern man." What you end up with in the missal is not a plethora of ancient sources but a carefully filtered and rewritten 1960s "take" on them. Ratzinger recognized this quite clearly: "The new Missal was published as if it were a book put together by professors, not a phase in a continual growth process. Such a thing has never happened before. It is absolutely contrary to the laws of liturgical growth, and it has resulted in the nonsensical notion that Trent and Pius V 'produced' a Missal four hundred years ago. The Catholic liturgy was thus reduced to the level of a mere product of modern times."[10] This chronological snobbery is perfectly conveyed in a memorandum from the Consilium in charge of the liturgical reform, dated September 9, 1968:

> It is often impossible either to preserve orations that are found in the [1962] Roman Missal or to borrow suitable orations from the treasury of ancient euchology. Indeed, prayer ought to express the mind of our current age, especially with regard to temporal necessities like the unity of Christians, peace, and famine. . . . In addition, it seems to us that it is not always possible for the Church on every occasion to make use of ancient orations, which do not correspond with the doctrinal progress visible in recent encyclicals such as *Pacem in Terris* and *Populorum Progressio*, and in conciliar documents such as *Gaudium et Spes*.[11]

---

[10] Joseph Ratzinger, *The Feast of Faith: Approaches to a Theology of the Liturgy*, trans. Graham Harrison (San Francisco: Ignatius Press, 1986), 86. Note how Archbishop Arthur Roche, in an interview on November 14, 2021, stated exactly the erroneous viewpoint described by the Bavarian: "What was produced in 1570 was entirely appropriate for the time. What is produced in this age [i.e., the Novus Ordo] is also entirely appropriate for the time." Quoted in Hannah Brockhaus, "Vatican archbishop: Traditional Latin Mass 'experiment' not successful in reconciling SSPX," *Catholic News Agency*, November 16, 2021.
[11] Schema 306 (*De Missali*, 52), September 9, 1968, p. 7, trans. Matthew P. Hazell, *The Post-Communion Prayers in the Ordinary Form of the Roman Rite: Texts and Sources* (n.p.: Lectionary Study Press, 2020), xxi–xxii. This mentality of *aggiornamento* found consummate and deceptively modest expression in the *General Instruction of the Roman Missal*, which states near the end of the Introduction: "On account . . . of the same attitude toward the new

Or again, when some people made "urgent requests to tone down some of the wording" of the ancient Good Friday intercessions that had a "bad ring to them," Bugnini gladly obliged: "It is always unpleasant to have to alter venerable texts that for centuries have effectively nourished Christian devotion and have about them the spiritual fragrance of the heroic age of the Church's beginnings. Above all, it is difficult to revise literary masterpieces that are unsurpassed for their pithy form. It was nevertheless thought necessary to face up to the task, lest anyone find reason for spiritual discomfort in the prayer of the Church."[12] In keeping with this policy, only 13 percent of the prayers of the old missal, once the backbone of Roman Catholic worship, found their way into the new missal unchanged: 165 out of 1,273 orations. Another 24.1 percent (307) were edited. A further 16.2 percent (206) were centonized with other prayers (combining parts of multiple prayers into a new oration). Fully 52.6 percent (669) of the prayers in the *usus antiquior* were excluded from the modern liturgy, memory-holed by the Consilium.[13] Does this mean that 87 percent of the orations were defective or in need of an update? The truly religious man never thinks this way; such is the thought process of a thoroughly irreligious person. How this can be considered acceptable to any Catholic conscience is completely beyond me.

The work of Lauren Pristas has demonstrated in embarrassing detail that the Collects of the missal were systematically rewritten to downplay or eliminate dogmatic, moral, and ascetical elements considered to be distasteful to "modern man," and to inculcate new, timelier principles. Thus, mentions of fasting, bodily maceration, and contempt of the world, prominent in the season of Lent, were purged and replaced with inoffensive

---

state of the world as it now is, it seemed to cause no harm at all to so revered a treasure if some phrases were changed so that the language would be in accord with that of modern theology and would truly reflect the current state of the Church's discipline. Hence, several expressions regarding the evaluation and use of earthly goods have been changed, as have several which alluded to a certain form of outward penance which was proper to other periods of the Church's past."

[12] Annibale Bugnini, *The Reform of the Liturgy 1948–1975*, trans. Matthew J. O'Connell (Collegeville, MN: The Liturgical Press, 1990), 119.

[13] This information comes from Matthew Hazell's detailed statistical analysis, accompanied by full documentation: "'All the Elements of the Roman Rite'? Mythbusting, Part II," *NLM*, October 1, 2021.

generalities.[14] It is as if the reformers, perhaps tired of the growing dishar-
mony between tradition and modernity, wanted to replace literal fasting
and abstinence with metaphorical fasting from the banquet of Catholic
ceremonial and abstinence from the meat of traditional prayers.

The scholars, with their scissors and paste, were busy rejecting or rewriting most of what they came upon. The editing process was ruthless, removing most of the references to "detachment from the temporal and desire for
the eternal; the Kingship of Christ over the world and society; the battle
against heresy and schism, the conversion of non-believers, the necessity of
the return to the Catholic Church and genuine truth; merits, miracles, and
apparitions of the saints; God's wrath for sin and the possibility of eternal
damnation."[15] Gone are most references to the struggle against our sinful
fallen nature, offenses against the Divine Majesty, wounds of the soul, worthy repentance, remorse, and reparation; the need for grace in order to do
any good acts; the mystery of predestination; the relics of saints; the subor-
dination of the secular sphere to the sacred, and of this world to the next;
the snares of the enemy; victory over hostile forces, including the pagans;
beautiful orations specifically addressed to Jesus Christ as God.

How, exactly, can a missal missing all these old riches be said to represent
"a richer selection of prayers"? On the contrary, the selection—precisely
because it is a selection by 1960s "experts"—is theologically narrower,
culturally thinner, and spiritually impoverished. The old missal's prayers
express much more of the full height and depth of the divine mysteries and
the variegated human response to them.

What Professor Pristas showed concerning the Collects of the Sundays
in Proper Seasons can be and has been shown in regard to every other area
of the liturgy. One could look at the ancient Sundays after Pentecost, on
the Gospels of which Saint Gregory the Great preached, bearing witness
that this cycle of readings goes back to the sixth century, and most likely
earlier still. It was taken away by the modern reformers, and was replaced
with their own brainchild. The preface of Apostles was transformed from

---

[14]   See especially her work *Collects of the Roman Missals.*
[15]   Michael Fiedrowicz, *The Traditional Mass: History, Form, and Theology of the Classical
Roman Rite*, trans. Rose Pfeifer (Brooklyn, NY: Angelico Press, 2020), 239, with ample notes
there.

a deprecatory into a declarative text: whereas before the Church begged that the Lord, through the Apostles' intercession, would not desert His Church, now she arrogantly assumes He will not, regardless of how badly she behaves.[16] The rite of baptism, indeed the rites of all the sacraments, were modified nearly past recognition. The list goes on and on. Everywhere one looks, one sees tradition suppressed, development rejected, and novelty gaily pursued. How can anyone, confronted with this vastitude of evidence, claim that there has been "no rupture," or that the rupture is at the level of indifferent details?

Our world is obsessed with low-fat this and low-calorie that; Paul VI, seeming to anticipate the Zeitgeist, gave us a low-fat, low-calorie liturgical diet. Almost every significant change in the liturgy went in the direction of simplifying, suppressing, abbreviating, and amputating. But Almighty God thinks very differently about the kind of worship we are to give *Him*, and the kind of sustenance He wishes to provide for *us*. In the book of Ezekiel, He tells us: "The priests and Levites . . . shall come near to me, to minister to me: and they shall stand before me, to offer me the fat, and the blood" (Eze 44:15). In Leviticus, succinctly: *Omnis adeps, Domini erit* (Lev 3:16), "all fat is the Lord's." *Deo optimo maximo,* "to God, most good, most great," nothing should be offered except that which is greatest and best. The Psalmist says: "May He be mindful of all thy sacrifices: and may thy whole burnt offering be made fat," *holocaustum tuum pingue fiat* (Ps 19:4), and again in the book of Daniel: "As in holocausts of rams, and bullocks, and as in thousands of fat lambs: so let our sacrifice be made in thy sight this day, that it may please thee" (Dan 3:40). When we give to God the best of the sacrifice, He feeds us in turn with the best of Himself: "And he fed them with the fat of wheat, and filled them with honey out of the rock" (Ps 80:17)—a verse that supplies the Introit of the Mass of Corpus Christi: *Cibavit eos ex adipe frumenti.* One of the great psalms sung at Lauds puts it best: *Sicut adipe et pinguedine repleatur anima mea, et labiis exsultationis laudabit os meum,* "Let my soul be filled as with marrow and fatness: and my mouth shall praise thee with joyful lips" (Ps 62:6).

---

[16] See p. 222 n. 4.

The fat of the sacrifice is not only Jesus Christ, Son of God and Son of Mary, who is the best and greatest gift from God; it is also *our* efforts inspired by God and united with Christ, the fullness of our prayers and praises, fine arts and servile arts, our physical movements and spiritual elevations, our devotions and allegories. The development of the traditional liturgical rites of East and West is Divine Providence's most special endowment upon the Church, because He deserves, demands, and delights in the richest offering we men can make to Him, and He therefore *provides* us with the sacrifice—not only in the naked elements of bread and wine but in the lavishly clothed, royally adorned, and symbolically dense act of worship that He caused to appear in the midst of His temple by a long history of cultural concentration, refinement, and interpretation.[17] *This* is the *whole* burnt offering. Our liturgical rites should indeed be like "thousands of fat lambs."[18]

When we look with care and piety, we find that what tradition has bequeathed to us is far better than anything we might create on our own, no matter how many "experts" we cram on to a committee and how much papal muscle we put behind them. The age-old Divine Office—let us say,

---

[17] Joseph Shaw: "This, then, is the paradox of the development of tradition. The richer the tradition, the more there is to contemplate, to inspire art, music, and poetry: and all this can be taken in different directions. At the same time the tradition binds us, and the central meaning, reiterated in a hundred ways by generations of commentators, is rendered the more emphatic. The view of Jungmann and other critics of the tradition since the sixteenth century is that the elaboration of tradition—'accretions' is a favorite word of this school of thought— serves to obscure the original and authentic meaning of the liturgy. For those on the inside of a community of belief, however, unless they think that neither Providence nor the Church officials charged with weeding out heterodox developments had any effectiveness, this is a puzzling claim. Those developments, rather, must be understood as building upon, commenting on, elaborating and clarifying the authentic meaning: even, of constituting the 'authentic' meaning in cases where there is no useful 'original' meaning, as perhaps is the case of using an elevated voice for the phrase 'nobis quoque peccatoribus.'" "Traditions, Liberation, and Meaning," *The European Conservative*, October 31, 2021. The striking imagery of Ezekiel 47 depicts not only the inundation of divine grace but also the unfolding of revelation and tradition.

[18] A moral aspect to this question is how we "spend" our personal resources. In keeping with the principle of *nihil operi Dei praeponatur* [let nothing be put before the work of God, i.e., divine worship], we should give the best of ourselves and of our day to God in the liturgy, as priests and religious once did (and still do if they adhere to the traditional rites). The postconciliar man has, instead, kept the fat of his time, his work, and his energy, for himself, alternating between anthropocentric activism and lazy self-indulgence, and thus depriving God of the sacrifice we owe Him by divine right.

monastic Lauds or Vespers as sung by traditional Benedictine monks or nuns—furnishes an irrefutable example of the more-than-human magnificence of a slowly-matured manner of singing the high praises of God. The undulating verses of the psalms, chanted in the eight Gregorian tones with their subtly varying terminations and framed by lovely antiphons; the gentle build-up to a chapter, a hymn, a versicle, the Benedictus or Magnificat antiphon, the Gospel canticle, and concluding prayers . . . Nothing we could ever invent sitting around a table would be able to compare with it for musical inventiveness, structural coherence, aptness of content, scriptural saturation, and integration with the Mass. And could any orator do justice to the immeasurable riches of countless polyphonic settings of the Office, the Mass, and devotional texts of every description, the sublime architecture of the buildings made to house these rituals and reverberate with their music, the frescoes, sculptures, and windows that fill them with silent companions and speechless narratives, innumerable vestments, vessels, and furnishings made for the altar of sacrifice, where the King and Center of All Hearts reigns victorious from His Cross?

The Latin liturgy assimilated and absorbed the intellectual and artistic riches that it found in its triumphant course through the world, dominating every culture with its own prepossessing *gravitas*. The liturgical reform, on the contrary, in the name of accessibility and adaptability to various cultures, Indonesian or Polynesian, Californian or Nebraskan, stripped the liturgy of its own distinctive clothing, ornaments, and symbols of authority, leaving it a naked slave to whatever agenda desired to press it into service. We may rightly call this an exercise in *de*culturation, since the result was not an enrichment or a renovation, but a destitution, an evacuation. In the words of the prophet Jeremiah: "Can a virgin forget her ornaments, or a bride her attire? Yet my people have forgotten me days without number" (Jer 2:32). Whatever the problems may have been prior to the Council, they were as nothing compared to the state of affairs afterwards: when this room of public worship was swept clean and put in rational order, it was infested with seven demons worse than the first (cf. Mt 12:43–45).

Such maneuvers are nothing less than a frontal assault on the truth of the Christian tradition and its trustworthiness for men of every condition and era. It would have been different had the Roman missal merely been augmented with some new Mass Propers for new saints, or ferial readings for Advent. But the revisers dismantled and reconfigured the entirety of the missal, breviary, *Rituale,* and *Pontificale,* retaining, rewriting, or discarding material *ad libitum,* according to their private theological opinions. Extreme centonization, or the reconfiguration of old texts into new prayers, became a death-defying sport to which the reformers gleefully abandoned themselves.

The divergence between the classical and modern rites is so great that it is possible to celebrate the New Mass—assuming its new readings, new antiphons, use of a Eucharistic Prayer other than the Roman Canon, etc.— in a way that would involve less than 10 percent of overlap with the old rite. Would a Byzantine Christian think he had worshiped God properly if he were thrust into a liturgy that contained less than 10 percent of one of the transmitted forms of the Divine Liturgy? Impossible!

Let us run with this thought experiment for a moment. Imagine the Divine Liturgy of Saint John Chrysostom as our starting point. Now, take away most of the litanies; substitute a newly-composed anaphora (with only the words of consecration remaining the same); change the troparia, kontakia, prokeimena, and readings; greatly reduce the priestly prayers, incensations, and signs of reverence; and while we're at it, hand cup and spoon to the laity, so they can tuck in like grown-ups.

Would anyone in his right mind say that this is *still* the Byzantine Divine Liturgy in any meaningful sense of the term? Sure, it might be "valid," but it would be a *different* rite, a different liturgy. Just for good measure, let's say we also remove the iconostasis, turn the priest around, take away some of his vestments and substitute ugly ones, and replace all the common tones of the ordinary chants with new melodies reminiscent of Broadway show tunes and anti-Vietnam folk songs. Now we'd have not only a different rite but a totally different *experience.* It is not the same phenomenon; it is not the same idea (in Newman's sense of the word "idea"); it is not the expression of the same worldview; indeed, it is not the same *religion,* if we take the word in the strict meaning of the virtue by which we give honor to God through external words, actions, and signs.

The danger of hyperpapalism

That strange scenario, which has (to my knowledge) never taken place in the East,[19] is, tragically, exactly what we are dealing with in the West. There is no way to maintain that the Missal of Paul VI is a "form" of the Roman rite. It is a new and different rite that bears some loose connections with the Roman rite. This is why Klaus Gamber called it the "modern rite," *ritus modernus*.[20]

Should this bother us? Absolutely! Of course, if the liturgy is just a service cobbled together by a group of men and subsequently actualized into validity by the stroke of a papal pen, it shouldn't bother us because, on that view, liturgy is no more than a moment's construction, an artistic creation subject to our theories and whims, as long as the untouchable "sacramental form" is kept inviolate.[21] This has never been and can never be the view of orthodox Christians. It expresses a hyperpapalist, neo-ultramontanist legal positivism that sees the pope as creator of tradition *ex nihilo* or as the one who endows it with value rather than as guardian of the Christian continuity of *paradosis*, the "handing down" of what we have received, *as it has really come down to us*—not as it should, or could, or might have existed in the distant past or as it should, or could, or might exist in the distant future. The hyperpapalist view, popular since around the time of the First Vatican Council, transmogrifies the pope into a "combination Delphic oracle, globetrotting superstar, dynamo of doctrinal development, and standard meter bar of orthodoxy,"[22] whose mind and will are, in and of themselves, always right, true, holy, and laudable. This view of the papacy is

---

[19] With the exception of the Maronite and Syro-Malabar rites, where altars and priests were foolishly turned *versus populum*. See my article "The Maronite Liturgy's Corruption under Modern Western Influence," *NLM*, September 27, 2021. At least among Syro-Malabar Christians there is an effort being made to restore *ad orientem*, although habituation to bad custom has provoked resistance.

[20] See Klaus Gamber, *The Reform of the Roman Liturgy: Its Problems and Background*, trans. Klaus D. Grimm (San Juan Capistrano, CA: Una Voce Press and Harrison, NY: The Foundation for Catholic Reform, 1993), 23–26, 91–95.

[21] In actual fact, not even these words were kept inviolate by Paul VI, who removed the phrase *mysterium fidei* from the formula over the chalice and made it an isolated fragment to which the faithful make a so-called "memorial acclamation." See chapter 9.

[22] See "When Will Catholics Wake Up and See the 'Mess' Pope Francis Has Made?" in Kwasniewski, *The Road from Hyperpapalism*, vol. 2, ch. 20.

contradicted not only by the actual teaching of Vatican I but also and more obviously by the sins, offenses, and negligences of postconciliar popes. It will suffice to mention only a few words: *Ostpolitik*; Bugnini; Assisi; Koran; Kasper; Maciel; McCarrick; Scalfari; *Amoris Laetitia*; death penalty; Abu Dhabi; Pachamama.

The view of liturgy that follows upon hyperpapalism—namely, that the form and content of liturgy is totally subject to the papal will—is no less erroneous. The pope, as sovereign as he is, does not have the ontological power to decree tradition not-really-tradition, to decree an innovation more-or-less-tradition, to decree that destruction and innovation shall be called "reform," or to decree an open, proclaimed, and lauded discontinuity a secret continuity. He can apply force in various ways, but he cannot make realities *not* be what they *are*[23]—and thus, for example, cannot declare that the *usus antiquior* is not the *lex orandi* of the Roman rite when, objectively, it is the very substance of that rite's *lex orandi*. Not even God has the power to change the past or to violate the principle of non-contradiction, and presumably, the pope's power is inferior to the Almighty's.

As we receive Catholic doctrine from our forefathers, so we receive our worship, and while we may enhance or augment this worship even as we expound Catholic doctrine in sermons, catechisms, and treatises, we may not *modify* it in such a way that it ceases to be recognizably the same and yet call it the same. As Saint Vincent of Lérins would say, the Church welcomes *profectus*, growth, but not *permutatio*, mutation, and should mutation occur, the result is not an improvement but a deformity. Ecclesiastical tradition is augmentative or additive: as our worship develops, its meaning is more clearly articulated and manifested. Authentic liturgical development in the age of the Holy Spirit—that is, the time from Pentecost to the Parousia—is teleological: it achieves a fuller, more striking, more adequate expression of the mysteries.

In short, liturgy is perfected over time, and unless we wish to say that Our Lord spoke falsely when He promised to be always with His Church until the end of the world, or unless we wish to say that the Holy Spirit

---

[23] I owe part of my formulation here to a forgotten dialogue partner on Facebook; whoever you are, I heartily thank you for it.

did *not* lead the Church into the fullness of truth but instead allowed her to get seriously lost and mixed up *for centuries*, we will not dare to abolish or radically alter the liturgy. Such abolition or radical alteration would contradict the meaning the Church has come to understand and express in these rites, in all their particularity.[24] The liturgical expression of the faith is not, in other words, like a set of premanufactured Lego bricks that can be endlessly reconfigured according to the ideas or tastes of each one who plays with them. Like the Creed we recite, it is something fixed and stable, and while we can *expand* a Creed (as that of Nicaea was expanded by that of Constantinople), we cannot reduce it or abolish it.

The French Dominican priest, Father Roger-Thomas Calmel (1914–1975), who refused to celebrate the Novus Ordo, correctly represented the Vincentian point of view regarding *profectus* and *permutatio*:

Our Christian resistance as priests and laity is a very painful resistance, for it forces us to say no to the pope himself about the modernist manifestation of the Catholic Mass. Our respectful but unshakable resistance is dictated by the principle of total fidelity to the living Church of all time; or, in other words, from the principle of living fidelity to the development of the Church. Never have we thought of holding back, or even less of impeding, what some (with very ambiguous words, for that matter) call "progress" in the Church; we'd call it rather the homogeneous growth in doctrinal and liturgical matters, in continuation with Tradition, in sight of the *consummatio sanctorum*. As Our Lord has revealed to us in parables, and as St. Paul teaches us in his Epistles, we believe that the Church, over the course of the centuries, grows and develops in harmony through a thousand adversities, until the glorious return

---

[24] The claim that Pope Pius V "removed lots of sequences" is something of an urban legend. With classically Roman conservatism, the Missal of the Roman Curia, the medieval predecessor of the Missal of Saint Pius V, simply had not received many sequences to begin with. After 1570, as churches passed over from their own local uses to that of Rome, they dropped the sequences because they were not in the Roman book. The same thing happened with some who, though retaining their proper uses, like the Premonstratensians, recast them in imitation of the Roman Missal. It is consistent with piety to regret the loss of some great medieval poetry; certainly we may work for its incorporation into the liturgy. True liturgical renewal includes the intelligent recovery of elements lost through forgetfulness or pragmatic decisions.

of Jesus Himself, her Spouse and our Lord. Since we are convinced
that over the course of centuries a growth of the Church is occurring, and since we are resolute in our desire to become part of
this mysterious and uninterrupted movement as integrally as possible, as far as it is up to us, we reject this supposed progress that
refers [solely] to Vatican II and which in reality is mortal deviation. Going back to St. Vincent of Lérin's classical distinction, the
more we desire good growth—a splendid *profectus*—the more do
we reject, uncompromisingly, a ruinous *permutatio* and any radical
and shameful alteration whatsoever; radical, since it comes from
modernism and denies all faith; shameful, since the denial of the
modernist sort is shifty and hidden.[25]

Ten years after the motu proprio *Ecclesia Dei*, Cardinal Ratzinger made
this fine observation in a speech he gave to the bishops of Chile:

> It is good to recall here what Cardinal Newman observed, that the
> Church, throughout her history, has never abolished nor forbid-
> den orthodox liturgical forms, which would be quite alien to the
> Spirit of the Church. An orthodox liturgy, that is to say, one which
> expresses the true faith, is never a compilation made according to
> the pragmatic criteria of different ceremonies, handled in a posi-
> tivist and arbitrary way, one way today and another way tomor-
> row. The orthodox forms of a rite are living realities, born out of
> the dialogue of love between the Church and her Lord. They are
> expressions of the life of the Church, in which are distilled the
> faith, the prayer, and the very life of whole generations, and which
> make incarnate in specific forms both the action of God and the
> response of man.[26]

---

[25] In the magazine *Itinéraires* of June 1971, cited by Roberto de Mattei, *Love for the Papacy*,
2–3.

[26] Joseph Ratzinger, "Ten Years of the Motu Proprio *Ecclesia Dei*," given on October 24,
1998, at the Ergife Palace in Rome. Ratzinger continues: "Such rites can die, if those who
have used them in a particular era should disappear, or if the life-situation of those same
people should change. The authority of the Church has the power to define and limit the use
of such rites in different historical situations, but she never just purely and simply forbids
them! Thus the Council ordered a reform of the liturgical books, but it did not prohibit the
former books." I am still wondering why this important address from 1998, which contains

Would the laws of logic or metaphysics permit us to invert these judgments of Newman, Calmel, and Ratzinger? Could we say that if an orthodox liturgical form is abolished or forbidden, then it cannot be the Church that has done it but rather churchmen abusing their authority? Could we say that a liturgy which is a "compilation made according to pragmatic criteria . . . handled in a positivist and arbitrary way" is, for that very reason, not an orthodox liturgy? Could we say that any liturgy *not* "born out of the dialogue of love between the Church and her Lord" but rather assembled by academic experts and *avant-garde* bishops in dozens of study groups orchestrated by a secretary with decidedly anti-traditional views is not a "living reality," an "expression of the life of the Church" that "distills the faith, the prayer, and the very life of whole generations"?[27] Could we say, in the end, that this form of worship, whatever else it may be, is very far from being "an incarnation of the action of God and the response of man"?

Yes, we can say all of these things. This only shows the magnitude of our crisis. One cannot create a living whole out of lots of scholarly pieces glued together. One cannot assign to an "on-the-spot fabrication" a complex, nuanced history of centuries of formation just by wishing it were so, any more than one can magically produce a nation called Esperance, home to a race of Esperanti, for whom Esperanto has been a centuries-old native tongue. The Novus Ordo is like Esperanto: a perfectly rational organization of language functions, spoken natively by no one and lacking any history or culture except that of its intentional community of specialists. Meanwhile, the truly beautiful, irregular, and rich Latin language and its incomparable

---

a wealth of reflections on the liturgy, was omitted from volume 11 of Ratzinger's *Collected Works* edited by Cardinal Müller and published in English by Ignatius Press. It is a peculiar omission, as anyone will see for himself by studying the text, which is available online. In the course of narrating an Easter Sunday Mass filmed in 1941 at the Church of Our Lady of Sorrows in Chicago, Msgr. Fulton J. Sheen echoes Newman: "It is a long established principle of the Church never to completely drop from her public worship any ceremony, object, or prayer which once occupied a place in that worship."

[27] As Benedict XVI wrote to Cardinal Müller on July 31, 2017: "In the confused times in which we are living, the whole scientific theological competence and wisdom of him who must make the final decisions seem to me of vital importance. For example, I think that things might have gone differently in the Liturgical Reform if the words of the experts had not been the last ones, but if, apart from them, a wisdom capable of recognizing the limits of a 'simple' scholar's approach had passed judgment." Translation published at *Rorate Caeli*, January 2, 2018.

musical setting in Gregorian chant were left aside. Never has it been proved more true that experts are like wells—they are deep in one spot, but narrow and cold—while tradition, home of the common man, is like the ocean—irresolvably vast, incomparably deep, fearful, sublime, teeming with fertility and nourishment, beckoning endless journeys.

In his address to the German Parliament at the Reichstag in Berlin on September 22, 2011, Pope Benedict XVI distinguished between mere success, which technique can acquire, and wisdom, which comes only from the assimilation of tradition. The pope quotes Saint Augustine's description of government without justice as a "highly-organized band of robbers," in which *might* is separated from *right*. The same judgment may be rendered on Bugnini and the Consilium: they assembled plenty of technical expertise, and their finished product was endorsed by the *might* of the reigning pope, but they lacked—indeed, they repudiated—the wisdom of tradition, and thus forfeited their *right* to handle the Church's sacred liturgy. In the end, the Consilium was a highly-organized band of robbers. Or, in the colorful language of Archbishop Robert J. Dwyer, a participant in all four sessions of the Council, writing in 1971: "The great mistake of the Council Fathers was to allow the implementation of the Constitution on the Sacred Liturgy to fall into the hands of men who were either unscrupulous or incompetent. This is the so-called 'Liturgical Establishment,' a Sacred Cow which acts more like a White Elephant as it tramples the shards of a shattered liturgy with ponderous abandon."[28]

Healing the Wounded Body

As Bishop Athanasius Schneider has eloquently said, the Mystical Body of Christ on earth is suffering from self-inflicted wounds.[29] How do we staunch these wounds? Can they be healed? The only way to do so is to address the underlying condition. The wounds can be bandaged up, but they will not heal until the body is healthy again. Since the very life of the Mystical Body is expressed and built up in the liturgy, no health is possible

---

[28] *The Tidings*, July 9, 1971, cited in Michael Davies, *Pope Paul's New Mass* (Kansas City, MO: Angelus Press, 2009), 651.

[29] See Peter Kwasniewski, *Resurgent in the Midst of Crisis: Sacred Liturgy, the Traditional Latin Mass, and Renewal in the Church* (Kettering, OH: Angelico Press, 2014), 94–111.

until (and to the degree that) the liturgy itself is healthy—when the Holy Sacrifice of the Mass, the praises of the Divine Office, and all the other sacramental and liturgical rites are as they should be. And how should they be? The way they were before the modern vice of "tinkeritis" dominated the minds of churchmen in the twentieth century.

Romano Guardini in his 1918 work *The Spirit of the Liturgy* talks about the importance of receiving an objective, impersonal, stable liturgy from "the Church." At the time he wrote, he could take it for granted that all his readers would understand what he was talking about: when you go to Mass or some other liturgy, you always see the clergy carrying out the rites entrusted to them and determined for them by the Church. If we look at the Novus Ordo, we can see that what Paul VI gave us is no longer something objective, impersonal, and stable, but a contrived blend of objective and subjective elements, a sort of Push-Me-Pull-You of impersonal and personalized, a liturgy that cannot be stable because it is a prisoner to mandatory optionitis and invasive inculturation.[30]

One cannot and must not identify any given pope with "the Church." Paul VI is not the Church; indeed Pius V or Pius X is not the Church. Guardini's argument, which matches the realities of Catholic theology and history, makes sense only if "the Church" means the body of Christ endowed with the deposit of faith and the fullness of the Holy Spirit, preserving Tradition with love and handing it down with authority. There is obviously a sphere over which popes have sway, but it cannot extend to the full-grown limbs and organs of the liturgical body. If a pope *does* touch these organic parts, amputating or performing plastic surgery or swapping in bionic limbs, his work will be offensive before God and man, and destined for failure.

Once again, it cannot be overemphasized that the method of reform adopted after the Council, with its assumptions and results, stems from

---

[30] Perhaps the most powerful cause of the atomizing and destabilizing nature of the new rites is their polymorphous vernacularization into hundreds of modern languages. This, in and of itself, dealt a death blow to the unity of Catholic worship, *pace* the "hermeneutic of continuity" fantasy of *Liturgiam Authenticam* (2001). Whatever may be the case with Eastern liturgies, in the West the sacred liturgy is *Latinate*, and its Latinity, after 1,600 years, is not a mere accident but a property of its being. There can no more be a Roman rite in the vernacular than there can be a Byzantine rite without litanies, leavened bread, and "The doors! The doors! In wisdom let us be attentive!"

the modernist praxis of theology as described in Pope Pius X's encyclical *Pascendi*. This soft modernism permeates the reformed liturgy and, moreover, inculcates an unconscious contempt for tradition among the faithful who pray according to it. Just as people who drink contaminated tap water or ingest bits of asbestos or lead paint suffer from the intake, whether they know it's happening or not, the Catholic who receives a mangled *lex orandi* is suffering from the lack of nutrition and the presence of foreign chemicals.

Thus, although most Catholics today are in a state of invincible ignorance about the liturgical reform, they too passively support the rending asunder of tradition by praying with rites that are wanting in their transmission of it. This is the reason why, when God grants a Catholic the grace of awakening to the problems of the liturgical reform and the grace of suffering under the burden of that knowledge, He is asking him at the same time to turn and be reconciled with tradition by making a principled commitment to the recovery and use of the traditional liturgy. The one, be he cleric, religious, or lay, who refuses this gracious invitation risks becoming an active contributor to the incoherence and collapse of the Catholic Church. Such a commitment to the *usus antiquior* need not imply that he must immediately sever himself from the modern rite and pray exclusively with the preconciliar one. It does, however, imply that he would be stunting his spiritual growth and impeding the advance of the common good of the Church by not embracing the traditional liturgy as much as possible. A moment will come, sooner or later, when the Catholic will say: "I cannot bear up any longer under pretense and fiction; I must have only what is true, authentic, traditional."[31]

The reform does not need reform; it needs repudiation with repentance. It is not enough to set aside abuses or to reintroduce traditional elements pell-mell—a little incense here, a fiddleback there, an introit today, *ad orientem* tomorrow. This is like piling up plasters on a gangrenous wound, or treating a cancer with multivitamins. No, something much more radical is required.

The account of the golden calf in the book of Exodus ends with a very peculiar verse. Often paraphrased in translation, the verse literally says: "And the LORD sent a plague upon the people, because they made the

---

[31] For a real exchange of letters with a priest who arrived at this moment, see Peter Kwasniewski, "Discovering Tradition: A Priest's Crisis of Conscience," *OnePeterFive*, March 27, 2019.

calf which Aaron made" (Ex 32:35). This verse illuminates a truth about complicity: even if Aaron was responsible for fashioning the golden calf, the people consented to what he did, and therefore shared his guilt. Similarly, Catholics conscious of the Church's departure from tradition and capable of returning to it who nevertheless adhere to the Novus Ordo that Montini made signify their acceptance of its deficiencies. Granted, a majority do not realize there is any alternative, but neither do unbelievers who have never heard the Gospel of Christ—yet unbelievers really do suffer from the lack of graces they would receive if they were actual members of His Mystical Body. In like manner, "mainstream" Catholics suffer from the lack of many good and important things of which the liturgical reform has deprived them. When a person becomes *aware* of these good things, he has an obligation to seek them out, analogous to the obligation an unbeliever has to seek membership in the Church. For indeed the Church herself is found in her most concentrated form in the sacred liturgy.

"Not every one that saith to me: Lord, Lord, shall enter into the kingdom of heaven; but he that doeth the will of My Father who is in heaven, he shall enter into the kingdom of heaven" (Mt 7:21). The liturgy in its broad lines of development is the will of the Father. Therefore the liturgical reformers went against His will. Just because the reformed rites cry out "Lord, Lord" does not mean they will be efficacious or lead souls to the pastures of eternal life. It is not about saying or singing "Lord," it is about adhering to the Father's will as He providentially reveals it to us in history, in our inheritance, in our personal lives. Naturally, those who did not *intentionally* "break their bonds asunder and . . . cast away their yoke" (cf. Ps 2:3) are not personally responsible for disobeying God's will, but once they come to know that the reformed liturgy represents a sin against the Father, they are required to obey His will by uttering "Lord, Lord" in accordance with the tradition.

Over the past fifty years and more, there have always been voices crying out in the wilderness about the reform's deviations and defects.[32] There

---

[32] Fine examples would include Marie-Madeleine Martin's *Immortal Latin* (1966, published for the first time in English by Arouca Press, 2022); Tito Casini's *Torn Tunic* (1967) and Fr. Bryan Houghton's *Mitre and Crook* (1979), both reprinted in Angelico Press's Catholic Tradi-

has not been much of an excuse for ignorance on the part of the educated. But today, we are in a new phase of what Louis Bouyer once referred to as "the decomposition of Catholicism": rampant ecclesiastical corruption and attacks on tradition from the Vatican have had the effect of the screaming sirens of London during the German air raids, urging all citizens to run for cover and hide in a safe place. The Church is being bombarded, and we too must run for cover and hide in a safe place—the traditional doctrine, morality, and liturgy of the Catholic Church, which no man, not even a pope, can rightfully take from us. That is why the pontificate of Francis has truly been a moment of grace, a time for waking up, an opportunity for acknowledging that we have squandered our heritage and now must repent of our folly.

As for the objection "The postconciliar liturgical reform must have been good since it was promulgated by a saint!" I refer the reader to my chapter "Animadversions on the Canonization of Paul VI" and to the other chapters in the book *Are Canonizations Infallible? Revisiting a Disputed Question* (Arouca Press, 2021). Even if Paul VI were a saint, that could not be taken as an equipollent canonization of his *ritus modernus*. Pius V, whose sanctity is beyond dispute, took far more pains to "canonize" the Tridentine rite with the extravagant language of his Apostolic Bull *Quo Primum*, and yet, say the liberal liturgists, this rite has been retired and replaced. If that is true, *a fortiori* Paul VI's product enjoys no special guarantee of sanctity, irreformability, or longevity (*pace* Francis and company). If that is not true and *Quo Primum* still abides in force, as I believe it does—not so much *qua* papal instrument as because of its permanent witness to the Church's perennial faith and morals as expressed in her traditional rites—then Paul VI's *ritus modernus* could be, at best, an alternative rite, and, at worst, an illicit one.[33]

---

tionalist Classics series; and Michael Davies's *Cranmer's Godly Order* (first ed., 1976).

[33] See, for further argumentation on these lines, Peter Kwasniewski, *True Obedience in the Church: A Guide to Discernment in Challenging Times* (Manchester, NH: Sophia Institute Press, 2021), 38–42, and my essay "Does *Traditionis Custodes* Lack Juridical Standing?" in Kwasniewski, ed., *From Benedict's Peace to Francis's War: Catholics Respond to the Motu Proprio* Traditionis Custodes *on the Latin Mass* (Brooklyn, NY: Angelico Press, 2021), 74–78. For a full treatment of the question of the licitness of the Novus Ordo, see John Lamont, "Is

Fidelity versus infidelity

Just as infidelity led to modernity, fidelity leads to tradition. The obverse is true as well: tradition embodies fidelity, and therefore encourages, nourishes, and rewards it; while modernity embodies several centuries of infidelity, and therefore encourages, nourishes, and rewards it. Those who follow the modern path will get their paltry rewards in this life and their eternal punishment in the next if they do not repent. The more modern they are, the more they will increase and multiply their temporal satisfactions. Those who follow the traditional path will surely bear their crosses in this life and reap an eternal reward in the next if they persevere with God's grace. But even in this life, as Our Lord promises, they will already see and taste the spiritual fruits of His goodness.

What we must realize is this: Christ continues His presence among us not only in His Eucharistic Body and Blood, as if in abstraction, but in the liturgy He raises up in His Mystical Body, which is the image of His divine attributes and His interior life, unfolded before our eyes over the progress of ages. That liturgy is the *home* of His royal priestly presence. How tragic it is when iconoclastic churchmen damage this holy image, reaping for themselves the somber judgment from the Last Gospel read at the end of nearly every traditional Mass: "He came unto His own, and His own received Him not" (Jn 1:11). For us, it can and should be different: "But as many as received Him, to them gave He power to become sons of God" (Jn 1:12).

The fundamental error of modern man is his conception of himself as being so *different* from what man has been in other periods of history that he considers himself unable to submit humbly to tradition. By subscribing to this error, the modern Catholic bestows on himself a "pass" to step outside the common inheritance of the Church and to create his own peculiar structures, which always flatter his ego and satisfy his passions. His vaunted differentness, which in fact is nothing other than a lack of self-knowledge propped up by a scaffolding of slogans, becomes over time a state of alienation and isolation due to the habitual indulgence of disordered concupiscence. To become convinced of our unchanging human nature, fallen but

the Mass of Paul VI Licit?" *Dialogos Institute*, March 20, 2022, http://dialogos-institute.org/blog/wordpress/disputation-on-the-1970-missal-part-1-dr-john-lamont/.

redeemed, requires a sustained effort of self-control, silent meditation, and surrender to ritual prayer—in other words, exactly what the traditional Latin liturgy abundantly provides for. Thus we face the inevitable paradox that the Novus Ordo, in spite of being created for modern man, does not challenge his vanity and hubris, whereas the ancient liturgy, truly so remote in its origin and development, provokes modern people to confrontation with God and themselves through its disciplined regimen of prayer, gesture, chant, and symbol. Its very density, opaqueness, and solemn indifference provoke a response in those who are jaded with entertainment and education.[34] It summons us to an encounter with the Real, exposing the cheerful lies of modernity.[35] As Martin Mosebach observes:

> The movement for the old rite, far from indicating aesthetic self-satisfaction, has, in truth, an apostolic character. It has been observed that the [classic] Roman Rite has an especially strong effect on converts, indeed, that it has even brought about a considerable number of conversions. Its deep rootedness in history and its alignment with the end of the world create a sacred time antithetical to the present, a present that, with its acquisitive preoccupations, leaves many people unsatisfied. Above all, the old rite runs counter to the faith in progress . . . that is now curdling into anxiety regarding the future and even a certain pessimism.

---

[34] As the great theologian Matthias Scheeben recognized, in words rich with liturgical implications: "The truths of Christianity would not stir us as they do, nor would they draw us or hearten us, and they would not be embraced by us with such love and joy, if they contained no mysteries. . . . When the heart thirsts after truth, when the knowledge of the truth is its purest delight and highest joy, the sublime, the exalted, the extraordinary, the incomprehensible all exercise an especial attraction. A truth that is easily discovered and quickly grasped can neither enchant nor hold. . . . The more exalted an object is, the more its beauty and greatness impress us and the more it compels our admiration, the more even the slightest glance that we dare fix on it captivates us. In a word, the charm of truth is proportionate to its abstruseness and mystery. . . . Does not Christianity impress us so powerfully just because it is one vast mystery, because it is the greatest of mysteries, the mystery of God? . . . What captivates us is the emergence of a light that had been hidden from us. . . . There must be truths that baffle our scrutiny not because of their intrinsic darkness and confusion, but because of their excessive brilliance, sublimity, and beauty, which not even the sturdiest human eye can encounter without going blind." *The Mysteries of Christianity*, trans. Cyril Vollert (St. Louis: B. Herder, 1946), 4–6.

[35] As I have argued in *Noble Beauty, Transcendent Holiness: Why the Modern Age Needs the Mass of Ages* (Kettering, OH: Angelico Press, 2017), especially chapter 1.

This contradiction with the spirit of our present age should not be lamented. It betokens, rather, a general awakening from a two-hundred-year-old delusion. Christians always knew that the world fell because of original sin and that, as far as the course of history is concerned, it offers no reason at all for optimism. The Catholic religion is, in the words of T. S. Eliot, a "philosophy of disillusionment" that does not suppress hope, but rather teaches us not to direct our hope toward something that the world cannot give. The liturgy of Rome and, naturally, Greek Orthodoxy's Divine Liturgy of St. John Chrysostom open a window that draws our gaze from time into eternity.[36]

Youths today may well be confused about a lot of things. But those who wish to be serious Catholics are clear about one thing: there is no future for a futuristic religion that already seems dated and dull. This is why they want the old, beautiful, meaningful liturgy of the Church. In a world where nothing seems certain, this liturgy is a stable rock on which to build one's spiritual life, social life, and family life. It is a rock in the desert from which fresh spiritual waters are ever flowing.

It should be clear, then, why we must resist the temptation to say that our adherence to the old rite is a matter of "personal preference": you like chocolate, I like vanilla; you like English, I like Latin; you like the Novus Ordo, I like the Vetus Ordo. This is nothing other than liturgical relativism based on papal absolutism. It presupposes that the only way we have a legitimate liturgy is by papal fiat, and whatever a pope establishes is *ipso facto* worthy of choice. Because Pius V approved the Tridentine missal and Paul VI approved the modern missal, either can be chosen, based on one's inclinations.[37] This subjectivist approach masks the fact that the old rite

---

[36] Martin Mosebach, *Subversive Catholicism: Papacy, Liturgy, Church*, trans. Sebastian Condon and Graham Harrison (Brooklyn: Angelico Press, 2019), 100.

[37] That was, at any rate, how things might have seemed under *Summorum Pontificum*. With *Traditionis Custodes*, Francis has renewed Paul VI's original attitude of intolerance and contempt for the truth that tradition is constitutive of Catholicism (as opposed to being merely a "charism" for a select few). Too many who grew comfortable under *Summorum Pontificum* have responded to this new attack with appeals to the good of liturgical diversity and freedom, without seeming to recognize how this "live and let live" attitude is a gigantic avoidance mechanism.

and the new rite are based on *different and contrary principles*, and that the new rite is founded on erroneous principles that have damaged the Church and deserve to be set aside.

Seen historically and theologically, that which Benedict XVI called the "*Ordinary* Form of the Mass" is the *indult*, the exception that has been permitted to occupy territory rightly owned by another, while that which he called the "Extraordinary Form" is, in reality, the unbroken custom that was never abrogated and could never be abrogated. The one is a Johnny-come-lately, with a tenuous purchase on its status; the other is an immemorial rite, with an unshakeable hold on our allegiance. What a privilege, what a blessing that we have been led, by an inscrutable Providence, to know and to love this inestimable treasure, for no merits of our own, but solely "for the praise of His glory" (Eph 1:12). "To Him be glory in the Church, and in Christ Jesus, unto all generations, world without end. Amen" (Eph 3:21).

I. Callot fecit

On this point, after a period of diplomatic silence, I need to make myself clear: I am one of those who believe that our [the Institute of the Good Shepherd's] absolute rejection of Paul VI's Mass is not affective, disciplinary, charismatic, etc. It is theological, dogmatic, and moral. In a word, it is absolute! The original sin of this detestable liturgical quarrel in the Church is the unbelievable and insane audacity of Pope Paul VI in promulgating a new *ordo missae* based on the research of experts, of Freemasons, and of Protestants, and to throw out (albeit with quivering voice) the Mass of the pontiffs Leo the Great and Gregory the Great. The Catholic liturgy can and should only be a transmission of the patrimony of the Apostles. A Mass concocted nineteen centuries later can only be a Promethean ambition, a romantic-libertarian chimera, populism in bad taste, unworthy of the Church of Jesus Christ.

—Fr. Philippe Laguérie

Today's reactionary has a satisfaction which yesterday's did not: to see modern programs end not only in disaster but also in ridicule.

—Nicolás Gómez Dávila

4

Revisiting Paul VI's *Apologia* for the New Mass

As 2019 came and went, so did the fiftieth anniversary of the promulgation of the *Novus Ordo Missae* by Pope Paul VI's Apostolic Constitution *Missale Romanum* of April 3, 1969, the provisions of which took effect in the same year on November 30, the first Sunday of Advent. When we look back a half-century later at this monstrous masterpiece of liturgical "reform"—and, truth be told, it is no longer only self-proclaimed traditionalists who lament a job badly done—we feel moved to ask the simple question: *Why?* Why was it deemed necessary to make such sweeping changes in the Mass?

For an explanation, we must look to the pope who, more than any other figure, was responsible for pushing forward the liturgical reform, handing down not only a new rite of Mass but also, in like manner, new rites for all of the sacraments and indeed new versions of almost everything to be said or done in church—a figurative "sack of Rome" that throws the work of Alaric and Charles V into the shade. In the world episcopacy or Roman curia in the 1960s, there was almost no one who was more willing to see the liturgy radically changed than Pope Paul VI, and of course, no one else had the sheer official power to force it through, extravagantly expending centuries of accumulated political capital and sucking dry the funds of ultramontanism. As Yves Chiron demonstrates in his biography of Annibale Bugnini, even that scheming architect of the reform would never have been able to get away with what he did had not the pope supported and encouraged him every step of the way until his sudden and mysterious downfall in 1975.[1]

Where can we look to find the pope's explanation? There are, as one would expect, a plethora of addresses, letters, and other documents that allow us not just a glimpse into the mind of Montini, but a leisurely review; he was frank and outspoken about liturgical reform, which had been his passion long before ascending the Chair of Peter and remained so during his pontificate. Above all, however, we ought to look carefully at three general audiences in the 1960s: the first from March of 1965, concerning the epochal shift from Christian Latin to modern vernaculars; and two from November of 1969, on the even greater shift from the Roman Catholic Mass to the Roman Consilium Mass.

Before descending into the details of these general audiences, however, I would like to introduce a different side of Montini to the reader, because I think it is valuable to see the "Dr. Jekyll/Mr. Hyde" we are dealing with, who seems to give with one hand what he takes away with the other. The psychological portrait is complex, contradictory, and torturous. It is fair to say that this psychology has, in many ways, passed into the bloodstream of the postconciliar Church, which is trapped in a vain dialectic between tradition and innovation, without the commitment to principle by which it could be transcended and peace could be restored to the body ecclesiastic.

Paul VI as traditionalist

Chapter 2 formulated laws and corollaries of organic liturgical development, which we may summarize as follows: "Under the guidance of the Holy Spirit and through the piety of the Christian people, the sacred liturgy tends toward greater articulation, enrichment, and perfection over time, and tends as well to become more determinate, stable, and unchanging." The pope who presided over the single greatest violation of these laws and corollaries nevertheless seems at times to have understood something of their truth and to have acted on them haphazardly, like the figure of

---

[1] Or perhaps no longer so mysterious? See Fr. Charles Murr, *The Godmother* and *Murder in the Thirty-Third Degree*, as well as his interviews published by *Inside the Vatican* and reproduced at *Rorate Caeli*.

Hamlet to which he was compared by John XXIII as well as by himself.[2] Surely one of the most remarkable examples of this phenomenon is the Instruction *Memoriale Domini* of May 29, 1969, issued by the Congregation for Divine Worship "at the special mandate of the Supreme Pontiff Paul VI" and "duly approved by him." In this document, we read as follows about the custom of distributing Communion on the tongue to the kneeling faithful:

> In view of the state of the Church as a whole today, this manner of distributing Holy Communion must be observed, not only because it rests upon a tradition of many centuries, but especially because it is a sign of the reverence of the faithful toward the Eucharist. The practice in no way detracts from the personal dignity of those who approach this great Sacrament, and it is a part of the preparation needed for the most fruitful reception of the Lord's Body.
>
> This reverence is a sign of Holy Communion not in "common bread and drink" but in the Body and Blood of the Lord. . . .
>
> In addition, this manner of communicating, which is now to be considered as prescribed by custom, gives more effective assurance that Holy Communion will be distributed with the appropriate reverence, decorum, and dignity; that any danger of profaning the Eucharistic species, in which "the whole and entire Christ, God and man, is substantially contained and permanently present in a unique way," will be avoided; and finally that the diligent care which the Church has always commended for the very fragments of the consecrated bread will be maintained: "If you have allowed anything to be lost, consider this a lessening of your own members."

---

[2] "Pope John XXIII . . . described Montini as 'un po' Amletico' (a bit Hamlet-like). Just as the prince endlessly hesitated to avenge his father's murder, so Montini was wavering, indecisive and ambiguous. He even asked himself, 'Am I Hamlet or Don Quixote?' This is the key question for an assessment of Paul VI's papacy. Were there too many compromises and half-decided issues?" Paul Collins, "Pope Hamlet: Paul VI's indecisive, wavering papacy," *National Catholic Reporter*, October 13, 2018. For a masterful, archivally-researched biography of Giovanni Battista Montini, see Yves Chiron, *Paul VI: The Divided Pope*, trans. James Walther (Brooklyn, NY: Angelico Press, 2022).

This exemplary passage invokes the principle of longstanding tradition; quotes four Fathers of the Church, Augustine, Justin, Irenaeus, and Cyril of Jerusalem; uses scholastic and Tridentine language; recognizes the principle that liturgical actions should avoid seeming commonplace and accentuate the divine mystery at hand; and lists the many spiritual and practical benefits the custom has, which more than suffice to explain its universal adoption. Yet in spite of this unanswerable demonstration, the same document allows episcopal conferences to permit Communion in the hand wherever it had already been introduced, and Paul VI did nothing to stop the illegitimate spread of this practice—nor did his successors. *Memoriale Domini* had died before it ever lived, another toothless Vatican velleity.[3]

A related and equally good example is the encyclical letter *Mysterium Fidei*, promulgated in September of 1965. This document reaffirms in the clearest possible way both Thomistic doctrine and Tridentine dogma about the Holy Eucharist, copiously citing Church Fathers and Doctors, upholding transubstantiation and the Real Presence, defending the true sacrificial nature of the Mass, the celebration of "private Masses," and the benefits of Eucharistic Adoration, and condemning in no uncertain terms the false Eucharistic theologies running rampant in the Church at the time.

A most interesting aspect of the letter is the pope's defense of preserving within the Church the modes of expression developed and handed down over the centuries—precisely what he will abandon a few years later when it comes to *liturgical* modes of expression, which are no less central to Christian identity and no less a matter of *paradosis* than doctrinal ones. He writes:

> Having safeguarded the integrity of the faith, it is necessary to safeguard also its proper mode of expression, lest by the careless use of words, we occasion (God forbid) the rise of false opinions regarding faith in the most sublime of mysteries. . . . "We . . . must speak according to a fixed norm, lest the lack of restraint in our speech

---

[3]   See Kwasniewski, *Holy Bread of Eternal Life: Restoring Eucharistic Reverence in an Age of Impiety* (Manchester, NH: Sophia Institute Press, 2020), 92–93, 124–26, 131–33, and the further references given there.

result in some impious opinion even about the things signified by the words themselves" (St. Augustine). . . .

The Church, therefore, with the long labor of centuries, and, not without the help of the Holy Spirit, has established a rule of language and confirmed it with the authority of the councils. This rule, which has more than once been the watchword and banner of orthodox faith, must be religiously preserved, and let no one presume to change it at his own pleasure or under the pretext of new science. Who would ever tolerate that the dogmatic formulas used by ecumenical councils for the mysteries of the Holy Trinity and the Incarnation be judged as no longer appropriate for men of our times and therefore that others be rashly substituted for them?

In the same way it cannot be tolerated that any individual should on his own authority modify the formulas which were used by the Council of Trent to express belief in the Eucharistic mystery. For these formulas, like the others which the Church uses to propose the dogmas of faith, express concepts which are not tied to a certain form of human culture, nor to a specific phase of human culture, nor to one or other theological school. No, these formulas present that part of reality which necessary and universal experience permits the human mind to grasp and to manifest with apt and exact terms taken either from common or polished language. For this reason, these formulas are adapted to men of all times and all places. But the most sacred task of theology is, not the invention of new dogmatic formulas to replace old ones, but rather such a defense and explanation of the formulas adopted by the councils as may demonstrate that divine Revelation is the source of the truths communicated through these expressions. . . .

Thus the understanding of the faith should be advanced without threat to its unchangeable truth.

Everything Pope Paul VI says here is applicable, *mutatis mutandis*, to the sphere of the liturgy. With the long labor of centuries and the help of the Holy Spirit, the Church has established for her public worship a rule of

language and confirmed it with the authority of councils; it must be religiously preserved; who would dare to judge it no longer appropriate for
men of our times? After all, it is made up of elements not tied to a certain
form of human culture nor to a specific phase of human culture, nor to one
or other theological school, but drawn from divine revelation, apostolic
tradition, natural religious instincts, and the cumulative piety of centuries.
For this reason, the hallowed liturgical rites are adapted to men of all times
and all places. The task of liturgists is not to invent new rites to replace old
ones but to defend and explain the rites we have inherited, advancing our
understanding without threatening the liturgy itself.

A third example is the apostolic letter *Sacrificium Laudis* of August 15,
1966, in which Paul VI praises monks and nuns for remaining faithful
to the "fixed and unceasing manner of prayer" that constitutes their daily
horarium, criticizes some of them who "wish to use the vernacular within
the choral office" or "exchange that chant which is called Gregorian for
newly-minted melodies," and chides those who "even insist that Latin
should be wholly suppressed." He writes:

> We have been somewhat disturbed and saddened by these requests.
> One may well wonder what the origin is of this new way of think-
> ing and this sudden dislike for the past. . . . What is in question
> here is not only the retention within the choral office of the Latin
> language—though it is of course right that this should be eagerly
> guarded and should certainly not be lightly esteemed, since this
> language is, within the Latin Church, an abundant wellspring of
> Christian civilization and a very rich treasure-trove of devotion—
> but also of preserving unharmed the quality, the beauty, and the
> native strength of these prayers and canticles. . . . The traditions of
> the elders, your glory throughout long ages, must not be belittled.
> Indeed, your manner of celebrating the choral office has been one
> of the chief reasons why these families of yours have lasted so long,
> and happily increased. It is thus most surprising that under the
> influence of a sudden agitation, some now think that it should be
> given up.

In present conditions, what words or melodies could replace the forms of Catholic devotion which you have used until now? You should reflect and carefully consider whether things would not be worse, should this fine inheritance be discarded. . . . One can also wonder whether men would come in such numbers to your churches in quest of the sacred prayer, if its ancient and native tongue, joined to a chant full of grave beauty, resounded no more within your walls. We therefore ask all those to whom it pertains, to ponder what they wish to give up, and not to let that spring run dry from which, until the present, they have themselves drunk deep. . . .

Moreover, those prayers, with their antiquity, their excellence, their noble majesty, will continue to draw to you young men and women, called to the inheritance of our Lord. On the other hand, that choir from which is removed this language of wondrous spiritual power, transcending the boundaries of the nations, and from which is removed this melody proceeding from the inmost sanctuary of the soul, where faith dwells and charity burns—We speak of Gregorian chant—such a choir will be like to a snuffed candle, which gives light no more, no more attracts the eyes and minds of men. . . .

We are unwilling to allow that which could make your situation worse, and which could well bring you no slight loss, and which would certainly bring a sickness and sadness upon the whole Church of God. Allow Us to protect your interests, even against your own will.[4]

It will be the same pope who, only a few years later (as we shall see), advocates the complete removal of Latin and Gregorian chant from the reformed liturgy, making no distinctions between religious and parochial contexts and failing to recognize the healthy influence monastic liturgy has always exercised on the rest of the Church by setting an ideal of plenitude

---

[4] Translated by Fr. Thomas Crean and published at https://lms.org.uk/sacrificium_laudis; slightly modified.

and beauty. In any event, he seems never to have lifted a finger to defend or implement this apostolic letter after it was published—once again, the Hamlet syndrome so familiar to those who have studied the life of Paul VI. Almost without exception, all of the religious orders abandoned both Latin and Gregorian chant, while he stood by on the sidelines, watching.[5]

One last example. In an address at Castel Gandolfo on August 13, 1969—thus, three and a half months prior to the mandated introduction of the Novus Ordo—Paul VI offers a description of the interplay between liturgy and personal piety that, so far from seeming applicable to the revised liturgical rites, calls powerfully to mind the experience of Catholics today with the rediscovered classical Roman rite:

> The liturgy has a primacy and fullness, an effectiveness of itself, that we should recognize and promote. But the liturgy, by its nature public and official in the Church, should not come to replace or impoverish personal spirituality. The liturgy is not ritual alone; it is mystery and by that fact calls for all who share in it to be consciously, fervently wrapped up in it. The liturgy demands faith, hope, charity, and so many other virtues and sentiments, acts and conditions—like humility, repentance, pardoning offenses, intention, attention, inward and vocal expression—disposing the believer for immersion into the divine reality that liturgical celebration makes present and active. Personal religion, because it is within the reach of everyone, is the indispensable condition for a genuine and aware liturgical participation. But that is not all: personal religion is also the result, the consequence of such participation, which is meant precisely to sanctify souls and to strengthen in them the sense of union with God, with Christ, with the Church, with all humanity.[6]

---

[5]   It has been told to me by an elderly Benedictine monk who studied in Rome in the 1970s, and who met Bugnini, that it was Rembert Weakland who persuaded Paul VI not to enforce *Sacrificium Laudis*. Nor was this document ever placed in the *Acta Apostolicae Sedis*, which means it never acquired the force of law.

[6]   Quoted by Anthony Ruff, "Paul VI on Liturgical Reform, Part 3," *PrayTell* weblog, August 4, 2018.

In terms of my own life as a Catholic, I would have had no idea what Paul VI was talking about *until* I began to attend the traditional Mass. It was *this* Mass that opened up the mystery of Christ, awakened my interior life, taught me how to pray, prompted fervor, acquainted me with penance (both as a virtue and as a sacrament).

Four examples of Montini's more "tradition-friendly" side have been cited, but of course there are many more. The plentiful stock has allowed conservatives to cherry-pick their favorite Paul VI quotations in order to present him as a pope in the classic mold of a Pius V or a Pius X, when he was nothing of the sort. It is difficult to see how a man of Catholic sensibilities and beliefs could have said the things he did in the three addresses to which we now turn.

General audience of March 17, 1965

The first address was delivered on March 17, 1965,[7] ten days after Paul VI celebrated the first-ever Italian-language Mass at the Church of All Saints (Ognissanti) in Rome.[8] In spite of official rhetoric, there is little evidence that the people rejoiced; a plaque memorializing the event in Ognissanti was vandalized so many times that a new plaque finally had to be placed high on the wall, out of reach of disgruntled parishioners.[9] Paul VI was in

---

[7]   The texts of the three audiences on which we are now commenting may be found in full in the appendix. In my commentary on the audience of March 17, 1965, I cite the translation printed in *L'Osservatore Romano* (posted at the weblog *Views from the Choir Loft* on March 26, 2014), but in the appendix, a fresh translation is provided.

[8]   At the Angelus in St. Peter's Square on March 7, 1965, Pope Paul VI addressed these words to the faithful: "Today is a memorable Sunday in the spiritual history of the Church: the vernacular, as you have perceived this morning, has officially taken its place within liturgical worship. The Church has judged this measure—raised and debated at the Council—to be necessary to make its prayer understandable and grasped by all. The good of the faithful calls for this kind action, making possible their active share in the Church's public worship. The Church has sacrificed its native tongue, Latin, a language that is sacred, measured, beautiful, richly expressive, and graceful. The Church has made the sacrifice of an age-old tradition and above all of unity in language among diverse peoples to bow to a higher universality, an outreach to all peoples. That means you, the faithful, so that you may be able to unite yourselves more closely to the Church's prayer, [and] pass over from being simply spectators to becoming active participants. If you can truly respond to this kindness of the Church, you will find the great joy, reward, and blessing of a genuine spiritual renewal" (*DOL* n. 26, p. 114).

[9]   See Gregory DiPippo, "The Liturgist Manifesto," *NLM*, November 29, 2014. For more on the Ognissanti event, see Dom Alcuin Reid, "March 7th, 1965—'An extraordinary way of celebrating the Holy Mass,'" *NLM*, March 7, 2015; Peter Kwasniewski, "'Backwards vs. For-

a bad mood at this juncture because the liturgical reform was encountering stiff resistance from the laity, whose spiritual plight was, after all, the main reason given for the reform, and who were expected to be its grateful beneficiaries.[10] "Power takes as ingratitude the writhing of its victims," Rabindranath Tagore reminds us.

It is hard to know what to be more astonished about: the sheer contempt for the common man with which the audience drips or the sheer fantasyland into which the pope enters when describing the anticipated benefits of the "new liturgy" that was unveiled at Ognissanti. (Remember, this was not the Novus Ordo, which was four years away, but a simplified Tridentine Mass conducted in Italian except for the Canon, with the celebrant facing the people, standing at a temporary altar placed outside of the sanctuary. Communion was distributed on the tongue, but the faithful were to remain standing for it.[11])

The pope says there have been negative reactions and positive reactions. The negative reaction is one of "a certain confusion and annoyance": "Previously, they say, there was peace, each person could pray as he wished, the whole sequence of the rite was well known; now everything is new, startling, and changed; even the ringing of the bells at the Sanctus is done away with; and then those prayers which one doesn't know where to find; Holy Communion received standing; Mass ending suddenly with the blessing; everybody answering, many people moving around, rites and readings which are recited aloud. . . . In short, there is no longer any peace and we now know less than we did before; and so on."

This does not seem an altogether unreasonable reaction. As far as the pope is concerned, however, Catholics who react this way have a paltry understanding of what they are doing: "We shall not criticize these views because then we would have to show how they reveal a poor understanding of the meaning of religious ceremonial and allow us to glimpse not a true devotion and a true appreciation of the meaning and worth of the

---

wards'—What Does It Mean?," *NLM*, May 4, 2015; Kwasniewski, "Just Say No to '65!," *NLM*, March 1, 2014; and the article mentioned two notes below.

[10] See Yves Chiron, *Annibale Bugnini: Reformer of the Liturgy*, trans. John Pepino (Brooklyn, NY: Angelico Press, 2018), 118–24.

[11] See the description in "The 50th Anniversary of Paul VI's First Italian Mass: Some hard truths about the '1965 Missal' and the Liturgical Reform," *Rorate Caeli*, March 7, 2015.

Mass, but rather a certain spiritual laziness which is not prepared to make some personal effort of understanding and participation directed to a better understanding and fulfillment of this, the most sacred of religious acts, in which we are invited, or rather obliged, to participate."

One wonders when a pope has ever said something more self-righteous, presumptuous, insensitive, and unjust? I suppose everyone, before the glorious revolution, was spiritually lazy, unprepared to make even "some" effort to understand, and altogether bereft of participation in the mysteries. The popularity of Liturgical Movement authors like Dom Prosper Guéranger, Pius Parsch, and Ildefonso Schuster, whose commentaries on the Mass instructed and inspired precisely those laymen who were startled and disturbed by the changes of the 1960s, is passed over in utter silence.[12]

Montini continues by explaining that reform always upsets people because deeply rooted religious practices are being tampered with, but that's okay—soon everyone will love it. And we'll make sure that no one can settle back again into silent devotion or laziness. "The congregation will be alive and active!" he says: everyone must participate. Now one must listen and pray (apparently they were doing neither before). Activity is the order of the day, the name of the game! We will finally have a liturgy that is not mummery ("performed merely according to its external form") but "an immense wing flying toward the heights of divine mystery and joy." An immense wing . . . Excuse me while I reach for the airsickness bag.

The positive reaction, on the other hand, is, according to Paul VI, that of a majority of Catholics, young and old, uneducated and scholarly, the earnestly devout and the urbanely cultured, insiders and outsiders, who greet the changes with "enthusiasm and praise." At last, they say, "one can understand and follow the complicated and mysterious ceremonial." (The pope declines to explain how simplification and easy accessibility fit with

---

[12] Pope Benedict XVI, whose intelligence, fairness, courtesy, and realism greatly exceeded those of Paul VI, noted precisely this fact in his letter to bishops *Con Grande Fiducia*, which accompanied the motu proprio *Summorum Pontificum* of July 7, 2007: "Afterwards, however [i.e., in the period after the introduction of the new missal], it soon became apparent that a good number of people remained strongly attached to this [older] usage of the Roman rite, which had been familiar to them from childhood. This was especially the case in countries where the Liturgical Movement had provided many people with a notable liturgical formation and a deep, personal familiarity with the earlier form of the liturgical celebration."

"complicated and mysterious," unless his meaning is that a ceremonial that was once complicated and mysterious will henceforth cease to be either.) At last, "the priest speaks to the people." (But wait: I thought the liturgy was addressed primarily to God?)

One old gentleman, the pope says, gushed to a priest that "at last" in this new way of celebrating Mass, he fully participated in the sacrifice—indeed, possibly for the first time in his life. Some say this excitement will quiet down and turn into habit. But Pope Paul expresses the hope that the "new form of worship" will continue to stir up "religious enthusiasm" so that "the gospel of love" will be realized in "the souls of our time."

Although generally well-read, Montini does not seem to be aware of Msgr. Ronald Knox's critique of religious enthusiasm. It is just this hankering for feelings of enthusiasm or excitement that has led to ever-repeated efforts to stir up or stimulate congregations ever since the sixties, with ever-diminishing returns. The number of full-blown enthusiasts for the reforms was meager, while the number of Catholics who quit going to church throughout the entire period of reform was significantly greater; a majority went along with it because, frankly, they had no choice.[13] The message of the pope was clear: "For your own good, you will participate actively in these various ways—and you will like it!" What we are seeing in this audience, then, can be summed up as "special pleading." Meanwhile, at just this time, early in 1965, the association Una Voce, dedicated to the preservation of Latin and Gregorian chant, was founded in Paris, and soon numbered chapters around the world.

This purple passage on enthusiasm for the reform cannot help but remind us today of the "results" of the survey of bishops with which Pope Francis tried to justify the draconian policies of *Traditionis Custodes*,[14] or

---

[13] I do not deny, obviously, that there were many social and cultural factors involved in the exodus of Catholics from the Church in the sixties and seventies, but as Stephen Bullivant recognizes in his authoritative study *Mass Exodus: Catholic Disaffiliation in Britain and America since Vatican II* (New York: Oxford University Press, 2019), the liturgical and disciplinary changes cannot be absolved of a serious role in diminishing Catholic identity and the attractiveness and rewards of belonging to a community of coherent belief and practice.

[14] See the three articles by Diane Montagna: "*Traditionis Custodes*: Separating Fact from Fiction," *The Remnant* online, October 7, 2021; "*Traditionis Custodes*: More Facts Emerge (What the Bishops of the World Actually Told Francis)," *The Remnant* online, October 28, 2021; "*Traditionis Custodes*: A Weapon of Mass Destruction," *The Remnant* online, November 29, 2021.

the conveniently scripted dubia to which the Congregation for Divine Worship provided goodthinkful responses on December 18, 2021. Over the decades, we have been subjected to a deceitful narrative in regard to the "success" of the liturgical reform and the wickedness of Catholics who cling to tradition—a veritable propaganda machine that deserves to be fully documented someday.

The 1965 papal address we have been considering is notable for the number of times it uses the word "new": "new, startling, changed"; "new order"; "new scheme of things"; "new liturgical books"; "new form" (twice); "new liturgy" (twice); "new habit"; "liturgical innovation." If we add them up, eleven times. Some Catholics today are critical of traditionalists who speak of the "Novus Ordo," but here we have a pope identifying the *interim missal* of 1965 as a novel thing, when it was vastly less of a novelty than the missal of 1969! I think we owe it to Pope Paul VI to use his terms when we talk about his reforms. He did not try to hide the fact that there had been a sea change. As the same pope said: "The important words of the Council are newness and updating . . . the word newness has been given to us as an order, as a program."[15]

Many notable Catholics of this period, such as Evelyn Waugh and William F. Buckley Jr., left us records of their less-than-enthusiastic impressions of the "new Mass" of 1965, which in retrospect turned out to be a half-way house. Dietrich von Hildebrand wrote in 1966:

> The basic error of most of the innovations is to imagine that the new liturgy brings the holy sacrifice of the Mass nearer to the faithful, that shorn of its old rituals the Mass now enters into the substance of our lives. For the question is whether we better meet Christ in the Mass by soaring up to Him, or by dragging Him down into our own pedestrian, workaday world. The innovators would replace holy intimacy with Christ by an unbecoming familiarity. The new liturgy actually threatens to frustrate the confrontation with Christ, for it discourages reverence in the face of mystery, precludes awe, and all but extinguishes a sense of sacredness.[16]

---

[15] *L'Osservatore Romano*, July 3, 1974.

[16] Dietrich von Hildebrand, "The Case for the Latin Mass," originally published in *Triumph*

General audience of November 19, 1969

Now we turn to a pair of general audiences given four and a half years later, in the month of November 1969.[17] As mentioned at the start, the *Novus Ordo Missae* was officially implemented on the first Sunday of Advent, which fell on November 30 that year.

The pope was feeling the heat at this moment. He had promulgated the text of the *Novus Ordo Missae* seven months earlier, on April 3. The *Short Critical Study of the New Order of Mass*, more commonly known as the "Ottaviani Intervention," was completed by June 5 but not published until a few months later; somehow it did not come to Paul VI's knowledge until September 29.[18] The popular press picked up the story and made a great deal of it. Paul VI sent the *Short Critical Study* to the Congregation for the Doctrine of the Faith, whose prefect, Cardinal Šeper, reported to him on November 12 that, in his opinion, the Study was essentially worthless. This was only one week prior to the general audience of November 19. We must bear in mind, then, that this and the following week's address are Paul VI's attempt to defend the entire project of the Novus Ordo in the face of its critics and for posterity. It is his *apologia pro Missa sua*.[19]

What is perhaps most striking about these addresses is the pope's penchant for gratuitous assertion and his stark authoritarian tone. He wants us to believe that nothing really central has changed, while at the same time listing, and doubling down on, one enormous change after another. For those who take seriously that a developed liturgical rite is a kind of body-soul composite in which one cannot readily separate what it is from how it is done, how it looks, sounds, smells, and feels, the case he makes for essential identity is far from convincing.

---

magazine, October 1966, and reprinted in *The Charitable Anathema: Essays and Addresses by Dietrich von Hildebrand* (Ridgefield, CT: Roman Catholic Books, 1993), 39. See Alcuin Reid, ed., *A Bitter Trial: Evelyn Waugh and John Carmel Cardinal Heenan on the Liturgical Changes* (San Francisco: Ignatius Press, 2011); William F. Buckley Jr., *Nearer, My God: An Autobiography of Faith* (New York: Doubleday, 1997), ch. 6: "Disruptions and Achievements of Vatican II," 91–108.

[17] Full texts are given in the appendix.

[18] See Chiron, *Bugnini*, 143.

[19] It is also worth noting that in response to the *Short Study* and other critiques, the pope pushed through a number of significant modifications to the *Institutio Generalis*.

On November 19, again the pope does not shy away from the language of novelty: he speaks of "a new rite of Mass" (four times), "a new spirit," "new directions," "new rules," "new and more expansive liturgical language," "innovation" (twice). He closes with bombastic sentimentality: "Do not let us talk about 'the new Mass.' Let us rather speak of the new epoch in the Church's life." In a colossal understatement, the pope says "the Mass will be celebrated in a rather different manner from that in which we have been accustomed to celebrate it in the last four centuries, from the reign of St. Pius V, after the Council of Trent, down to the present."

He shows admirable candor in getting right to the point: "This change has something astonishing about it, something extraordinary. This is because the Mass is regarded as the traditional and untouchable expression of our religious worship and the authenticity of our faith. We ask ourselves, how could such a change be made? What effect will it have on those who attend Holy Mass?"

His answer is feeble. Just pay attention to the explanations you will get from the pulpit and in religious publications, and trust that "a clearer and deeper idea of the stupendous and mysterious notion of the Mass" is just around the corner, thanks to the new missal. Again, he shows candor in admitting that the faithful will have "spontaneous difficulties."

Paul VI claims that the new missal "is due to the will expressed by the Ecumenical Council held not long ago." This claim is questionable, to say the least—particularly in view of what the pope will say one week later, when he openly contradicts *Sacrosanctum Concilium* on any number of points. But here, the new missal is said to be four things, each of which is surprising: "It is an act of obedience. It is an act of coherence of the Church with herself. It is a step forward for her authentic tradition. It is a demonstration of fidelity and vitality, to which we all must give prompt assent."

It is left quite unclear how the "coherence of the Church with herself" is to be achieved by breaking with much of what the Church had been doing in her most important actions for centuries. It is quite unclear how exactly a radically revised missal counts as a "step forward" (whatever that means) for the Church's "authentic tradition" (whatever that means). I do not think it would be unfair to call this doublespeak. According to Edward

Herman, "What is really important in the world of doublespeak is the ability to lie, whether knowingly or unconsciously, and to get away with it; and the ability to use lies and choose and shape facts selectively, blocking out those that don't fit an agenda or program."[20] Again, one is left speechless at the claim that the *Novus Ordo Missae* is "a demonstration of fidelity and vitality, to which we all must give prompt assent." Fidelity—how so, precisely? Vitality—just because papal muscle can be flexed to push through the biggest raft of changes in the history of the Church's worship?

The speech continues in a tone almost feverish and certainly imperious, as if the pope were feeling the total inadequacy of his account: "It is not an arbitrary act. It is not a transitory or optional experiment. It is not some dilettante's improvisation. It is a law. It has been thought out by [wait for it] authoritative experts of sacred liturgy; it has been discussed and meditated upon for a long time [that is, for a few years of extremely hasty and busy committee work]. We shall do well to accept it with joyful interest and put it into practice punctually, unanimously, and carefully."

These are not the words of a man who is especially at peace about what he has done, or confident in the power of the product to win over the customers. One suspects a psychiatrist could have a field day analyzing this language.

Pope Paul VI then says that the reform he has imposed "puts an end to uncertainties, discussions, arbitrary abuses. It calls us back to that uniformity of rites and feeling proper to the Catholic Church." Can irony have no limits? The febrile atmosphere of uncertainty, discussion, and abuse was in no way stifled but rather stirred up by the Vatican's practically annual changes to the liturgy from the 1950s through the 1960s. It was the official insistence on liturgical reform that shattered the uniformity of rites and feeling that the Church had enjoyed in relative peace from the end of the Council of Trent to the twentieth century. Moreover, one of the most characteristic features of the Novus Ordo is its lack of uniformity from one celebration to another, and its multiplication of Catholic "identities."

---

[20] Cited at https://en.wikipedia.org/wiki/Doublespeak. A similar Montinian phrase shows up in an Address to a Consistory, May 24, 1976: "For our part, in the name of tradition [!], we beseech all our children and all Catholic communities to celebrate the rites of the restored liturgy with dignity and fervent devotion."

The second part of the address goes into "what exactly the changes are." Whether from ignorance or from duplicity, the pope states that the changes "consist of many new directions for celebrating the rites," not adverting to the fact that the principal change is in the substance of the texts themselves: for example, only 13 percent of the orations of the old Roman Missal survived intact in the new missal. He then has the temerity to say: "Keep this clearly in mind: Nothing has been changed of the substance of the traditional Mass." I wonder how many people in 1969 believed this; I wonder how many still believe it today.

A passage in Saint Irenaeus of Lyons, directed against the arbitrary interpretations of the Gnostics, seems to me to capture perfectly what was done in our times with the Roman rite, as well as the subterfuge of saying: "This *is* the Roman rite" or worse, "This is now *tradition.*" Saint Irenaeus writes:

> Their manner of acting is just as if, when a beautiful image of a king has been constructed by some skillful artist out of precious jewels, one should then take this likeness of the man all to pieces, should rearrange the gems, and so fit them together as to make them into the form of a dog or of a fox, and even that but poorly executed; and should then maintain and declare that this was the beautiful image of the king which the skillful artist constructed, pointing to the jewels which had been admirably fitted together by the first artist to form the image of the king, but have been with bad effect transferred by the latter one to the shape of a dog, and by thus exhibiting the jewels, should deceive the ignorant who had no conception of what a king's form was like, and persuade them that that miserable likeness of the fox was, in fact, the beautiful image of the king.[21]

---

[21] Saint Irenaeus of Lyons, *Against Heresies*, Bk. I, ch. 8, trans. Alexander Roberts and William Rambaut, in *Ante-Nicene Fathers*, vol. 1, ed. A. Roberts, J. Donaldson, and A. C. Coxe (Buffalo, NY: Christian Literature Publishing Co., 1885), rev. and ed. for New Advent by Kevin Knight. It is worth pointing out that, true to his name, Saint Irenaeus (in the words of Eusebius of Caesarea) "fittingly admonished" Pope Victor I, who was trying to stamp out an ancient custom in Asia Minor of celebrating Easter on a different day than was observed elsewhere. How small a matter this is compared to the attempt to suppress the entire ancient Roman rite!

Returning to the general audience, we find Paul VI—as if detecting the misgivings his words up to this point might generate in a listener—going on the defensive:

> Perhaps some may allow themselves to be carried away by the impression made by some particular ceremony or additional rubric [this is what he says, but in fact the transition from old to new is mostly a matter of *lost* rubrics, not *additional* ones], and thus think that they conceal some alteration or diminution of truths which were acquired by the Catholic faith for ever, and are sanctioned by it. They might come to believe that the equation between the law of prayer, *lex orandi*, and the law of faith, *lex credendi*, is compromised as a result.
>
> It is not so. Absolutely not. Above all, because the rite and the relative rubric are not in themselves a dogmatic definition. Their theological qualification may vary in different degrees according to the liturgical context to which they refer. They are gestures and terms relating to a religious action—experienced and living—of an indescribable mystery of divine presence, not always expressed in a universal way. Only theological criticism can analyze this action and express it in logically satisfying doctrinal formulas.

In a spectacular instance of neoscholastic reductionism, we are told that only dogmatic definitions pertain to the essence of the Catholic Faith, since rites and rubrics have to do with experiences and actions that vary according to place and time; the only expression of truth is a "logically satisfying doctrinal formula." In these words, Paul VI has obliterated the *lex orandi* as a reality unto itself and has denied liturgy as *theologia prima*, a mode of conveyance of revelation.

He continues: "The Mass of the new rite is and remains the same Mass we have always had. If anything, its sameness has been brought out more clearly in some respects." As Shakespeare says, "The lady doth protest too much, methinks." To belabor the point that the Mass is the same establishes that it isn't; the obvious need not be said. In order to agree with the sameness hypothesis, one would first have to adopt the perspective that the Roman rite is nothing but a generic outline—an introduction, some readings, an anaphora with valid words of consecration, Communion, conclusion.[22]

As if to offer proof of his claim, the pope rather pathetically turns to the oneness of the Lord's Supper, the Sacrifice on the Cross, and the representation of both in the Mass, which he says all remains true for the Novus Ordo. Apart from the somewhat odd claim that the Mass is a representation of both the Cross and the Last Supper—which is not what the twenty-second Session of the Council of Trent teaches—this, it must be said, is placing the bar of liturgical continuity pretty low. Far from supporting the claim that the Novus Ordo is still the same Roman rite, it demonstrates only that the Novus Ordo is a valid liturgical rite, like any other liturgy, Eastern or Western, offered by a validly ordained priest using the correct matter and form. By this logic, one could argue that the Novus Ordo is the same as the Divine Liturgy of St. John Chrysostom.

Still clutching at straws, Paul VI says that the new rite brings out more clearly the relationship between the Liturgy of the Word and the Liturgy of the Eucharist[23] but fails to explain how this is so, and, as can be shown both theoretically and practically, the opposite proves to be true.[24] He makes one last plug for the joy of active participation, then, as if running out of steam, declares: "You will also see other marvelous features of our Mass." Why

---

[22] Such a remote or abstract sameness would not, in all probability, convince either the simple and childlike or the sophisticated and cultured—the two demographics most heavily alienated from the Church during this period—that the Mass was the same. Continuity of rites has to be verified at the level of *specifics*, not at that of generalities. I recall a commenter at *PrayTell* who first presented a chart in which he lined up the *parts* of the classic Roman rite and of the Novus Ordo, and then said: "Look, not so much difference after all!" This is like saying "we read some of the Bible," instead of asking "which readings do we use for the Sunday Epistles and Gospels?," or "the annual calendar is organized around Christmas and Easter," instead of asking "How are the seasons and feasts articulated and liturgically observed?" At the level of airy generalities, it is barely possible to discriminate even between (say) Coptic, Byzantine, and Latin, since everyone does *basically* the same kinds of things: they chant or sing, they read readings, they have litanies or petitions, they have an anaphora, they recite the Lord's Prayer, etc.

[23] Incidentally admitting that the age-old nomenclature of "the Mass of Catechumens" and "the Mass of the Faithful," matching up to ancient practice and followed by hundreds of commentators over the centuries, has therewith been jettisoned.

[24] On this point, see my articles "Why 'Mass of Catechumens' Makes Better Sense Than 'Liturgy of the Word,'" *NLM*, December 29, 2014; "Why the 'Word of God' for Catholics Is Not Only the Bible, But More Importantly, Jesus Himself," *LifeSiteNews*, August 29, 2019.

exactly does this plural—"*our* Mass"—suddenly appear? Is it the papal "we": our modern papal rite? Is it an oblique reference to the Consilium: our committee Mass that we now present to a Catholic world panting in expectation? Or is this the "we" of the collectivity that would subsequently find in the *Novus Ordo Missae* the incentive, and indeed the invitation, to celebrate itself?

Then, another desperate attempt to ram home the sameness thesis: "But do not think that these things are aimed at altering its genuine and traditional essence." We are left once more with the stubborn question that will not go away: What is "the genuine and traditional essence" of a liturgy? Is it whatever the pope decides it is, however minimal that may be, or can we trust the broad lines of its historical development and its universal reception in the Church, as the Council of Trent so obviously did? In short, it is hard to imagine two more opposed visions of liturgy than Trent's and Montini's.

At the end, he invokes a favorite word, "pastoral," as justification, and he expresses his desire that "the faithful will participate in the liturgical mystery with more understanding, in a more practical, a more enjoyable, and a more sanctifying way." To my ear, the language here smacks of urban planning and social engineering. How curious, then, that he refers to "the Word of God which lives and echoes down the centuries"—that very Word whose ongoing embodiment in the organic development of the liturgy is being repudiated—and then opines that the faithful will better "share in the mystical reality of Christ's sacramental and propitiatory sacrifice," even though the Novus Ordo has purged the liturgy of its palpable mysticism and its unmistakable accentuation of the propitiatory sacrifice of Calvary!

The address is Montini all over: cold logic, stiff manner, overbearing tone, occasional Maritainian poetic flourishes, and, above all, a baffling obliviousness to the sheer magnitude of what he is doing, as if the dropping of bombs were like playing a game of chess.

General audience of November 26, 1969

One week later, the pope continues his *apologia*. Once again, notice how relentlessly Paul VI underlines the newness of what he is imposing on the

Church. In the opening sentence, he speaks of "the liturgical innovation of the new rite of the Mass." The phrase "new rite" is mentioned seven times; the words "new," "newness," or "renewal," seven more times; "innovation" twice; "novelty" twice. That makes a total of eighteen times.

In classic Montini fashion, his second paragraph lingers regretfully over what is to be lost:

> A new rite of the Mass: a change in a venerable tradition that has gone on for centuries. This is something that affects our heredi- tary religious patrimony, which seemed to enjoy the privilege of being untouchable and settled. It seemed to bring the prayer of our forefathers and our saints to our lips and to give us the comfort of feeling faithful to our spiritual past, which we kept alive to pass it on to the generations ahead. It is at such a moment as this that we get a better understanding of the value of historical tradition and the communion of the saints.

As incredible as it may seem, the pope appears to be saying that when we give up our hereditary religious patrimony, we feel most keenly the value of that tradition and of the communion of saints with whom we once prayed in common! This seems to me a sadistic maneuver, like telling a child: "You will appreciate your mother more if we take her away from you and you never see her again." He continues, resuming themes from his March 1965 address: "This change will affect the ceremonies of the Mass. We shall become aware, perhaps with some feeling of annoyance, that the ceremonies at the altar are no longer being carried out with the same words and gestures to which we were accustomed—perhaps so much accustomed that we no longer took any notice of them. This change also touches the faithful. It is intended to interest each one of those present, to draw them out of their customary personal devotions or their usual torpor."

If I am not mistaken, Paul VI is arguing that ritual stability causes people to stop paying attention to what is going on and to fold in on themselves in subjectivism or laziness. If this were true, it would explain the obsession of modern liturgists with constantly changing things up: as I once remarked, paraphrasing Heraclitus, "you can never step in the same Novus Ordo twice." In the experience of many, on the contrary, stability in ritual makes possible a deep intimacy with the Church's prayer, and thereby heads off unhealthy private *or collective* subjectivism.[25]

In any case, the pope seems to be under no illusions about the shake-up when he writes in paragraphs 4 and 5: "We must prepare for this many-sided inconvenience. It is the kind of upset caused by every novelty that breaks in on our habits. We shall notice that pious persons are disturbed most, because they have their own respectable way of hearing Mass, and they will feel shaken out of their usual thoughts and obliged to follow those of others. Even priests may feel some annoyance in this respect. . . . This novelty is no small thing. We should not let ourselves be surprised by the nature, or even the nuisance, of its exterior forms."

Paul VI would never have succeeded as a salesman. It is no wonder so many Catholics stopped going to Mass and a further wave of priests and religious suffered from spiritual disorientation when their supreme Shepherd thought it was a good idea to cause especially pious persons and priests a "many-sided inconvenience," "upset," "disturbance," "annoyance," "nuisance," as they struggled to figure out what in Hades was going on with the "exterior forms"—not to say internal spirit—of the Church's liturgy! Noteworthy, too, is the pope's denigration of habits. How different was the attitude of Jacques Maritain, in accord with the perennial wisdom of Saint Thomas: "Habits are, as it were, metaphysical letters patent of nobility, and just as much as inborn talents make for inequality among men, the man with a habit has a quality in him for the lack of which nothing can

---

[25] See my article "The Fixity of Liturgical Forms as an Incentive to Prayer and *Lectio Divina*," *NLM*, January 23, 2017. How healthy was the attitude found among the more conservative members of the Liturgical Movement! "It would be a severe strain on us if every time we approached God we had to think out how to set about it. We would feel the responsibility appalling and the claim on our emotions too great, particularly at times when we did not feel very religious, but turned to prayer straight from the bustle of everyday life. One function of ritual, therefore, is to canalise our prayer, to insure against the ups and downs of our moods and the wayward vulgarities of fashion. A ritual that is formed by long tradition, and which enshrines the deepest truths of our religion in a setting worthy of their grandeur, carries us along on its tide; it leads and forms our prayer in a sacred mould rather than waiting upon any burst of personal inspiration. It is there already to hand, and we have only to enter into it, to take it up and try to make it personal, to make it our own." Fr. John Coventry, *The Breaking of Bread: A Short History of the Mass* (New York: Sheed & Ward, 1950), 2.

compensate, as nothing can take its place. Other men are defenceless, he is armour-clad, but his armour is the living armour of the spirit."[26]

In the face of this upcoming challenge, what does Paul VI recommend? Like a dreamy intellectual far removed from ordinary Christians, he suggests that we need to prepare ourselves for "this special and historical occasion" by, don't you know, doubling down on our study of books and articles that explain the motives for "this grave change." Recognizing again the inherent weakness of his position, he invokes "obedience to the Council"—well he knows the lesson of totalitarian propaganda that the only thing needed to establish a falsehood as truth is to repeat the same lies calmly, boldly, and frequently—and adds to it, for good measure, "obedience to your bishops." He is confident that all the bishops will be lining up in good ultramontanist (or should we say ultra-Montini-ist) fashion.[27] In a moment of almost Montanist *afflatus*, he concludes paragraph 6: "It is Christ's will, it is the breath of the Holy Spirit which calls the Church to make this change. A prophetic moment is occurring in the Mystical Body of Christ, which is the Church. This moment is shaking the Church, arousing it, obliging it to renew the mysterious art of its prayer."

In paragraphs 7 through 14—the largest thematic section of the discourse—Paul VI offers a defense of the practical abolition of Latin.[28] He still seems to be smarting under the lash of Tito Casini's 1965 book *La Tunica Stracciata* (*The Torn Tunic*), in which that popular Italian author attacked the introduction of the vernacular into the Mass.[29]

The pope's point of departure in this section is the claim that because "the faithful are also invested with the 'royal priesthood' . . . they are qualified to have supernatural conversation with God" (§6). From this truth—which no one had ever denied, in theory or in practice—Paul VI deduces the necessity of replacing Latin with the common spoken language; for otherwise, the people are not able to have a supernatural conversation with

[26] Jacques Maritain, *Art and Scholasticism with Other Essays*, trans. J. F. Scanlan (New York: Charles Scribner's Sons, 1924), 9.
[27] This was prior to the heroic stance taken up by Archbishop Marcel Lefebvre, which was to bring out the worst in Paul VI. But that is a story for another time.
[28] See also the Angelus address from March 7, 1965 (quoted in n. 8 on p. 117), which is like an abstract of the present audience.
[29] The English translation was republished in 2020 by Angelico Press.

God (?). The pope starts up his familiar hand-wringing routine, in which he will first tell us how great a loss will be incurred by the new rite:

> The introduction of the vernacular will certainly be a great sacrifice for those who know the beauty, the power, and the expressive sacrality of Latin. We are parting with the speech of the Christian centuries; we are becoming like profane intruders in the literary preserve of sacred utterance. We will lose a great part of that stupendous and incomparable artistic and spiritual thing, the Gregorian chant. We have reason indeed for regret, reason almost for bewilderment. What can we put in the place of that language of the angels? We are giving up something of priceless worth. But why? What is more precious than these loftiest of our Church's values?

It is at this point that Paul VI shows his cards, advocating a kind of epistemological nudism or "free and simple" philosophy: "The answer will seem banal, prosaic. Yet it is a good answer, because it is human, because it is apostolic. Understanding of prayer is worth more than the silken garments in which it is royally dressed. Participation by the people is worth more—particularly participation by modern people, so fond of plain language which is easily understood and converted into everyday speech."[30]

As our earlier quotation from Dietrich von Hildebrand pointed out, we see here a humanistic, horizontal, and anthropocentric understanding of liturgy that is opposed, paradoxically, to liturgy's very effectiveness as a means of spiritual transformation, drawing the soul up to the infinite God and into communion with the Mystical Body of Christ, past, present, and eternal. The Latin language is effective precisely *because* of its "beauty,

---

[30] In a homily preached four months later, on March 27, 1966 at the Parish of Mary Immaculate in Rome, Paul VI spoke of "the remarkable sacrifice of Latin, the priceless repository of the Church's treasure," for which he claimed conciliar justification—in the meantime, insulting generations of Catholics: "The Council has taken the fundamental position that the faithful have to understand what the priest is saying and to share in the liturgy; to be not just passive spectators at Mass but souls alive. . . . No longer do we have the sad phenomenon of people being conversant and vocal about every human subject yet silent and apathetic in the house of God. . . . In this way the Sunday Mass is not just an obligation but a pleasure, not just fulfilled as a duty, but claimed as a right" (*DOL* n. 33, p. 125). As we see again and again, Paul VI was not above selectively citing and creatively reconstructing the teaching of the Council to serve his purposes.

power, and expressive sacrality," its "sacred utterance," its "priceless worth," the loftiness of its associations, and the "stupendous and incomparable artistic and spiritual thing" that clothes it in music, Gregorian chant.

Participation in the sense of the immediate comprehension of "plain language, easily understood, in everyday speech" is the least and lowest sense in which the faithful participate in the awesome mysteries of Christ. Sociologists have pointed out that dense, impenetrable, to some extent off-limits religious rituals are a powerful motivator for belief and devotion. Fr. Aidan Nichols observes: "The notion that the more intelligible the sign, the more effectively it will enter the lives of the faithful is implausible to the sociological imagination. . . . A certain opacity is essential to symbolic action."[31] Psychologists note that archetypal symbolism conveyed in gestures, clothing, and other physical phenomena, not to say the superrational language of music, are at least as communicative as words, if not more so. The power of the liturgy to affect the soul depends to a very great extent on such non-verbal elements and the subtle factor that may be called, for lack of a better term, atmosphere or ambiance.

Yes, the faithful should have some grasp of the content of the Mass (and, of course, acquaintance with more of the Catholic liturgy than just the Mass, which is the font and apex, but not the totality); about this, Dom Guéranger and the *pars sanior* of the Liturgical Movement were right.[32] But what draws men to liturgical worship is the prospect of an encounter with

---

[31] Aidan Nichols, *Looking at the Liturgy: A Critical View of Its Contemporary Form* (San Francisco: Ignatius Press, 1996), 61. See also Uwe Michael Lang, *Signs of the Holy One: Liturgy, Ritual, and Expression of the Sacred* (San Francisco: Ignatius Press, 2015); Michael Fiedrowicz, *The Traditional Mass: History, Form, and Theology of the Classical Roman Rite*, trans. Rose Pfeifer (Brooklyn, NY: Angelico Press, 2020), 191–231. It boggles the mind that Paul VI could be making such remarks at the same time as the popularity of Carl Jung via Joseph Campbell was reaching new heights. If anyone has ever misread the "signs of the times," it was Montini, who built a giant shrine to modernity at the very moment post-modernity was achieving ascendancy.

[32] It is distressing to see some of today's would-be advocates of tradition exalting a "devotionalism of ignorance" and a strict bifurcation between lay spirituality and the rites of the sanctuary. On this topic, see "When Piety Is Mistaken for Passivity, and Passivity for Piety," in my book *Ministers of Christ: Recovering the Roles of Clergy and Laity in an Age of Confusion* (Manchester, NH: Crisis Publications, 2021), 141–51; cf. Peter Kwasniewski, *Noble Beauty, Transcendent Holiness: Why the Modern Age Needs the Mass of Ages* (Kettering, OH: Angelico Press, 2017), 89–94, 205–8 and my article "Living the *Vita Liturgica*: Conditions, Obstacles, Prospects," *NLM*, April 16, 2018.

the mysterious and the ineffable, the strangely beautiful that opens our minds to the transcendent and offers a glimpse of heaven. In this way, it was exactly *anti*-apostolic to invert the Church's priorities by placing a superficial notion of popular engagement above the more profound immersion in prayer that the ancient liturgy, properly celebrated, had always offered to the faithful, and still does.

In one of the most hauntingly ironic statements in papal history, Paul VI noted with some melancholy in his 1975 Apostolic Exhortation *Evangelii Nuntiandi*: "Modern man is sated by talk; he is obviously tired of listening, and what is worse, impervious to words."[33] This observation was made only five years after he had imposed on the Church a liturgy outstanding for its non-stop verbosity, huge doses of Scripture, lack of silence, and paucity of non-verbal ritual.

Back in the 1969 address, Pope Paul proceeds to dig himself into a hole: "If the divine Latin language kept us apart from the children, from youth, from the world of labor and of affairs, if it were a dark screen, not a clear window, would it be right for us fishers of souls to maintain it as the exclusive language of prayer and religious intercourse?"

The most dramatic decline in Mass attendance in the decade after the Council (that is, from the first introduction of the vernacular and *versus populum* to the imposition of the Novus Ordo) was found precisely among the laborers, as English sociologist Anthony Archer demonstrated.[34] Furthermore, it is by no means clear that the "world of affairs" ever favored the liturgical reform. I have already mentioned Casini, von Hildebrand, Waugh, and Buckley, but the most embarrassing sign of the lack of support among educated people came in 1971, with a petition urging the preservation of the traditional Latin Mass, signed by fifty-six of the most eminent cultural figures of Great Britain—"many of the foremost writers, critics, academics, and musicians of the day, as well as politicians from Britain's then three main parties, and two Anglican bishops"[35]—which John

---

[33] *Evangelii Nuntiandi* §42.

[34] In his book *The Two Catholic Churches: A Study in Oppression* (London: SCM Press, 1986); see Joseph Shaw, "A sociologist on the Latin Mass," *LMS Chairman* weblog, June 26, 2013.

[35] Joseph Shaw, ed., *The Case for Liturgical Restoration: Una Voce Studies on the Traditional Latin Mass* (Brooklyn, NY: Angelico Press, 2019), 213–16. There were, in fact, two nearly

Cardinal Heenan presented to Pope Paul VI, an intervention that led to the "English Indult" (sometimes called the "Agatha Christie Indult") for the continued use of the old Mass, which was, in retrospect, the first step in a long process of backtracking on the overblown claims that had been made for the "new epoch" to be ushered in by the liturgical reform.[36] Lastly, Paul VI's mention of "children and youth" may remind us of what is perhaps the sharpest irony of all: while the average number of children born to mainstream Catholics and the average retention rate of young adults continue to be alarmingly low, the numbers of large families in the traditional Mass movement and its overall youthfulness tell a very different story about what attracts people to Christ and what pushes them away.

In paragraphs 13 and 14, the pope throws a sop to Latin-lovers by reminding them that the new rite of Mass *allows for* the people to sing together in Latin the Ordinary of the Mass—an allowance that was almost never to be actualized in practice—and that Latin will still remain the official language of Vatican documents, cold comfort if ever there was any. With no hint of intentional irony, he says: "Latin will remain . . . as the key to the patrimony of our religious, historical, and human culture. If possible, it will reflourish in splendor." Yet if Latin is really the key to our Catholic patrimony, why are we making the one move most calculated to destroy its living presence in the Church? How will this help Latin "reflourish in splendor"?

In paragraph 15, Paul VI takes up his theme from the previous week that the Mass hasn't really changed, because "the fundamental outline of the Mass is still the traditional one, not only theologically but also spiritually."

---

simultaneous petitions, one limited to the fifty-six signatories from or living in the UK, and another, published in Italian, that added an additional forty-two signatories from around the world. See Joseph Shaw, "50 Years Ago: Non-Catholics Petitioned the Pope for the Latin Mass," *OnePeterFive*, November 8, 2021, https://onepeterfive.com/non-catholics-petition-pope-latin-mass/; Shaw, "Other Petitions in Favour of the Ancient Mass," *Gregorius Magnus* 12 (Winter 2021): 41–44, https://issuu.com/gregoriusmagnus/docs/gads1591_gregorius_magnus_12_winter_web_2021_ame/s/13650010; the same issue contains several additional pieces connected with these petitions.

[36] The crucial milestones in this process are well known: the English Indult of 1971, *Quattuor Abhinc Annos* of 1984 (cleverly named to sound like a response to and replacement of *Tres Abhinc Annos* of 1967), *Ecclesia Dei Adflicta* of 1988, *Summorum Pontificum* of 2007, and *Universae Ecclesiae* of 2011. Tragically, this glacially slow progress was abruptly interrupted by Francis's *Traditionis Custodes* of 2021, which, many predict, will have a short life-span.

If by "fundamental outline" one means that some kind of penitential thing comes first, some kind of Eucharistic prayer comes around the middle, and some kind of gesture indicating the end of the service comes last, one can agree with the pope's assessment. The ways in which the structure, theology, and spirituality of the new missal clearly differ or depart from those of the old missal are practically innumerable and have been well described in copious literature.[37] But it takes little more than attendance at the *usus antiquior* to begin to see for oneself that the application of the word "traditional" to the reformed liturgical rites of Paul VI is precisely the sort of "abuse of language, abuse of power" about which the philosopher Josef Pieper, who lived under the National Socialist regime in Germany, wrote so eloquently.[38]

Then Paul VI has either the naïveté or the shamelessness to assert: "Indeed, if the rite is carried out as it ought to be, the spiritual aspect will be found to have greater richness. The greater simplicity of the ceremonies, the variety and abundance of scriptural texts, the joint acts of the ministers, the silences which will mark various deeper moments in the rite, will all help to bring this out."

As long as everyone "participates profoundly," he says, the Mass will become "more than ever a school of spiritual depth and a peaceful but demanding school of Christian sociology. The soul's relationship with Christ and with the brethren thus attains new and vital intensity." In lines like this, we see Paul VI abandoning himself to full-scale fantasyland.

---

[37] It is clear, at any rate, to those who *compare* them, although one is permitted to wonder how well acquainted Paul VI was with every liturgical book published at his behest. According to Archbishop Bugnini, on the one hand Paul VI read each draft of the *Ordo Missae* with painstaking care, underlining in multiple colors and annotating the margins in small print (Chiron, *Bugnini*, 135), while on the other hand he returned the text of the new lectionary with a note saying he had not been able to study it but assumed that the experts had done their work properly. See Annibale Bugnini, *The Reform of the Liturgy 1948–1975*, trans. Matthew J. O'Connell (Collegeville, MN: The Liturgical Press, 1990), 420; cf. my article "Who Was Captain of the Ship in the Liturgical Reform? The 50th Anniversary of an Embarrassing Letter," *NLM*, June 24, 2019.

[38] We see another spectacular example of it in Paul VI's Address to Cardinals, May 24, 1976: "They [the traditionalists] cast discredit on the authority of the Church in the name of a Tradition for which only material and verbal respect is shown. . . . In the name of Tradition itself we ask all of our sons and all the Catholic communities to celebrate, with dignity and fervor, the rites of the renovated liturgy."

The last three paragraphs, 17 through 19, form a bizarre coda that conveys, even to us at a distance of half-a-century, something of the feeling of slapdash haste and scarcely-controlled chaos that surrounded the entire project of liturgical reform: "But there is still a practical difficulty, which the excellence of the sacred renders not a little important. [What an expression!—*PK*] How can we celebrate this new rite when we have not yet got a complete missal, and there are still so many uncertainties about what to do?"

Good question, Holy Father. It was a question that had rarely left the lips of clergy and laity for a good fifteen years by this point, as rubrics, texts, music, language, nearly everything continued to evolve on an almost annual basis. What we see in this madness for sacramental reform, starting regrettably under Pius XII, is the very negation of the correct Catholic attitude toward tradition, which is that of a gardener, not that of an industrialist or a real estate developer who knocks down the old mansion to make way for modern flats. If I might adapt some recent words of Fr. John Hunwicke: the pope needs "to remember the aperçu of Blessed John Henry Newman, that the ministry of the Roman Church within the *oikoumene* is to be a barrier, a *remora*, against the intrusion of erroneous novelty. It is: to hand on the Great Tradition unadulterated. In an age when the adjective 'negative' has unpopular vibes, we need a reappropriation at the very highest level within the Church of the central, fundamental importance of a negative and preservative papacy. *Tradidi quod et accepi* implies *Quod non accepi non tradam.*"[39]

Having posed the question, Paul VI answers it with rather more technical detail than one would expect in a general audience. The takeaway is that Latin liturgy is definitely on its way out—and that, by the pope's express will. By November 28, 1971, there are to be no more Latin liturgies from the old missal or even from the new one. And if a priest expects to find himself in various places, offering Mass alone as well as with a congregation, he had better invest in a stout wagon for carrying all the liturgical books he will need. The old days when an altar missal sufficed are hereby excluded in the name of "greater simplicity of rites."[40]

[39] "'The worst pope ever'?" *Fr Hunwicke's Mutual Enrichment*, March 16, 2019.
[40] To use the language of the Synod of Pistoia—and of Paul VI.

The address closes with a final subtle irony—a quotation from one of Paul VI's favorite authors, the Swiss priest and theologian Maurice Zundel (1897–1975), from the preface to the second edition of *Le Poème de la Sainte Liturgie* of 1934, which was published in English in 1939 under the title *The Splendor of the Liturgy*: "The Mass is a Mystery to be lived in a death of Love. Its divine reality surpasses all words. . . . It is the Action par excellence, the very act of our Redemption, in the Memorial which makes it present."[41]

I do not know what Zundel, who died in 1975, thought of the *Novus Ordo Missae*, but I can say with confidence that anyone who reads *The Splendor of the Liturgy*—a profound work of mystical theology, which, from start to finish, is steeped in the prayers and ceremonies of the classic Roman rite—enters into a world of luminous wonder and fiery devotion, the epitome of a Church securely and gratefully rooted in her tradition. This world was doomed by Paul VI's interim missal of 1965 and banished by the deceptively named *Missale Romanum* of 1969. To a poor layman or priest attending the general audience on November 19 or November 26 of that fateful year, the glorious and intimate world described in Zundel—or, for that matter, by Prosper Guéranger, Nicholas Gihr, Pius Parsch, Fernand Cabrol, Ildefonso Schuster, or any of the large number of liturgical commentators in the nineteenth and twentieth centuries who labored tirelessly to advance understanding and reanimate participation in the liturgy of the Church in its traditional (i.e., handed down) form, not as it might be reinvented by engineers in laboratories—seemed on the verge of being lost forever.[42]

Revisiting these addresses more than five decades later is important for many reasons, but I would like to mention one in particular. Proponents of the "Reform of the Reform," no doubt in good faith, cling to a narrative

---

[41] The wording of the opening phrases as quoted by the pope is somewhat different from that which is found in the English edition published by Sheed & Ward: "The Mass is a mystery, which must be made our living experience. And that experience is no less than a death for love."

[42] For a poignant memoir of the feelings of this time, see Bryan Houghton, *Unwanted Priest: The Autobiography of a Latin Mass Exile* (Brooklyn, NY: Angelico Press, 2022).

in which the *Novus Ordo Missae* came hot off the Vatican press clothed in Latin as with a garment, ready to be celebrated in splendor and solemnity to the noble strains of Gregorian chant, in perfect fulfillment of the conciliar constitution *Sacrosanctum Concilium*—and then the Mass got "hijacked" by European and American progressives, who flatly contradicted the good intentions of Paul VI.[43]

A basic problem with this narrative is that it's false. The three general audiences indicate that Paul VI never thought or wished that the Novus Ordo would be celebrated widely in Latin; he never expected Gregorian chant to survive in the parishes; he never wanted "our Mass" to look or sound like the inherited Roman liturgy. He calmly noted that Latin and Gregorian chant would disappear; the old way of celebrating Mass might as well perish from the face of the earth. A sign that the chants were no longer intended to be seen as integral to the modern Roman rite—contrary to Vatican II's explicit statement in *SC* 116—is that Paul VI's new Mass was rolled out in 1969, five years before a new *Graduale* could be published for it by the monks of Solesmes in 1974. This is one sign among many that the Low Mass had been taken as the model: liturgy reduced to text alone, contrary to its origins and structure.[44] No one who cared about the integrity of the rite or of maintaining any kind of continuity would have rushed to release a missal for which the corresponding chants were not ready to hand. Judging from his audiences, Paul VI, at least, sought rupture, not the continuity for which his successor Benedict XVI became the spokesman.[45]

---

[43] Proof that I am not making this up: see Dr. Philippa Martyr's article "The Novus Ordo was meant to be a Latin Mass," *The Catholic Weekly* online, July 11, 2021.

[44] The traditional liturgy's paradigm is the solemn pontifical Mass, of which solemn Mass (with priest, deacon, and subdeacon) is a reduction, and a *Missa cantata* (with only a priest) a further simplification, and the low Mass the last distillate. In the Novus Ordo, by contrast, the low Mass of a single priest is taken as the model, and extrapolations or adaptations are made depending on which other ministers happen to be present. The traditional way harks back to the episcopocentric liturgy of apostolic times, while the modern way, ironically, stems from the much-maligned private devotional Mass of medieval origin—one of many ironies of the "reform," especially in view of the Council's encouragement of solemn sung liturgy (*SC* 112–13).

[45] The only exception was Paul VI's counsel to monks and nuns whom (as we saw in the apostolic letter *Sacrificium Laudis*) he encouraged to retain their chanted Latin Divine Office. However, he never enforced this plea, in keeping with his weak and ambivalent mode of governance, and watched from the papal apartments as all of the great religious orders collapsed, taking their choral office and sung Mass into the tomb with them.

Paul VI could have heartily endorsed the words of influential liturgist and Consilium member Joseph Gelineau, SJ: "Let those who like myself have known and sung a Latin-Gregorian High Mass remember it if they can. Let them compare it with the Mass that we now have. Not only the words, the melodies, and some of the gestures are different. To tell the truth, it is a different liturgy of the Mass [*c'est une autre liturgie de la messe*]. This needs to be said without ambiguity: the Roman rite as we knew it no longer exists [*le rite romain tel que nous l'avons connu n'existe plus*]. It has been destroyed. [*Il est détruit.*]"[46]

It is evident that Paul VI's operative principle was accommodationism: the liturgy must be accommodated to the mentality and purported needs of Modern Man.[47] To this hungry Moloch of modernization, every other consideration had to yield; indeed, the first sacrificial offering to be placed in its mouth was the Council's Constitution on the Sacred Liturgy. It requires no towering intelligence to see that some of *Sacrosanctum Concilium*'s clearest and most important provisions were not only ignored but negated. Perhaps Martin Mosebach is too kind when he evaluates *SC* as a modest document, but his view is surely the one held by most of the Fathers who voted for it: "The Second Vatican Council had once again comprehensively and expressly confirmed the theology of the Mass that had been handed down; it solemnly recognized sacral language, sacred music—Gregorian Chant, which floats between Occident and Orient and belongs to no single sphere of culture—and only encouraged a cautious review of the liturgical books, as was common practice once every few hundred years."[48]

In an exercise of hyperpapalism that has no other historical equivalent and probably never will, Paul VI unilaterally acted against the provisions

---

[46] From *Demain la liturgie: Essai sur l'évolution des assemblées chrétiennes* (Paris: Cerf, 1976), 9–10. Gelineau continues: "Some walls of the former edifice have fallen while others have changed their appearance, to the extent that it appears today either as a ruin or the partial substructure of a different building."

[47] On the motives of the reform and its revolutionary nature, Michael Davies's *Pope Paul's New Mass* (Kansas City, MO: Angelus Press, 2009) and Anthony Cekada's *Work of Human Hands: A Theological Critique of the Mass of Paul VI* (West Chester, OH: Philothea Press, 2010) remain indispensable, even if they must be supplemented by more recent publications.

[48] Martin Mosebach, *Subversive Catholicism: Papacy, Liturgy, Church*, trans. Sebastian Condon and Graham Harrison (Brooklyn: Angelico Press, 2019), 105.

signed by 2,147 bishops and major superiors.[49] In this way, he exhibited an extreme megalomania that could be summed up in the phrase: *L'église, c'est moi.* The single most influential person in the destruction of the Roman rite was not Bugnini or any other liturgist, but Paul VI himself, without whose constant backing the Consilium's lame ideas would have died the death of most scholarly theories and pastoral plans.

Mosebach, whose work I admire so much and with whom it pains me to disagree, has claimed that Paul VI's reformed liturgy was innocent of the anti-Latin, anti-chant, anti-*ad orientem* mentality that overtook it in the late sixties. For example, he writes:

> There can be no question that the council fathers regarded the Roman Canon as absolutely binding. The celebration of the liturgy *ad orientem*, facing eastward to the Lord who is coming again, was also uncontested by the majority of council fathers. Even those who undertook the Pauline reform of the Mass and who swept aside the will of the council fathers didn't dare touch this ancient and continuous practice. It was the spirit of the 1968 revolution that gained control of the liturgy and removed the worship of God from the center of the Catholic rite, installing in its place a clerical-instructional interaction between the priest and the congregation. The council fathers also desired no change in the tradition of church music. It is with downright incredulity that one reads these and other passages of the Constitution on the Sacred Liturgy, for their plain sense was given exactly the opposite meaning by the enthusiastic defenders of post-conciliar "development."[50]

This may be true to a degree, assuming the most conservative possible interpretation and use of the new liturgical books, the normative editions

---

[49]   As Archbishop Robert J. Dwyer of Portland (present at all four sessions) recalled: "Who dreamed on that day [when *SC* was promulgated] that within a few years, far less than a decade, the Latin past of the Church would be all but expunged, that it would be reduced to a memory fading into the middle distance? The thought of it would have horrified us, but it seemed so far beyond the realm of the possible as to be ridiculous. So we laughed it off." *Twin Circle*, October 26, 1973. Cited in Michael Davies, *Liturgical Timebombs in Vatican II* (Rockford, IL: TAN Books, 2003), 65.

[50]   Mosebach, *Subversive Catholicism*, 93; cf. 80–81. See my article "*Sacrosanctum Concilium*: The Ultimate Trojan Horse," *Crisis Magazine*, June 21, 2021.

of which are always in Latin, with rubrics that imply eastward orientation,[51] and a few pages, here and there, of notated chant. However, the manifest intention of the legislator points in the opposite direction. The three addresses of Paul VI discussed above establish beyond the shadow of a doubt that *his* intention was to see the end of the 1,600-year reign of Latin, the end of the centrality of chant, and the turning of altars "toward the people." He set the potent example from the throne of Peter; he provided the spurious rationale; he gave free rein to the national episcopacies in their mad pursuit of relevance and accessibility; he acted vigorously to suppress traditional "resistance." In all these ways, we cannot understand the reformed liturgical books without seeing them through the lens of their maker, governor, and judge.

These three addresses illustrate a more general trend. We can see an exact parallel to them in the manner in which the Vatican after the Council discouraged culturally Catholic nations from preserving special constitutional recognition of the Church, and in the disastrous policy toward the Communist countries known as *Ostpolitik*, which has resurfaced in Pope Francis's sell-out to the Chinese government. We see it in the encouragement of ugly modern art, with the Paul VI audience hall, opened in 1971, as its preeminent monument. We see it in the discouragement of clerical attire and large families. In other words, we are looking at a comprehensive program of secularization, of conformity to the liberal Western world forged in the anticlerical Enlightenment and repackaged after World War II as optimistic humanism. This was the defining *ethos* of the Vatican II period as interpreted and advanced by and under Pope Paul VI. And this is and was contrary to the fundamental demand of Christianity according to Saint Paul in the Epistle to the Romans: "Do not be conformed to this world"—that is, the world as fallen angels and sinful men have made it in their rebellion against God—"but be transformed by the renewal of your mind, that you may prove what is the will of God, what is good and acceptable and perfect" (Rom 12:2).

---

[51] See Kwasniewski, "The Normativity of *Ad Orientem* Worship According to the Ordinary Form's Rubrics," *NLM*, November 23, 2015.

The great nineteenth-century American Catholic writer Orestes Brown-son wrote in July 1846:

> The Church is not here to follow the spirit of the age, but to con-
> trol and direct it, often to struggle against it. They do her the great-
> est disservice who seek to disown her glorious past, and to modify
> her as far as possible, so as to adapt her to prevailing methods of
> thought and feeling. It is her zealous but mistaken friends, who,
> guided by a short-sighted policy, and taking counsel of the world
> around them, seek, as they express it, to *liberalize* her, to bring her
> more into harmony with the spirit of the age, from whom we, as
> good Catholics, should always pray, *Libera nos, Domine!*[52]

Martin Mosebach speaks of "the defective liturgical development that was encouraged by a mentality antagonistic to spiritual realities."[53] This, in fact, is what we see in Paul VI: a mentality so preoccupied with modernity, with evangelization, and with accessibility that it ends up becoming antag-onistic to spiritual realities—the set-apartness of the sacred; the primacy of God and the things of God; the otherworldly itinerary of Christ in His passion, death, resurrection, and ascension; and the conquest of this world for Christ the King, seizing it from Satan's empire and sanctifying it with, in the words of the Council of Trent, her "mystic benedictions . . . derived from apostolic discipline and tradition."[54] As Johann Adam Möhler justly observes: "If one cannot trust tradition, then Christians would rightly despair of ever learning what Christianity really is; they would rightly despair that there is a Holy Spirit which fills the Church, that there exists a common spirit and sure knowledge of Christianity. . . . This is the state in which those who reject tradition find themselves, and for them there can be no such thing as an objective Christianity."[55]

---

[52] "Newman's Development of Christian Doctrine," *Brownson's Quarterly Review* 3.3 (July 1846).
[53] Mosebach, *Subversive Catholicism*, 95.
[54] Council of Trent, Session 22, ch. 5.
[55] Quoted in Antoine Arjakovsky, *What is Orthodoxy? A Genealogy of Christian Under-standing* (Brooklyn: Angelico Press, 2018), 267–68.

The problem of the new Missal lies in its abandonment of a historical process that was always continual, before and after St. Pius V, and in the creation of a completely new book, although it was compiled of old material, the publication of which was accompanied by a prohibition of all that came before it, which, besides, is unheard of in the history of both law and liturgy. And I can say with certainty, based on my knowledge of the conciliar debates and my repeated reading of the speeches made by the Council Fathers, that this does not correspond to the intentions of the Second Vatican Council.

—Joseph Ratzinger (1976)

Even when he assisted tradition therefore, Benedict XVI had to wrap his actions in subterfuge. Thus the old Mass could only be restored under the description of the "Extraordinary Form" of the Roman rite (a phrase for which a very short life expectancy may be predicted), and with the pretence that it was "the Mass of Blessed John XXIII" rather than the liturgy of the Catholic centuries. Such signs exemplify the continuing gap in the Church between reality and official professions; but no institution can survive on pretences, and the Church of Christ least of all. Sooner or later, eternal reality will recover its rule, because there is no other standard to which the Church can conform.

—Henry Sire (2015)

Two "Forms": Liturgical Fact or Canonical Fiat?

E very Catholic in the world—if only he knew it—is indebted to Pope Benedict XVI for "liberating" the traditional Latin Mass with the motu proprio *Summorum Pontificum*, even if that motu proprio was ungraciously snuffed out while its author continued to live nearby; for its positive effects have been numerous and profound, and will outlast in their power the temporary setback of *Traditionis Custodes*.

As Martin Mosebach noted, we may complain about various things Pope Benedict did not do that we feel he ought to have done, but we must never fail to be grateful for the courageous steps he took in matters in which nearly the entire hierarchy of the Church stood opposed to him.[1] It was deeply against his nature to impose anything that would not be welcomed by at least a large number of bishops, and in this act, he stood nearly alone. The motu proprio has caused innumerable flowers to flourish, and countless fruits to be harvested. In this chapter, I do not wish either to praise or to bury Pope Benedict but rather to examine an operative assumption in the motu proprio, to wit, that Paul VI's *Missale Romanum* of 1969 (the "Novus Ordo") is, or belongs to, the same rite as the *Missale Romanum* last codified in 1962, or, more plainly, that the Novus Ordo can be called "the Roman rite" of the Mass. This, I shall argue, cannot withstand critical scrutiny. Although I will be referring primarily to the Roman missal and

---

[1] See Mosebach's foreword to Peter Kwasniewski, *Noble Beauty, Transcendent Holiness: Why the Modern Age Needs the Mass of Ages* (Kettering, OH: Angelico Press, 2017), "For Pope Benedict XVI, On His Ninetieth Birthday." For a critique of the weaknesses of Benedict's motu proprio, see my lecture "Beyond *Summorum Pontificum*: The Work of Retrieving the Tridentine Heritage," *Rorate Caeli*, July 14, 2021.

the Mass, my argument would apply, *mutatis mutandis*, to the rites of the other sacraments, to blessings and rituals, and to the Divine Office and its substitute, the Liturgy of the Hours.

As a preliminary, we should define the terms *rite* and *use*, since they play a prominent role in any interpretation of *Summorum Pontificum*.[2] Apart from rarefied liturgical circles, very few Catholics ever speak of "uses." We tend to say "rite" of a host of different phenomena: (1) a family of related liturgies, as in the statement "the Roman rite includes the Sarum use"; (2) a specific *member* of that family, as when we say "the Missal of Pius V contains the Roman rite of Mass" or "the Dominican rite is making a comeback today"; (3) any particular liturgical service, as when we talk of "the rite of baptism" or "the rite of confirmation." These ways of speaking are analogous applications of the word *ritus*, which originally simply meant "ceremony," especially of a religious type.[3]

The distinction between "rite" and "use" has never been officially laid out by Church law, but we are on safe ground if we take "rite" as the broader of the two terms, referring to a constellation of liturgy, doctrine, spirituality, history, culture, language, and law proper to a certain church.[4] A "use," on the other hand, is a variation or local tradition *within* a certain rite. For instance, in the Byzantine rite, there is the Greek tradition and the Slavonic tradition, which differ considerably in their features, but both are clearly Byzantine, as we see in their adherence to the Divine Liturgies of Saint John Chrysostom and Saint Basil the Great and the Liturgy of the Presanctified Gifts. In the Western or Latin sphere of Christianity, history has known a variety of uses that may be considered

---

[2]   For this paragraph, I am indebted to Dom Cassian Folsom, OSB, "Two 'Laws of Praying,' One 'Law of Believing': A Reflection on the Motu Proprio *Summorum Pontificum*," *Antiphon* 24.1 (2020): 19–30, as well as Gregory DiPippo, "The Legal Achievement of *Summorum Pontificum*," *NLM*, July 5, 2017.

[3]   Suetonius equated *ritus* and *caeremonia*. Forcellini gives as the definition of *ritus*: "mos et approbata consuetudo, et praecipue in sacrificiis administrandis." See William W. Bassett, *The Determination of Rite: An Historical and Juridical Study* (Rome: Gregorian University Press, 1967), 22–23.

[4]   I am working off of the helpful can. 28 §1 of the *Code of Canons of the Eastern Churches* of 1990: "A rite is the liturgical, theological, spiritual, and disciplinary patrimony, culture, and circumstances of history of a distinct people, by which its own manner of living the faith is manifested in each Church *sui iuris*."

variants of the Roman rite (broadly speaking), such as the Sarum use, the use of Lyons, the use of Braga, and the uses of religious orders such as the Cistercians, the Carthusians, and the Dominicans.[5] One might compare a rite to a species of flower, and a use to a varietal, or perhaps a color variation due to soil.

To identify a certain use as belonging to the Roman rite, one need only verify that the essential characteristics of the Roman rite are present in it. This would include the structure of the Divine Office and the structure of the *Ordo Missae* (not only the Canon, but also the Introit, Kyrie, Gloria, Collect, Epistle, Gradual, Alleluia, etc.). With minor variants—usually of order, rather than of text—the vast bulk of the material will be the same from use to use as well.[6] One who looks though every single Missal or antiphonary of every use of the Roman rite will find the Introit *Ad te levavi* on the first Sunday of Advent, *Populus Sion* on the second, and so forth, and all with very similar chant melodies. Moreover, granting that there were many regional accents or local touches, it is obvious that the doctrine, spirituality, history, culture, language, and law distinctive of the Roman church permeated all these liturgical uses throughout Western Europe.

What we commonly refer to nowadays as "the Roman rite" is not synonymous with all of the various Latin liturgical uses;[7] rather, people tend to

---

[5]   Before the Tridentine reform, variants were almost always referred to as "uses." For example, the frontispiece of the Sarum Missal reads: "Missale *ad usum* insignis et celeberrimae ecclesiae Sarum." After Trent, the term "use" became rare, and "rite" was used in its place.

[6]   As a consequence, any proper Mass or Office written for the one can be transposed into any of the others with no difficulty at all. For example, Saint Thomas Aquinas wrote the Office and Mass of Corpus Christi according to the medieval French use followed by the Order of Preachers: nine responsories at Matins, rather than eight, a versicle between Matins and Lauds, etc. Almost nothing needed to be done to adjust these texts for the "use of the Roman Curia," which became the basis of the Missal and Breviary of Saint Pius V. However, when the same Mass was added to the Ambrosian *rite*, all kinds of adjustments had to be made: the addition of a first reading, the antiphon after the Gospel, the *oratio super sindonem*, and the *transitorium*, none of which exist in the Roman rite, as well as the removal of the Sequence, which has never existed in the Ambrosian rite. Vice versa, if one wanted to take the Ambrosian Mass in honor of Saint Ambrose and transpose it into the historical Roman rite, one would need to mutilate it very badly, adding a Psalm verse and Gloria to the *ingressa*, removing the first reading, the antiphon after the Gospel, the *oratio super sindonem* and *the transitorium*, etc.

[7]   The uses of Braga, Lyons, and Sarum continue to be used occasionally either for the Mass or for the Divine Office or for both; the Premonstratensian use has reappeared; the Carthusian exists in a semi-reformed condition. The Dominican use is experiencing a renaissance

mean by it the use of the Roman curia that formed the basis of the Missal of Pope Saint Pius V. In the remainder of this chapter, "Roman rite" will refer to the use of the papal court that was extended to the whole Catholic world by the Bull *Quo Primum* of 1570, implementing the wishes of the Council of Trent, and which, for that reason, is often referred to as the "Tridentine" liturgy, the adoption of which was obligatory in any setting where a distinctive liturgical use of at least two hundred years' standing could not be demonstrated.

The problem

Now, we are all aware that Pope Benedict asserted, or established, or proposed, in *Summorum Pontificum* and in its accompanying letter to bishops *Con Grande Fiducia*, that there are "two forms" of the Roman rite and that the newer form is in continuity with the older form. He speaks also of a "twofold use of one and the same rite" and "two usages of the one Roman rite." He said, moreover, that "there is no contradiction between the two editions of the Roman Missal. In the history of the liturgy there is growth and progress, but no rupture." What does this claim of unity and continuity actually amount to? Can it be sustained?

Let me begin by stating the obvious. Never before in the history of the Roman Church have there been two "forms" or "uses" of the *same* local liturgical rite, simultaneously and with equal canonical status. That Pope Benedict could say that the older use had never been abrogated *proves* that Paul VI's liturgy is something novel rather than a mere revision of its precursor—*pace* progressives who wanted us to believe that it was but a new version of what came before; indeed, *pace* Paul VI, who seemed to think the new *Missale Romanum* was to replace the old *Missale Romanum*, just as every earlier edition since 1570 had been replaced by every subsequently promulgated *editio typica* (as, in our own times, the edition of 1920 was replaced by that of 1962).[8] When Benedict XVI recognized that the for-

---

among the younger generations of friars.

[8] A major edition of a liturgical book is called an *editio typica*. The *Missale Romanum* in the form promulgated by Pius V in 1570 has seen five subsequent *editiones typicae*: 1604 (Pope Clement VIII), 1634 (Pope Urban VIII), 1884 (Pope Leo XIII), 1920 (Pope Benedict XV), and 1962 (Pope John XXIII). The editions of the *Missale Romanum* from 1924, 1939,

mer Missal had never been abrogated and that its use may be continued *ad libitum*, he intensified Paul VI's resemblance to an autocrat: never before had a pope dared to change the Roman rite to such an extent that it could be treated by a later pope as if, for all intents and purposes, it were a new liturgy, not a revision or new edition of the same one. As we saw in the last chapter, Paul VI himself offered abundant support for this view. Joseph Shaw gives a knock-down argument based on the language of the motu proprio:

> The traditional Mass is called the "former [earlier, older] liturgical tradition": *traditio liturgica antecedens* (from Article 5). This tradition is not "expressed" by the Novus Ordo; if it were, people attached to it would be attached to the Novus Ordo, which is not the sense of the passage. On the contrary, it seems this is a *different* liturgical tradition: there are two, in fact, an older and a newer one. The fact that there is some important difference between the older tradition and the Novus Ordo is implied in an even more important way by the claim in *Summorum Pontificum* that the 1962 Missal has never been abrogated (*numquam abrogatam*, Article 1). Normally, each edition of the Roman Missal is replaced by the next; that this had happened to the 1962 Missal was a very common argument made by canonists before 2007, and this was the reason it was supposed that celebrations of it required an indult or special permission. *Summorum Pontificum* says that this did *not* happen. The explanation is not made explicit in the document, but it is clear enough: the 1970 Missal is not simply a new edition of the *Missale Romanum* like all the earlier (and, indeed, later) ones. Something different happened: it was a new Missal in the sense of being a new start, a new tradition, and therefore it did not replace and exclude ("obrogate") the earlier Missal.[9]

1953, etc. are called *editiones "post typicam,"* that is, with minor modifications. Similarly, the changes approved in 1964 and 1967 could be considered variations on the 1962.

[9] Joseph Shaw, "Is the Novus Ordo an Authentic Expression of the Tradition?," *LMS Chairman*, December 14, 2013. The missal Paul VI approved in 1969 did not have its full first edition until 1970, hence Dr. Shaw's mention of the latter year.

One winces at the palpable oxymoron of a "new tradition," a philosophically incoherent notion.[10]

Thus, while Benedict asserts that there is no contradiction and no rupture, at the same time, and startlingly, he allows for the coexistence of *two* canonically equal forms of one and the same liturgical rite—an unprecedented and, in many ways, unintelligible situation. As we have seen, there have always been many different "uses" in the Latin Church, but that the use of Rome should be thus doubled has never been seen before. Such a contradiction within the Church can be likened to a case of dissociative identity disorder.

In reality, as Msgr. Klaus Gamber argued so many years ago in a book praised by Cardinal Ratzinger,[11] the modern rite *cannot* be regarded as the Roman rite or a use thereof, regardless of what Paul VI, Benedict XVI, or anyone else wishes to call it. To unpack the significance of this statement will require a critique of the inadequate mode of theologizing about the liturgy that has dominated the West for several centuries and has prevented us from recognizing our errors, repenting of our follies, and restoring our authentic traditions.

Neoscholastic reductionism

The principal objection likely to be raised to any claim of rupture between the classical rite and the modern rite will go something like this: "All of the differences you are pointing to are incidental; after all, if the consecration happens, it's the sacrifice of Christ, and the rest is window-dressing." Often summed up in the trite statement "The Mass is the Mass, after all," this objection is built upon a neoscholastic reduction of the Eucharistic liturgy to the moment of consecration. This ahistorical and rationalistic

---

[10] A German canonist, Markus Graulich, argued for a distinction between a liturgical book's abrogation or derogation and the removal of a cleric's permission to utilize that book: see "Vom Indult zum allgemeinen Gesetz: Der Gebrauch des Messbuchs von 1962 vom Zweiten Vatikanischen Konzil bis *Summorum Pontificum* in kirchenrechtlicher Perspektive," in *Zehn Jahre* Summorum Pontificum: *Versöhnung mit der Vergangenheit—Weg in die Zukunft*, ed. Graulich (Regensburg: Verlag Friedrich Pustet, 2017), 13–54. Such a hair-splitting distinction may explain what Pope Benedict believed he was doing in *Summorum*: having admitted that the old missal had never been abrogated, he granted a universal permission or faculty to all clergy in good standing to avail themselves of it. In my opinion, this distinction fails to reach to the fundamental issues involved.

[11] Published in English as *The Reform of the Roman Liturgy: Its Problems and Background*.

reductionism deserves to be rejected because it dismisses the constitutive role of historically articulated tradition in God's self-revelation to mankind.[12] It vitiates any notion of identifiable families of rites derived from apostolic churches, with venerable texts, chants, gestures, and ceremonies, handed down within irreducibly distinct traditions of theology, spirituality, and custom that interpret, enrich, and contextualize the sacrificial offering while instructing and nourishing the faithful who take part in it. *All* of this—the rites, their specific content, and the understanding and way of life that go along with them—deserves religious respect and preservation, in deference toward our predecessors and in charity for ourselves and our descendants. In the words of Joseph Ratzinger: "The 'rite,' that form of celebration and prayer which has ripened in the faith and the life of the Church, is a condensed form of living Tradition in which the sphere using that rite expresses the whole of its faith and its prayer, and thus at the same time the fellowship of generations one with another becomes something we can experience, fellowship with the people who pray before us and after us. Thus the rite is something of benefit that is given to the Church, a living form of *paradosis*, the handing-on of Tradition."[13]

Opposed to this holistic vision is the neoscholastic reductionism that defines the "essence" of the Mass as "having a valid consecration," which can be seen to be a major premise or prerequisite of liturgical progressivism. In almost any conversation about whether and to what extent the rite of the Mass can or should change, the proponent of tradition is immediately challenged with: "But you can't prove that the Novus Ordo [or any fabricated, experimental liturgy] is bad. It has the words of consecration." If one adopts this reductive vision of Mass, nothing will be left of liturgy *as such*. The "essence" will be identified with a particular formula and act of God,

---

[12] As I noted in chapter 1, "tradition" in its broadest sense encompasses even Sacred Scripture, which records the historical deeds and sayings of Israel (old and new), and is passed down within the Church. All of God's revelation to mankind comes in the form of *paradosis* or *traditio*, something handed down from above to the people, and from one generation to the next. The error under consideration here has radical implications: see my article "'All That Matters at Mass is Jesus': Responding to Liturgical Heresy," *OnePeterFive*, February 16, 2022; cf. Peter Kwasniewski, *Reclaiming Our Roman Catholic Birthright: The Genius and Timeliness of the Traditional Latin Mass* (Brooklyn, NY: Angelico Press, 2020), 193–204, 262–65.
[13] Foreword to Dom Alcuin Reid, *The Organic Development of the Liturgy*, 2nd ed. (San Francisco: Ignatius Press, 2005), 11.

and the substance in which the essence resides, together with the multitudinous accidents by which the essence expresses its full meaning and power, will be lost.[14] It would be like defining man as his intellect rather than as a body-soul composite of a given sex and a given race, existing in space and time. Akin to the human person, the liturgy is a hylomorphic composition, not a disembodied consecration.[15] Again, Ratzinger identifies the problem with his usual perspicacity, warning us

> against the wrong path up which we might be led by a Neoscholastic sacramental theology that is disconnected from the living form of the Liturgy. On that basis, people might reduce the "substance" to the material and form of the sacrament and say: Bread and wine are the matter of the sacrament; the words of institution are its form. Only these two things are really necessary; everything else is changeable. . . . As long as the material gifts are there, and the words of institution are spoken, then everything else is freely disposable. Many priests today, unfortunately, act in accordance with this motto; and the theories of many liturgists are unfortunately moving in the same direction. They want to overcome the limits of the rite, as being something fixed and immovable, and construct the products of their fantasy, which are supposedly "pastoral," around this remnant, this core that has been spared and that is thus either relegated to the realm of magic or loses any meaning whatever. The Liturgical Movement had in fact been attempting to overcome this reductionism, the product of an abstract sacramental theology, and to teach us to understand the Liturgy as a living network of Tradition that had taken concrete form, that cannot be

---

[14] See chapter 1 for the full argument, and chapter 6 on the consequences.

[15] Sadly, the Divine Office has fared even worse under the influence of liturgical reductionism, since the Office has nothing equivalent to the confection or conferral of a sacrament under a definite form and matter. Because it is purely a set of texts to be sung or recited, the possible extent of its deformation and corruption is almost endless. The *only* thing that could hold back the violent hand is respect for tradition, e.g., that such-and-such psalms have always been prayed at particular hours on particular days. We know that such respect was not a notable characteristic of the liturgical revolutionaries; it was even lacking in Pius X's extreme revision at the start of the twentieth century. The Liturgy of the Hours promulgated by Paul VI bears at best a vague resemblance, at worst none at all, to the Divine Office as it has been prayed for most of the Church's history.

torn apart into little pieces but has to be seen and experienced as a living whole. Anyone who, like me, was moved by this perception at the time of the Liturgical Movement on the eve of the Second Vatican Council can only stand, deeply sorrowing, before the ruins of the very things they were concerned for.[16]

Since nearly everyone who came to the Second Vatican Council or who worked for the Consilium had been brought up on this neoscholastic reductionism, they felt free to rip apart and reconfigure the Roman rite as long as they kept the words of consecration (more or less) intact. In this regard, they were lab technicians committed all along to the result of a valid Mass without feeling themselves ethically bound to any particular content or process. Indeed, the arrogance of the reformers could not stop at the threshold of the holy of holies but went so far as to tamper with the formula of the consecration of the wine by removing the phrase *mysterium fidei* from within it, even though these words were uttered at that moment for as far back as we have written records of the Mass, which explains why Saint Thomas Aquinas in the thirteenth century could plausibly claim for them apostolic pedigree.[17]

Reducing the Mass to a valid consecration is like reducing the nuptial act to a successful conception of a child. I sincerely hope no one is foolish enough to *define* the nuptial act as the conception of a child. The nuptial act is naturally *ordered to* the conception of a child, to be sure, but it has its own reality, its own meaning, that comprises more than conception; it is an expression of spousal love, which is designed to culminate in new life. By God's institution, life is supposed to proceed from love; *both* elements—the unitive and the procreative—are included in the definition of the act. If the sole meaning or value of the union of man and woman were a viable

---

[16] Reid, *Organic Development*, 11. Ratzinger says at one point in this foreword that "modernists and traditionalists are in agreement" on this reductionism. I am not quite sure what he means. Undoubtedly, before the Council, everyone was teaching about sacraments in a reductive neoscholastic manner, but once it became clear that the progressives had embarked on a process of dismantling and reconstruction that would not honor any of the existing forms, a genuine *traditionalist* movement was born that took with utter seriousness the organic, holistic, aesthetic, and historical dimensions of liturgy. The figure of Dietrich von Hildebrand comes immediately to mind, as does the learned Abbé Franck Quoëx.

[17] See chapter 9.

zygote, the Church would have no reason to oppose *in vitro* fertilization. In like manner, the Mass is a privileged microcosm of unitive prayer with a Eucharistic finality. The presence of the sacrificial victim who is to be our divine food is conceived, as it were, by the liturgy in its totality. Even if the consecration takes place at a certain moment,[18] it has been prepared for and will be followed by a manifestation of love that suits us to receive the Lord and rejoice in His presence. When this does *not* happen, we are dealing with the specter of what might be called "*in vitro* transubstantiation." The lab technicians, Ratzinger seems to imply, would raise no objection.[19]

In sum, the problem with the neoscholastic reductionist approach is that it falsifies the reality of a liturgical rite as a concrete embodiment of apostolic tradition existing over the course of history—a history fraught with meaning and value, establishing a cumulative *lex credendi* (law of believing) for successive generations. The faithful are permitted to enter into this inheritance on condition of remaining humble recipients; all the more is this true for the clergy. The moment anyone dares to stand before a liturgical rite as its master and possessor, he forfeits his claim to its fruits.

Each rite has its own deep characteristics that make it irreducibly itself. No one would dream of defining the Byzantine Divine Liturgy of Saint John Chrysostom as "essentially" a valid consecration to which a multitude of florid prayers and hymns have been attached in order to give the people and the deacons something to do. In like manner, no one with a modicum of sense could define the Roman rite of Mass apart from the Roman

---

[18] As a Thomist, I hold that there *is* a moment of consecration: see Peter Kwasniewski, *Holy Bread of Eternal Life: Restoring Eucharistic Reverence in an Age of Impiety* (Manchester, NH: Sophia Institute Press, 2020), 53–56. But if one looks at *Summa theologiae* III, q. 83, one will see that Saint Thomas is far from being a liturgical reductionist. His method of starting with the complexity of the Mass as he finds it and discerning the meaning and value of *each* of its parts implies the respect in which it ought to be held by those who worship using it. Scholastic precision does *not* have to devolve into neoscholastic reductionism.

[19] Geoffrey Hull well expresses the problem: "One of the most pernicious consequences of the Latin West's downgrading of *theologia secunda* is its concern for validity, the automatic product of doctrinal orthodoxy, to the neglect of authenticity, the natural fruit of orthopraxis. Differently put, this is making text all-important and context a matter of indifference. Indeed most Catholic debate about the liturgical revolution has centred on the question of whether the new official text makes the Mass and sacraments valid or not; the cultural packaging of the same rites is meanwhile relegated to the realm of relatively unimportant 'externals.'" Geoffrey Hull, *The Banished Heart: Origins of Heteropraxis in the Catholic Church* (New York: T&T Clark, 2010), 38.

Canon, which is its defining feature, or insist on the insertion of an explicit *epiclesis* when it never had one and does not need to have one. These rites are what they are—and thanks be to God for that.

What makes the Roman rite itself?

Consequently, we need to start over again with better questions. We should ask, not: What is it that makes transubstantiation happen? but: What is it that makes a liturgy to be a *Christian* liturgy? Even more importantly, what makes *this* liturgical rite to be *itself*—Roman, Ambrosian, Mozarabic, Byzantine, Syro-Malabar, etc.—and no other? When these are the questions we pursue, we find rich answers that show us the fittingness, and the beautiful complexity and sufficiency of each rite of apostolic derivation, and therefore, expose the anti-liturgical, anti-ritual, and ultimately anti-Catholic nature of the liturgical reform.

Obviously, there are elements more and less central to a given rite; our list could be longer or shorter depending on how general or detailed a consideration we make. Some things can belong to the core identity of a certain rite and yet not be restricted to that rite, being found also in several other rites or even in all traditional Christian rites.[20]

What, then, belongs to the "personality," the identity or inner core, of the Mass of the Roman rite? I propose at least nine crucial elements: (1) the Roman Canon; (2) the use of Latin; (3) Gregorian chant; (4) the lectionary; (5) the calendar; (6) the Offertory; (7) the *ad orientem* stance; (8) parallelism of liturgical action; (9) the separate Communion of the priest. The first six are, in content, specific to the Roman rite, although all traditional rites, Eastern and Western, have something analogous to them; while the last three of these elements, which describe not so much content as manner of worship—eastward orientation, parallelism of action, and the separate Communion of the priest—are found in *all* traditional liturgical rites. These three deserve to be included here because they, too, sharply distinguish the Roman rite from its modern impostor. I shall now expand a little on each of these elements.

---

[20] This is the approach I took in chapter 2 when contrasting the Novus Ordo with *any* traditional liturgy.

First and most importantly, the Roman Canon, the sole anaphora of all uses of the Roman rite for 1,500 years, which goes back in its elements to the earliest centuries. So monolithic is the connection between this anaphora and this rite that we may safely formulate the rule: where there is the Roman rite, there will necessarily be the Roman Canon; and—outside of the special case of the diocese of Milan[21]—where there is the Roman Canon, there is the Roman rite. No Roman Canon, no Roman rite.[22]

Second, the use of the Latin language, which began in the West in the middle of the second century and was completed in the fourth century under Pope Damasus. Instead of referring to this process as the "vernacularization" of an originally Greek liturgy, as modern liturgists do,[23] it would be far more accurate to speak of the "Westernization" or even "Romanization" of liturgy, when it ceased to be tethered to the ancient Greek world and was firmly implanted in the Roman world as it had developed in contradistinction to the East.[24] From this point onwards, Western liturgies would remain in Latin for over 1,600 years, as befitted a culture and a civilization that always retained a fundamental unity in its marvelous variety. (Thus we speak tellingly of "Romance" languages and of "Latin" America.) The use of a single language of worship throughout the sphere of Roman Catholicism both reflected its unity and continually effected it: it expressed a true

---

[21] The Ambrosian rite also features the Roman Canon. There is still a lack of scholarly consensus on the question of whether this Canon was always used in it or whether it was "imported" at some point to replace an earlier specifically Ambrosian anaphora. Our sources for the Ambrosian rite are far fewer and later than the ones we have for the Roman rite.

[22] See chapter 8.

[23] This way of speaking is deceptive, both because it appears that Latin forms were developed somewhat independently of Greek forms and because the Latin itself was a specialized Christian Latin developed for the purpose, with an elevated hieratic register and biblical literalism; it was by no means the common or "vulgar" language of the people. See Christine Mohrmann, *Liturgical Latin: Its Origins and Character* (London: Burns & Oates, 1959); Michael Fiedrowicz, *The Traditional Mass: History, Form, and Theology of the Classical Roman Rite*, trans. Rose Pfeifer (Brooklyn, NY: Angelico Press, 2020), ch. 8: "Sacred Language," 153–78.

[24] As Patrick Owens notes: "The elevated register of Christian Latin ultimately replaced Greek in the sacred rites of the West, in part because it was more palatable to the educated Roman elite than Greek or vulgar Latin. The evangelization of the Roman cultural aristocracy was the primary impetus behind the development of Rome's own liturgical idiom." In Roberto Spataro, *In Praise of the Tridentine Mass and of Latin, Language of the Church*, trans. Zachary Thomas (Brooklyn, NY: Angelico Press, 2019), 8.

commonality and impressed it on the people wherever they lived and what-ever vernacular they spoke.[25]

Third, the liturgical "vesture" of Gregorian chant, which is not a mere add-on or ornament but the liturgy-as-sung, the liturgy in tones, rhythms, and cadences. The chant stands to the liturgy as bone of its bone, flesh of its flesh. The Proper and Ordinary chants articulate the shape of the rite, fill its content, sustain its spirituality, and guarantee its substantial conti-nuity from one age of the Church to another. Without the non-negotiable presence of Gregorian chant in the sung liturgy, and without an identifiable and stable body of chanted texts for the Introits, Graduals, Alleluias, Tracts, Offertories, and Communions, we may safely conclude that we not look-ing at the Roman rite any more.[26]

Fourth, the cycle of readings—namely, the lessons and Gospels at Mass.[27] This is a topic on which much has been written in recent years; here it suffices to note that the Roman lectionary, almost as venerable in its antiquity and universality as the Roman Canon, was supplanted by the novelty of a multi-year lectionary constructed by "experts" for the Missal of Paul VI. The old and new lectionaries have surprisingly little overlap as liturgical books.[28]

Fifth, the calendar, with its particular clusters of Roman saints and its rhythm of Sundays, Holy Days, Ember and Rogation Days, vigils, octaves, and seasons, including Epiphanytide, Septuagesimatide, Passiontide, Ascensiontide, the eight days of Pentecost, and the Sundays after Pentecost.

---

[25]   It is true that in rare cases the Latin liturgy existed in non-Latin forms, e.g., the Glagolitic Mass, the Slavonic Mass, and the Iroquois Mass. But these were the rare exceptions that proved the rule. Latin was always the dominant, nearly exclusive custom, and it was jealously guarded and valued as such.

[26]   Even the Low Mass bears witness to this normativity of the chants of High Mass by requir-ing the recitation of the texts of the chants, although this is somewhat like a two-dimensional drawing versus a three-dimensional sculpture. A more positive way of looking at the Low Mass would be to see it as a kind of corporate, sacramental *lectio divina.*

[27]   For a thorough discussion and critique of the new lectionary, see my lecture "The Reform of the Lectionary," in *Liturgy in the Twenty-First Century: Contemporary Issues and Perspec-tives,* ed. Alcuin Reid (New York: Bloomsburg, 2016), 287–320; also published (without its notes) at *Rorate Caeli* on May 24, 2019, under the title "When the Yearly Biblical Readings of Immemorial Tradition Were Cast Away."

[28]   See my foreword, "Not Just More Scripture, But Different Scripture," in Matthew P. Hazell, *Index Lectionum: A Comparative Table of Readings for the Ordinary and Extraordinary Forms of the Roman Rite* (n.p.: Lectionary Study Press, 2016).

While it is true that the calendar had a lengthy development,[29] it developed organically in certain distinctively Roman ways that were always preserved until various reforms of the twentieth century mutilated the calendar almost past recognition, beginning with the abolition of most of the octaves and vigils by Pius XII in 1955 and ending with the imposition of a new calendar in 1969.[30]

Sixth, the great Offertory of the Mass, which originated in the Middle Ages (among its oldest prayers is the *Suscipe, sancta Trinitas*, which is attested for the first time in the Echternach Sacramentary of 895). By "Offertory" here, I mean of course a true and proper Offertory characterized by prolepsis, wherein the sacramental immolation of the victim is anticipated in oblative language that sets aside the gifts solely for a sacred use and firmly establishes the priest's intention to offer an expiatory sacrifice for the honor and glory of the Most Holy Trinity. Prolepsis is a figure of speech that means representing something as existing before it actually does; thus the Offertory speaks of "the immaculate victim" while the unconsecrated bread is being held aloft. Such ways of speaking are universal in liturgical traditions: in the chanted antiphon, which has always been called the Offertorium; in the Secret prayers; in the Canon, prior to the consecration.[31] Taken *en bloc*, the Roman Offertory prayers are unique. No other use has the first three prayers, or if they do appear, it is the result of a process of Romanization. The other elements all appear in the majority of uses, but mixed up in various orders. The *Suscipe, sancta Trinitas* is by far the most widely used. Although the wording varies, the substance is always the same. The Roman Offertory is deeply in accord with the genius of the rite and

---

[29] See Dom Gregory Dix, *The Shape of the Liturgy* (New York: Continuum, 2005), ch. 11, "The Sanctification of Time," 303–96.

[30] The situation is rendered even worse by the constant "adaptations" that episcopal conferences are permitted to make. To take two familiar examples in the United States, it is sheer liturgical nominalism to "transfer" the Ascension and the Epiphany to the nearest Sundays. By divine revelation, we know that Our Lord's ascension takes place forty days after the resurrection, and therefore on a Thursday. Epiphany is celebrated twelve days after Christmas. It is one thing to celebrate the feasts on their proper days and then add so-called "external solemnities" on a nearby Sunday (this is rather like repeating Masses during an octave), but quite another to abolish the proper days and simply shift them to the nearest Sunday. This is the liturgical equivalent of rewriting history: it is doing violence to the nature of things.

[31] The Byzantine rites use prolepsis on an extravagant scale: see Gregory DiPippo, "The Theology of the Offertory, Part 4: An Ecumenical Problem," *NLM*, March 28, 2014.

was universally received and inflexibly maintained. In light of the principle of organic development, it may be compared with a branch successfully grafted into a tree so that it loses all foreignness and becomes a major part of the flourishing organism. Its removal in 1969 was not like a haircut but like the amputation of an arm or a leg; its replacement—a quasi-Jewish presentation of gifts, in which their divine, natural, and human origins are called to mind, and the people respond with a generic acclamation—is like nothing ever seen in Christian liturgical history.

Seventh, the *ad orientem* stance. We have no way of knowing just how early on this stance became normative, but we know that by the time the Church emerged from persecution into favor with the Roman state, *ad orientem* was already a universal practice in East and West, which could never have happened were it not apostolic in origin, as indeed the Church Fathers claimed. For example, Saint Basil the Great in his treatise *On the Holy Spirit* (375) argues that we should take seriously the divinity of the Holy Spirit *for the same reason* that we take seriously the celebration of the liturgy eastwards—namely, that it was handed down to us from the Apostles, and therefore is not subject to dispute. In other words, Basil takes *ad orientem* as an uncontroversial basis on which to defend the controverted divinity of the Third Person of the Blessed Trinity! Offering liturgical prayer facing east belongs to the original configuration of all of the great historic rites of Christianity. Without it, a liturgy is no longer in actual continuity with apostolic tradition, however much it may enjoy a technical validity of the reductive sort mentioned earlier.

Eighth, parallelism of liturgical action.[32] Even as eastward orientation is found in all liturgies of Eastern and Western Christendom, so too is the presence of many-layered simultaneous actions on the part of different ranks of clergy and laity. Because liturgy is an act of God in man, and of man toward God, rather than a human activity directed to the people, its prayers and rituals are frequently not intended to be seen or heard by the congregation but are offered up directly to God. Traditional liturgy is not linear, discursive, and modular, but circuitous, intuitive, and organic.

---

[32] See Jared Osterman, "Twentieth-Century Reform and the Transition from a 'Parallel' to a 'Sequential' Liturgical Model: Implications for the Inherited Choral Repertoire and Future Liturgical Compositions," *Sacred Music* 142.1 (Spring 2015): 8–21.

There is a progression from beginning to end, but it is the progress of a differentiated people toward a heavenly city—that is, the image of a hierarchical society moving toward its exemplar. The modern rite is sequential, like an agenda for a business meeting (in other words, usually only one thing is supposed to be happening at any given time, and everyone's attention is supposed to be fixed on it); the classical rite builds up layer upon layer of action, which is done for God's eyes and ears.[33] The one is a self-enclosed circle, rational and verbose, in which someone is always in charge; the other is eccentric, ecstatic, superrational, in which many are busy with their work and no one stands over against the group.

Ninth, the Communion of the priest prior to, and in a manner ceremonially differentiated from, that of the people. His Communion is *required* for the completion of the sacrifice; the people's is desirable but optional. Again we see the same distinction between clerical Communion and lay Communion in all traditional rites. It expresses the dogmatic truth that the priest acts *in persona Christi capitis* by virtue of a sacramental character of priesthood that sets him apart from (and hierarchically above) the simple baptized.[34] The ritually bifurcated Communion of priest and people is the liturgy's way of representing the dogmatic distinction between the "objective redemption" that Christ accomplished in full on the Cross—re-presented in the Body and Blood offered and consumed by the Lord's minister, thus completing the sacrifice in and of itself (no one else need be present)—and the "subjective redemption" of Christians, which occurs through the application of the merits of Christ's passion to as many souls as seek communion with Him, for which the distribution of the host suffices.[35]

It should go without saying that a liturgy is far more than a collection of texts in a book, the doctrinal orthodoxy of which one might evaluate in a philosophical vacuum. A liturgy comprises the chant melodies to which

---

[33] I do not deny, of course, that parts of the liturgy are for the people, but there is no part that is *simply* for the people, the way the "Liturgy of the Word" in the new rite is designed to be. The way the old liturgy serves the needs of the people is by relentlessly ordering them to the divine. See my article "'Moments of Liturgical Action': Recovering the Sacramentality of Biblical Lections," *NLM*, January 24, 2022.

[34] See my comments on the importance of the "Confiteor" before the people's communion as marking a definite *caesura* in the rite: "Why the Confiteor Before Communion Should Be Retained (or Reintroduced)," *NLM*, May 27, 2019.

[35] See Saint Thomas, *ST* III, qu. 80, art. 12, ad 2 and ad 3.

texts have been sung, century after century; it includes vestments, ceremonies, gestures, postures, actions. For example, the celebration of liturgy *ad orientem* is part of its nature, part of the ensemble of symbols that constitute the rite; it is no superficial, indifferent accident. A liturgy *versus populum* would be a different liturgy, even if the texts were the same.

The modern rite is not the Roman rite

Now, it cannot escape the notice of anyone that, in regard to all of the foregoing elements, the modern rite of Paul VI is a striking departure from the Roman rite. It is *possible* for it to be celebrated in a way that follows *some* of the rite's precedents (never all of them), but it is equally possible for it to be celebrated in a way that is at variance with *all* of them. A very great number of celebrations, certainly the vast majority, are at variance with the Roman tradition, because

- the Roman Canon is not used;
- Mass is not offered in Latin;
- the liturgical texts are not recited or chanted; e.g., the Propers and Ordinary are absent, mangled, or delivered in a way inconsistent with their origins;
- the multi-year lectionary, that novelty of novelties, is employed;
- a severely reduced calendar is followed;
- the traditional Offertory is lacking;
- Mass is not said *ad orientem*;
- the liturgy is sequential, a sure sign of the influence of Enlightenment rationalism; and
- the priest's and faithful's Communions are conflated.

Proponents of "mutual enrichment" or "the Reform of the Reform" might object that I am portraying a worst-case scenario. Surely, if the Novus Ordo were celebrated *ad orientem* with the Roman Canon and chanted Ordinary and Propers, would we not have a rite that is recognizably Roman? My response is that it would have (to some degree) the *appearance* of the Roman rite, but not the inner essence, for two reasons. First, it would still favor the sequential over the parallel, it would still lack a true and proper

Offertory, and it would still follow both a novel calendar and a novel lectionary. Second, and more importantly, it would achieve these appearances of continuity only by means of the celebrant's *choice*. That is, its continuity would be *willed* as a possible realization rather than received as a necessary rule of prayer. In this way, the liturgical action remains the voluntaristic product of its users, even if its "externals" were borrowed from the Roman tradition with impeccable taste. One could also make this argument in a slightly different way: since the modern missal permits not only the Roman Canon (albeit in modified form[36]) but also alien life-forms like the "Eucharistic Prayers for Reconciliation," we must judge the modern missal by the deviations it officially permits, not by the illusion of continuity it may support in the generous hands of Oratorians. This is simply an application of the proverb that a chain is only as strong as its weakest link. It is not by an Oratorian Novus Ordo with a Latin Roman Canon, etc., that we must evaluate the missal of Paul VI, but by the most discontinuous celebration *still permissible by the rubrics* (e.g., one that is said *versus populum*, in the vernacular, with no Propers, no Confiteor, the second Eucharistic Prayer, Communion in the hand, etc.). Such a Mass is *no less perfectly* the Novus Ordo than the most glorious smells-and-bells Mass. Put differently, what is most characteristic of the Novus Ordo is not this or that configuration but its *ad libitum* configurability. For this reason alone it has no claim to be in the family of the Roman rite. Instead, it is the modern papal rite, which happens to allow the Roman Canon and so forth as options.

Another way of seeing the same truth is to examine what scholars like to call the "euchological material" of the missals—namely, the content of the orations: the Collects, Secrets, and Postcommunions. As has been mentioned before, only 13 percent of the Collects of the old *Missale Romanum* survived unchanged in the missal of Paul VI.[37] Let's ponder this a moment. If my body lost 20 percent of its parts, I might still be alive, as long as those parts were external limbs, but if my body lost 87 percent of its parts, I would no longer exist. A liturgy that has lost 87 percent of its euchological material is no longer the same rite as its predecessor; it is a different entity.

---

[36]   See chapters 8 and 9.
[37]   See Matthew Hazell, "'All the Elements of the Roman Rite'? Mythbusting, Part II," *NLM*, October 1, 2021.

Or one could argue from the analogy of DNA. Nothing in a liturgical rite is merely "external" any more than a person's face, voice, or skin color is merely external. These things well up from our DNA, which carries the detailed instructions by which they are produced.[38] If we did a forensic DNA profiling of the "two forms of the Roman rite," would we find them to be fraternal twins? Could a court of law establish the kinship?

Moreover, it would make no difference even if every prayer newly incorporated into the Novus Ordo had been taken verbatim from some ancient sacramentary. (Of course, this is not the case: almost nothing was left unedited, "negative" or "difficult" language was systematically removed or dampened, and many particular elements were fabricated from scratch. But let us assume the premise for the sake of argument.) There would *still* be rupture and discontinuity with the Church at prayer, with the real incarnate Church as she existed and exists, with her *lex orandi*, with the actual dispositions of the Holy Spirit. There would still be the ravages of an artificial and arbitrary antiquarianism; there would still be the rejection of the liturgy as it matured in the faith-life of the Church.[39] Even in this best-case scenario, we could excoriate such a reform as unfitting, uncatholic, untraditional, and un-Roman. In actual fact, what happened in the abattoir of the Consilium was not the best-case scenario but very nearly the worst.

At this point, we could also "pull a Michael Davies" and appeal to the well-documented fact that those who were most closely involved in the liturgical reform made no attempt to hide their glee (Bugnini, Marini, Braga, Gelineau, et al.) or their chagrin (Bouyer, Martimort, Antonelli) at the retirement and replacement of the classical Roman rite, while those who deeply loved this rite (Lefebvre, Gamber, Dobszay, et al.) deplored the obvious rupture and discontinuity of the new liturgical books.[40] Martin Mosebach comments:

---

[38] The phenotype derives from the genotype interacting with environmental conditions. The entire physical dimension is, moreover, the metaphysical counterpart of the individual rational soul, which is expressed through them.

[39] See chapters 2 and 7 on the role played by false antiquarianism in the liturgical reform.

[40] All one needs to do is to study the books by Annibale Bugnini, his amanuensis Piero Marini, and liturgists like Andrea Grillo and John Baldovin to find brash and boastful acknowledgments of the revolutionary nature of the changes. Those who are most steeped in the liturgical books and their history understand that we are not looking at mere superficial adjustments.

No one who has eyes and ears will be persuaded to ignore what his own senses tell him: these two forms are so different that their theoretical unity appears entirely unreal. It is my experience that the pros and cons of "Mass reform" in the Church actually cannot be debated dispassionately. The opposing sides on this question have long faced each other with equally irreconcilable and fixed resolve: there can be no question of debate. Those who refused to accept that what had been *everything* was now *nothing* formed a tiny circle: in the words of the theologian Karl Rahner they were "tragicomic, peripheral human failures." They were mocked, and at the same time regarded as highly dangerous.[41]

Putting the myth to bed

So much for the myth of "two forms of one Roman rite."[42] When Roman Catholics attend the Novus Ordo, they are getting a Mass—but not the Mass of the Roman rite. They are getting what Klaus Gamber called "the modern rite," whose genesis and scope are well described by liturgist John F. Baldovin: "The implementation of the reform, under Bugnini's tutelage and involving dozens of experts in the fields of history, theology, and pastoral practice, resulted in the complete vernacularization of the liturgy, reorientation of the presiding minister vis-à-vis the assembly, an extensive and even radical reform of the order of Mass, and a major overhaul of the liturgical year, not to mention a complete revision of every sacramental liturgy and daily liturgical prayer."[43]

---

[41] Martin Mosebach, *The Heresy of Formlessness: The Roman Liturgy and Its Enemy*, rev. ed. (Brooklyn, NY: Angelico Press, 2018), 163.

[42] DiPippo ("The Legal Achievement of *Summorum Pontificum*") defends Benedict XVI's inventiveness by noting that he was attempting a stable canonical solution to a uniquely intractable problem. Had he established that there were two Roman *rites*, the liberalization of the Vetus Ordo would have instantly granted biritual faculties to 400,000 priests, but calling them *uses* would have falsified the historical meaning of the term. He therefore invented the new concept of "form," as if recognizing an absolutely anomalous situation in which two rites or uses have much in common generically and yet are radically different in detail.

[43] "The Twentieth-Century Reform of the Liturgy: Outcomes and Prospects," *Institute of Liturgical Studies Occasional Papers* 126 (2017): 1–13, at 4–5; cited in the brilliant article by Tomasz Dekert, "Tradition, the Pope, and Liturgical Reform: A Problematization of Tradition in the Catholic Church and Catholic–Orthodox Rapprochement," *Nova et Vetera* (English ed.) 20.1 (2022): 101–31.

It is worth noting that Baldovin is by no means an opponent of the reform, so he is not intending, in a polemical way, to exaggerate postconciliar changes.[44] Baldovin's research supports the statement read at a press conference on January 4, 1967, by Annibale Bugnini:

> A reform of Catholic worship cannot be accomplished in a day or a month, nor even in a year. The issue is not simply one of touching up, so to speak, a priceless work of art; in some areas, entire rites have to be restructured *ex novo*. Certainly this involves restoring, but ultimately I would almost call it a remaking and at certain points a creating anew. Why a work that is so radical? Because the vision of the liturgy the Council has given us is completely different from what we had before. . . . We are not working on a museum piece, but aiming at a living liturgy for the living people of our own times.[45]

The mentality at work is aptly skewered by Louis Bouyer: "If there is one fantasy absorbing us moderns, it is that of pure futurity. We would fain believe that the future, an untrammeled, creative future, is everything, and in order to enter upon it we are prepared cheerfully to sacrifice our entire past."[46] Or, as Bishop Rob Mutsaerts of 's-Hertogenbosch put it more succinctly: "We want to be relevant, apparently, at the expense of our own identity."[47]

Regardless of whether one *likes* or *dislikes* this modern rite, we should at least agree to not call it "the Roman rite." Calling something that which it is not is an abuse of language, which stems from an abuse of power and further perpetuates it.[48] Calling something that which it is not only strengthens the relativistic mentality of our age, which considers that whatever can be *pronounced* corresponds to something real. One is feeding the

---

[44] For additional statements of this kind from Baldovin, see above, pp. 70–71.

[45] *DOL* n. 37.

[46] Cited in Keith Lemna, *The Apocalypse of Wisdom: Louis Bouyer's Theological Recovery of the Cosmos* (Brooklyn, NY: Angelico Press, 2019), 52.

[47] "For the Record—Dutch Bishop: 'In the synod, nonsense that would embarrass Luther and Calvin: and the Pope is looking on,'" *Rorate Caeli*, October 23, 2019.

[48] See Josef Pieper, *Abuse of Language, Abuse of Power*, trans. Lothar Krauth (San Francisco: Ignatius Press, 1992).

illusion that the power to *say* the words "2 + 2 = 5" makes the statement *true*.[49] As the philosopher Charles De Koninck puts it: "One can say and write things that one cannot think. One can say, 'It is possible to be and not to be at the same time and in the same respect'; 'the part is greater than the whole,' though one cannot think such things. But yet, they are grammatically correct phrases. Transcendent power of language: one can say both the thinkable and the unthinkable. . . . I can say: 'I do not exist.' And with that, I can found 'I exist' on pure non-being. I say it! Who will stop me?"[50]

We see how real and extensive is the damage wrought by the mentality of neoscholastic reductionism. It is the only atmosphere in which the outrageous enterprise of creating a modern rite in the 1960s could have sprung up. The same mentality has, over time, propagated itself to other areas of Catholic life as well. For example, that people today ask whether adulterers and sodomites may receive Holy Communion, as if the answer were not already obvious from Catholic tradition, shows that the Most Holy Eucharist has been reduced in the minds of many to a mere sign of belonging, foodstuff for the "table of plenty"—not a supernatural mystery that requires the full commitment of one's mind, heart, soul, and strength to Jesus Christ really present, against whom one mortally sins by unworthily receiving Him.[51] Such moral and disciplinary reductionism is not, however, surprising against the backdrop of the wave of liturgical reductionism that went before, the "poster child" of which is the removal from the new lectionary of Saint Paul's warning against unworthy Communions in 1 Corinthians 11:27–29, which, in contrast, was and is read at least three times each year in the traditional Roman rite.[52] Our age

---

[49] On Fr. Antonio Spadaro's claim that in theology, 2+2 can make 5, see George Weigel, "Theology Isn't Math; But It *Is* Theology," *First Things* online, January 25, 2017.

[50] Charles De Koninck, *On the Primacy of the Common Good*, trans. Sean Collins, *The Aquinas Review*, vol. 4 (1997), 86–87.

[51] "Worthy reception" does not mean that we are already perfect (that will never be the case in this life!), but, as John Paul II explains in *Ecclesia de Eucharistia*, that we are free from the guilt of mortal sin through confession and have an intention of living according to all the commandments of God. In *Veritatis Splendor*, the same pope reaffirms the teaching of Trent that only the grace of Christ—received in baptism, strengthened by daily prayer, recovered through penance—can empower us to live according to this standard. That is the very meaning of the *newness* of the New Covenant, as Saint Thomas teaches (*ST* I-II, qq. 106–8).

[52] See *Holy Bread*, ch. 13: "The Omission That Haunts the Church," 181–95.

has provided a nearly scientific demonstration of the axiom *lex orandi, lex credendi, lex vivendi.*

It is more necessary than ever for Catholics to work for two great goods that stand or fall together: the recovery of a sound Eucharistic theology and the reestablishment of the actual Roman rite of the Mass.[53] Good theology and authentic liturgy work together to unveil to the eyes of faith the presence of Our Lord Jesus Christ in the *entire* liturgy[54] and, above all, in the miracle of the host and chalice, in such a way that Catholics will be able to experience once more the terrible beauty and challenging joy of Eucharistic communion, and will strive to order their lives and their societies according to Its demands.

Positivism versus tradition

The fundamental divide today is between a positivistic understanding and a traditional understanding of what liturgy is and what constitutes it *as* liturgy. If you adopt positivism, you can swallow the Novus Ordo or anything thrown at you, as long as it is done by so-called "legitimate authority." If you hold fast to tradition, you will never be able to accept the Novus Ordo as a use of the Roman rite and will adhere to the rite worthy to be called Roman.

---

[53] I have targeted neoscholastic reductionism, but what of Saint Thomas Aquinas? Does he not bear some of the responsibility for this reduction of the Mass or the Eucharist to transubstantiation, about which he speaks at such great length, defending in detail the proposition that "the words of consecration" are the sole cause of the miracle (*ST* III, qq. 75 and 78)? Thomas had a metaphysical mind that was uniquely qualified to tackle the thorniest difficulties in sacramental theology, but he does not deny the larger biblical and patristic framework of the entire discussion; indeed, he shows himself to be aware of it (as in III, q. 83, on the rite of Mass), even though he is far more eager to dig into the philosophical perplexities. In any case, it is important not to take Saint Thomas as the be-all and end-all of theology. He is the Common Doctor, our guide to the discipline of theology, but he himself would be the first to command us to sit at the feet of the authors of Sacred Scripture and the great Fathers of the Church to whom he looked as constant reference points. He does not repeat what they have done but develops into a system the principles and conclusions to which they bear witness. We still and always have need of the *original data* in the *original manner of its proclamation.* Scholasticism will aid us in our search for the truth, focusing our minds and purifying them; it will not substitute for a lifelong apprenticeship to the liturgy, the Bible, and the Fathers.

[54] This theme is found throughout the writings of Mosebach: see *Heresy of Formlessness* and *Subversive Catholicism.*

I once saw a billboard along a highway. It had the names of a bunch of Christian denominations printed all over it in smaller letters, and then in the middle, in big letters: "Which is the real Jesus?" (Evidently, the toll-free phone number was meant to connect you with the real Jesus, or at least with those who presumed to speak for Him.) Then I began to think about a similar billboard that would have on it a bunch of liturgical rites, old, new, and imaginary, with "Which is the real liturgy?" printed on it. We don't have a toll-free number to call, so how do we know which is the real liturgy? How *could* we know, apart from tradition? Even the papacy is something contained in and handed down by tradition. If a liturgy cannot be traced back step by step over centuries of gradual development, we can recognize it as a rupture, a construct, an imposture, not a real liturgy in the full sense of the word.

Although still whispered rather than proclaimed out loud, this negative assessment is becoming more widespread among thoughtful Catholics—and they are acting on it. For example, the number of places that have quietly returned to the pre-1955 Holy Week is an astonishing advance that one could barely have imagined fifteen years ago. *Summorum Pontificum* has set in motion a reform, the logical principles of which will lead back before the time of Pacelli and Bugnini.

We must, indeed, go back. Unlike modernity, Christianity is not based on the supposedly self-evident truth that we must always be "moving ahead." The Christian Faith is a permanent tension between, on the one hand, memory—*hoc facite in meam commemorationem*, lingering over the life of Our Lord and entering into the transtemporal mysteries of His factual, incarnate, historical life, preserving at every step our bond with what has been handed down—and, on the other hand, looking forward not to a man-made future but to the second coming of Christ from the East. The modern notion of progress is foreign to Christianity—even antithetical to it. As believers, we are always striving to be *equal* to our past, to be humble and grateful inheritors of it; we are not *better* than our past, and thinking ourselves to be better will only make us guilty of the sin of pride. As John Henry Newman candidly states:

It is a fault of these times (for we have nothing to do with the faults of other times) to despise the past in comparison of the present. We can scarce open any of the lighter or popular publications of the day without falling upon some panegyric on ourselves, on the illumination and humanity of the age, or upon some disparaging remarks on the wisdom and virtues of former times. Now it is a most salutary thing under this temptation to self-conceit to be reminded, that in all the highest qualifications of human excellence, we have been far outdone by men who lived centuries ago; that a standard of truth and holiness was then set up which we are not likely to reach, and that, as for thinking to become wiser and better, or more acceptable to God than they were, it is a mere dream.[55]

At the same time as we look to our *antecessores*, those who have run the race before us and are therefore *ahead* of us, we are striving to prepare ourselves for the coming of the Lord and the establishment of a new heaven and a new earth (cf. Rev 21:1), which is *His* prerogative, not *our* product. This continual preparation or receptivity by which we allow the soil of our souls to be cultivated and sown with the givenness of Christian religion is what makes us bear fruit—thirtyfold, sixtyfold, a hundredfold—the more we receive and then transmit what we have received, enriched with whatever offerings the Lord has enabled us to add to it. A fruitful development is certainly possible, but only on condition of fidelity, reverence, and awe toward our inheritance. A saying I heard comes to mind: "The only one who can have true knowledge of a thing is he who stands in awe before it."

The liturgical reformers rejected many prayers (e.g., the Offertory) as useless accretions; they saw them as pointless or even erroneous and therefore harmful. This attitude and the actions to which it led are reprehensible, the badge of unwisdom; indeed, one must say that they are, at best, a thumbing of one's nose at the Holy Spirit and His working over the preceding nineteen centuries and, at worst, a kind of blasphemy. "By their fruits you shall know them" (Mt 7:20). The Novus Ordo has been afflicted with a spirit of narcissism, dryness, and boredom, an astounding lack of fruitfulness, and an appalling dearth of vocations to priestly and religious

---

[55] "Use of Saints' Days," *Parochial & Plain Sermons*, vol. 2 (1835), Sermon 32.

life in proportion to the number and needs of Catholics.[56] Can we not see this as the Lord's just and disciplinary punishment for the repudiation of the rites He inspired in His Church? To lovers and haters of liturgical tradition may be fitly applied the words of the psalmist: "With the holy, thou wilt be holy; and with the innocent man thou wilt be innocent. And with the elect thou wilt be elect: and with the perverse thou wilt be perverted. For thou wilt save the humble people; but wilt bring down the eyes of the proud" (Ps 17:26–28). The fact that vocations and large families abound wherever the traditional liturgy flourishes *ought* to be sufficient cause for a radical reexamination of the entire approach of the past sixty years, with its vain quest for contemporary relevance. The abuse of power, like the abuse of language that cloaks and sanitizes it, cannot last very long; it is like a man sitting in a tree, sawing off the branch on which he is sitting. If the Lord intends the Church to endure in this world, a time must come when tradition is vindicated and the project of modernization is exposed as the Satanic ploy it has always been.

I come, now, to several conclusions.

It is not any pope's authority that makes the Church's liturgy to *be* her liturgy. Papal authority may establish the edition of a liturgical book for the sake of unanimity of usage, but it is *tradition* that makes a liturgy to be itself. We know this to be true because Christians were celebrating their liturgies for over 1,500 years before any pope ever legislated a missal. The fact that Saint Pius V legislated a revised missal in 1570 does not mean

---

[56] Denying God the honor due to Him by stripping the Church's rites of already-existing prayers and ceremonies is a standing insult, doomed to failure. For it is one thing *not* to have those prayers and ceremonies at an earlier phase, and quite another to remove them once they are firmly settled in place. The former is an unintentional absence, but the latter is an intentional omission. It is like the difference between not having the technology to provide nutrition and hydration for a patient and removing these from a patient when already in place. The former is a lack of means to help a person continue living; the latter is a withdrawal of means that leads to a person's death. In like manner, not having the offertory prayers in the Roman rite of the first millennium is a lack of the perfection of the fully developed rite as it would later come to fruition, but actively *removing* them from the liturgy is a case of maiming, deforming, and disemboweling. If the Novus Ordo is the Roman rite, then it is the Roman rite violently damaged, depriving the Lord of signs of reverence, depriving the celebrant of his spiritual nourishment, and depriving the people of opportunities to pay homage to the Divine Majesty. See Jeremiah 17:5–8 for the contrast between the barren tree and the fruitful tree, which hinges on whether it is man's prudence or God's providence that is trusted.

that popes always implicitly had the authority to establish or revoke liturgy at their whim or that, after 1570, they explicitly have the authority to do so. Rather, Saint Pius V was codifying an *existing* apostolic rite, with such minor modifications as he deemed pastorally necessary. There was no question of a wholesale recasting of the rite from the ground up; no one would have dreamed of such a thing. It was literally unthinkable—and so it remains.[57] As Michael Fiedrowicz writes:

> Even the highest authority of the Church may not change at will the ancient and venerable liturgy of the Church. This signifies an abuse of power (*abusus potestatis*). The authority of the bull of promulgation *Quo Primum* is especially grounded in the fact that here a pope regulated the liturgy in the exercise of the fullness of his papal power and in complete consensus with the vote of an ecumenical council, and in addition, he found himself in accordance with the unbroken tradition of the Roman Church, as well as—regarding the fundamental parts of the Missal—in accordance with the Universal Church. Above all, the fact that the *Missale Romanum* of 1570 was intended to be the most perfect liturgical expression of the Catholic teaching on the Eucharist, as the Council of Trent had defined it for all times over against Protestant errors, is a significant argument that the Missal itself, as well as the dogmatic definition of Trent, should remain substantially unchanged for all time.[58]

What Paul VI did was *ultra vires papae*, beyond the legitimate authority of the pope.[59] He created a pseudoliturgy or a paraliturgy that resembles

---

[57] See Joseph Shaw, "St. Pius V and the Mass," *Voice of the Family* Digest (online) no. 24, October 6, 2021.

[58] Fiedrowicz, *Traditional Mass*, 36.

[59] Some (like Karl Rahner) make a distinction between legal authority and moral authority, saying that a pope may legally create a new rite of Mass wholly disconnected from previous rites but that he would sin gravely in doing so, for he has not the moral authority to act outside of the tradition he is to receive and promote. One might question that distinction: if authority exists for a good end, its limits cannot extend beyond what is good/morally right. See Peter Kwasniewski, "The Pope's Boundedness to Tradition as a Legislative Limit," in Kwasniewski, ed., *From Benedict's Peace to Francis's War: Catholics Respond to the Motu Proprio Traditionis Custodes on the Latin Mass* (Brooklyn, NY: Angelico Press, 2021); John Lamont, "Is the Mass of Paul VI Licit?" *Dialogos Institute*, March 20, 2022.

the Roman rite; in no sense did he "revise the Roman rite." He *replaced* the
Roman rite with a new ritual that maintains sacramental validity but lacks
honorable parentage. By the arguments set forth, one must consider it a
prayer service with a consecration, which confects the Body of Christ in
an extra-ordinary fashion and not as the culminating point of an authentic
historic liturgical rite of apostolic derivation. In this sense, it would have
been far more accurate to call the Missal of Paul VI the "extraordinary
form" and the Missal of John XXIII the "ordinary form," since the latter is
still largely in continuity with preceding editions of the missal, while the
former falls outside of this missal tradition.[60] The classical Roman Mass is
a true liturgical rite, with all of the qualities or properties needed to merit
that distinguished title; the modern Mass is a sacramental delivery system
made up of parts manufactured by committee and newly configured by
each celebrant's set of choices.

Like the entire Church, the pope, too, *receives* the liturgy as an inheritance, and even as he is supposed to conserve and defend doctrine in faith
and morals, so too, and for precisely the same reason, he is supposed to
conserve and defend the liturgical rites. Thus, the difference between Pius
V and Paul VI comes down to this: Pius V *recognized* a rite as that of
the Church, whereas Paul VI attempted to *constitute* a rite as that of the
Church. It belongs to the Church to *regulate* rites but not to *create* rites,
as Joseph Ratzinger acknowledges: "After the Second Vatican Council, the
impression arose that the pope really could do anything in liturgical matters, especially if he were acting on the mandate of an ecumenical council.
Eventually, the idea of the givenness of the liturgy, the fact that one cannot do with it what one will, faded from the public consciousness of the
West. . . . The pope's authority is bound to the Tradition of faith, and that
also applies to the liturgy. It is not 'manufactured' by the authorities. . . .
The authority of the pope is not unlimited; it is at the service of Sacred
Tradition."[61]

---

[60] As indicated by the omission, for the first time since Pius V, of the text of *Quo Primum*—
an admission that this edition of the missal is not in continuity with all of its predecessors.
[61] Joseph Ratzinger, *Spirit of the Liturgy*, trans. John Saward (San Francisco: Ignatius Press,
2000), 165–66; comm. ed., 179–80; *Collected Works*, 11:102–3.

Pentecostal hermeneutics

This leads me to a final broad thesis. The Second Vatican Council was billed as a "new Pentecost."[62] But a new or second Pentecost is impossible. Pentecost is the mystery of the Church's identity and vitality down through all ages until Christ returns in glory; Pentecost is not a human event like a Fourth of July fireworks display, repeatable at will, but a permanent dynamism, expressed in the perennial freshness of the liturgy over which "the Holy Ghost . . . broods with warm breast and with ah! bright wings,"[63] warmly remembered in all those Sundays after Pentecost that fill the authentic Roman calendar with bright green. Abbot Ansgar Vonier cannot find forceful enough words to drive home this truth:

> The advent of the Spirit is as complete at the first Pentecost as will be the coming of the Son of God in the glory of the Father at the end of the world. . . . It is on account of this full measure of presence since Pentecost that the Kingdom of God is truly said to be with us on this earth, because the Spirit abides with us in the fulness of His divinity, not with a transient and provisional economy. . . . No one ever came with such completeness as did the Spirit; no one ever arrived with such a resolve to abide for ever as did the Paraclete. For it is in the very nature of His coming that He should abide. . . . He came finally, totally, permanently, establishing the Kingdom of God of which there shall be no end. . . . The finality of the advent of the Spirit is one of the pivotal truths that make Catholicism what it is. . . . The Holy Ghost, like the Word, came once; He does not come a second time; after His coming He abides in the Church, and it is this abiding presence that is the constant renewal of life; there is no fresh advent like that of the first Pentecost.[64]

---

[62] For references to statements of John XXIII and others, see Thomas Hughson, "Interpreting Vatican II: 'A New Pentecost,'" *Theological Studies* 69 (2008): 3–37.

[63] Gerard Manley Hopkins, "God's Grandeur."

[64] Anscar Vonier, *The Collected Works of Abbot Vonier* (London: Burns Oates, 1952), vol. 2, pp. 9, 10, 13, 69. See also Cardinal Charles Journet, "The privileges of the Apostles as founders of the Church," in *The Theology of the Church*, trans. Victor Szczurek (San Francisco: Ignatius Press, 2004), 116–22, 156–57.

There can be a new Pentecost only if the old one has failed, and in like manner, there can be a new liturgy only if the old one has failed.[65] If there can be a new Pentecost, there can be a new form of Catholicism, with new doctrines, new morality, a new liturgy, for a new humanity in a new creation—all of which can be openly in conflict with their old counterparts.[66]

Martin Mosebach eloquently diagnoses the problem:

> The "spirit of the Council" began to be played off against the literal text of the conciliar decisions. Disastrously, the implementation of the conciliar decrees was caught up in the cultural revolution of 1968, which had broken out all over the world. That was certainly the work of a spirit—if only of a very impure one. The political subversion of every kind of authority, the aesthetic vulgarity, the philosophical demolition of tradition not only laid waste universities and schools and poisoned the public atmosphere but at the same time took possession of broad circles within the Church. Distrust of tradition, elimination of tradition began to spread in, of all places, an entity whose essence consists totally of tradition—so much so that one has to say the Church is nothing without tradition. So the post-conciliar battle that had broken out in so many places against tradition was nothing else but the attempted suicide of the Church—a literally absurd, nihilistic process.
>
> We all can recall how bishops and theology professors, pastors and the functionaries of Catholic organizations proclaimed with a confident victorious tone that with the Second Vatican Council a new Pentecost had come upon the Church—which none of those famous Councils of history which had so decisively shaped the development of the Faith had ever claimed. A "new Pentecost" means nothing less than a new illumination, possibly one that would surpass that received two thousand years ago; why not

---

[65] In fact, a "new liturgy" is a contradiction in terms; the Church has no mandate to institute such a thing. Even the Apostles developed their liturgy out of the pre-existing Jewish temple and synagogue rituals and the Passover as modified by Christ. No true rite is the work of a committee that treats all previous liturgical data as raw material over which they exercise superior judgment and control.

[66] See the discussion of "Nietzschean Catholicism" in chapter 11.

advance immediately to the "Third Testament" from the *Education of the Human Race* of Gotthold Ephraim Lessing? In the view of these people, Vatican II meant a break with the Tradition as it existed up till then, and this breach was salutary. Whoever listened to this could have believed that the Catholic religion had found itself really only after Vatican II. All previous generations—to which we who sit here owe our faith—are supposed to have remained in an outer courtyard of immaturity.[67]

What we have seen in the past six decades is a clumsy revival of the medieval Joachimite heresy by which the Church would have supposedly entered the third and final age, a new age of the Spirit, which leaves behind the Old Covenant of the Father, represented by the tables of the decalogue and the animal sacrifices, and the New Covenant of the Son, represented by the Constantinian conjunction of Church and State and the Holy Sacrifice of the Mass. The new age ecumenically and interreligiously "moves beyond" commandments and Christendom and traditional divine worship. With Paul VI's liturgical reform, we move beyond the inherited liturgical tradition. With John Paul II's Assisi meetings, we move beyond the absolute difference between the true religion and false religions. With Francis's *Amoris Laetitia* and Abu Dhabi declaration, we move beyond the rigid confines of the Decalogue and the Gospels.

So many and such great novelties have all the appearances of a new religion, and a new religion could only be a false religion. The peculiar features of the "new Pentecost" or "new springtime" are manifestations of a neo-Joachimite heresy incompatible with confessional Catholicism. The collapse of the Church in our times has been the divine stamp of disapproval on the deliberate departure and the passive drifting away from Scripture, Tradition, and (yes) Magisterium,[68] in these decades when amnesia has replaced anamnesis and sacrilege has supplanted sacredness. As obvious as the collapse has been—and it threatens to become only more earthshaking with each passing year—many are the blind eyes and deaf ears that register

---

[67] Mosebach, foreword to Kwasniewski, *Noble Beauty*, xii–xiii.

[68] See my article "How Protestants, Orthodox, Magisterialists, and Traditionalists Differ on the Three Pillars of Christianity," *OnePeterFive*, May 26, 2022.

nothing but a narrowly-construed institutional self-interest. The ones who have noticed and responded to the unfolding ecclesiastical chastisement are the faithful equipped with that *sensus fidei* by which one can discern between orthodoxy and heterodoxy, right worship and its deviations.[69] As an online writer noted:

> It is the general untrustworthiness of much of the official Catholic media and printing houses that has made blogs so popular. This is especially true regarding the obvious cognitive dissonance any serious Catholic feels between the placidity and jolliness of the official media, and the reality seen on the ground, from the abuse of children to the abuse of sacraments, from the abuse of liturgy to the abuse of confidence, from the promotion of dissidents to the hiding of the statistics of the general collapse of Catholic demographics and practice in most of the world since this wintriest of springtimes began.[70]

Today the Church on earth suffers from heart disease: she is lethargic from fatty tissue and clogged arteries. She needs a heart transplant—but instead of getting a *different* heart, she needs to get rid of the artificial mechanical heart installed by her ill-informed doctors and take back the heart of flesh that her tradition grew within her. When this occurs, we shall witness, not a *new* Pentecost, but a renewal of the age-old and ever-youthful Christian worship of God in spirit and in truth, even as Our Lord prophesied and has already delivered to us in His unfailing Providence. Dom Paul Delatte, abbot of Solesmes from 1890 to 1921, wrote of the Church's traditional sacred liturgy: "In it the Holy Spirit has achieved the concentration, eternalization, and diffusion throughout the whole Body of Christ of the unchangeable fullness of the act of redemption, all the spiritual riches of the Church in the past, in the present, and in eternity."[71] No wonder Dom

---

[69] See Roberto de Mattei, "Resistance and Fidelity to the Church in Times of Crisis," in *Love for the Papacy and Filial Resistance to the Pope in the History of the Church* (Brooklyn, NY: Angelico Press, 2019), 105–30; Peter Kwasniewski, *True Obedience in the Church: A Guide to Discernment in Challenging Times* (Manchester, NH: Sophia Institute Press, 2021), 43–51.

[70] "Alternative Catholic Media: Into the Catacombs," *Rorate Caeli*, May 2, 2014.

[71] *The Rule of St. Benedict: A Commentary by the Right Rev. Dom Paul Delatte*, trans. Dom Justin McCann (London: Burns Oates & Washbourne, 1921), 133.

Guéranger said that "the Holy Ghost . . . has made the liturgy the center of His working in men's souls."[72] *This* is where our Pentecost is to be found; this is where the Church is perpetually reborn in her youth, finding ready to hand one common language with which to praise, bless, glorify, and adore her heavenly King, until He returns from the east in glory. "I will go up to the altar of God, to God, who giveth joy to my youth."

---

[72] *The Liturgical Year*, vol. 1: *Advent*, 17.

The infallibility of the pope does not mean in any way that he enjoys unlimited and arbitrary power in matters of government and teaching. The dogma of infallibility, while it defines a supreme privilege, is fixed in precise boundaries, allowing for infidelity, error, and betrayal. Otherwise in the prayers for the Supreme Pontiff there would be no need to pray "*non tradat eum in animam inimicorum eius*" [that he may not be delivered into the hands of his enemies]. If it were impossible for the pope to cross to the enemy camp, it would not be necessary to pray for it not to happen. The betrayal of Peter is the example of possible infidelity that has loomed over all of the popes through the course of history, and will be so until the end of time. The pope, even if he is the supreme authority on earth, is suspended between the summit of heroic fidelity to his mandate and the abyss of apostasy that is always present.

—Roberto de Mattei

The law of prayer is the law of faith: the Church believes as she prays. Liturgy is a constitutive element of the holy and living Tradition. For this reason no sacramental rite may be modified or manipulated at the will of the minister or the community. Even the supreme authority in the Church may not change the liturgy arbitrarily, but only in the obedience of faith and with religious respect for the mystery of the liturgy.

—*Catechism of the Catholic Church*

6

How Much Can the Pope Change Our Rites— and Why Would He?

In discussions of whether or not the pope has the authority to radically change the Church's liturgy, one popular Catholic speaker—relying on the hypothesis that early Christians all used leavened bread for the Eucharist and that at some point a pope was responsible for shifting the West to unleavened bread—made the following objection against my stance: "If a pope can modify the bread from leavened to unleavened and then limit reception to one species—which both pertain to the very substance of the sacrament!—then of course he can do anything else to the rite by which it is confected." I want to explain why this claim is a *non sequitur*.

Before proceeding, I will note that there is no good historical evidence that all ancient liturgies used leavened bread until at some point a pope flexed his pontifical muscle to say: "No more! We Latins must be different." The comprehensive article on "Azymes" by Church historian Dom Fernand Cabrol in the authoritative *Dictionnaire d'Archéologie Chrétienne et de Liturgie* (vol. 1, cols. 3254–60) says nothing about such a purported papal change.[1] We need to be careful not to fall into the trap of the common assumption (which in the field of liturgy is totally unjustified) that everything in the East is much more ancient than everything in the West, and that the East never changes; ergo, if the East uses leavened bread, and the West uses unleavened bread, that must be because the older and "original"

---

[1] The article may be read at https://gallica.bnf.fr/ark:/12148/bpt6k3044526w/f901.item.r=a zymes.

custom was to use leavened bread, and the West must have changed it. In any case, evidence does not support the idea that any shift that may have occurred was due to simple papal fiat.[2] Early Church history is generally a lot more complicated and polymorphic—and, it's always humbling to remember, a lot less documented—than we with our tidy scholastic mental habits might wish it were.

Be that as it may, let's assume, for the sake of argument, that a pope could make such a change of matter in the sacrament. Similarly, he may permit or not permit Communion under both kinds; he may add or not add the Filioque; and any number of other discrete changes of that sort. The interesting question is: How much does it matter, and what does it prove?

Bread of Life, Bread of Truth

If I receive consecrated leavened bread, I receive Jesus. If I receive consecrated unleavened bread, I receive Jesus. Both types of bread are fitting for different reasons. If I receive Communion under two species, I receive Jesus whole and entire. If I receive Communion under the species of bread alone, I receive Jesus whole and entire. Nothing is lacking in the divine gift, the Bread of Life. Neither of these cases affects the sacrament of the Eucharist, which is the "axis" or "center" of the Divine Liturgy. Substantially, the two scenarios are the same.

But there is much more to a liturgical rite than the sacrament it houses; in fact, as all are aware, there are liturgies that are not sacramental, such as the Divine Office, which have always been considered of the highest importance in the Church. If we want to understand what is right and

---

[2] The old *Catholic Encyclopedia* entry under "altar breads" includes this passage, which gives a sense of the variety of opinions out there: "It is probable that Christ used unleavened bread at the institution of the Blessed Eucharist, because the Jews were not allowed to have leavened bread in their houses on the days of the Azymes. Some authors are of the opinion that down to the tenth century both the Eastern and Western Churches used leavened bread; others maintain that unleavened bread was used from the beginning in the Western Church; still others hold that unleavened or leavened bread was used indifferently. St. Thomas ([*Sent.*] IV, Dist. xi, qu. 3) holds that, in the beginning, both in the East and West unleavened bread was used; that when the sect of the Ebionites arose, who wished that the Mosaic Law should be obligatory on all converts, leavened bread was used, and when this heresy ceased the Latins used again unleavened bread, but the Greeks retained the use of leavened bread."

wrong in terms of rites—the Bread of Truth, so to speak—we must look at how they convey the truth of the faith, how they impart doctrine, how they doxologize.

Imagine a Eucharistic liturgy that has matured slowly to its full perfection. It lavishes praises on the Holy Trinity and on the Word made flesh. It frequently invokes the Mother of God and the saints. It expresses clearly that the Mass is a true and proper sacrifice, offered in propitiation for our sins and for the good estate of the living and the dead. Its orations express all the dogmas of the Faith, without abridgement or embarrassment: they speak of merits, intercessions, miracles, apparitions of the saints; of detachment from earthly goods and the longing for the eternal; of the struggle against heresy and schism, the conversion of unbelievers, and the necessity of returning to the Catholic Church and to unadulterated truth; of God's wrath against sin and the possibility of eternal damnation.[3] In its readings, the rite does not shy away from difficult sayings of Scripture, including the warning against unworthy Communion with the Body of Christ. Lastly, the rite profoundly venerates the altar, the tabernacle, the crucifix, and the reliquaries, and lavishes signs of adoration on the Most Holy Eucharist, not only at the moment of its consecration, but even in preparing it beforehand and distributing it afterwards. In all these ways, the rite presents the full biblical and traditional doctrine of the Faith, informing the Christian mind and preparing the soul for the worthy and fruitful reception of Christ.

Now, imagine another Eucharistic liturgy that was quickly composed by a committee, using old and newly-invented material filtered through uncertain scholarly hypotheses and based on a theory of what people need at a very particular moment in history. This liturgy severely reduced mentions of or gestures toward the Trinity, the Incarnation, the Mother of God, and the saints, whose feasts it heavily diminished. It removed much of the language of altar, sacrifice, and propitiation, preferring table, meal, and community. Its prayer for the dead is gladsome rather than solemn. Its orations retained only a fraction of the orations traditionally prayed, and in their place substituted orations that omit fundamental mystical and

---

[3] Here I am following some of the language of Michael Fiedrowicz, "They Do Not Even Know What Has Been Taken from Them," *Rorate Caeli*, August 30, 2021.

ascetical themes and downplay distinctively Catholic doctrines deemed difficult or offensive. The Scripture readings were likewise edited to avoid "difficult" passages, such as the warning against unworthy Communion. Signs of veneration and adoration were severely curtailed. Overall, the rite does not present the full biblical and traditional doctrine of the Faith. On account of all these things taken together, those who attend this liturgy will not be formed as well in the Faith, or prepared as well for a worthy and fruitful reception of Holy Communion.

Can it be denied for a moment that a transition from the first liturgy to the second one—even if both are valid—is much more drastic, much more influential, than the transition from leavened to unleavened bread, or from two species to one? The liturgical rite is where the theological reality and moral-spiritual implications of the Bread of Life are made clear: what we must believe and profess about it, how we must behave toward it, how we are to prepare for communing with it, and what are the desired effects of this divine gift. The type of wheat bread or the species under which it is distributed means far less than the totality of prayers, gestures, readings, chants, incense, etc., that tell us what we are actually doing.

A liturgical rite inadequately expressive of the Church's faith—an inadequacy that could result from a number of causes: omissions, ambiguities, excessive material, lack of useful repetition—could lead over time to the loss of the orthodox faith among the people. The attenuation of dogma, the silence on difficult truths, the feeble testimony to the Real Presence—all these things would undermine the faith that is foundational to active participation in and fruitful reception of the sacraments.

How to sabotage the Catholic faith

In order to pursue the argument further, it's time for a thought experiment.

If a team of saboteurs wanted to undermine faith in the Real Presence of Christ, they would set about decentering the Mass from the Eucharist and re-centering it on the "celebrating community," on the "presider" and the "assembly," so that it was no longer apparent that everything is focused on Him at the altar.[4] The awesome silence of the Roman Canon that helps

---

[4]   The reason Christ deserves to receive all the attention is that He alone is the One who

everyone to be aware that something extraordinary and supernatural is taking place would have to go too, and for this purpose, the mantra "everyone should hear and understand everything" would come in handy.[5] Under the specious excuse of "removing useless repetitions," they would cut down on the number of kisses made to the altar, the number of genuflections toward the Blessed Sacrament, the many bows and signs of the cross, the threefold "Lord, I am not worthy . . .", the many prayers said by the priest to prepare himself for Communion. Under the pretext of "simplifying the rites" (is it because Modern Man is too busy and impatient to be in church, or too stupid to follow something complex and non-linear?), they would cut out the many poignant passages of Scripture found throughout the Order of Mass that accentuate the seriousness of the act of worship, from Psalm 42 at the beginning to the Prologue of John at the end. With the excuse of "returning to ancient practice," they would jettison one of the most vivid signs of faith in the Real Presence in the Western liturgy—namely, kneeling at the altar rail to receive the Body of Christ on the tongue, something we would never do for ordinary food or a mere symbol. Instead, they would insist that all remain standing and take the host into one's hands and then feed oneself, an irresistible juggernaut of desacralization.[6] If they wanted

makes us the Mystical Body in our union with Him. If we were not worshiping Christ and He did not truly come among us, we would be just a bunch of people doing some kind of community-building self-help therapy that terminated on a natural level. Which, come to think of it, is how a lot of modern worship services look.

[5] Not paying regard to the reality that almost nothing in the Mass is capable of being perfectly understood by us, so why foster an illusion—unless you want to undermine faith in the supernatural and convert Christianity into a natural religion of pure reason?

[6] No one has better explained the reason for this destructiveness than Martin Mosebach: "Kneeling was medieval, they said. The early Christians prayed standing. Standing signifies the resurrected Christ, they said; it is the most appropriate attitude for a Christian. The early Christians are also supposed to have received Communion in their hands. What is irreverent about the faithful making their hands into a 'throne' for the Host? I grant that the people who tell me such things are absolutely serious about it all. But it becomes very clear that pastors of souls are incredibly remote from the world in these matters; academic arguments are completely useless in questions of liturgy. These scholars are always concerned only about the historical side of the substance of faith and of the forms of devotion. If, however, we think correctly and historically, we should realize that what is an expression of veneration in one period can be an expression of blasphemy in another. If people who have been kneeling for a thousand years suddenly get to their feet, they do not think, 'We're doing this like the early Christians, who stood for the Consecration'; they are not aware of returning to some particularly authentic form of worship. They simply get up, brush the dust from their trouser-legs and say to themselves: 'So it wasn't such a serious business after all.' Everything that

to undermine faith in the Mass as the mysterious re-presentation of the Sacrifice of the Cross, they would strip the liturgy of mentions of sacrifice, oblation, immolation, victim, propitiation, and the like so that it would not be able to offend a broad-minded Calvinist.[7]

The foregoing paragraph could be extended into a book describing all the changes that saboteurs of the Catholic Faith would make if they wanted to destroy the traditional faith of Catholics as dogmatically defined at the Council of Trent.

Fortunately, such a book has already been written, and more than once. I will mention only three: Michael Davies's *Pope Paul's New Mass*; Anthony Cekada's *Work of Human Hands*; and Michael Fiedrowicz's *The Traditional Mass*. For the sobering reality is that the liturgical reform after Vatican II did every one of the things mentioned above. Even before the Novus Ordo went into effect, Cardinals Bacci and Ottaviani had put their signatures on a cover letter to a short study of its deficiencies—the famous "Ottaviani Intervention"—and showed how it would lead Catholics astray, how it failed to express clearly the Church's faith and would poorly transmit it. One might say Bacci and Ottaviani had predicted well in advance that, under the Novus Ordo regime, faith in the Real Presence would erode, as we can see in the 2019 Pew Research Study that showed a whopping sixty-nine percent of self-described US Catholics—and thirty-seven percent of *weekly Mass-going* Catholics (!)—do not believe in the Real Presence (and if people were asked whether the Mass is a true and proper sacrifice, surely the same results, or worse, would be found). The reaction to this study should not have been wide-eyed surprise and calls for better and slicker video catechesis, but ashes and sackcloth, widespread book-burnings, and Latin Mass training sessions.

---

takes place in celebrations of this kind implies the same thing: 'It wasn't all that serious after all.' Under such circumstances, anthropologically speaking, it is quite impossible for faith in the presence of Christ in the Sacrament to have any deeper spiritual significance, even if the Church continues to proclaim it and even if the participants of such celebrations go so far as to affirm it explicitly." Martin Mosebach, *The Heresy of Formlessness: The Roman Liturgy and Its Enemy*, rev. ed. (Brooklyn, NY: Angelico Press, 2018), 14–15.

[7] See Sharon Kabel, "Catholic fact check: Jean Guitton, Pope Paul VI, and the liturgical reforms," https://sharonkabel.com/post/guitton/, December 7, 2020.

Let us not forget, too, that the first and most basic form of active partic-ipation is the physical bodily presence of faithful in the pews. During the period of volatile liturgical change, the faithful began their exodus from the churches, and, despite Paul VI's papal insistence that the new rite would renew the People of God, the hemorrhaging has never ceased, as fewer and fewer show up for the "full, conscious, active participation that is their right and duty" (*SC* 14). Paul VI may have been prophetic about contraception, but he was no prophet when it came to liturgy: "Through an intense and prolonged religious movement, the liturgy—crowned, and, as it were, can-onized by Vatican II—has gained a new importance, dignity, accessibility, and participation in the consciousness and the spiritual life of the people of God and, we predict, this will continue even more in the future."[8]

The rite is the locus of catholicity

Given my analysis above, no one should be surprised at this result—or at the parallel phenomenon of growing Latin Mass congregations (at least, wherever violence is not used to suppress them). If the new rite lowers our horizon to the horizontal, it will have no staying power against secular culture, which far more successfully appeals to our fallen human nature. If the other rite draws us up "vertically" into the worship of the transcendent Triune God and compels us to pay homage to Christ our King, it woos and wins the heart longing for the divine and for redemption from this world of sin.

Why, during the period of COVID panic and lockdown, was it primar-ily the traditional priests who kept Masses going, even in secret if necessary, and the traditional faithful who went out of their way to get to Mass—while the Novus Ordo world (again, generally speaking) went into hiberna-tion? Why were the laity attached to tradition ready to go to Mass in person and yet, if the bishop had forbidden Communion on the tongue, equally

---

[8] General Audience at Castel Gandolfo, August 13, 1969 (*DOL* 45). It was a fantasy to which this pope was to yield countless times. Another example: "The choral prayer of the Mystical Body, which the Church is, is reaching and stirring the people of God, who are consciously becoming a community and experiencing an increase in faith and grace. Therefore, super-natural faith is reawakening, eschatological hope is guiding ecclesial spirituality, charity is reassuming its life-giving, active primacy. And all of this in a pagan, worldly century, deaf to the cries of the soul" (General Audience at Castel Gandolfo, September 3, 1969 [*DOL* 47]).

ready to not receive the Body of Christ, out of deepest regard for what is right and fitting? Why, when the bishops said everyone was freed of the Sunday Mass obligation, did traditionalists still try to go to Mass, often at great inconvenience? And why, once the dust settled and the obligation was reactivated, did the mainstream churches not recover their pre-COVID congregations, while the traditional communities pulled out folding chairs for the overflow?

The Novus Ordo, a product of simplification and banalization, lends itself to cancellation. The logic of reductionism is severe and indiscriminate: all who take the scissors will perish by the scissors. Regarding centuries-old prayers as useless repetitions will lead to regarding private Masses as useless repetitions and ultimately to regarding the sacramental life itself as a useless repetition.

We are looking here at *concrete practical results* of two different liturgies: one of them manifestly centered on the Holy Sacrifice and the Real Presence, the other decentered from both. Clergy believe and behave as each liturgy forms them to, and the same is no less true of the laity. In the hour of trial, instincts and habits formed over the decades showed themselves. "Breeding will tell."

If you change the rite of Mass—the content of its prayers, its ceremonies, its music and silence, and so forth—you will change the faith of the people: what they believe Mass is, and what they are doing (or not doing) at Mass. This is exactly what happened in the 1960s and 1970s, and the fallout has not subsided, nor has the obvious remedy changed.

Looking past the surface to the common tradition

In the course of my life I have assisted frequently at the Byzantine Divine Liturgy. Superficially, it is very different from the traditional Latin Mass that is my home and heritage as a Roman Catholic. In the Byzantine rite, I receive Communion standing, after making a profound bow—but the priest (and only he) delivers the precious Body and Blood, under the forms of leavened bread soaked in wine, directly into my mouth, on a spoon. In the Roman rite, I kneel to receive on my tongue the Body of Christ under the form of a host of unleavened bread. In both cases, I receive my Lord and my Savior, for the forgiveness of my sins and for life everlasting. What became utterly clear to me over time, however, is that the traditional rites of East and West, be they ever so different in appearances, are profoundly united in their traditional qualities: in the seriousness and solemnity of the act of worship as communicated in the texts, music, and ceremonial; in the resounding orthodoxy of the prayers; in the obvious theocentricity of the rites, the offering of a holy sacrifice to God, and the sense of His heavenly Kingdom breaking into our world. Moved by this realization, I published an article at *New Liturgical Movement* entitled "The Byzantine Liturgy, the Traditional Latin Mass, and the Novus Ordo—Two Brothers and a Stranger."[9]

In any traditional rite, we worship God in the beauty of holiness, in the truth of orthodoxy, in the adequate (not perfect—that is saved for heaven) expression of the mysteries we are enacting and receiving. I came to realize over many years that, tragically, this is not what is happening with the Novus Ordo. It is inherently and fundamentally lacking in the traditional qualities of the liturgy as practiced by apostolic Christianity; worse than that, it is fashioned in such a way as to act as a solvent, over time, of the faith of the people, unless heroic supplementary efforts are made to fill in the gaps from the outside.[10] It is inadequate to its task.

---

[9] This article appears as Chapter 10 in this book, with a slightly different title.

[10] Since we know that "God desires all men to be saved and to come to the knowledge of the truth" (1 Tim 2:4), we also know that He will find or create ways to lead the faithful back to the truth if the official Church has misled them, and ways back to the means of salvation if these are being neglected. This, it seems to me, explains several phenomena characteristic of postconciliar Catholicism. Because the Novus Ordo was patently inadequate to remind the faithful of the Sacrifice of the Mass and unite them to it, Divine Providence made use of the Divine Mercy chaplet: "Eternal Father, I offer to Thee the most precious Body and Blood, Soul and Divinity, of Thy dearly beloved Son, Our Lord Jesus Christ, in atonement for our sins and those of the whole world"; "For the sake of His sorrowful Passion, have mercy on us and on the whole world." These prayers cultivate a sense of seriousness about the central mystery of salvation history and thereby keep alive a belief that the liturgy is not correctly transmitting. Similarly, the Luminous Mysteries brought the wedding feast at Cana and the institution of the Eucharist to the fore, both of which are treated negligently in the new liturgy. (See my articles "Basking in the Glow of Epiphany: The Wedding Feast at Cana," *Rorate Caeli*, January 13, 2018, and "Why We Should Revive the Octave of Corpus Christi in the *Usus Antiquior*," *NLM*, May 31, 2021.) In the same way, the rediscovery and growth of Eucharistic Adoration outside of Mass was a heaven-sent means of sustaining faith in the Real Presence when the liturgy itself was doing a disgraceful job of it. There are reasons to criticize some of these paraliturgical devotions or the manner in which they are sometimes pursued,

My own "pew research" was conducted from the pews (or, more often, the choir lofts) I inhabited for decades, and it brought me to a conclusion and a resolution several years ago: whatever others may choose to do, I can neither actively promote nor lend my passive approval to an ersatz liturgy that undermines the Catholic Faith. There is, and there must only be, traditional worship. And no pope has the authority to abolish it.

It is, consequently, a much bigger deal for a pope to radically change a liturgical rite—the *lex orandi* that enshrines and instills the *lex credendi*—than it would be for him to change the type of wheat bread or the species under which Communion is distributed. And that is why it doesn't follow that just because the pope may have the authority to do the latter, therefore he would have the same to do the former. The pope's authority is for edification, not for destruction. Tellingly, the decree *Laetentur Caeli* (1439) of the Council of Florence states: "We define that the body of Christ is truly effected with either unleavened or leavened wheaten bread; and that priests must confect the body of the Lord in one way or the other, namely, each following the custom of their Church, whether Western or Eastern."[11] Note that what is normative is precisely *tradition*, in this case liturgical custom, with the question of leavened or unleavened being decidedly secondary. What priests must do—and popes, no less—is follow their own tradition and what it dictates.

In the years when I lived in Austria, I used to see a popular bumper sticker that read: "Der Weg ist das Ziel"—"the way is the goal." This statement has been attributed to Confucius, although it might sound like the motto of a postmodern German relativist who does Yoga on the weekends and, having spurned the Cardinal Marxes of the world, directs her church tax to the upkeep of the EU. If, moreover, one is fortunate enough to have an Audi, a Mercedes, or a BMW, as many Germans and Austrians do, one might be

---

yet we should not fail to see how they have been used by God to maintain the faith in spite of the official Church's deviations.

[11] See Heinrich Denzinger, *Enchiridion symbolorum definitionum et declarationum de rebus fidei et morum*, 43rd ed., ed. Peter Hünermann, Robert Fastiggi, Anne Englund Nash (San Francisco: Ignatius Press, 2012), n. 1303.

tempted to drive with no particular goal in mind. But here I should like, perhaps unexpectedly, to suggest that this motto admits of a special application to Catholic liturgy.

Unlike a business trip where the whole point is to get to a meeting or conference and the journey stands somewhere between a necessary evil and an inconvenience, liturgy is not just about getting a certain result or outcome. "Results" there may and should be, of course: the Eucharist may be confected, Holy Communion may be consumed, a newly-wed couple may walk out of the church, a new priest may step forth into the sunshine, a body may be carried off to the cemetery. But such results do not exhaust, much less cancel out, the *intrinsic* reasons why we worship, and the inherent needs and demands of that worship.

Liturgy—the formal, solemn, public *cultus* of God, wherein the Church, on behalf of mankind and all of creation, adores, blesses, glorifies, and gives thanks to the Most Holy Trinity—is the reason we do liturgy. The way is the goal. If liturgy truly is our participation in the heavenly worship of the angels and saints gathered around their High Priest in the sanctuary not made by human hands, then we are participating in this heavenly worship *now*, and, depending on *how* we worship, will be participating well or poorly. What Our Lord expects of us in worship is not that we get something or get somewhere but that we *be* a certain way in His presence, that we know and love Him in a certain way. This is the precondition for being fitted to receive any gift He wishes to give, most especially His Body in the Eucharist. In that sense, if we do not take seriously the *way*, we are not taking seriously the goal, either. We do not reach the goal except by the way thither, and, in the spiritual realm, our behavior or attitude on the way determines our worthiness or fitness to come to the goal, both here and in the hereafter.

Liturgy mirrors our earthly pilgrimage. If we expect to come to heaven, the only determining factor is how we live our lives *en route*. It's not as if we can live a slipshod life and die a godless death and then expect to be rewarded for it with beatitude. It's not as if we're given another chance after death.[12] The way we live is the way we die. If we live for God *now*, even

---

[12] See Dom Pius Mary Noonan, *Whilst It Is Day: Shedding Light on the Eternal Stakes of Life*

the now that verges on death, we are already at the goal: union with God in love. As Pope Leo XIII says in his encyclical *Divinum Illud Munus*, the difference between a soul in the state of grace and a soul in the state of glory is the hiddenness of the presence of God: in this life His indwelling is invisible to us, while in the next we see Him face-to-face in the beatific vision. But in both states He is truly present in us, and we in Him. In a sense, then, one may say of the Christian life as a whole what one may say of the liturgy: the way is the goal.

Where we see this truth most splendidly is the Divine Office, which is pure verbal incense, burned up in the presence of the Lord, and for His sake. This is not to say that we do not benefit from it; quite the contrary. Saint Thomas Aquinas says plainly enough that since we cannot improve *God* by our worship, any benefits must accrue to *us*.[13] But the benefit consists in the very *doing* of it, not in something other than the doing of it. Perhaps this is why the Office has fallen on such hard times: for pragmatic, utilitarian, materialistic people such as we modern Westerners are—even, at times, in spite of our best intentions—the Office fails to "deliver the goods." Where's the *thing* we get at the end of it? The ashes, palm branch, host, anointing, bulletin? We tend to look at the Office through the lens of the Mass and find it wanting, because it seems to be unable to compete with the latter's sacramental results.

What is needed, rather, is to see the Mass through the lens of the Office. We need to see the Mass as a sweet-smelling sacrifice of praise offered up in psalms, hymns, and spiritual canticles, thanking God for His great glory, adoring, placating, supplicating Him. Only after that does it make sense to see it as a banquet to which we are invited. We are invited to a *sacrifice* of

---

(Colebrook, Tasmania: Cana Press, 2020).

[13] *ST* II-II, qu. 81, art. 7: "We pay God honor and reverence, not for His sake (because He is of Himself full of glory to which no creature can add anything), but for our own sake, because by the very fact that we revere and honor God, our mind is subjected to Him; wherein its perfection consists, since a thing is perfected by being subjected to its superior, for instance the body is perfected by being quickened by the soul, and the air by being enlightened by the sun." See also qu. 91, art. 1: "We employ words, in speaking to God, not indeed to make known our thoughts to Him Who is the searcher of hearts, but that we may bring ourselves and our hearers to reverence Him. Consequently we need to praise God with our lips, not indeed for His sake, but for our own sake; since by praising Him our devotion is aroused towards Him."

which we may then partake if we are properly disposed; we reap spiritual fruit in proportion to how well we have been prepared by the very liturgical action in which we have participated.[14]

I never cease to feel amazed that there are Catholics who, having been exposed to the traditional liturgy or having some awareness that it exists and is richer than its streamlined modern counterpart, still shrug their shoulders and say, in effect, "it's not such a big deal." The only way I can make sense of this strange attitude is by assuming in their souls an implicit or explicit acceptance of a reductionistic conception of the Mass that equates it with the consecration: as long as we have Jesus in the Eucharist, that's all that matters.[15]

It sounds plausible, and yet it is not, for several reasons.

The Mass is not a utilitarian process designed to maximize the efficient delivery of goods. The Mass is not, as such, a Communion service. It is a complex ceremony of repentance, adoration, petition, and thanksgiving, with a sacramental sacrifice at its core. It was given to us by Our Lord and His Church as the highest form of prayer, which *prepares for, culminates in, and gives thanks for* the gift of His Most Holy Body and Blood. It does not begin and end with that gift.

So, the first problem with the *Novus Ordo Missae* is that, owing to its impoverished content and ceremonial, it tends not to cultivate and prompt acts of repentance, adoration, petition, and thanksgiving nearly as well as the old Mass can do. The next problem, intimately linked with the foregoing, is that it does not prepare us for the reception of the Most Holy Eucharist as well as the old rite does. Hence, it falters even if we view the Mass under the more restricted aspect of being an opportunity for sacramental Communion.[16]

---

[14] See my article "The Priority of Religion and Adoration over Communion," *NLM*, October 9, 2017.

[15] For more on this point, see the preceding chapter; also Peter Kwasniewski, *Reclaiming Our Roman Catholic Birthright: The Genius and Timeliness of the Traditional Latin Mass* (Brooklyn, NY: Angelico Press, 2020), 103–10, 198–201. Readers may charge me with being unfair by suggesting that Catholics who frequent the Novus Ordo suffer from this mentality. But I have seen it countless times in discussions: "If the Eucharist is present, what more do you want? What more do we need?" The fact that this is such a *common* reaction suggests a systemic problem in our way of thinking, since the Church has never held to such reductionism.

[16] For a detailed exposition of the claims of this paragraph, see my series "Time for the Soul

Think of it this way: If you were Mary of Bethany, sitting at the feet of Jesus and soaking in His words, would you want to sit there quietly, for quite some time, preparing yourself deeply for the spiritual marriage with Him—"the marriage of the Lamb is come, and his wife *hath prepared herself*" (Rev 19:7)—or would you want to listen for a few minutes, jump up, give Him a hug and a kiss, and be off to the next thing? Or worse, what if Mary greeted Him with a smile, said "Need to finish something—be with you in a moment," busied herself with a few more chores, and then came back with hors d'oeuvres, in order to be "actively participating" in this colloquy? Meanwhile, Jesus would patiently and humbly sit there, waiting for Mary to stop distracting herself and sit down. In the contemporary Church, it's mostly Martha, very little Mary; mostly busyness, little contemplation; efficiency in place of wasteful love.

Beyond this devotional angle, we must consider the Mass in its diachronic continuity. The Mass is handed down to us from apostolic tradition, developed over the centuries of faith by the real devotional life of the People of God. It is therefore like a living, breathing, growing organism, reflecting and, in a mysterious way, sharing in the divine and human life of the Son of God and of His Mystical Body. The Mass is something we gratefully and humbly *receive*, just as we receive our human nature in conception and our supernatural life in baptism. Thus, even if *per impossibile* the Mass were no more than a glorified Communion service, we would *still* have no right, no business, deconstructing and reconstructing the inherited form of this service in the Roman rite, a deposit of faith-filled prayer that the Church always considered it her duty to guard and protect.

It was and is a crime for Church leaders to treat the Church's tradition in such a contemptuous way; it was and is an incalculable loss for the spiritual vitality and sanctification of her members; it was and still is the principal cause of the crisis of faith through which we have been passing in the decades since the Council. The only way we will restore an integrally Catholic way of life is with an integral liturgy, the liturgy that the Holy Spirit built up over twenty centuries with the living stones of clergy, religious, and

---

to Absorb the Mysteries" at *NLM* (December 4, 11, 18, and 27, 2017; January 3, 2018), and *Reclaiming Our Birthright*, ch. 19, "Good and Bad Liturgical Parenting," 255–65.

laity, with the breath of their orations, lections, and chants, with the fire of the Spirit poured forth upon the Church at Pentecost. No matter how valid a new sacramental rite may be, no one can create for it a history *ex nihilo*, no one can make it to be a treasure handed down when it is not. No matter how valid it may be, if it is defective in regard to the *way* of worship, it will be defective also in leading people to the *end* of worship. A good end does not necessarily sanctify, or justify, any means taken. The way and the goal cannot be divorced: "What therefore God hath joined together, let no man (and no committee) put asunder."

In short: the Mass is not just about Communion. It is a many-sided service of prayer, including a careful preparation for Communion and thanksgiving after it[17]—and it is a prayer handed down to us along the line of the apostolic tradition to which we belong. For both of these reasons, a stripped-down, heavily redacted, modified, and innovated rite of Mass cannot be said to be other than a bad thing for the life of the Church and the life of individual Catholics, regardless of whether or not the consecration is valid.

Let us consider this fact. It would have been a lot "simpler" if Jesus had remained among us under His natural appearances until the end of time. He surely could have done that; the Ascension was not necessary, in the strict logical sense of necessity. He chose nevertheless to depart and to communicate His grace and truth to us in other ways—in specifically sacramental, liturgical, ecclesial ways, which therefore deserve our trust, our homage, our best efforts, and our gratitude.

The liturgy is not a mere shell for the Real Presence, like a monstrance holding a host, nor is it a mere container for a product, like a tube full of toothpaste; *it is the privileged way He becomes present to us and we to Him.* And that way is not a modern highway along which we speed as quickly as we can to reach our exit, paying scant attention to the road; it is a path *along which* we are sanctified, prepared to reach our goal worthily.[18]

---

[17] See Peter Kwasniewski, *Holy Bread of Eternal Life: Restoring Eucharistic Reverence in an Age of Impiety* (Manchester, NH: Sophia Institute Press, 2020), 87–88.

[18] See, for an application to the *usus antiquior*, "Two Modest Proposals for Improving the Prayerfulness of Low Mass," *NLM*, November 12, 2018.

Allow me to draw out a corollary from the foregoing discussion. A liturgical rite is *constituted by* its particular texture and content of chants, texts, ceremonies, the language it has made its own, the stance of the priest, the motions of the ministers, and so forth. These things are not supplementary to or decorative of the liturgy; they simply *are* the liturgical rite. Thus, it can be said with precision that the Novus Ordo is not a form of the Roman rite; it is not the same liturgy as the Roman rite. For it is possible to have a Novus Ordo celebration in which almost *nothing* said and done is held in common with what is said and done in the Roman rite as it historically existed: one can have different proper antiphons (or none at all), different orations, different readings, a different anaphora, the contrary stance of the priest, etc.; and even if all of the "right" options were chosen, they remain essentially "at option" and thus not inherent and constitutive of the rite.

So the next time someone says: "It doesn't matter which Mass you go to, the 'Ordinary Form' or the 'Extraordinary Form'—Jesus is present in both!" (which is usually said with a triumphant assurance that this is the end of the discussion, when in fact the real discussion hasn't even begun), slow him down and ask him what his conception of the Mass is. Might he be reducing it to consecration and Communion? We may be dealing here with a sort of Catholic parallel to the popular Protestant notion of "salvation by faith alone"—namely, "liturgy by Eucharist alone." To the oft-posed Fundamentalist question "Have you accepted Jesus Christ as your personal Lord and Savior?" would correspond the sacramentally reductionist question: "Has your Mass transubstantiated bread and wine?" If such a position were true, the ultimate *Novus Ordo*—the *Novissimus Ordo*, as it were—would start off with a priest standing over bread and wine, who, right after a greeting, immediately says the words of consecration, distributes Communion, and closes with a blessing. Over and done with in less than three minutes (particularly if armies of "extraordinary ministers of Holy Communion" are called upon), and, don't you know, "we've got Jesus." What more could we ask for?[19]

---

[19] Indeed, it would be even "better"—from this reductionist vantage—for a priest to consecrate a bushel or two of hosts at a given location, and then to allow lay ministers to distribute communion daily for the next several months. This would at once solve the problem of the priest shortage *and* empower laity with new forms of active participation! Absurdity aside,

Our Lord Himself gives us the kernel of a response: "I came, that they may have life—*and have it in abundance*" (cf. Jn 10:10). This abundance is the garden of mysteries of His human and divine life, unfolded and elaborated, made real and present for us, in the sacred liturgy developed and delivered over twenty centuries. The faithful children of the Church should settle for nothing less, as they continue to resist the liturgical reform's brutal reductionism.

---

what we see is that the Catholic Faith demands the figure and function of the priest to remain what it is and to carry on the worship to which we are deputed in our baptism. Therefore, we are obliged to seek the liturgical form that most fully reflects the sacramental identity and unique activity of the priest, and to resist anything that dilutes it or farms it out to those to whom it is foreign.

For even as he would be guilty of falsehood who would, in the name of another person, proffer things that are not committed to him, so too does a man incur the guilt of falsehood who, on the part of the Church, gives worship to God contrary to the manner established by the Church or divine authority, and according to ecclesiastical custom. . . . The various customs of the Church in the divine worship are in no way contrary to the truth: wherefore we must observe them, and to disregard them is unlawful.

—St. Thomas Aquinas

In the light of the invasion of secularism, of the atrophy of the spiritual life, of the drying up of vocations, of the vast loss of influence and respect suffered by the Church, the conclusion on practical grounds must be that the modernisers were wrong. They were wrong because of the aggressive imposition of their policy; they were wrong because of their ideological priorities at the expense of genuine pastoral concerns; they were wrong because their reformism was reckless of orthodoxy and tradition; they were wrong in their pseudo-ecumenism which ignored the Eastern tradition of Christianity; and they were wrong above all in their determination to blur the line between the Catholic faith and the Protestant denial of it.

—Henry Sire

7

Growth or Corruption? Catholic versus Protestant-Modernist Models

From one point of view, liturgy is a freely-devised human work—really a gigantic gathering of works—that changes over time because of concrete decisions made by individuals. These decisions can be either good or bad, can be evaluated as improvements or corruptions depending on their merits or demerits. The fact that we are not dealing with a purely spontaneous natural phenomenon like the growth of a plant or an animal rules out a naïvely literal application of the terms "organic" and "inorganic" to the history of the liturgy.[1] What, then, is the objective basis for the long-standing habit of using these terms in this field of discourse?

I propose that "organic" is a metaphor for a set of qualities. In a famous passage quoted earlier, Saint Vincent of Lérins compares the "growth of religion" with the "growth of the body": personal identity, structure, and purpose remain the same although the parts are enlarged and refined.[2] Now, clearly the development of doctrine is not something that happens

---

[1] See Gregory DiPippo, "Against 'Organic Development,'" *NLM*, December 3, 2021; "Rethinking 'Organic Development,'" *NLM*, December 8, 2021. See also "On Liturgical Development and Corruption" in Peter Kwasniewski, *Tradition and Sanity: Conversations and Dialogues of a Postconciliar Exile* (Brooklyn, NY: Angelico Press, 2018), 43–51.

[2] Saint Vincent of Lérins, *Commonitorium*, ch. 23, nn. 55–56, trans. C. A. Heurtley, in *Nicene and Post-Nicene Fathers*, Second Series, vol. 11, ed. Philip Schaff and Henry Wace (Buffalo, NY: Christian Literature Publishing Co., 1894), rev. and ed. for New Advent by Kevin Knight, quoted above on pp. 36–37.

automatically, spontaneously, or involuntarily, as the growth of a body does. But the metaphor is useful because, in Church history, it is *as if* certain developments unfold with an inevitableness that suggests the growth of an organism. In the midst of the Trinitarian and Christological disputes, no one would have said "this is an organic process," since at the time it would have seemed like a bar-room brawl, but in retrospect, when one looks at the great lines of the debates, one sees a progression from topic to topic that seems compellingly logical—almost inevitable.

Once a given question was raised about Christ, someone was bound to raise the next one, and the next one. Are there two natures in Christ? Yes. Well then, are there two wills in Christ? Yes. Well then, are there two energies in Christ? One can see lines of thought unfolding like this in regard to many areas of Christian doctrine. The unfolding is never perfectly logical, since human free agents are involved, not to mention surprises like wars, disasters, and famines, but looking back one sees why the developments happened as and when they did. That is why Newman could write his *Essay on the Development of Christian Doctrine.* When you look at it from a later vantage point, growth in doctrine or dogma seems like the growth of an organism: it has an appearance of right, proportionate, and necessary growth, in spite of the intervention of so many individual human wills, and that is why Vincent's comparison can be understood and approved, even if, when pressed too hard, taken too literally, it would fall apart.

Perhaps the profound root of this metaphor is our conviction that the Church is the Mystical Body of Christ—a mystical organism that does have an inner principle of motion and rest, of movement toward goals and rest in them (at least partial rest; eternal rest is not for this world). It is not only bishops, popes, and councils that run the gardening operation; Providence is the ultimate gardener that tends and prunes this mystical vine, which is composed of rational beings but is governed by the God who, without violating their freedom, can guide them along paths He has preordained, while also permitting evils to occur.

Moving over to the sphere of liturgy, it seems to me that what we mean by "organic" is not "mindless" or "necessitated" but rather "in accord with the reality's inner principles" and therefore, in a way, explicable given its own nature. It is crucial for this metaphor's efficacy that the rate of change, or at least the rate of most changes and of perceived change, be relatively slow—measured in centuries, as was the case with the Roman rite prior to Pius X, rather than in mere decades or years, as occurred in the twentieth century, with increasingly hasty and wide-ranging reforms. When significant changes happen by individual intellects and free choices only once in a while—a new Sequence here, a new feast there (think of Corpus Christi, added in the thirteenth century)—the broad picture will be that of a gentle and gradual process, the way leaves grow on a tree, and then buds, and then fruits. Each day brings a little more growth, but you don't notice it as growth. It's not like the magic lamp-post in *The Magician's Nephew*, which grows up in real time out of the ground before your very eyes.

In short, what is organic is not so much the individual change to the liturgy as the entire trajectory of changes over long periods. Instead of saying "the feast of Christ the King was an organic development," when we know perfectly well that it was a pope crowned only a hundred years ago, Pius XI, who willed to insert a new feast into the calendar (a voluntary phenomenon, not a natural one), we should apply the label "organic" to the overall sanctoral and temporal cycles of the Roman rite, which have developed much over sixteen centuries but which have preserved all along the core elements and embellished them in ways that are appropriate (or at least not inappropriate) to the original spirit and purpose of such cycles. The devotion to Christ as King is, as Pius XI himself notes in *Quas Primas*, something present in Scripture and Tradition and seen in countless works of art from all ages, and accordingly, this liturgical insertion, made at a specific time for specific reasons, is in continuity with elements already present. It accentuates those elements; it does not bury them or distort them. In contrast, what Paul VI did to these cycles (not to mention what he did to Pius XI's feast!) can in no way be reconciled with this spirit and purpose, nor with the attitude of respect that Catholics have instinctively felt it is right to give to the results of the history through which we have passed.[3]

---

[3] On the significant changes, see my articles "Should the Feast of Christ the King Be Celebrated in October or November?" *Rorate Caeli*, October 22, 2014; "Between Christ the King and 'We Have No King But Caesar,'" *OnePeterFive*, October 25, 2020; cf. Michael P. Foley, "A Reflection on the Fate of the Feast of Christ the King," *NLM*, October 21, 2020.

Let's take a more controversial example: Communion received on the tongue while kneeling. The double shift from standing to kneeling and from receiving in the hand to receiving on the tongue is certainly a change that had to be willed by various local churches before it became a universal custom, but the rationale behind this change is easy to see. It was always profound reverence for Our Lord present in the Blessed Sacrament that was dictating the Church's policy in regard to its reception, and as awareness grew and spread that there were better ways to express this reverence and to avoid dangers in the use of the sacrament, to that degree did the new practices take hold and become universal. They did so, in other words, not because of an all-powerful pope in Rome saying to every local church: "You must receive Communion in thus-and-such a way"—before the sixteenth century the Church did not legislate universally in that manner about liturgy—but because a custom with evident benefits, a *lex orandi* with a better claim to conveying the *lex credendi*, had sprung up here and there, and spread from one local church to the next.[4] It spread by its own inherent rightness, its superiority over what had been done before.

That is the kind of development that looks, in retrospect, "organic": though the result of human wills, it popped up here and there like seeds sprouting, and spread like seeds carried by the wind, and gradually covered the Catholic world, until it seemed inevitable. We see that it is *dignum et justum*. There would certainly never be a reason to go backwards artificially to pick up an earlier practice that was rightly discarded.[5]

Consider one more example: the "sacerdotalism" of the old rites, in which the clergy—bishops, priests, deacons, subdeacons, those in minor orders or their substitutes—are manifestly the primary agents executing the services, and the congregation attends, or to use an old-fashioned term, "assists" in a mostly quiet and apparently passive way. Modern liturgists uniformly deplore what they see as a form of clericalism and a separation or exclusion of the people from the liturgical action. Yet they fail to

---

[4]   On all these points, see Peter Kwasniewski, *Holy Bread of Eternal Life: Restoring Eucharistic Reverence in an Age of Impiety* (Manchester, NH: Sophia Institute Press, 2020), 89–145.

[5]   See Peter Kwasniewski, *Reclaiming Our Roman Catholic Birthright: The Genius and Timeliness of the Traditional Latin Mass* (Brooklyn, NY: Angelico Press, 2020), ch. 10, "The Problem of False Antiquarianism," 149–60.

grasp the paradox—frequently experienced by attendees of the traditional rites—of the intense spiritual involvement, attraction, and even fascination provoked by the hieratic "distance" of the clergy in the sanctuary, the architectural boundaries and barriers that turn spaces into symbols, and the entrustment of rites to men who exemplify the worship of God in their ceremonial vesture, scripted words, and carefully-controlled motions. In other words, a phenomenon that is routinely assumed to be anti-participational and anti-corporate is nothing of the kind. The "sacerdotalizing" development that took place in history accentuated features already clearly present in the old covenant and continued in the new covenant, which was pre-interpreted in a private upper room, consummated on a hill cut off from the city, achieved in the torturous separation of body and blood, echoed in the *Nolite me tangere* of the risen Lord who must ascend beyond us that we may follow Him: *Trahe me, post te curremus.*[6] We should not be too quick to trust the examples of corruption furnished by the class of professional liturgists.

There are equally obvious cases of changes that call for the metaphorical description "inorganic." In the seventeenth century, Pope Urban VIII, a classicizing poet who disdained medieval verse, ordered that 952 "corrections" be made to the 98 hymns then contained in the breviary. A scholar of the subject explains:

> Urban's most lasting legacy had nothing to do with his nepotism, or his extravagance, or his condemnation of Galileo. That legacy was the damage done to the Latin hymns of Catholicism, which were revised and rewritten, not only under Urban's orders, but also with his active participation. . . . The repertory of hymns which fell victim to Urban's ill-advised revision contained some material

---

[6] "Do not touch me" (Jn 20:17); "Draw me, we will run after thee" (Song 1:3). See Peter Kwasniewski, *Ministers of Christ: Recovering the Roles of Clergy and Laity in an Age of Confusion* (Manchester, NH: Crisis Publications, 2021), passim; *Reclaiming Our Birthright*, 28–33, 56–58, 174–77; and my articles "How the Clergy's 'Distance' from the People Facilitates the Laity's Offering," *OnePeterFive*, September 1, 2021; "The Priest Praying for Himself at Mass," *OnePeterFive*, September 8, 2021. For two examples "in the wild" of the modern liturgists' point of view, see Fr. Jeffrey Moore, "Liturgical Participation," https://frmoore.com/2020/02 /01/february-02-2020-liturgical-participation; Timothy P. O'Malley, "Assessing the Council's Liturgical Reforms," *Our Sunday Visitor*, February 21, 2022.

which had been in more or less continuous use for almost a thousand years. . . . Some hymns were almost totally rewritten, and
many thoughts and ideas expressed in the original texts of hymns
were totally lost. . . . Sometimes the rewriting by Urban and his
associates appears so very unnecessary that the logic behind the
change is totally incomprehensible. . . . It is now almost universally
conceded that the seventeenth-century revision of the Latin hymnal was a mistake, and that the despoiling of these ancient hymns
cannot possibly be defended or justified. The so-called improvements which were made to the texts were, in fact, no improvement
whatsoever. One commentator has wisely observed that "Ambrose
and Prudentius took something classical and made it Christian; the
revisers and their imitators took something Christian and tried to
make it classical. The result may be pedantry, and sometimes perhaps poetry; but it is not piety." . . . Even though he was motivated
by the best of intentions, and even though he and his colleagues
were eminently suited for the task which they adopted, the revision
of the hymn texts was a tragic mistake. All that the Barberini pope
really succeeded in doing was to impose a seventeenth-century
view of Latin poetical construction on subsequent generations of
Roman Catholics.[7]

Can anyone seriously maintain that the body of Latin hymn texts possessed
by the Church needed to be rewritten in a classicizing manner? I mean,
was there a principle within Christendom that dictated that ancient pagan
Roman verse should be asserted as normative? Or was this the hobby-horse
of a particular pope who abused his papal authority to promote his personal poetic preferences? Our answer may be found in the fact that, citing
the privilege of exemption, the Benedictines, Cistercians, Carthusians, and
Dominicans refused to change their hymn texts when Pope Urban enforced
them on the rest of the Church, and about 350 years later, when new Latin
hymn texts were published by the Vatican, the original texts were restored
(unfortunately, by that time almost no one was using Latin anymore, so it

---

[7]   Vincent Lenti, "Urban VIII and the Revision of the Latin Hymnal," *Sacred Music* 120.3
(Fall 1993): 30–33.

was an example of redress that took too long and came too late). To this day, traditional clergy and religious who use the Breviary of Pius X are shackled with Pope Urban's neo-pagan hymnody—yet another incentive to become a Benedictine oblate in order to pray the monastic office!

We could say something similar about the utterly failed "Bea psalter" (named after Cardinal Augustin Bea, SJ), a new and supposedly more "elegant" Latin version of the psalms that Pius XII introduced with the intention of displacing the age-old translation by Saint Jerome that had been prayed by innumerable monks, nuns, and clerics. Critics said: "adauget latinitatem, minuit pietatem" (it increases Latinity but diminishes piety).[8] It seems to me that no one will ever look back at history and say "Urban VIII's imposition of classicized hymns and Pius XII's introduction of a classicized psalter were changes prompted, nay, demanded, by the inner nature of Catholic worship, and better expressed it."

In chapter 2, I formulated five laws of "organic liturgical development": (1) there is true development in regard to liturgical rites; (2) authentic development begins from and remains faithful to what the Lord entrusted to the Apostles; (3) the "truth" into which the Holy Spirit guides the Church includes the development of her liturgy; (4) as the liturgy develops, it becomes fuller and more perfect; (5) to the extent that a liturgy is perfected, its changes will be proportionately incidental or accidental. The fourth law has three corollaries: (i) the rate of liturgical change decreases over time, as the rite achieves the plenitude intended for it by Divine Providence; (ii) one should expect a rite, after a certain point, to be relatively permanent and immobile so that it is a compliment rather than a criticism to say of it that "it has hardly changed for centuries"; (iii) the clergy offering and the faithful assisting at a particular rite can see that it is appropriate for a rite to have the qualities of permanence and immobility.

Earlier I quoted Saint Vincent of Lérins on doctrinal development, and then applied his teaching to the liturgy. Someone might object that doctrine is one kind of thing and liturgy is another; doctrine of its nature

---

[8] On the "Bea psalter," see Yves Chiron, *Annibale Bugnini: Reformer of the Liturgy*, trans. John Pepino (Brooklyn, NY: Angelico Press, 2018), 37–39. Just as John XXIII celebrated the pre-55 Good Friday ceremonies instead of following Pius XII's "Solemn Afternoon Liturgical Action," so too he let the Bea Psalter drop into oblivion.

concerns the truth, which never changes in itself, whereas liturgy concerns practical actions, which can and even should change over time. However, as we must always remind over-eager papal apologists, nothing of any significance in the liturgy can ever be considered "merely disciplinary"; the liturgy always bears doctrinal content or testimony. And therefore changes in liturgy will have doctrinal implications, either for good or for ill, as Michael Davies memorably demonstrated in his work *Cranmer's Godly Order*. The comparison to a growing body holds to the same extent for dogma and for liturgy, a point Newman recognizes in passing:

> It appears then that there has been a certain general type of Christianity in every age, by which it is known at first sight, differing from itself only as what is young differs from what is mature, or as found in Europe or in America, so that it is named at once and without hesitation, as forms of nature are recognized by experts in physical science; or as some work of literature or art is assigned to its right author by the critic, difficult as may be the analysis of that specific impression by which he is enabled to do so. And it appears that this type has remained entire from first to last, in spite of that process of development which seems to be attributed by all parties, for good or bad, *to the doctrines, rites, and usages in which Christianity consists*; or, in other words, that the changes which have taken place in Christianity have not been such as to destroy that type,—that is, that they are not corruptions, because they are consistent with that type.[9]

Given the foregoing, I think we can say why the concluding premise of *SC* 23 ("there must be no innovations unless the good of the Church genuinely and certainly requires them; and care must be taken that any new forms adopted should in some way grow organically from forms already existing"), although well-intentioned or, at any rate, designed to reassure nervous bishops that they were not being asked to vote away Catholic tradition, is thoroughly implausible, considering the larger context. When a

---

[9] John Henry Newman, *Essay on the Development of Christian Doctrine* (London: Longmans, Green, and Co., 1909), ch. 7, p. 323, emphasis added.

council asks for many simultaneous revisions (recall the frequent refrain "a new rite is to be drawn up" for this and that and the other[10]), and then the body entrusted with the realization of the desiderata makes a thousand more changes in the course of just a few years—all on a scale, quantitatively and qualitatively, never seen in any natural process except perhaps for volcanic eruptions and atomic explosions, to which the human analogy would be times of great political upheaval such as the French Revolution (to which indeed Cardinal Suenens compared the Second Vatican Council)— it is perfectly obvious that such an affair could *never* have the appearance of "growing organically from forms already existing"! At that point one has entirely left behind the remotest resemblance to change over time "as if" by a natural process; by no stretch of imagination can the Consilium's work be called "organic," even allowing for the most elastic metaphors. Rather, it looks decidedly violent, which, as Aristotle shows, is the opposite of natural.[11] And that is why Cardinal Joseph Ratzinger could famously write in his foreword to Dom Alcuin Reid's book on our subject:

> Growth is not possible unless the Liturgy's identity is preserved. . . . Proper development is possible only if careful attention is paid to the inner structural logic of this "organism": just as a gardener cares for a living plant as it develops, with due attention to the power of growth and life within the plant and the rules it obeys, so the Church ought to give reverent care to the Liturgy through the ages, distinguishing actions that are helpful and healing from those that are violent and destructive. . . . With respect to the Liturgy, he [the pope] has the task of a gardener, not that of a technician who builds new machines and throws the old ones on the junk-pile.[12]

This quotation suggests that at least one of the reasons people use the term "organic" is to contrast the liturgy with a machine—the contrast between something alive that follows its own internal principles and something we build solely by our own lights and are very willing to throw on the junk pile

---

[10]   See *SC* 13, 21, 58, 68, 69 (twice), 71, 80, 89, 98, 101.

[11]   Aristotle, *Physics*, Bk. 4, ch. 8; Bk. 5, ch. 6; Bk. 8, ch. 4.

[12]   Dom Alcuin Reid, *The Organic Development of the Liturgy*, 2nd ed. (San Francisco: Ignatius Press, 2005), 9, 11.

when we come up with the next model. For indeed the liturgy is a living reality, not because it itself is an organism, but because it has the living God for its author and animator, and makes Him present to us and unites us with Him in praise and in sacrament.

The liturgy is also living because it bears within itself content that was caused by the living God at every stage of the Church's life across time. From that point of view and in that specific sense, the "reformed" liturgy after Vatican II, which repudiates so much of that history, cannot be said to be alive or to have the living God as its author. It has God for its author in the general sense in which any being—such as the bullet of a criminal and its flight through the air to the heart of an innocent victim—has God for its author; it also has God for author in the validity of the sacramental action narrowly construed.

The parallel here with doctrine is evident: we can speak of "the living Magisterium" in the sense of the teaching authority that is one and the same, consistent with itself across all ages because it emanates from the ever-living Christ. But we cannot speak of a "living Magisterium" in the sense of a "Magisterium of the moment," ever changing to reflect the whims of the chair's current incumbent.

The elephant in the room here is, without a doubt, the centralization of authority in the hands of the pope and of the Vatican. Popes have always made contributions to the liturgy, but the history of the subject shows that, until the Tridentine period, Rome was perhaps as often reacting to changes elsewhere as it was inducing change itself (e.g., we know that Rome received back its own rite enriched by its sojourn among the Carolingians, and that Rome added a Creed rather late, after everyone else had done so)—and most of all, the popes were just not in the habit of changing things on a regular basis, and certainly not "for the good of everyone," with that arrogant populist attitude that dictates what the people need best, whether they know it or not.

The simple fact that, for most of the Church's history, liturgical books had to be laboriously copied by hand and were therefore rare and valuable, together with the slowness of communication, meant that local custom would be tenacious. A new liturgical custom had to fight for its turf; if it was found appealing within the customary piety of the community, it was then neatly inked into the margin or in between lines of an altar missal that might be several centuries old. The combined invention of the printing press and the massive reassertion of sovereign papal authority during the Protestant Revolt opened the way to a tinkeritis that only grew worse with the passage of time, like an itch that worsens when scratched.

After the problems that come with centralization, the second major issue that people overlook is the pope's boundedness to tradition, meaning, the moral obligation he has, in virtue of his office, to receive and preserve the inherited rites—with or without printing presses at his disposal. I have spoken about this at length elsewhere, so I will not dilate upon it here.[13]

Liturgical history is not primarily people cooking up new ideas, trying them out, and responding to whether they succeed or fail. Liturgical history, especially as time goes on, is much more about retaining and handing down what is already there, accumulating over time. It would be *wrong* and arguably illicit for a pope to, for example, abolish the subdiaconate or create female "ministries." New things are added somewhat in the manner of ornaments to a great big Christmas tree—a tree that abides. What happened in Paul VI's reform was more like planting a new tree that looks a bit like the old tree and then building a wall to keep people away from the old tree.

Indeed, it's worth pointing out that the image that comes most readily to mind for organic growth in the liturgy is that of a tree. Unlike animals that grow quickly and die after a few years, trees can live for hundreds and even thousands of years. They grow far more slowly than animals—so much so that their major growth is imperceptible in the short term. Although they put out more and more branches and leaves and fruits, they remain rooted in one place.

Every analogy limps, and the comparison of the liturgy to a tree limps too, but there are some striking parallels. The liturgy is rooted in divine revelation and apostolic tradition. It remains itself while it gets larger and bigger. Like the mustard seed, its beginning is modest, but its final, fully perfected

---

[13] See Peter Kwasniewski, "The Pope's Boundedness to Tradition as a Legislative Limit," in Kwasniewski, ed., *From Benedict's Peace to Francis's War: Catholics Respond to the Motu Proprio* Traditionis Custodes *on the Latin Mass* (Brooklyn, NY: Angelico Press, 2021), 222–47.

form is massive and grand, with the lush foliage of the riches of culture as we
see them in the great cathedrals, the baldachins and choir stalls, the gold and
silver vessels, the ornate vestments, the chant and polyphony, and so on and
so forth. The same as ever, and yet more itself than ever. We can see, once
again, why the modern liturgical reform could never be called organic: it
moves in the opposite direction (well, it claims to wish to do so, though it is
highly inconsistent in its pursuit of paleo-Christian authenticity). As Hugh
Ross Williamson memorably put it: "The return to the 'primitive' is based
on the curious theory of history, sometimes referred to as 'Hunt the Acorn.'
That is to say, when you see a mighty oak you do not joy in its strength and
luxuriant development. You start to search for an acorn compatible with
that from which it grew and say: 'This is what it ought to be like.'"[14]

Yet that is the opposite of the truth: as Jean Borella says, "The most objective truth of the seed is the tree into which it will transform itself."[15] That is
because it belongs to the essence of a thing capable of change from within
to aim for its goal or purpose (*telos*)—namely, that in which it achieves
perfection and finds rest. The end or final cause is the "cause of causes": it
is the reason something begins to move, the reason it has its peculiar form
and matter. That is why the seed, as potent as it is, is called imperfect, while
the tree is perfect: the former is inherently ordered to the latter, as potency
to act, as promise to fulfillment.

For all these reasons, I am convinced that the language of organic and
inorganic retains its value as long as we recognize it to be metaphorical and
not metaphysical—descriptive of patterns (as are sociological or economic
laws) and not deterministic (as are scientific laws).

The claim that the liturgical reform under Paul VI was "Protestant" or
"Protestantizing" is one that is both frequently made by its critics and
strenuously resisted by its defenders. To some traditionalists, it is enough to

---

[14] Cited in Joseph Pearce, *Literary Converts: Spiritual Inspiration in an Age of Unbelief* (San
Francisco: Ignatius Press, 2000), 353.
[15] Jean Borella, *Love and Truth: The Christian Path of Charity*, trans. G. John Champoux
(Brooklyn, NY: Angelico Press, 2020), 71.

point to the presence of Protestant observers at the Consilium; others find support in the striking admission of the pope's close friend Jean Guitton, a well-respected philosopher, who stated in a live conversation:

> First of all, Paul VI's Mass is presented as a banquet, and empha-
> sizes much more the participatory aspect of a banquet and much
> less the notion of sacrifice, of a ritual sacrifice before God with the
> priest showing only his back. So, I don't think I'm mistaken in
> saying that the intention of Paul VI and the new liturgy that bears
> his name is to ask of the faithful a greater participation at Mass;
> it is to make more room for Scripture, and less room for all that
> is, some would say magical, others, transubstantial consecration,
> which is the Catholic faith. In other words, there was with Paul VI
> an ecumenical intention to remove, or at least to correct or to relax
> what was too Catholic, in the traditional sense, in the Mass, and,
> I repeat, to bring the Catholic Mass closer to the Calvinist Mass.[16]

Yet it seems that the Protestant observers at the Consilium played a fairly minor role, participating more actively only during discussions of the expanded lectionary,[17] and, in scrupulous fairness, one should not unquestioningly accept a man's interpretation of his friend's motives.

Nevertheless, it is impossible to deny the basic agreement of historical vision between the modern liturgical reformers and the Protestant Reformers. Both regarded the post-Constantinian history of the Catholic Church as one of progressive darkening and pagan relapsation, a deviation from the pure, simple, authentic springtime of the early Christians who met in homes to "break bread" and remember Jesus, the wonder-working carpenter from Nazareth. This deviation, according to such reformers, reached its nadir in the Middle Ages, which then transmitted a superstitious cult

---

[16] Yves Chiron, with François-Georges Dreyfus and Jean Guitton, "Entretien sur Paul VI" (Niherne: Éditions Nivoit, 2011), 27–28, provided by Kabel in "Catholic fact check: Jean Guitton, Pope Paul VI, and the liturgical reforms." Translation mine. Just how close a friend Paul VI considered Guitton may be inferred from the fact that the former asked the latter to suggest ideas for his inaugural encyclical and, a couple of years later, asked him (along with Jacques Maritain) to draft the various "messages" that the pope would deliver at the end of the Second Vatican Council. See Yves Chiron, *Paul VI: The Divided Pope*, trans. James Walther (Brooklyn, NY: Angelico Press, 2022), ch. 7.

[17] See Chiron, *Bugnini*, 162–65.

to succeeding centuries, embellished along the way by the courtliness of the Baroque, until the clericalist dumb-show known as the Tridentine Mass achieved maximum rigidity. The fiery breath of the Pentecostal spirit melted this paradigm and replaced it with forms of worship more in tune with the living faith of Christians: first in the Reformation, then, much later, in the period of Vatican II and the sweeping reforms it ushered in.

There is practically no mainstream book on liturgy from about 1965 to about 1985 that does not express something like this viewpoint, with varying degrees of mockery for the past and of confidence for the future of vernacular, accessible, lay-inclusive worship. It simply becomes the unquestioned summary of where the Church has been and where she is going.

Now, this is a Protestant account if ever there was one. A friend pointed out to me the following passage from a popular Protestant homeschooling textbook, *World History and Cultures in Christian Perspective*, published by Abeka:

> The pagans who flooded the imperial church [after the Edict of Milan] inundated it with heathen beliefs, practices, and traditions. Public worship was described by Justin Martyr in the second century as a simple meeting of believers on the Lord's Day to hear the Scriptures read and explained along with the singing of hymns, the offering of prayers, the celebrating of the Lord's Supper, and the receiving of gifts.
>
> The influence of paganism began to change the worship service into elaborate rites and ceremonies with all the trappings of heathen temple worship. The presbyters now became *sacerdotes* who offered up the Lord's body and blood as a sacrifice for the living and dead. Little by little, these errors and distortions grew and developed into the false teachings and practices of the medieval church. . . . Some devout followers even purchased and worshipped relics. . . .
>
> The demands of their religion led the people to regard Christ as a stern and merciless Judge rather than a compassionate and loving Savior. They sought to placate the Son's wrath against their sins by praying to His mother, the Virgin Mary, and seeking her intercession. Because even Mary sometimes seemed unapproachable, they also prayed to the long-departed apostles and other saints (deceased Christians officially recognized by the Church as holy because of martyrdom, miracles, or

other merits). But the Bible clearly teaches that there is only one mediator between God and man, Jesus Christ (1 Tim 2:5).

We may wince and groan at this caricature of ancient Catholicism, but it is sobering to discover tempered versions of it in Liturgical Movement authors writing in the twentieth century, paving the way for *Sacrosanctum Concilium* and the Pauline reform. In their different ways, Cardinal Ottaviani and Cardinal Bacci over fifty years ago in their *Short Critical Study*, and Cardinal Ratzinger in his lecture at the Fontgombault conference of July 2001, recognized this Protestantization of Catholic liturgical thinking. Ratzinger noted that almost no academic theologian in Europe defends anymore the notion of the Mass as a true and proper sacrifice; even Catholics have come around to agreeing with Martin Luther.[18]

It is therefore no exaggeration to say that the postconciliar liturgical reform rests on a Protestant understanding of Church history and liturgy. To accept it is to accept, to a greater or lesser extent, its foundation in the textbook Protestant vision of Catholicism as a history of obscurantism, mystification, ritualistic clericalism, and systematic exclusion from the liberties of the Gospel—in a word, a history of corruption. And the way out of this corruption is always presented as "returning to a simpler, more ancient form, like the early Christians had." Dom Prosper Guéranger writes:

> All sectarians without exception begin by claiming the rights of antiquity. They wish to free Christianity of all that has sunk into falsehood and has become unworthy of God because of man's error and passions. They only wish for the primordial and they assert the claim that they are returning back to the cradle of Christian institutions. To this end they shorten, obliterate, and cut away. Everything falls under their blows; whoever expectantly wishes to see before his eyes divine worship in its original purity finds himself besieged with new formulas which are but a day old and indisputably penned by men, as their authors are still living.[19]

---

[18] Joseph Ratzinger, "Theology of the Liturgy," in *Theology of the Liturgy: The Sacramental Foundation of Christian Existence* (*Collected Works of Joseph Ratzinger*, vol. 11), ed. Michael J. Miller (San Francisco: Ignatius Press, 2014), 11:542–49.

[19] *Institutions liturgiques* I (Paris [i.a.]: Société générale de librairie catholique, 1878), 399,

Guéranger nicely identifies the irony that those who claim to be reviving a pristine liturgy are, in fact, creating a new liturgy that never really existed and certainly has little enough to do with the actual history of the Church at prayer. It is, in that sense, a pure novelty that loses all the benefits of ageless and anonymous antiquity!

Could we say that a recurrent problem within Protestantism (admittedly, I paint here with a broad brush) is that it does not place a positive value on the working of the Holy Spirit in history, over the course of time? There seems to be no inherent weight to the witness of time, the sum total of the contingent, the course of development. Anything good about time or history is purely coincidental or extraneous. For example, in a certain year, say, 1780 or 1843 or 1921, there may be a camp revival somewhere, and that's great as far as it goes, but it has nothing to do with the Christian religion as such. For Protestants, all dynamism takes place at the level of the individual man, inside the heart, where the Spirit moves; there is no relationship between the Spirit and a visible Church as a temporal/transtemporal whole. History is, in that sense, irrelevant, except perhaps as an empty space within which conversions or charisms can happen, causally linked (if at all) by the conjunction of a preacher and his audience.

The Catholic, on the other hand, sees the Faith as an historical, social, visible, incarnate reality, living a life that develops and unfolds, and that retains its earlier phases within itself while it grows beyond them. This is why the view John Henry Newman arrived at in his *Essay on the Development of Christian Doctrine* is so profoundly un-Protestant:

> The following Essay is directed towards a solution of the difficulty which has been stated,—the difficulty, as far as it exists, which lies in the way of our using in controversy the testimony of our most natural informant concerning the doctrine and worship of Christianity, viz. the history of eighteen hundred years. The view on which it is written has at all times, perhaps, been implicitly adopted by theologians, and, I believe, has recently been illustrated by several distinguished writers of the continent, such as De Maistre and Möhler: viz. that the increase and expansion of the Christian Creed and

quoted in Michael Fiedrowicz, *The Traditional Mass: History, Form, and Theology of the Classical Roman Rite*, trans. Rose Pfeifer (Brooklyn, NY: Angelico Press, 2020), 211.

Ritual, and the variations which have attended the process in the case of individual writers and Churches, are the necessary attendants on any philosophy or polity which takes possession of the intellect and heart, and has had any wide or extended dominion; that, from the nature of the human mind, time is necessary for the full comprehension and perfection of great ideas; and that the highest and most wonderful truths, though communicated to the world once for all by inspired teachers, could not be comprehended all at once by the recipients, but, as being received and transmitted by minds not inspired and through media which were human, have required only the longer time and deeper thought for their full elucidation.[20]

In fairness, we may assume that many or most of the Catholics involved in the liturgical reform would have said they agreed with Newman and not with a purely Protestant view, but it can escape no one's notice that their attitude is at best *semi-Protestant*, in the sense that they think and act on the basis of a profound skepticism about most of the history of the Church, from the middle of the first millennium to the end of the second millennium—the period from which they felt free to discard whatever features they deemed "corrupt" or "redundant" or "obscure" or "outmoded." For example, a progressivist writer at *PrayTell* who compares liturgy to a window through which we can glimpse God then goes on to say: "Of course, the window itself is neither irrelevant nor unimportant. A dirty or foggy window will distort or obscure the view. The reform of the liturgy promoted by the Second Vatican Council was intended to clean the windows after centuries of grime."[21]

In other words, their conception of faith is *not* the incarnational and pneumatological confidence in the unfolding of tradition that Catholics have always held, but, like Protestants looking for the stirring up of the heart in the revival tent meeting, they bring to bear a set of subjective criteria based on what they deem "effective" or "relevant." In this way, they have a basic stance of skepticism toward tradition that is incompatible with Catholicism. A passage from Vladimir Soloviev is remarkably pertinent:

---

[20] Newman, *Essay*, Introduction, §21 (p. 29).
[21] Elizabeth Harrington, "Liturgy Lines: Liturgy is a Window," *PrayTell*, April 17, 2018.

How unreasonable is he who, seeing in the seed neither trunk nor branches, neither leaves nor flowers, and hence concluding that all the other parts are only applied later and artificially from the outside, and that the seed has not the force to issue forth these parts, totally denies that the tree will appear in the future, admitting only the existence of the single seed. Just as unreasonable is the person who denies the most complex forms or manifestations in which divine grace appears in the Church and wants absolutely to return to the form of the early Christian community.[22]

It is only apparently paradoxical that antiquarianism and modernism go hand-in-hand. Cardinal Newman perceived this connection when he claimed that dogmatic Protestantism, which took as its justification the proclamation of the "original uncorrupted" Gospel, has a tendency, due to hermeneutical subjectivism, to degenerate into liberal Protestantism, which in turn tends to degenerate into ethical rationalism, agnostic naturalism, and atheistic secularism. In short, Protestantism has a way of self-destructing. Once one starts down this path, one will reach the end of it, unless one is fortunately inconsistent or rescued by divine intervention. Hence, if the liturgical reform adopted the same mental framework toward historical and traditional Catholicism that dogmatic Protestantism did in the sixteenth century, it is only a matter of time before this newer version of Catholicism will enter its liberal mid-life and move on from there to ethical, agnostic, and atheistic decrepitude.

In fact, a good case can be made that, like a time-lapse film of a tree losing its foliage in the fall, the Church (in the main) has already passed through the second phase and is well advanced in the final one. When a pope prioritizes environmental ethics, gives interviews to atheist-communist journalists, and eviscerates Scripture of its supernatural sense, we are already looking at the frightening prospect of a Church of Latter-day Socinians.[23] It took our separated brethren centuries to separate themselves from Christ as God, from

---

[22] Quoted in Cardinal Charles Journet, *The Theology of the Church*, trans. Victor Szczurek (San Francisco: Ignatius Press, 2004), 145.

[23] Born out of the chaos of the Protestant Revolt and named after Lelio and Fausto Sozzini (in Latin the last name is Socinus), Socinianism was a sixteenth-century heresy that denied the Trinity and, accordingly, the divinity of Christ, and can be seen as one of the historical roots of Unitarianism.

God as real, and, at last, from man as man. Catholics after Vatican II, goaded perhaps by an inferiority complex, have done it in a matter of decades.

The Modernists against whom Popes Pius X and Pius XII battled had, of course, their own version of the "corruption claim." For them, however, it was not the inadequacy of the medieval church but the inadequacy of premodern Christianity *as a whole*, from the death of the last Apostle to the advent of the first paleontologist, that compelled a fundamental shift in understanding and practice. In response to a defrocked priest whom he calls "Fr. G.," Teilhard de Chardin wrote on October 4, 1950: "Basically I consider—as you do—that the Church (like any living reality after a certain time) reaches a period of 'mutation' or 'necessary reformation' after two thousand years; it is unavoidable. Mankind is undergoing a mutation, how could Catholicism not do the same?"[24]

This mutation of Catholicism from its dogmatic-liturgical essence to a loosely-defined moral therapeutic deism in symbolic pantomime has happened, is happening, and will continue to happen for as long as the Protestant distrust of incarnational ecclesiology and the Modernist skepticism of divine revelation and apostolic tradition continue to exercise their sway in the Vatican, the academies, the chanceries—and upon the altars of our parishes.

There is, however, a solution for the Church of the Latin Rite, a solution as obvious as it is demanding: to leave behind the *faux ancien*, crypto-Protestant, congenitally modern[25] papal rite of Paul VI and to return confidently, totally, and exclusively to the Tridentine liturgy—rich fruit of a continuous, organic, millenium-striding, providential, and Pentecostal development.

---

[24] For this and other quotations, see my article "Teilhard de Chardin: Model of Ambiguity for a Future Pope," *OnePeterFive*, January 16, 2019.

[25] These three adjectives are not groundless besmirching but simply what the architects of the Novus Ordo said and what its defenders today repeat: that this rite, stripped of its medieval and Baroque clutter, is more like early Church worship (e.g., Saint Justin Martyr's *First Apology*), which is just what the Protestant reformers claimed for *their* revised rites, and, moreover, in a curious coincidence, that the reform more perfectly meets the mentality of modern Western people, which is surprising considering how far removed that mentality is from the liturgical asceticism and mysticism of the Fathers. For examples of such claims on behalf of the Novus Ordo, see Anthony Cekada, *Work of Human Hands: A Theological Critique of the Mass of Paul VI* (West Chester, OH: Philothea Press, 2010), 13–47; Michael Davies, *Pope Paul's New Mass* (Kansas City, MO: Angelus Press, 2009), 71–145; Kwasniewski, *Reclaiming Our Roman Catholic Birthright*, 149–79.

The Canon is, through its origin, antiquity, and use, venerable and inviolable and sacred. If ever a prayer of the Church came into existence under the special inspiration of the Holy Ghost, it is assuredly the prayer of the Canon.

—Fr. Nicholas Gihr

I regard the Roman Canon as part of the complex of traditions which characterized the life of the Church as it emerged from the centuries of persecution: a shared rule of faith in the creeds, a shared rule of what constituted Scripture, a shared rule of holy order, and a shared rule of prayer. I do not believe that any part of the Church in later centuries has any authority to alter these canons.

—Michael Moreton

The first characteristic of the anti-liturgical heresy is hatred of tradition as found in the formulas used in divine worship. One cannot fail to note this special characteristic in all heretics, from Vigilantius to Calvin, and the reason for it is easy to explain. Every sectarian who wishes to introduce a new doctrine finds himself, unfailingly, face to face with the Liturgy, which is Tradition at its strongest and best, and he cannot rest until he has silenced this voice, until he has torn up these pages which recall the faith of past centuries. As a matter of fact, how could Lutheranism, Calvinism, Anglicanism establish themselves and maintain their influence over the masses? All they had to do was substitute new books and new formulas in place of the ancient books and formulas, and their work was done.

—Dom Prosper Guéranger

8

The Roman Canon:
Pillar and Ground
of the Roman Rite

O f all the prayers with which the Latin-rite Church offers the sacrifice
of praise to Almighty God, the one that stands out the most as a
touchstone of divine faith, a foundation of immovable rock, a treasure of
ages, is the Roman Canon—the unique anaphora or Eucharistic prayer of
the Roman Church (and eventually of the Western patriarchate in general), from the misty centuries before Saint Gregory the Great (d. 604)
until the fateful end of the 1960s. Fr. Guy Nicholls writes of this remarkable Canon:

> There are very few human phenomena or institutions with a his-
> tory stretching back something approaching two thousand years,
> that have not changed constantly, or at least frequently during
> most of that time. The Catholic Church, viewed within the
> dimension of history, is such an institution. She has changed in
> many ways, and frequently throughout the long course of her life.
> But within the human life of the Church is a divine heart. It is
> this heart which does not change, and the human aspect wishes
> to make that changelessness its own. The heart of the Church,
> her *fons et culmen*, is the Sacred Liturgy, in which *terrenis caelestia,*
> *humana divinis iunguntur* [earthly things are joined to heavenly,
> and human to divine]. There is, therefore, a deep instinct in the
> human members of the Church to find in the Sacred Liturgy the

signs of that heavenly worship to which she aspires on earth, and in which she shares this *pignus futurae gloriae* [pledge of future glory]. Therefore, in the natural order of things, one would expect to find at the most sacred centre of the most holy meeting-place between Almighty God and redeemed man, a still point in a moving world. The Roman Canon of the Mass has exercised this symbolic role of stillness for virtually fifteen hundred years. This is a remarkable fact when you bear in mind that it is at the heart of something done, something acted many times a day in different circumstances throughout the world. It is not like a megalith, or a pyramid, which remains virtually unchanged by virtue of being an artefact. The liturgy of the Mass, and especially the Roman Canon, ought, humanly speaking, to change as human speech changes, sometimes quickly, sometimes imperceptibly, but always inexorably, from one generation to the next.[1]

The Roman Canon was, and was always seen as, an apostolic heritage to be lovingly received, jealously guarded, and diligently handed on. We may imagine it as a kind of sacred "baton" passed from one generation to the next, to insure the continuity of the race we are running in the footsteps of the Apostles Peter and Paul, as we strive to attain the heavenly prize.

This was a baton with which the Protestant heretics wanted to have nothing to do. For them, the Roman Canon was the embodiment of all that was superstitious, corrupt, works-oriented, regressively pagan, popish, and medieval. Well aware of this contemptuous (and, one might add, historically and theologically untenable) attitude, the Council of Trent took special pains to praise the Roman Canon, in words quoted earlier but well worth quoting again:

> Since it is fitting that holy things be administered in a holy manner, and of all things this sacrifice is the most holy, the Catholic Church, to the end that it might be worthily and reverently offered

---

[1]   Guy Nicholls, "The History of the Prayers of the Roman Canon," in *Theological and Historical Aspects of the Roman Missal*, Proceedings of the Fifth International Colloquium of Historical, Canonical, and Theological Studies on the Roman Catholic Liturgy (Kingston & Surbiton: CIEL UK, 2000), 29–52; here, 29–30.

and received, instituted many centuries ago the holy canon, which
is so free from error that it contains nothing that does not in the
highest degree savor of a certain holiness and piety and raise up to
God the minds of those who offer. For it consists partly of the very
words of the Lord, partly of the traditions of the Apostles, and also
of pious regulations of holy pontiffs.[2]

In short, the Roman Canon is a monument and repository of all that is
truest, holiest, most ancient, and most efficacious in the Church founded
by Christ. It may with good reason be called the "pillar and ground" of
the Roman rite. A pillar can be a symbol of doctrine, since a pillar stands
tall in supporting the vaults above it and points heavenward to the permanent truths of our Faith, while the ground can serve as an image of sound
morals, on which the Christian life rests and without which it is so much
hot air.

This chapter, then, will have two parts. The first and more substantial
part focuses on twelve dogmatic truths transmitted by the Roman Canon—
truths either totally absent from the neo-anaphoras of the Missal of Paul VI
or significantly muted in them.[3] This will demonstrate the extent to which
the Canon is indeed a pillar of doctrine. The second part will consider some
moral implications of having shifted the ground of Catholic worship by
optionalizing the Roman Canon into a state of near oblivion.

I. Dogmatic Truths

For each of the twelve dogmatic truths, I will state the truth in question,
quote the pertinent passage in the Canon, and then offer my commentary.

---

[2]   Council of Trent, Session 22, ch. 4.
[3]   Unique elements beyond these twelve could be adduced. Any one of the sections that follow
could be expanded into a full treatment of its theme as we find it throughout the *usus antiquior*
liturgical books and as we *fail* to find it in like manner in those of the *usus recentior*. Translations of the Roman Canon are taken from the *Campion Missal* and the *Baronius Missal*.

1. The Church's unity and other perfections are gifts we pray to receive from God.

Te igitur, clementissime Pater, per Iesum Christum, Filium tuum, Dominum nostrum, supplices rogamus ac petimus: uti accepta habeas, et benedicas hæc ✠ dona, hæc ✠ munera, hæc sancta ✠ sacrificia illibata: in primis quæ tibi offerimus pro Ecclesia tua sancta catholica; quam pacificare, custodire, adunare, et regere digneris toto orbe terrarum . . .

[We therefore humbly pray and beseech Thee, most merciful Father, through Jesus Christ Thy Son, Our Lord, to receive and to bless these gifts, these presents, these holy unspotted sacrifices, which we offer up to Thee, in the first place, for Thy holy Catholic Church, that it may please Thee to grant her peace, to guard, unite, and guide her, throughout the world . . .]

The very opening of the Canon combines profound humility with earnest pleading that the Father would receive this most solemn offering of the Church and would make it, by His almighty paternal command, the unspotted *sacrifices* of Christ. (Note the plural, a sign of this prayer's great antiquity, for the early Christians when referring to the Mass spoke of "the mysteries," "the sacrifices," and "the sacraments"—the latter usage reappearing in the ablution prayers—whereas later authors tend to speak of the mystery, the sacrifice, and the sacrament.)

The Roman Canon prioritizes the purpose of the offering by stating at the outset that it is being made *by* the Mystical Body *for* the Mystical Body, and not in a vague way, but with respect to its hierarchical structure—something lacking in the newly-fashioned anaphoras that hold off on the ecclesial purpose of the offering until after the consecration. Indeed, the pseudo-scholarly critics of the Roman Canon in the middle of the twentieth century complained that it began with the Church and her structure rather than starting with something "more theological" like the Trinity, or "grander" like the plan of salvation, or "historically germane," like the Last Supper. These criticisms show scant regard for the centrality of the Church as the very Body that is offering and is offered, in union with her

Head and Lord, Jesus Christ, who became man in order to pour forth the Church from His wounded side; scant regard for the Church as the locus in which the mystery of the Trinity is revealed and glorified; scant regard for the Church as the underlying principle of continuity in salvation history, as Saint Augustine demonstrated in *The City of God*. More prosaically, the Canon reflects both Greek philosophical wisdom, which says that the final cause or purpose is the "cause of causes" (that is, the cause that explains all the other causes) and Patristic theology, which always emphasizes the ecclesial setting of the liturgy. This is the sacrifice *of* the Church, *for* the Church, always in union with its Head, Our Lord Jesus Christ, who is at once high priest, victim, and altar.

The Roman Canon speaks of "Thy holy Catholic Church," the one and only Bride of the Lord; and yet the priest pleads with the Father to *unite* her, to *guard* and *guide* her, and to *grant* her peace. Surely, one would have thought such petitions unnecessary. Is she not already indestructibly one? Is she not perpetually guarded from harm and guided safely by Divine Providence? Could He ever abandon her? These are serious questions to ask at a time like ours, when the unity of the Church on earth appears more shattered than ever, when harm to the People of God is widespread and obvious, and when the captaining of Peter's barque seems scarcely better than that of the *Exxon Valdez*, with similar catastrophic results impending.

The Canon transmits here a sobering doctrine. It is not to be "taken for granted" that the Church will be well-governed on earth; that she will follow peacefully in the right path; that she will remain safe from the evils of ignorance, error, and sin; even that she will remain in visible unity. Saying that "the Church is indefectible" does not mean that *your* soul, *your* local church, or *your* regional anything is indefectible. Your soul and mine can be lost forever; your local church and mine can be swallowed up by Muslims, militant atheists, homosexual activists, or crippling civil action; your episcopal conference can fall off the cliff into open heresy. All this is well within the realm of possibility, just as branches can be lopped off of trees without the tree itself dying. The Canon says to us that peace, protection, unity, and wise governance are goods to be *impetrated*, petitioned and obtained from the Lord in His mercy, and by means of the Cross—not only by the Sacrifice of the Cross objectively re-presented in the Mass, but also by taking this Cross upon ourselves in our prayer, penance, conversion, and fidelity.[4]

All of these goods are gifts from God, who may, in His wisdom and justice, deprive the Church on earth of the enjoyment of these goods if the faithful or their rulers should be so unfortunate as to be lukewarm in performing the *opus Dei*,[5] or worldly in their attitudes, or cowardly in their preaching. The Church will always have real existence in this world until the end of time, but she may disappear from my life or yours, in my country or yours, in my national hierarchy or yours. Think of the bishops under Henry VIII who fell like bowling pins before his threats. In a matter of years, the hierarchy had essentially vanished.

As with ancient Christianity in general, so here in this Anaphora, there is an utter absence of presumption. The members of the Church on earth do not presume that they are already the perfect, spotless Bride of Christ; rather, they beg to have those qualities. (The same sort of prayer recurs in the "Domine, Jesu Christe" after the Agnus Dei: "Look not upon my sins, but upon the faith of Thy Church, and vouchsafe to grant her peace and unity according to Thy will.")

2. The Sacrifice is offered for Catholics who hold the true faith, and they are its beneficiaries.

... una cum famulo tuo Papa nostro N., et Antistite nostro N., et omnibus orthodoxis, atque catholicæ et apostolicæ fidei cultoribus.

[... in union with Thy servant *N.*, our pope, and *N.*, our bishop, and with all orthodox men: indeed, with those who cultivate (foster, promote, support) the Catholic and apostolic faith.][6]

---

[4]   Similarly, the traditional form of the Preface of the Apostles, which dates back to (at least) the Verona Sacramentary containing material from the fifth and sixth centuries, "humbly begs the Lord not to desert His flock, but that He may keep it through His blessed Apostles under endless protection." The liturgical reformers in the 1960s rewrote the text so that instead of being deprecatory it is merely indicative: "Lord, you do not desert your flock but you keep it under protection . . .": as if it's something that can be taken for granted. The shift of mentality is decisive and revealing. See Fr. John Hunwicke, "The Preface of the Apostles," *Fr Hunwicke's Mutual Enrichment*, January 25, 2022.

[5]   That is, the liturgical worship of God.

[6]   As John Pepino pointed out to me, the *atque* is a strong conjunction that adds something (often a greater specificity) to what came before; it isn't just a synonym for *et*. It's as though the

Continuing the same petition, the priest states that he is offering the sacrifice for the hierarchs of the Church, and, indeed, for all orthodox Catholics—an implicit prayer that we may always be and remain such.

Noteworthy here is the emphasis on doctrinal orthodoxy, which, for the ancient Christians who first prayed this prayer, was *incomparably* the first and most important thing you had to know about someone: Does he adhere to the true faith? Not: Is he a nice person, does he pay his bills and volunteer to coach football and recycle his garbage, but: Does he profess the universal faith that comes to us from the Apostles?[7] Even the question of charity is secondary to this one, since true charity, the infused theological virtue, requires the infused virtue of faith as a foundation. Otherwise it is mere philanthropy, do-goodism, niceness, or pagan virtue, none of which inherits the kingdom of heaven.

Hence the Roman Canon places emphasis on *orthodoxy as the basic condition of Church membership*, instead of the diffuse semi-moral quasi-virtues that are substituted for it today. This part of the Canon teaches that the Holy Sacrifice is offered not vaguely for a universal brotherhood of mankind or an ecumenical alliance but for right-believing Catholics who profess the faith handed down to us. It challenges us to take dogmatic truth as seriously as all the saints have taken it, to be willing to lay down our lives rather than dissent from one jot or tittle of the *depositum fidei*. No sacrifice can be offered for our salvation, and we will not in fact be saved, if we are dissenters, heretics, schismatics, apostates, or infidels.[8]

There is a further implication, one especially pertinent to our times. The Canon is not asserting that the pope and the local bishop *are* orthodox, as if naming them at this moment in the Canon must magically mean they

---

text says that we are in communion with all who hold the correct faith, and moreover, with those who actively promote the correct faith. This could well be an echo of the Arian crisis.

[7]   The Byzantine Divine Liturgy of Saint John Chrysostom expresses exactly the same thing: "Again we pray for the people here present who await Your great and bountiful mercies, for those who have been kind to us, and for all orthodox Christians." And later: "May the Lord God remember you and all orthodox Christians in His Kingdom, now and ever and unto ages of ages." Again: "We implore You, remember, O Lord, every orthodox bishop who rightly teaches the Word of Your truth."

[8]   The omission, in the neo-anaphoras, of any reference to the "orthodox, Catholic, and apostolic" Faith is quite telling: the most basic feature of Modernism is its denial that there even is such a thing as a determinate, time-transcending "orthodox, Catholic, apostolic" Faith.

could never fall away. Rather, we are praying for them *as long as* they are orthodox. That is, we offer the sacrifice "for *all who are orthodox* in belief and who *profess* the Catholic and apostolic faith." In the ancient Church, it was common practice for bishops to strike off the names of other bishops who had fallen away from the Faith into heresy. A bishop who had excommunicated another bishop would drop his name off of the diptychs, as if to say: "We are not praying for you, and we will not pray for you, until you repent and return to orthodoxy." This is the "tough love" practiced by the early Church, the heroic age of martyrs, towering theologians, and desert monks.

I am not sure exactly how bishops today could put into practice this supernatural common sense that regarded public prayer as offered only for the orthodox and not for heretics or schismatics, but it is certainly getting to be the case, more and more, that we can no longer *assume* that when we pray the Roman Canon—be it prayed in the most insignificant or the most powerful diocese—we are praying efficaciously for the man who appears to be occupying the local see. We dare to hope. Of course, until there is an ecclesiastical decision of some sort, such as the judgment of an ecumenical council or even of an imperfect council, God alone would know whether the Mass is able to be offered for the named figures, or whether they are outside of the Church that prays and is benefited in turn by the prayers. Prayer should continue to be made in communion with and on behalf of the recognized incumbent until he dies or unless he has been deposed or replaced.

The reader may be asking himself: What is the spiritual benefit of thinking about these things? The benefit is simply this: we must recognize, with full seriousness and sobriety, that the Church in her public prayer does not *presume* that she will be at peace, united, under good leadership, and heading in the right direction. She *begs* for it. And we must imitate her, we must internalize the same attitude. We are repeatedly and earnestly seeking these goods from the Lord in His mercy, and His answer partly depends on the faith and fervor with which we ask Him for them. We are warned by the Canon that without holding fast to the Catholic and orthodox faith, entire and inviolate, we cannot be saved, nor can our shepherds.

The traditional Litany of Saints contains petitions that confirm the foregoing interpretation: "That thou wouldst deign to rule and preserve Thy holy Church, we beseech thee, hear us . . . That thou wouldst deign to preserve the pope and all the ecclesiastical orders in holy religion. . . That thou wouldst deign to grant peace and unity to all Christian people . . ." The second of these petitions is especially interesting: we are asking God to preserve the pope in the virtue of religion, or in keeping the Catholic faith. There would be no point in asking for this if it were not the kind of thing that could be absent or lost due to men's sins and God's just judgment.

3. Faith and devotion are prerequisites to participating in the Mass.

Memento, Domine, famulorum famularumque tuarum N. et N.: et omnium circumstantium, quorum tibi fides cognita est et nota devotio, pro quibus tibi offerimus: vel qui tibi offerunt hoc sacrificium laudis . . .

[Be mindful, O Lord, of Thy servants, N. and N., and of all here present, whose faith and devotion are known to Thee, for whom we offer, or who offer up to Thee, this sacrifice of praise . . .]

Here the Canon singles out two qualities that *must* be present in anyone who would assist at the Holy Sacrifice without sin—namely, faith and devotion. According to Saint Thomas, the worst sin, simply speaking, is that of infidelity, the refusal to submit one's mind to God's Revelation.[9] Faith is the root of the entire Christian life: "without faith, it is impossible to please God" (Heb 11:6). Note: not that it is "difficult" or "harder" to please God without faith, but *impossible*. Salvation is not within reach of those who do not profess the Christian faith. As the opening line of the Athanasian Creed says: "Whoever wishes to be saved must, before all things, hold fast the Catholic faith. For unless a man keep this faith whole

---

[9] See *ST* II-II, qu. 10, art. 3; although Thomas also argues that, in certain respects, despair, hatred of God, and schism are worse than unbelief (cf. II-II, qu. 20, art. 3; qu. 34, art. 2, ad 2; qu. 39, art. 2, ad 3).

and undefiled, without doubt he shall be lost forever." So the Canon fittingly singles out this virtue in remembering the living, as it will do later in remembering the dead.

Moreover, the Canon mentions "devotion," because, as Saint Thomas explains, no one may worthily offer the Sacrifice of the Mass or receive Holy Communion without *actual devotion.* "Actual" here means a conscious attitude in the moment rather than the mere possibility of it based on a habit. Here is how he explains the point:

> Since this sacrament perfects us by uniting us to the end [of all the sacraments, namely, Christ] . . . in order for it to have its own effect fully in the one who receives it, there must be actual devotion present. And since sometimes actual devotion can be impeded without mortal sin, since various distractions impede it, and venial sins destroy the act of the virtues, this sacrament's effect can be impeded *without* mortal sin, such that someone [going to Communion] *does not receive an increase of grace*; but neither would he have become guilty of mortal sin, but perhaps he would be guilty of venial sin, by the fact that he approaches the sacrament without proper preparation.[10]

Thus, it is at least a venial sin to offer or to receive in a totally distracted frame of mind, out of routine or convention, without explicit faith in the Real Presence accompanied by some act of adoration that wells up from our devotion to the mysteries. The Canon prompts us to think about how the liturgy itself should offer us the means to prepare ourselves properly for approaching so great a sacrament.

4. Mary is perpetually a Virgin, and Christ is true God.

Communicantes, et memoriam venerantes, in primis gloriosæ semper Virginis Mariæ, Genitricis Dei et Domini nostri Iesu Christi . . .

[Having communion with and venerating the memory, first, of the glorious Mary, ever a virgin, mother of Jesus Christ, our God and our Lord . . .]

---

[10] *In IV Sent.*, dist. 12, qu. 2, art. 1, qa. 3.

As befits its ancient provenance, the Canon calls to mind the dogma of the perpetual virginity of Our Lady, *semper Virgo—virgo ante partum, in partu, post partum,* virgin before birth, virgin during birth, virgin after birth—a feature missing from the new Eucharistic Prayers.[11]

However, more important still is the ringing testimony it gives to the divinity of Christ: "Jesus Christ, *our God* and our Lord." While the phrases "Christ our Lord" or "Christ your Son our Lord" are still plentiful in modern prayers, in none of them is this classic anti-Arian expression preserved, a loss that matches the removal from the Novus Ordo of many prayers in the *usus antiquior* that directly address Christ as God.[12] Christ is not just our Redeemer, our Savior, our Teacher, our Brother: He is our *God*—God from God, Light from Light, true God from true God, whom we worship with the adoration of *latria* that is reserved to God alone. As the great *Suscipe, sancta Trinitas* of the old Offertory makes clear (and as the Novus Ordo fails to make clear), the sacrifice of the Eucharist is offered not simply to the Father but to the *Triune God,* inseparably Father, Son, and Holy Ghost. In this way, the venerable Roman rite again coincides with the Byzantine tradition: "It is You who offer and You who are offered; it is You who receive and You who are given, O Christ our God" (prayer spoken during the Cherubic Hymn at the Divine Liturgy of Saint John Chrysostom).

5. We are protected by God owing to the merits of the saints.

. . . et omnium Sanctorum tuorum; quorum meritis precibusque concedas, ut in omnibus protectionis tuæ muniamur auxilio. . . . Intra quorum nos consortium, non estimator meriti, sed veniæ, quæsumus, largitor admitte.

[. . . and of all Thy saints, for the sake of whose merits and prayers do Thou grant that in all things we may be defended by the help of Thy protection. . . . Into their company do Thou, we beseech Thee, admit us, not weighing our merits, but freely pardoning our offenses.]

---

[11] Fortunately still found in the neo-Confiteor.
[12] For a more detailed analysis, see Peter Kwasniewski, *Resurgent in the Midst of Crisis: Sacred Liturgy, the Traditional Latin Mass, and Renewal in the Church* (Kettering, OH: Angelico Press, 2014), 79–93.

All of the approved anaphoras mention the communion and intercession of the saints, but only the Roman Canon specifies that it is their *merits* that obtain for us the Lord's protection. This element counterbalances the element toward the end about "not weighing our merits," with an implied contrast to those of the saints. Apart from a reference in Eucharistic Prayer II ("that . . . we may merit to be co-heirs to eternal life"[13]), the notion of merit is strangely lacking in postconciliar liturgical texts, most likely because it was in the interests of ecumenism to downplay one of the issues on which Catholics and Protestants most strongly disagree.[14]

Worthy of mention in this connection are the two extensive lists of saints in the Roman Canon. Given final form by Saint Gregory the Great, these lists are tightly crafted in their numerology and in their mingling of saints of universal import and saints locally venerated in Rome, as if to accentuate the universality of the *logos* that draws to itself all men who are "intelligent and seeking God" (cf. Ps 13:2) as well as the "scandal of the particular."[15] In the Roman Canon, forty saints beloved to the ancient Church of Rome are recalled and called upon: twenty-five saints before the consecration (a number to which Saint Joseph was added in 1962), and fifteen afterwards. Apart from Our Lady, who stands in a class by herself, and Saint Joseph, the list before the consecration includes two groups of twelve saints each. First, the Apostles: Peter and Paul, Andrew, James, John, Thomas, James,

---

[13] This phrase had been omitted from the original ICEL "translation," which was often no better than a loose paraphrase.

[14] With a *lex orandi* as defective as that, is not Pope Francis's absurd statement that "Catholics and Lutherans agree about justification" more understandable and a lot less likely to be recognized as poison?

[15] See Cardinal Charles Journet, *The Theology of the Church*, trans. Victor Szczurek (San Francisco: Ignatius Press, 2004), 128–29, for the relationship of Incarnation-Eucharist-Papacy. By "scandal of the particular," I mean that we are saved not by abstractions or formulas but by a flesh-and-blood Savior named Jesus of Nazareth, who lived at a certain place and time, and whom we encounter today in highly defined rituals that have been handed down from generation to generation. A lovely example of the "local feeling" we have in the Roman Canon is in the phrase that describes heaven in the memento for the dead: "locum refrigerii, lucis, et pacis," a place of coolness, light, and peace. *Coolness*, because this prayer originated in the hot climate of the Mediterranean, where everyone was seeking relief; indeed, the maniple was first worn as a handkerchief for wiping sweat off the brow. *Light*, because in a pre-industrial world, the most valuable of all things is the daylight by which men can live and work. *Peace*, because the world of the late Roman Empire was volatile, full of warfare and brigandage, and anything but peaceful.

Philip, Bartholomew, Matthew, Simon and Jude; then, the martyrs: Linus, Cletus, Clement, Sixtus, Cornelius, Cyprian, Lawrence, Chrysogonus, John and Paul, Cosmas and Damian. This double list is a deliberate numerological schema: adding 12 and 12 yields 24, the number of elders before the throne of God and the Lamb; multiplying 12 by 12 yields 144, putting us in mind of the 144,000 sealed children of Israel mentioned in the book of Revelation (7:4).[16]

In the second list, following the consecration, John the Baptist is mentioned first and should be taken as the head of this second choir of saints, on account of his unique relationship to the Church in Rome, as patron of the pope's Lateran cathedral. Two groups follow: seven men (Stephen, Matthias, Barnabas, Ignatius, Alexander, Marcellinus, Peter) and seven women (Felicity, Perpetua, Agatha, Lucy, Agnes,[17] Cecilia, Anastasia). Since the number 7, like 12, signifies perfection, fullness, completeness, we are put in mind here of the entire company of saints, male and female. Multiplied, 7 x 7 = 49 reminds us of the totality of the kingdom made holy by the descent of the Holy Spirit at Pentecost (49 + 1, where the *1* points to God, who sanctifies the saints and is magnified in them).

The Canon thus places twice before our eyes the entire communion of saints: those whose feasts we celebrate, those who are mentioned in the Martyrology, and the host whose names are known to God alone. Every time the traditional Mass is offered, forty-six saints are named: the forty-one already mentioned, plus Saint Abel, Saint Abraham, Saint

---

[16] In Scripture, twelve is the number of the tribes of Israel, the fullness of God's people. When the number is squared, its fullness is, so to speak, solidified. Multiplied by a thousand points to the unimaginable vastitude of the citizenry of the heavenly city. The inclusion of Saint Joseph in this list is problematic because it disturbs the harmony (both Mementos have a leader and then two equal groups), and he is the only one in the first list to whom martyrdom is not attributed in some fashion.

[17] Another lovely "irregularity" in the classical Roman rite is the presence of two feasts of Saint Agnes: her primary feast of January 21 and her "second commemoration" on the octave day of January 28, an arrangement unique among the saints. In the 1866 edition of Rev. Alban Butler's *The Lives of the Saints*, we read: "A second commemoration of St. Agnes occurs on this day in the ancient *Sacramentaries* of Pope Gelasius and St. Gregory the Great; as also in the true *Martyrology* of Bede. It was perhaps, the day of her burial, or of a translation of her relics, or of some remarkable favour obtained through her intercession soon after her death." A legend grew, saying that on this day Agnes, surrounded by virgins resplendent with light, appeared to her parents while they were praying at her tomb, which accounts for the choice of the Introit of the Mass, *Vultum tuum.*

Melchizedek, Saint Isaiah, and Saint Michael the Archangel.[18] These saints of the New Testament, the Old Testament, and the angelic order stand in for the vast multitude of every tribe and tongue and people and nation who sing the high praises of God in the kingdom of heaven. The apparent "arbitrariness" of these forty-six saints, when so many others could have been chosen, reinforces one of the fundamental lessons of divine revelation: "I will be gracious to whom I will be gracious, and will show mercy on whom I will show mercy."[19] God calls us by name, He does not redeem us in generalities. The ancient Greeks called a slave *aprosopos*, the one without a face. Jesus Christ, God's human face, restores to us *our* faces, our names, our dignity, in the midst of our brothers and sisters. The neo-anaphoras, in contrast, obliterate these lists of saints—the *pia memoria* of the Church of Rome—and, apart from obligatory mentions of Our Lady and Saint Joseph,[20] reflect industrial modernity's nameless masses by omitting the dignified names of individual persons.

6. God the Father is the Paterfamilias of the Church, His family; the priest is His head servant.

Hanc igitur oblationem servitutis nostræ, sed et cunctæ familiæ tuæ, quæsumus, Domine, ut placatus accipias . . .

[Wherefore, we beseech Thee, O Lord, graciously to receive this oblation which we, Thy servants, and with us Thy whole family, offer up to Thee . . .]

The antiquity and *Romanitas* of the Roman Canon can be seen in many features, of which the *Hanc igitur* is a vivid example. Here, God is the *Paterfamilias*, the one on whose Word hangs the life and death of all

---

[18] One might also say that the saints appealed to in various prayers by reference to their relics in or around the altar are also being invoked directly, albeit not with proper names. For commentary on all of the saints mentioned in the traditional Mass, see Most Rev. Amleto Cicognani, *The Saints Who Pray with Us in the Mass* (Kansas City, MO: Romanitas Press, 2017); Neil J. Roy, "The Roman Canon: *Deësis* in Euchological Form," in *Benedict XVI and the Sacred Liturgy*, ed. Neil J. Roy and Janet E. Rutherford (Dublin: Four Courts Press, 2010), 181–99.

[19] Ex 33:19; cf. Rom 9:15–18.

[20] The addition of the latter is a novelty for which we are beholden to Pope John XXIII.

members of the family. If the Father speaks the word of command, the sacrifice will occur; if He deigns to receive it, it will be efficacious. This is why
the Roman Canon has no *epiclesis*.[21] Predating the Macedonian controversy
over the divinity of the Holy Spirit, it reflects a Patricentric theology in
which the Father's good pleasure with the Son, together with His omnipotence,[22] furnishes a sufficient explanation of why the prayer of the Church
prevails and the Body and Blood of Christ come to be present on the altar.
"For the Roman Canon, Consecration means that we offer bread and wine
to the Omnipotent Father so that he, by accepting them, makes them the
Body and Blood of His Son in accordance with the words uttered by the
Incarnate Word. In Byzantium, the Priest, bidden by the Deacon, invokes
the Holy Ghost to descend upon the elements so that by His Transformation, they may be the Lord's Body and Blood. Each tradition is entitled to
its own integrity."[23]

The Church is comfortingly styled "God's family."[24] The priest asks the
Father to be pleased with *hanc oblationem servitutis nostrae*, literally, this
offering of our servitude—that is, a work done by servants of the household
because they are bidden to carry it out. The priest at the altar, then, is the
master's head servant or steward, an *architriclinus* who acts on His behalf
for the benefit of all the members of the family.[25] The Canon's language

---

[21] See Gregory DiPippo, "Reforming the Canon of the Mass: Some Considerations from Fr
Hunwicke," *NLM*, April 25, 2015; Peter Kwasniewski, "East-West Disagreements about the
Epiclesis and Transubstantiation," *NLM*, May 4, 2020; Brother André Marie, "Some Thoughts
on the *Epiclesis* in the Divine Liturgy," *Catholicism.org*, July 10, 2019. In this respect, I must
note a friendly disagreement with Mosebach's claim that the "Veni Sanctificator" in the Offertory is the *epiclesis* of the Roman Mass; nor is the theory that makes the "Supplices te
rogamus" an esoteric *epiclesis* more convincing.

[22] The divine attribute of omnipotence is given prominence in the Roman Canon. It is mentioned right before the consecration of the host, at the *Supplices te rogamus*, and in the doxology at the end. In the *usus antiquior* as a whole, the words "omnipotent" (which can also be
translated "almighty") or "omnipotence" is used sixteen times on a standard Sunday. In the
modern rite of Paul VI, the number ranges from nine, if the Confiteor *and* the Roman Canon
are used, to as few as six if they are not.

[23] "The Worst Evil of Uniatism?," *Fr Hunwicke's Mutual Enrichment*, June 30, 2019.

[24] This expression is confined to the Roman Canon and to Eucharistic Prayer III. The latter,
however, substitutes for its original Roman context the somewhat sentimental-sounding image of a father asked to "gather . . . all [his] children scattered throughout the world."

[25] As *Watson's Biblical & Theological Dictionary* explains: "αρχιτρικλινος, generally trans-
ated *steward*, signifies rather the master or superintendent of the feast; 'one,' says Gauden-
ius, 'who is the husband's friend, and commissioned to conduct the order and economy

unites hierarchy of authority with family intimacy, the special exalted place of the priest with his status as a servant of the community—companion truths that are often pitted against each other in theory and in practice in the imbalanced ecclesiologies of today, teetering between base-community populism and top-heavy papalism.

7. The default destiny of mankind is hell; the elect are predestined by God to eternal life.

. . . diesque nostros in tua pace disponas, atque ab æterna damnatione nos eripi, et in electorum tuorum iubeas grege numerari.

[. . . dispose our days in Thy peace; command that we be rescued from eternal damnation and numbered among the flock of Thine elect.]

The second part of the *Hanc igitur* enshrines the truth about human salvation taught by the Fathers, Doctors, and premodern popes of the Church, and thereby excludes the universalist mentality of our age, which assumes that all men will be saved—that salvation is the *default* position—unless they conscientiously and egregiously reject God. On the contrary, the consensus of Catholic theologians from ancient times until the early twentieth century was that man, due to his inheritance of original sin, cannot enter into the kingdom of heaven unless he dies and rises with Christ in baptism,[26] and that, accordingly, mankind is a *massa damnata* from whom individuals are rescued by the application to their souls of the fruits of His redemption. Christ came into the world to save sinners from the destruction due to sins, inherited and actual. The sole path to eternal life is to be clothed with Christ,[27] to be incorporated into His Mystical Body, and to die in a state of sanctifying grace. As Scott Hahn says in a lecture on the Gospel of John, "the history of salvation is also the history of damnation":

of the feast.' He gave directions to the servants, superintended everything, commanded the tables to be covered, or to be cleared of the dishes, as he thought proper: whence his name, as regulator of the *triclinium*, or festive board. He also tasted the wine, and distributed it to the guests." From www.studylight.org/dictionaries/wtd/a/architriclinus.html.

[26] Here I include baptism of desire and baptism of blood, as well as sacramental baptism with water. See Saint Thomas, *ST* III, qu. 66, arts. 11–12.

[27] Cf. Rom 13:14, Gal 3:27; cf. Mt 22:12; Acts 4:12.

Christ came into the world for judgment, to cause separation by revealing the truth and exposing darkness.[28] This is why the Roman Martyrology carefully records not only the names of each martyr but the names of their persecutors as well.

Moreover, in utter opposition to Pelagianism, the Church teaches that God, not man, takes the first step in the renewal of our life; that all our sufficiency is from Him (2 Cor 3:5); that no man comes to Jesus unless the Father draws him (Jn 6:44); that we become adopted sons of God by His predestinating purpose (Eph 1:5); that we persevere by His gift, not by our own efforts alone. In short, God must *number* us in the flock of His chosen ones; He knowingly and lovingly *chooses* us to be the "rational sheep" of His flock.[29] He does not, as it were, happen to find us there in the sheepfold and express pleasant surprise; He *brings* us there and *keeps* us there.

All this the Roman Canon succinctly transmits in words as simple as they are sobering, reminding us that the Catholic Church, like her Common Doctor St. Thomas, has always taught and still teaches the doctrine of predestination.[30] The petition from the *Hanc igitur* is a liturgical distillation of the teaching of the Apostle Paul, as found especially in Ephesians and Romans:

> Who hath predestinated us unto the adoption of children through Jesus Christ unto himself: according to the purpose of his will. . . . In whom we also are called by lot, being predestinated according to the purpose of him who worketh all things according to the counsel of his will. (Eph 1:5, 1:11)
>
> For whom he foreknew, he also predestinated to be made conformable to the image of his Son; that he might be the firstborn

---

[28] Cf. Jn 9:39; cf. Jn 3:16–21, 5:24–29; Lk 12:51.

[29] As the Byzantine Akathist hymn says.

[30] See *ST* I, qu. 23, with Réginald Garrigou-Lagrange's commentary *Predestination*. If anyone doubts that the Catholic Church still teaches the doctrine of predestination—obviously not one of the several erroneous Protestant notions of it, but the true notion—he would do well to start with the *Catechism of the Catholic Church* nos. 257, 600, 1007, 2012, 2782, and 2823; n. 600 steers clear of the Dominican-Molinist controversy by merely repeating multiple times the statements of Saint Paul, adding only this gloss: "To God, all moments of time are present in their immediacy. When therefore he established his eternal plan of 'predestination,' he includes in it each person's free response to his grace."

amongst many brethren. And whom he predestinated, them he also called. And whom he called, them he also justified. And whom he justified, them he also glorified. (Rom 8:29–30)[31]

The liturgy bears witness to the Church's faith in a number of places, such as the Sequence of the Mass for the Dead (*Dies Irae*). The Secret for the Twenty-Third Sunday after Pentecost expresses the doctrine of the Church to perfection: "May this sacrifice of praise that we offer to Thee, O Lord, be for an increase of our servitude [i.e., our service to Thee]: that what Thou hast begun without our merits Thou mayest mercifully bring to completion" [*ut, quod immeritis contulisti, propitius exsequaris*]. The Postcommunion for the *usus antiquior* Feast of the Holy Name of Jesus, a relatively recent addition from the sixteenth century (and incorporated into the general calendar in the eighteenth), reads thus: "O almighty and everlasting God Who didst create and redeem us, look graciously upon our prayer, and with a favourable and benign countenance deign to accept the sacrifice of the saving Victim, which we have offered to Thy Majesty in honour of the Name of Thy Son, our Lord Jesus Christ: that through the infusion of Thy grace we may rejoice that our names are written in heaven, under the glorious Name of Jesus, the pledge of eternal predestination."[32]

But why is this doctrine important to us spiritually?

---

[31] It makes little difference that the passages from Ephesians 1 and Romans 8 are contained in the new lectionary (e.g., Wednesday of Week 30 *per annum*, Year I; 17th Sunday *per annum*, Year A; Thursday of Week 28 *per annum*, Year II; Immaculate Conception, 2nd reading), since readings come and go, like birds at a bird-feeder, whereas the danger of damnation and the divine mercy of predestination are woven into the very fabric of the traditional Roman rite. Moreover, most of the prayers that point to predestination in the *usus antiquior* have been either removed or toned down in the *usus recentior* so that it would be much more difficult to establish that the revised liturgy clearly and unambiguously teaches this Scriptural and traditional doctrine.

[32] In yet another display of theological "neutralization," the Novus Ordo—from whose calendar the feast of the Holy Name had initially been purged by Paul VI, no doubt because it was a Baroque accretion, only to be reinstated later under John Paul II as an "optional memorial"—politely trims down this Postcommunion to an acceptable banality: "May the sacrificial gifts offered to your majesty, O Lord, to honor Christ's Name and which we have now received, fill us, we pray, with your abundant grace, so that we may come to rejoice that our names, too, are written in heaven." The doctrine is there, but as if muffled beneath sterile cotton.

In modern times, we are constantly being told how good we are and how well-intentioned, and yet how very much we are the innocent victims of the prejudicial environments that formed us, which (of course) entitles us to coddling compensations. We are reassured of the greatness of man, of his dignity and rights. But we are in sore danger of forgetting fundamental truths about our condition. We are fallen beings alienated from God, from our neighbors, even from our very selves. We have no rights to stand on before God; we are like "filthy rags," as Isaiah says (Is 64:4). We are dependent on the divine Mercy at every moment—for our very existence, for our conversion to good, for our repentance from evil, for our escape from damnation, and above all, for the gift of eternal life in Christ Jesus.

We stand at the edge of an abyss of never-ending misery into which we may fall at any moment by mortal sin, should our life be snuffed out before we have repented of it—if the Lord does not, in His mercy, prevent us from falling or, after we have fallen, grant us the gift of repentance. "Lead us not into temptation." Lead us not into the abyss. *Command that we be rescued from eternal damnation.* This is *reality*, as opposed to the shallow fantasy of egoism, the "broad path that leads to destruction," with which our contemporary culture envelops us.

We stand, too, at the edge of an upward abyss, that of the never-ending bliss of heaven, into which we are drawn up out of ourselves, in reverse gravity, to the supernatural grandeur of the sons of God. This, too, is a gift we could never have merited; Christ alone won it for us by shedding His Precious Blood upon the Cross, in the one supreme sacrifice that is made present at every offering of the Holy Mass. It is precisely on the verge of making this sacrifice newly present in our midst that we humbly beseech the Lord: *Command that we be numbered among the flock of Thine elect.* Number us, O Lord, with the good thief to whom Thou didst say: "This day thou shalt be with Me in paradise."

The doctrine of predestination rightly understood (and not, for example, Calvin's distortion of it) has as its positive spiritual effects an attitude of deep and abiding *thanksgiving* for the Lord's mercies without number, since He died for us while we were yet His enemies, that we might become His friends; a profound *humility* at having been chosen by God for no beauty of our own but solely that He might make us beautiful in His sight; a sober *watchfulness* and *earnestness*, lest our names be erased from the Book of Life; and, most of all, a constant *recourse to prayer*, that we may be established more and more in Christ and not in ourselves, for it is by "being made conformable to the image of His Son" (Rom 8:29), and in no other way, that our predestination is actually accomplished. In response to so great a mercy, the Church places the words of the Psalmist on the lips of her priests as they receive the Precious Blood, the price of our souls: "What shall I render to the Lord for all the things that He hath rendered to me? I will take the chalice of salvation, and I will call upon the Name of the Lord. Praising I will call upon the Lord, and I shall be saved from mine enemies."

It is therefore of immense importance for nourishing the right faith of the Church that the doctrine of predestination, transmitted pure and entire in the Roman Canon, be present to priests in their offering of the Mass and to the people in their participation in it.

8. The sacrifice we offer is rational; our faith is reasonable.

> Quam oblationem tu, Deus, in omnibus, quæsumus, bene✠dictam, adscri✠ptam, ra✠tam, rationabilem, acceptabilemque facere digneris: ut nobis Cor✠pus, et San✠guis fiat dilectissimi Filii tui, Domini nostri Iesu Christi.
>
> [Which oblation do Thou, O God, vouchsafe in all respects to make blessed, registered, ratified, rational, and acceptable, that it may become for us the Body and Blood of Thy most beloved Son, Jesus Christ our Lord.]

The legal language used here, also very Roman, conveys a strong sense of objectivity: we are asking the Father to grant that everything be properly done and noted as such, as if to imply that salvation is not a matter of impressions, feelings, subjective states, wishful thinking, amorphous longings, but a concrete, definite, known access to God by means of a "visible sacrifice such as the nature of man requires."[33]

---

[33] Trent, Session 22, ch. 1. On this part of the Canon, Fr. John Hunwicke comments: "The key to a balanced understanding here is the assumption integral to the Pentateuch, that the Sacrifices of Israel needed to be done exactly as the inspired texts directed. And that itself

In this way, the Roman Canon highlights the *rationality* of the Christian faith. The *Logos* became flesh in order to restore man's *logos*, his reason. We are given the privilege of a rational worship that, on the one hand, still contains the full reality of sacrifice (without which there is no religion, no adoration, no forgiveness of sins), and, on the other hand, is unbloody and spiritual, leading us from the sensible or earthly realm to the intelligible or celestial realm. Protestantism attacked Catholicism as a recrudescence of paganism or a Judaizing cult; modernity attacked Catholicism as irrational superstition and pre-scientific prejudice; postmodernity attacks Catholicism as an avaricious, chauvinistic, omniphobic, intolerant structure of self-serving power; but the Roman Canon serenely bears witness to the luminous rationality of the Faith, the majesty of its God, the excellence of its rites, the lofty aim of its rule of life.[34]

9. *The hands of Christ are holy and venerable—and so are the priest's.*

Qui pridie quam pateretur, accepit panem in sanctas ac venerabiles manus suas, et elevatis oculis in cælum, ad te Deum Patrem suum omnipotentem . . . Simili modo postquam cenatum est, accipiens et hunc præclarum calicem in sanctas ac venerabiles manus suas . . .

[Who the day before He suffered, took bread into His holy and venerable hands, and having lifted up His eyes to heaven, to Thee,

---

goes back to the very meaning of Covenant. This, quite simply, links the Faithfulness of our Covenant God (what we Latins call <u>his</u> *pietas*) with our obedience to His Law (what we Latins call <u>our</u> *pietas*). As Christine Mohrmann established, the legalistic character of Liturgical Latin goes back way beyond the fourth-century Latin which we find in the early Roman Sacramentaries. She discussed 'the almost juridical precision' of the Canon in terms of the surviving fragments of preChristian, preclassical Roman prayer texts used in agriculture as much as in warfare. She was not afraid to talk about 'this monumental verbosity coupled with juridical precision, which is so well suited to the *gravitas Romana* but which also betrays a certain scrupulosity with regard to higher powers.' 'A sacral style has been created which links up with the old Roman prayer of the official Roman cult.'" "Are the Institution Narratives of the Roman Rite legalistic? (2)," *Fr Hunwicke's Mutual Enrichment*, June 9, 2019.
[34] Again, we see how the Roman Canon parallels the language of the Byzantine Divine Liturgy of Saint John Chrysostom: during the Cherubic Hymn, "You were appointed our High Priest, and as Master of all, handed down to us the priestly ministry of this liturgical sacrifice without the shedding of blood"; at the Epiclesis: "We offer You this rational worship without the shedding of blood."

God, His almighty Father . . . In like manner, after He had supped, taking also into His holy and venerable hands this resplendent chalice . . .]

One of the most beautiful Catholic customs is that of kissing the hands of a newly-ordained priest, to express one's reverence for the Lord's minister and especially for *these* anointed instruments by which the sacraments—above all, the precious Body of the Lord—are conferred upon the people.

The dignity of Christ the High Priest, His inherent holiness, and the way in which the minister shares in this dignity and holiness are beautifully emphasized in the Roman Canon, when the priest, at the moment he picks up the host, says: "He took bread into His holy and venerable hands," and then uses the same words in reference to the chalice. The hands of the priest: why do so many Catholics no longer reverence them, no longer see them as uniquely suited to handling the Bread of Life? Surely it is because of a massive loss of faith in the Real Presence, which reduces this immortal gift to mere wafers to be distributed in the most convenient manner. Having lost sight of the One with "holy and venerable hands," the One "who lifts up His eyes to heaven," we have also lost sight of the distinctiveness of His minister, the responsibilities that belong to him as *alter Christus*, and the essentially sacred character of liturgical worship, by which we are to lift *our* eyes to heaven, not keep them fixed on the things of earth (Col 3:2)—or fixed upon each other in a "self-enclosed circle,"[35] as occurs whenever the Mass is celebrated toward the people rather than eastwards in a common orientation to Christ our God, who, as Scripture tells us, will come in judgment from the East.

Allow me to illustrate the power of these words by means of a true story. There was a certain priest who never used the Roman Canon, but only the neo-anaphoras. It happened that a friend asked him to celebrate Mass for a special occasion and requested that he pray this Canon. The day arrived, and when the priest came to speak the words "He took bread into His holy and venerable hands," he paused and started crying—because for the first

---

[35] Joseph Ratzinger, *Spirit of the Liturgy*, trans. John Saward (San Francisco: Ignatius Press, 2000), comm. ed., 94; original ed., 81; *Collected Works* 11:49.

time in his life he was aware that these words also referred to *his own* hands, as a representative of Jesus Christ at the altar. The priest took a moment to calm down and continued until he came to: "taking into His holy and venerable hands this resplendent chalice," and began to cry again. May this story rekindle our wonder at the tremendousness of the Holy Sacrifice, and the unique role the priest takes in it! Let us never forget that what the priest accomplishes at the consecration, with God's power, is not equaled by anything done by the natural power of any angel of the heavenly hosts, even Saint Michael the Archangel.[36]

10. All Masses are mystically the same as the one Sacrifice of Calvary.

> . . . accipiens et hunc præclarum calicem in sanctas ac venerabiles manus suas . . .
>
> [. . . taking also into His holy and venerable hands this resplendent chalice . . .]

The striking phrase *HUNC praeclarum calicem* forcefully asserts the unity of the present Mass with the one all-sufficient Sacrifice of Calvary, which the Lord anticipated in symbols on the night He was betrayed.[37] The first Mass on Maundy Thursday, the bloody oblation on Good Friday, and every one of the countless Masses celebrated since then, is one and the same sacrifice of the innocent Lamb of God who takes away the sins of the world. That is

---

[36] At the consecration, a miracle takes place. This miracle is multifaceted: not only the change of the whole substance of the bread into the Body of Christ (and of the wine into His Precious Blood), but also the *manner* in which it is accomplished, viz., with the accidents of bread and wine continuing, by the power of God, to be on the corporal and in the chalice *without any subject in which to inhere*. (There is no bread or wine of which they are the accidents, nor are they the accidents of the Body or Blood of Christ.) The priest, in uttering the words of consecration, is the instrumental cause, under God, of the transubstantiation itself and of the miraculous persistence of the accidents without a subject. Angels by their natural power cannot work a miracle in the strict sense—i.e., cannot produce an effect that lies outside the order of the whole of created nature (cf. *ST* I, qu. 110, art. 4). They can, of course, by the dazzling powers of their own nature, produce effects that surprise men (ad 2), and they can act as the servants of God when He works a miracle by His omnipotence—e.g., gathering the dust of bodies at the resurrection (ad 1).

[37] A case has been made that the *hunc* may indicate that at Rome the actual chalice from the Last Supper was used at the time of the composition of the Canon. See Janice Bennett, *St. Laurence and the Holy Grail: The Story of the Holy Grail of Valencia* (San Francisco: Ignatius Press, 2004). If so, that would be a fine example of a humano-apostolic tradition.

why the priest can say, with simultaneous poetic license and metaphysical exactitude, that Jesus took "THIS resplendent chalice," blessed it, and gave it to His disciples.[38] As a modern author says: "In Mass, space and time are annihilated. In Mass, eternity and infinity are brought to earth. Though Mass is celebrated at a thousand altars, there is but one Mass: one miracle, one coming; one Calvary, one sacrifice, in which all sacrifice is included."[39]

Moreover, the word *praeclarus* deserves attention. It means "splendid, bright, excellent, famous, illustrious, noble, distinguished." This word has both a causative and an explanatory force. On the one hand, it is because of what the Lord does to the wine that the vessel in which it is contained acquires nobility. This chalice *becomes* illustrious because the Lord's very Blood (together with His Body, Soul, and Divinity) come to be present within it. On the other hand, because Christ's followers subsequently *know* what is to become of the wine in the chalice, they strive through the ages to make the most beautiful, noble, splendid chalices that human art can contrive so that they will be worthy—or at least less *un*worthy—of their sacred content. Thus, it is entirely fitting that a priest should bow his head over (for example) an elaborate gold chalice studded with jewels and say *hunc praeclarum calicem*; the very vessel he handles, so different from secular cups, becomes an external sign of the internal reality that no mortal eye can see: "the chalice of eternal salvation." By challenging the Church to make her outward appearance point to inward realities, the Roman Canon raises the bar of ecclesiastical art to the highest possible level.

Shortly after the consecration of the chalice, the Canon uses the word *praeclarus* a second time—*offerimus praeclarae majestati tuae*, "we offer unto Thy resplendent Majesty"—echoing the words before the consecration of the chalice: *hunc praeclarum calicem*, as if to say: what is about to be within this chalice is at one with, and worthy of, the One to whom it is raised up. The Holy Sacrifice of the Mass collapses the distance between Creator and creation while emphatically affirming the infinite abyss bridged by Christ

---

[38] In both the ICEL 1973 translation and the one proposed in 1998, the phrase *accipien. hunc praeclarum calicem in sanctas ac venerabiles manus suas* was "translated" as "he took the cup"—that's it. The 2011 translation at least had the courtesy to translate what the Lati actually says.

[39] Michael Kent, *The Mass of Brother Michel* (Brooklyn, NY: Angelico Press, 2017), 264–65

alone, in His very Person. The Roman Canon is, therefore, as radically Christocentric as it is Patricentric: we receive no blessing and grace without the Son, without desire for communion with Him—a truth also underlined by the significant repetition of "Per Christum Dominum nostrum," which punctuates the Canon five times, in honor of the Five Wounds.

These "Per Christum Dominum nostrum" conclusions are sometimes written off as medieval accretions at odds with the literary and theological structure of ancient anaphoras. But this is to fail altogether to see their structural and symbolic functions, which even Jungmann indicates.[40] Moreover, they repeat like a refrain—as the Jesus Prayer does—that Christ is the one and only Mediator. There is no other way to God (cf. Acts 4:12); there is no other religion that pleases or placates God except the worship offered in the name of Jesus; God cannot be approached except through Him. This runs completely against the religious indifferentism and relativism of our age and has implications for social doctrine, affirming the Christocentrism of Pius XI's *Quas Primas* rather than the panreligious public square of *Dignitatis Humanae*. Some liturgists complain about the "useless repetition" of this formula, but how useless is it? If one says it meaningfully, it becomes the seal of approval on every prayer we offer, the guarantee that our words will be heard and answered with fire from heaven.

11. The Christians who offer this sacrifice
are the true children of Abraham.

Supra quæ propitio ac sereno vultu respicere digneris: et accepta habere, sicuti accepta habere dignatus es munera pueri tui iusti Abel, et sacrificium Patriarchæ nostri Abrahæ: et quod tibi obtulit summus sacerdos tuus Melchisedech, sanctum sacrificium, immaculatam hostiam.

[Vouchsafe to look upon them with a gracious and tranquil countenance, and to accept them, even as Thou wast pleased to accept the offerings of Thy just servant Abel, and the sacrifice

---

[40]   See Josef Jungmann, *The Mass of the Roman Rite: Its Origins and Development ("Missarum Sollemnia")*, trans. Francis A. Brunner (Notre Dame, IN: Christian Classics, 2012), 2:178–79, et passim.

of Abraham, our patriarch, and that which Melchizedek, Thy
high priest, offered up to Thee, a holy sacrifice, a victim without
blemish.]

The Roman Canon speaks of the sacrifice of Christ as the culmination of a
long history of holy sacrifices that foreshadowed it, with three being singled
out: Abel's offering of "the firstlings of his flock and of their fat" (Gen 4);
Abraham's offering of his beloved son, Isaac (Gen 22); and Melchizedek's
offering of bread and wine (Gen 14). Abraham, tellingly, is called "*our
patriarch*."[41]

   Not by descent of blood but by imitation of faith, Abraham is *our* patriarch, the patriarch of orthodox Christians—*not* the patriarch of the Jewish
people as an ethnic or religious group. As Saint Paul teaches in Galatians:
"it is *men of faith* who are the sons of Abraham" (Gal 3:7); "the promises
were made to Abraham and to his *seed*," that is, Christ (Gal 3:16), and
so, to all who belong to Christ in faith: "And if you are Christ's, then you
are Abraham's seed, heirs according to the promise" (Gal 3:29). And in
Romans: "For not all who are descended from Israel belong to Israel, and
not all are children of Abraham because they are his descendants. . . . It is
not the children of the flesh who are the children of God, but the children
of the promise are reckoned as descendants" (Rom 9:6–8). Abraham is the
patriarch of all who have faith in Christ—of the Hebrews, like himself,
who longed for the Messiah and who were delivered by Him from the
limbo of the fathers, as well as of the Jews and Gentiles from the time of
Christ down to the present who have been baptized into Christ and thus
become "the Israel of God" (Gal 6:16), the Catholic Church. The Jewish
people as an ethnic and/or religious group is no longer the chosen People of
God after their infidelity to their Messiah (cf. Deut 18:18–19; Heb 8:13).

   A prayer that Pope Leo XIII wrote for the consecration he made of the
human race to the Sacred Heart in the Holy Year 1900, which Pope Saint
Pius X ordered to be made annually, and which Pope Pius XI specified

---

[41] The 2011 English version of the Novus Ordo, far more accurate than the abysmal 1973
version, still retains the limp circumlocution "our father in faith" in order to avoid the loaded
word "patriarch" for reasons of political correctness, thereby obscuring part of the theological message of the text.

should be made each year on the Feast of the Kingship of Our Lord Jesus Christ, bears witness to the truth of supersessionism: "Turn Your eyes of mercy toward the children of that race, *once* Your chosen people. Of old they called down upon themselves the Blood of the Savior; may It now descend upon them as a laver of redemption and of life."

Supersessionism does not touch on how Jews ought to be treated in everyday life. There is no reason to treat them differently from the manner in which we ought to treat every neighbor—namely, with a charity that wishes for them life in Christ and the beatific vision. Indeed, they are a people deserving of special respect owing to the election of their ancestors and the weight of their prophecies of the Messiah, to which they continue to bear independent witness (as Saint Augustine argues[42]). But in the supernatural order, they are no longer the "Chosen People" or "the people of the covenant." To say otherwise is to reject "the unicity and salvific universality of Jesus Christ and the Church"[43]—that is to say, to reject Christ and His Church, period.[44]

---

[42] An excellent summary with ample quotations may be found in Thomas McDonald's "Unwilling Witnesses: St. Augustine and the Witness Doctrine," *Wonderful Things* weblog, August 28, 2013. As we learn from Romans 9–11, the Jews retain relevance for the history of salvation: God desires them to come to the full inheritance of the promises He made to them (even as we may say He desires the Orthodox to be reunited to Rome, and Roman Catholics to be reunited to their own tradition). It is piously believed that the Parousia is delayed until the conversion of the Jews.

[43] The quotation is the subtitle of the Congregation for the Doctrine of the Faith's Declaration *Dominus Iesus* (August 6, 2000).

[44] The common teaching of Christianity is well exhibited in the superb commentary on the Psalms compiled by J. M. Neale, who writes, concerning the verse *filii alieni mentiti sunt et claudicaverunt a semitis suis*: "*The strange children.* That is, the Jews: children indeed, as descended from faithful Abraham; but strange by rejecting Him whose day Abraham desired to see. It is thus that almost all the Fathers interpret the passage. . . . And they not only dissembled themselves, but were the cause of deceit in others. . . . S. Augustine, in expounding that passage, 'Many shall come from the east and the west, and shall sit down with Abraham, Isaac, and Jacob in the kingdom of heaven; but the children of the kingdom shall be cast out,' says with reference to this text: 'Children, not my own, but strange children, as it is written, Ye are of your father, the devil.'" *A Commentary on the Psalms from Primitive and Mediaeval Writers and from the Various Office-books and Hymns*, 3rd ed. (London: Joseph Masters, 874), 1:254.

12. The Mass is an earthly sacrifice united to, and uniting us with, the eternal liturgy in heaven.

Supplices te rogamus, omnipotens Deus, iube hæc perferri per manus sancti Angeli tui in sublime altare tuum, in conspectu divinæ maiestatis tuæ: ut quotquot [*osculatur Altare*] ex hac altaris participatione sacrosanctum Filii tui Cor✠pus et San✠guinem sumpserimus [*seipsum signat*] omni benedictione cælesti et gratia repleamur. Per eundem Christum Dominum nostrum. Amen.

[We humbly beseech Thee, almighty God, to command that these our offerings be borne by the hands of Thy holy angel to Thine altar on high, in the presence of Thy divine Majesty; that as many of us as shall, by partaking from this altar (*priest kisses altar*), receive the most sacred Body and Blood of Thy Son, may be filled with every heavenly blessing and grace (*priest signs himself with the cross*).]

In this sublime prayer, recited by the priest bowing toward the altar, we scent the mingling of two fragrances—that of Hebrew mysticism, as glimpsed in the elaborate dedication rites of Solomon's temple,[45] and that of Neoplatonic mysticism, which sees this visible realm as a dim reflection of or shadowy participation in the realm of true being, the realm of unchanging divine reality.

The priest asks God to command that the earthly offerings be carried up to a heavenly altar, into God's presence, by a holy angel who mediates between earth and heaven (this is why some commentators see this "holy angel" as Christ Himself, "the angel of the great counsel" [Is 9:6], "the one Mediator between God and man" [1 Tim 2:5][46]). We are praying that our particular time-bound sacrifice here below may be one with the eternal liturgy of the celestial fatherland; that our altar may become a channel through which to access the immortal food and drink of paradise, the fruit

---

[45] See 1 Kg 8; 2 Chron 5–7.
[46] See Nicholas Gihr, *The Holy Sacrifice of the Mass, Dogmatically, Liturgically, and Ascetically Explained* (St. Louis: B. Herder, 1949), 696–703, who rejects this opinion in favor of taking "angel" to mean a created spirit. However, Saint Thomas offers the Christic view as a possible interpretation: *ST* III, qu. 83, art. 4, ad 9; cf. Gihr, 699, n. 50.

of the tree of life. The all-holy Victim on the altar is put forward as both the *condition* for obtaining every blessing and grace given to the human race (this is why the sweet-smelling oblation must be borne on high, in the sight of God, who is pleased by it), and as the ultimate *content* of every blessing and grace we receive.

Yet in the end we must agree with the medieval deacon Florus of Lyons (d. 860): "These words of mystery are so profound, so wonderful and stupendous, who is able to comprehend them? Who would say anything worthy? They are more to be revered and feared than discussed."[47]

These twelve features present us with a distinctively Roman theology of the Mass. Holy Mass is an earthly sacrifice united to, and uniting us with, the eternal liturgy in heaven; all Masses are mystically the same as the one Sacrifice of Christ on the Cross, anticipated by the offering made by the holy hands of Jesus at the Last Supper, and renewed at the altar by the holy hands of the ministerial priest. God the Father is the *Paterfamilias* of the Church; His family, the true children of Abraham, approach Him with faith and devotion, begging to be numbered among the elect who are snatched from hell. The priest is His head servant, who offers this rational sacrifice of our reasonable faith, on behalf of all members of Christ's Church who hold the true faith, and to obtain for them unity and other perfections from God, through the prayers and merits of the saints, and above all those of the ever-Virgin Mary. How massive, how intricate, how lofty is the fundamental dogmatic content of the Canon! The Council of Trent's canons and anathemas on the Mass proceed naturally from the theology contained in the Roman Canon, as if prompted by meditation on it, and thereby reaffirm the principle that all expression and development of doctrine *must* be founded on what is already given in tradition.

The twelve truths I have summarized are clearly found in the Roman Canon but are absent from, or else barely present in, the ten neo-anaphoras included in the missal of Paul VI—that is, Eucharistic Prayers II through IV, the two "for reconciliation," and the four variations of the EP "for

---

47 Cited in Gihr, *Holy Sacrifice*, 701, n53.

various needs."[48] Nor was this an inexplicable oversight. In his candid and detailed account of nearly every aspect of the liturgical reform, Annibale Bugnini tells us outright that the reformers, in the name of "the principle of variety," sought to compose prayers as different as possible from the Roman Canon. *The Reform of the Liturgy* relates the impresario's well-nigh blasphemous words: "The decision to add other Eucharistic Prayers to the Roman liturgy was not an 'intolerable audacity' but a return to authentic tradition and a rejection of the deplorable impoverishment that had been a typical result of centuries of liturgical decadence."[49] Like most of what the reformers proclaimed, this assertion is an historical falsehood of the first order; there is no evidence of any kind that the Roman rite ever had any Eucharistic prayer other than the Roman Canon. In order to repair this "impoverishment," Bugnini says (speaking of what we now call Eucharistic Prayers II, III, and IV, prior to the addition of still others):

> It seems proper that while respecting the laws that every anaphora must obey, the new anaphoras should also have their own spiritual, pastoral, and stylistic characteristics that would distinguish them both from one another and from the Roman Canon. This kind of variety seems needed if the Roman liturgy is to have the greater spiritual and pastoral riches that cannot find full expression in a single type of text. As far as possible, therefore, concepts, words, and phrases from the Roman Canon have been avoided in the three new anaphoras [EP II–IV], and things found in one of the three have not been repeated in the other two. . . . Only by having three [more] did it seem possible to introduce into the [*sic*; maybe *this*?]

---

[48] One can almost hear the very timbre of the 1970s in the titles given to these four rarely-used prayers: "The Church on the Path of Unity," "God Guides His Church along the Way of Salvation," "Jesus, the Way to the Father," and "Jesus, Who Went About Doing Good." There are also three Eucharistic Prayers for Masses for Children (!) that have received ample and well-deserved mockery.

[49] Annibale Bugnini, *The Reform of the Liturgy 1948–1975*, trans. Matthew J. O'Connell (Collegeville, MN: The Liturgical Press, 1990), 449. Bugnini does not explain, for example, how it could be a "deplorable impoverishment" for the Roman Canon to mention in its an-amnesis the "blessed Passion, the Resurrection from the realm of the dead, and the glorious Ascension into heaven" whereas Eucharistic Prayer II, its most popular replacement, men-tions only "the Death and Resurrection" *tout simplement*. Examples like this abound.

part of the Roman liturgy the spiritual and pastoral riches required today.[50]

So, not only are the aforementioned twelve dogmatic truths largely or indeed nearly totally absent from all the new anaphoras, but this was by design. Moreover, it would be possible to show that all of these themes are diluted throughout the new liturgical books and prominent in the old ones. Since the Mass is at the heart of the worship of the Catholic Church, and the Canon is at the heart of the Mass, the fact that the *lex orandi* has been so heavily altered amounts to a betrayal of Tradition in the strict sense of the word and a cause of corruption in the *lex credendi*, with inevitable results in the *lex vivendi*.

Beyond these twelve truths, consideration should also be given to doctrines of the Catholic Faith that, while *present* in all the Novus Ordo anaphoras, are given *consummate expression* in the Roman Canon and find only a feeble echo in the others. A complete study would take us far afield. Suffice it to look at a crucial example: the *de fide* dogma that the Mass is a true and proper sacrifice. The Roman Canon may be said to insist on this truth, even to revel in it: "these gifts, these presents, these holy unspotted sacrifices . . . this sacrifice of praise . . . this oblation . . . this our oblation . . . a victim which is pure, a victim which is holy, a victim which is stainless . . . the sacrifice of Abraham, our patriarch . . . a holy sacrifice, a victim without blemish . . ." Here we are dealing with a question of relative emphasis rather than absence. Although one *can* find the language of oblation and sacrifice in the neo-anaphoras,[51] it is surprisingly exiguous in

---

[50] Bugnini, 452, referring to the following Coetus X documentation: "Ceterum libertas tria (vel quattuor) nova schemata proponendi admisit, immo suadebat diversitatem quoad singula, ita ut non idem in omnibus repeteretur, sed varietas quaedam adesset in dispositione, stilo, terminologia, et expressionibus." Schema 218 (De Missali 34), 19 March 1967, p. 46. Cipriano Vagaggini, OSB, one of the members of Coetus X, at least had the common sense in his 1966 book *The Canon of the Mass and Liturgical Reform*, trans. Peter Coughlan (Staten Island, NY: Alba House, 1967), exactly contemporaneous with the writing of Eucharistic Prayers II–IV, to state that a revision of the Roman Canon would "inevitably lead to an awful mess" (122). Because his three suggestions—retaining the Canon (albeit with "minor modifications"); providing an originally-composed canon with variable preface for *ad libitum* use; providing another canon with a fixed preface giving an exposition of salvation history (cf. 122–23)—are similar to what eventually transpired, I suspect that he more than anyone else was the driving force behind the Coetus's work on the new EPs.

[51] This I say because some traditionalist authors betray an embarrassing ignorance in claim-

comparison with the abundance and clarity of such language in the Roman Canon, which identifies the action taking place as an offering of sacrifice and speaks continually of the victim by whom God is placated. In the period around the Second Vatican Council, this kind of language met with academic disapproval and cultural scorn: surely, Modern Man does not believe in a "vindictive God who delights in the blood of sacrificial victims"? In thinking that this *was* the traditional view, they convicted themselves of a deplorable lack of theological understanding[52] and succeeded only in propagating superficial views of what the Mass is.

Given its thundering proclamation of traditional doctrine, it's no wonder, one regrets to say, that this Canon was the target of increasingly audacious critiques on the part of *soi-disant* liturgical scholars who claimed to find in it a rambling, disorganized mish-mash of ancient prayers no longer well-suited for "Modern Man" (that most useful of manikins), as if the Canon were like a gaudy antique wardrobe that deserved to be carried off to storage and replaced with a sleeker, more efficient furnishing of Bauhaus design.[53]

---

ing that the new Eucharistic Prayers do not express a theology of sacrifice. They do, sufficiently to defend them against the charge of heresy—but their content in this regard falls far short of what has always been present in the authentic Roman rite. Moreover, the language is often looser or less definite, in a way that Protestants would find easier to accept and to interpret in their own way, which fits in with the oft-stated ecumenical intention of the creation of the Novus Ordo. In any case, imposing committee-designed anaphoras by legal fiat is a problem in and of itself.

[52] For a more nuanced understanding of the Mass as a sacrifice, see Ratzinger's essay "Theology of the Liturgy."

[53] In his preface to Vagaggini's book, influential liturgist Fr. Frederick R. McManus explained that "the eucharistic prayer in the vernacular, however desirable, will make public something that has been overlooked except by liturgical and pastoral experts, namely, the defects of the Roman canon" and that "the limitations and defects will call for the evolution of new forms." The solution to these problems would be "the serious construction of new eucharistic prayers which reflect the progress of theological and liturgical science and which are meaningful—or can be made meaningful through study and reflection—to the twentieth-century Christian." *The Canon of the Mass and Liturgical Reform*, 10–11. One could note that the parlor-game of "reconstructing the original form of the Roman Canon" had already been underway for a long time, beginning with nineteenth-century German scholars. Fr. Adrian Fortescue takes it for granted that the prayers had previously been used in some other order, that an original *epiclesis* had fallen out of the text, etc.—all assumptions that more recent scholarship rejects. It is problematic that Fortescue's somewhat unreliable articles from the original *Catholic Encyclopedia* circulate widely via the internet.

This new teaching [on the need for a radical reform of the Church's liturgy] is not merely a deepening and forward-moving development, like a branch which sends forth new shoots as it matures and flourishes. Rather, it is literally superlative, standing above and outside of the preceding history of the liturgy and theology of the Church, and able to adjudicate retroactively in light of the new understanding. How can the central and most sacral part of the western Church's corporate worship, specifically attested to by the Fathers, unchanged and nearly universally used since AD 600, now be said to have contained serious defects and limitations? How can an official text of the Roman liturgy which has existed in verifiable form since the late fourth century now be said to "sin in a number of ways" against guidelines which were promulgated nine days after the burial of John F. Kennedy?[54]

In the mid-1960s, anxious Catholics were being told that, at very least, the Roman Canon would remain fixed and in Latin; only a few years later, a whole battalion of manufactured Eucharistic Prayers was released, intended to be said in the vernacular.[55] This was just the sort of 180° shift that caused Catholics to wonder if churchmen had lost their wits in the Woodstock era[56]—or if, perhaps, they had just been purveyors of mythology all along, profiteering from structures of power. In any case, it's awfully suspicious: a prayer that had served the Catholic Church in the West for well over 1,400 years was suddenly found to be inadequate to our needs! It would seem that the problem is more with *us* than with the prayer—even as it is

---

[54] See the two-part article "How Do You Solve A Problem Like the Canon?," *NLM*, February 11 and 16, 2022; this quotation from part 2. The internal quotation is from Vagaggini's *Canon of the Mass*, 90.

[55] It is beyond reasonable doubt that Paul VI believed that *SC* was *not* to be followed in the matter of retaining Latin for the fixed parts of the Mass, for he stated in a famous papal audience, for all intents and purposes, "goodbye to Latin." See chapter 4.

[56] A passage from Archbishop Marcel Lefebvre captures the spirit of the time: "The keynote of the reform is the drive against certainties. Catholics who have them are branded as misers guarding their treasures, as greedy egotists who should be ashamed of themselves. The important thing is to be open to contrary opinions, to admit diversity, to respect the ideas of Freemasons, Marxists, Muslims, even animists. The mark of a holy life is to join in dialogue with error." *An Open Letter to Confused Catholics*, trans. Fr. Michael Crowdy (Kansas City, MO: Angelus Press, 1986), 62.

no argument against monogamy if a man tires of only one wife and would like to try several more.

II. Moral Implications

Someone may object to my line of argument in two ways. First, they will say: "Did not Pope Paul VI have the authority to introduce new anaphoras? And having done so, must they not be valid, licit, and therefore worthy to be used?" Second, "is not the Roman Canon still part of the new missal, and thus the new missal is the same as the old—at least in this respect?"

Regarding the first objection, it should be denied, simply speaking, that a pope has the authority to institute a new canon of the Mass,[57] but affirmed *secundum quid* or in a manner of speaking. We must make a distinction between "power" and "authority."[58] Power refers to the ability to bring about some effect and to enforce it once effected. Authority (sometimes called "moral authority") refers to the *right* to do something, and may imply a duty to do it. Pope Paul VI used the power of his papal office to impose a new liturgy on Catholics, but he lacked true authority to enforce such a rupture from tradition; the act was *ultra vires*. He was, not surprisingly, able to leverage the power of his office and take advantage of habits of ultramontanist obedience, but he had no moral *right* to lay hands on the inherited sacred liturgy as he did and to substitute another rite for it, and, *a fortiori*, no capacity to require others to accept what he did. One might put it this way: it was not so much a *use* of his papal power as it was an *abuse* of it. The result of his exercise of power were liturgical rites that validly enact sacraments and contain no positive error—that is the best one can say about them. These rites are valid, but that is no reason to believe they are worthy to be used or even pleasing to God. In some respects, indeed, they may be displeasing to God and demeritorious.[59]

---

[57] See chapter 2; cf. Peter Kwasniewski, "The Pope's Boundedness to Tradition as a Legislative Limit," in Kwasniewski, ed., *From Benedict's Peace to Francis's War: Catholics Respond to the Motu Proprio* Traditionis Custodes *on the Latin Mass* (Brooklyn, NY: Angelico Press, 2021), 222–47, and Kwasniewski, *True Obedience in the Church: A Guide to Discernment in Challenging Times* (Manchester, NH: Sophia Institute Press, 2021), 33–42.

[58] See Eric Sammons, "Power vs. Authority in the Church," *Crisis Magazine*, December 30, 2021.

[59] See Peter Kwasniewski, "Does Pius VI's *Auctorem Fidei* Support Paul VI's Novus Ordo?"

Moving to the second objection, it is not quite accurate to say that "the Roman Canon" *as it existed until the mid-1960s* is found in the 1969 Missal of Paul VI. The first, most obvious, and in many ways most consequential difference in terms of the sacred phenomenology of the Mass is the abandonment of the silent Canon, which was the established custom in all rites, Eastern and Western, by the end of the eighth century—in spite of the Emperor Justinian's attempt to prohibit it in 565.[60] Patristic evidence points to silence during all or some part of the anaphora as a feature already familiar in the fourth century.[61] A stunning homily from the Syriac poet-theologian Narsai (d. 502) describes the anaphora of his day thus: "All the ecclesiastical body now observes silence, and all set themselves to pray earnestly in their hearts. The Priests are still, and the deacons stand in silence . . . the whole people is quiet and still, subdued and calm . . . . The Mysteries are set in order, the censers are smoking, the lamps are shining, and the deacons are hovering and brandishing [fans] in likeness of watchers [i.e., angels]. Deep silence and peaceful calm settles on that place: it is filled and overflows with brightness and splendour, beauty and power."[62]

Narsai goes on to report that a "herald" (perhaps a deacon?) cries out: "In silence and fear be ye standing: peace be with us. Let all the people be in fear at this moment in which the adorable Mysteries are being accomplished by the descent of the Spirit." Many scholars have noted that it was

---

in Kwasniewski, *The Road from Hyperpapalism to Catholicism: Rethinking the Papacy in a Time of Ecclesial Disintegration* (Waterloo, ON: Arouca Press, 2022), vol. 1, ch. 9.

[60] We must bear in mind that in ancient liturgies after the fourth century (at the latest), there was always *some* kind of symbolic "barrier" between the people and the clergy who were offering the Eucharistic prayer, whether it took an *architectural* form (e.g., a separated apse or an altar beneath a ciborium surrounded by curtains) or, as time went on, a *sonic* form (silence), or both.

[61] As we see with early Christian records in general, the first extant mention of something is often a passing reference suggestive of a much longer custom. For example, the first extant mention of subdeacons in Rome comes in a letter from 251, which indicates their matter-of-fact presence in the ecclesiastical hierarchy. Bishop Athanasius Schneider maintains that with Rome's famous stubborn conservatism, it's unlikely that the subdiaconate was a recent creation in the mid-third century, and far more likely that it stretched back to the apostolic or subapostolic period. See Peter Kwasniewski, *Ministers of Christ: Recovering the Roles of Clergy and Laity in an Age of Confusion* (Manchester, NH: Crisis Publications, 2021), xlii, 53–55.

[62] Quoted in Charles Harris, "Liturgical Silence," in *Liturgy and Worship: A Companion to the Prayer Books of the Anglican Communion*, ed. W. K. Lowther Clarke (New York: Macmillan, 1932), 779.

characteristic of the Protestants to insist upon the full audibility of all liturgical prayers, owing to their predominantly didactic and congregationalist
understanding of divine worship.[63] The Novus Ordo's rubrical instruction
that the Eucharistic Prayer be read aloud so that the people can follow
it,[64] especially taken together with the customary *versus populum* direction,
undermines the experience of the prayer *as* prayer (i.e., its theocentricity)
and of the mystery *as* mystery (i.e., its awe-inspiring transcendence over
nature and reason).[65] A Byzantine Catholic layman once made this per-
ceptive remark: "Some who support the praying of the Canon aloud claim
that they do so because these prayers are 'for us.' They're right, but in the
wrong way. The prayers are indeed for us but they are not for our education by hearing. They are for our salvation by praying."[66] As the multi-
dimensional value of the silent Canon has been the subject of frequent
discussion,[67] and, in any case, as experience is the best and perhaps the only
convincing proof of its rightness, I will not speak of it further.

Second, and no less troublingly, the formulas for consecration as they
had always existed in the Roman tradition were modified in order to make
them match Scriptural data more closely, in spite of the well-known fact
that none of the historic apostolic rites uses verbatim the wording of the

---

[63] The Novus Ordo does not go quite so far as to abolish private priestly prayers, but it reduces them to almost nothing in comparison with the *Ordo Missae* of the medieval Roman
rite as codified in 1570 (see Peter Kwasniewski, "The Priest Praying for Himself at Mass,"
OnePeterFive, September 8, 2021). Even at their greatest extent the personal prayers for the
celebrant were never very numerous in comparison to those of the more voluble Eastern
tradition, which makes their extreme reduction in the 1969 missal all the more harmful to
the spiritual life of the clergy and the overall spirit of the liturgy.

[64] See the *General Instruction of the Roman Missal* (2002 ed.), n. 30 and n. 32: "Among the
parts assigned to the priest, the foremost is the Eucharistic Prayer, which is the high point
of the entire celebration. . . . The nature of the 'presidential' texts demands that they be spoken in a loud and clear voice and that everyone listen with attention." For commentary, see
Matthew S. C. Olver, "A Note on the Silent Canon in the Missal of Paul VI and Cardinal
Ratzinger," *Antiphon* 20.1 (2016): 40–51.

[65] See my articles "The Silent Canon: Is Worship Supposed to be Aweful?" *NLM*, October 14,
2013; "The Silence of the Canon Speaks More Loudly Than Words," *NLM*, January 5, 2015.

[66] "A Byzantine Look at the Novus Ordo," *Rorate Caeli*, July 17, 2009.

[67] See Michael Fiedrowicz, *The Traditional Mass: History, Form, and Theology of the Classical
Roman Rite*, trans. Rose Pfeifer (Brooklyn, NY: Angelico Press, 2020), 285–91; Peter Kwas-
niewski, *Reclaiming Our Roman Catholic Birthright: The Genius and Timeliness of the Tradi-
tional Latin Mass* (Brooklyn, NY: Angelico Press, 2020), 32–33, 71–72, 146–47, 246; Joseph
Shaw, ed., *The Case for Liturgical Restoration: Una Voce Studies on the Traditional Latin Mass*
(Brooklyn, NY: Angelico Press, 2019), ch. 5, "Silence and Inaudibility," 31–35.

Last Supper accounts in the New Testament, which of course *postdate* the celebration of the Mass in early Christian communities. Evidently, a millennium and a half of unbroken daily practice in the Roman rite was not a sufficient barrier to the Consilium's urge to "improve." For the Host:

> *Vetus:* Hoc est enim Corpus meum.
>
> *Novus:* Hoc est enim Corpus meum, quod pro vobis tradetur.

For the Chalice:

> *Vetus:* Hic est enim Calix Sanguinis mei, novi et æterni testamenti: mysterium fidei: qui pro vobis et pro multis effundetur in remissionem peccatorum. (Hæc quotiescumque feceritis, in mei memoriam facietis.)[68]
>
> *Novus:* Hic est enim Calix Sanguinis mei, novi et æterni testamenti: ~~mysterium fidei:~~ qui pro vobis et pro multis effundetur in remissionem peccatorum. (~~Hæc quotiescumque feceritis, in mei memoriam facietis.~~ Hoc facite in meam commemorationem.)

Naturally, on Thomistic grounds, none of the changes affects the requirements of sacramental validity, but the gratuitous modifications speak for an entire mentality. One could remark upon some subtle points in these changes. Here it will be enough to draw attention to the worst change, namely, the removal of the phrase *mysterium fidei*—the placement of which in the consecratory formula of the wine was attributed to apostolic tradition and even to Christ Himself by all the great commentators on the Mass, including the Church's greatest theologian, Saint Thomas—and its transmogrification into an invitation for a people's "memorial acclamation" that has no basis whatsoever in the Latin tradition and introduces a phenomenological tension between the sacramental real presence and the anticipated bodily presence of Christ the Judge at the end of time.[69]

---

[68] The phrase in parentheses is not considered part of the form but is said when the chalice is replaced on the altar before the priest genuflects. The genuflection immediately after each consecration and prior to the elevation—a gesture than which nothing could be more *dignum et iustum*, expressive as it is of supernatural faith and prompted by intimate devotion—was abolished in the Novus Ordo.

[69] See the next chapter for a detailed examination of this change.

Third, the lists of saints and the structural and symbolic recurrences of "Per Christum Dominum nostrum" are bracketed as optional, which is a subliminal directive to omit them. The Roman Canon is sometimes felt to be an unwieldy text when recited out loud toward the people, and no wonder: it does not lend itself to this mode of delivery, but much more to silent recitation *versus Deum*.

Fourth, many of the priest's ceremonial actions, especially the signs of the cross and genuflections, have been stripped away (this was already done in the mid-1960s and carried over into the Novus Ordo). Since the Church's *lex orandi* finds expression not only in words but also in gestures, this ritual overhaul is by no means negligible. Fr. Hunwicke movingly describes the gesture at the start of the Canon:

> The priest introduces the Eucharistic Prayer by saying "Let us give thanks unto the Lord our God.". . . The celebrant thus calls upon us to join him in making the one all-availing thank-offering to YHWH of his Son's Body and Blood. In the Tridentine Rite the priest, at these words, joins his hands together, the liturgical sign of total self-humbling (as a captive or slave might offer his wrists to be bound). And he raises his eyes to heaven and then bows his head. What a shame it is that modern rites discard this wonderful reverencing of YHWH our creator God, the God of our forefathers Abraham, Isaac, and Jacob, the God to whom once we offered a twice-daily Tamid sacrifice of a lamb in His Temple and to whom now we offer the Immaculate Lamb.[70]

Fifth, in the missal of 1969, the entire doxology is to be said or sung aloud, even though this had not been done for very many centuries.

In these five ways, the Roman Canon as it appears in the Novus Ordo missal is not identical with the Roman Canon as received in the Latin liturgical tradition prior to the reform. But let us acknowledge, for the sake of argument, that we may consider the Roman Canon to be part of the new missal. There remains a much bigger problem, one that I would argue

---

[70] See "O LORD," *Fr Hunwicke's Mutual Enrichment*, March 26, 2018.

pertains to multiple moral virtues under the general heading of religion, the most excellent of these virtues.

Having rested on the rock-like solidity of a single anaphora from ancient times until the 1960s—so, a period of some fourteen to sixteen centuries—the Church transitioned suddenly from a uniquely solemn and solemnly unique Roman Canon that *defined* the Roman rite to a plethora of "Eucharistic Prayers" placed at the *ad libitum* volition of the celebrant, with no requirement as to when or how the prayers are to be used—a fact that distinguishes contemporary Roman practice sharply from traditional Byzantine practice, to which it is sometimes erroneously compared.[71] Multiple anaphoras in the West is a novelty pure and simple, a rupture with our actual lived tradition the magnitude of which has no equal in the history of any liturgical rite. That the Roman Canon is now an *option* contradicts its inner nature as a *canon*, a fixed rule or measure of the Church's worship.[72] We speak, for example, of the "canon of Scripture," and by this we mean a fixed set of books received by the Church as divinely inspired, inerrant, and incapable of being added to or substituted by anything else. While the Canon of the Mass is not divinely inspired in the same way, we know that it developed in the bosom of the Church over the first several centuries under the guidance of the Holy Spirit, until it was given its finishing touches by Saint Gregory, and that, from this point onwards, it was humbly received as a repository of apostolic faith and piety—something to be venerated with religious awe, which no one would dare to "edit" or "improve."[73] It

---

[71] To read more about how the shift from one Canon to many Eucharistic Prayers occurred, see Dom Cassian Folsom, "From One Eucharistic Prayer to Many: How it Happened and Why," first published in the *Adoremus Bulletin* 2.4, 2.5, and 2.6 (September, October, and November 1996; reproduced in full online at https://adoremus.org/1996/09/from-one-euc haristic-prayer-to-many-how-it-happened-and-why/). Fr. Cassian quotes an Italian liturgist on the Roman Canon: "its use today is so minimal as to be statistically irrelevant." (This was more true of the nineties than it is today, when younger clergy are more likely to use the Roman Canon, at least sometimes.) This rupture best illustrates the untenability of asserting that the *usus antiquior* and the *usus recentior* are merely two versions of "the Roman rite."

[72] Prof. Andrea Grillo of Sant'Anselmo in Rome bitterly complained about the "individualism" unleashed by *Summorum Pontificum*, because a priest could choose which form of the Roman rite to use. However, he oddly failed to explain why it is bad to choose a form in which everything is fixed but good to choose a form in which the priest is given the option to choose between radically different anaphoras (along with many other internal options). How is the use of a predetermined traditional rite individualistic but a "do-it-yourself" liturgy is not?

[73] In the words of Raymond Winch: "The anaphora of the Roman Mass is of great antiquity

was already, and was destined to be seen more and more as, a true *canon*, a rule or measure placed upon us like the "easy yoke" and "light burden" of the law of Christ.

It seems to me that the loss of a fixed rule of public worship is one of several points of departure for the fifty-year descent to *Amoris Laetitia*, with its undermining of exceptionless moral norms. In divine worship, the Catholic priest was once *required* to submit to a law that strictly governed all his words and actions. The ground on which he stood was holy ground, like Moses before the burning bush. Without the protective clothing of traditional forms of prayer, the priest would far too easily incur the guilt of irreverence, impertinence, subjectivism, or arbitrariness. *Apprehendite disciplinam, nequando irascatur Dominus, et pereatis de via justa.* "Take hold of discipline, lest at any time the Lord be angry, and you perish from the just way" (Ps 2:12). The crisis over natural law and divine law into which Francis's pontificate has plunged the Church did not come out of nowhere. It is the ultimate expression of the same hubris that was first displayed in the violence done to the core of our Western *lex orandi* in the inherited Eucharistic liturgy. If we can bring ourselves to do violence to this most sacred action, is there *anything* we will not subsequently violate, manipulate, adulterate, and corrupt? The rejection of an immobile center leads to the destabilization and centrifugal disintegration of everything else. In the words of the poet William Butler Yeats: "Things fall apart; the centre cannot hold; Mere anarchy is loosed upon the world."[74]

Cardinal Burke has spoken of antinomianism—that is, a dismissive or hostile attitude toward law and law-abidingness—as one of the great temptations and errors of our times.[75] Allowing a priest to choose *ad libitum* from various Eucharistic Prayers when celebrating Mass is ritualized

---

and provides a vital witness to the abiding tradition of the universal Church. . . . To make any changes in the canon in order to 'improve' its theology would be more reprehensible than to alter texts of the [Church] fathers on the presumption of superior spiritual insight." *The Canonical Mass of the English Orthodox*, cited by Fr. John Hunwicke, "The Worst Evil o Uniatism."

[74] "The Second Coming" (1919).

[75] See Raymond Leo Cardinal Burke, "Liturgical Law in the Mission of the Church," in *Sa cred Liturgy: Source and Summit of the Life and Mission of the Church*, ed. Alcuin Reid (Sa Francisco: Ignatius Press, 2014), 389–415, esp. 393–94; Burke, "New Evangelization an Canon Law," *The Jurist* 72 (2012): 4–30, esp. 20ff.

antinomianism. The very core of the Eucharistic liturgy, the heart of the *lex orandi*, has become a buffet from which one may choose a slice of this or a slice of that. I find it therefore no more possible to agree with Pope Benedict XVI that there are "two forms of the Roman rite" than to agree with his successor that there is only one—namely, the modern rite. In truth, there is the Roman rite in its full historical dimensions, stretching from the Upper Room to Pope Damasus through Pope Gregory to Popes Pius V and Pius X, and characterized by a growth toward perfection that culminates in stability of form and fixity of practice—and then there is a modern fabrication loosely based upon it, which, by design, like a chameleon, changes color to suit its environment, or, like a liquid, takes on the shape of whatever vessel contains it. This many-faced impostor may respond to many different names, but "Roman rite" is certainly not among them.

Hence it is hardly surprising that today's clergy are rather sharply divided into unequal groups: the minority that always or frequently prays the Roman Canon and the vast majority that always or frequently avoids it in favor of choosing any other Eucharistic Prayer on the menu (especially the Second or pseudo-Hippolytan, the "Drive-Thru" of anaphoras).[76] Consequently, the faithful under the care of the clergy are receiving two different formations in the prayer of the Church. One group of faithful hears—or, as the case may be, does *not* hear aloud—the Roman Canon regularly and is, very likely, familiar with it from well-thumbed hand missals; another group never or rarely encounters that Canon in the wild, as if it were a rarely-sighted endangered species. The theology of the Roman Canon, so ancient, so lush, so very Roman and even Jewish in feel, promises to form one kind of ecclesial, liturgical, and sacramental mind, while the neo-anaphoras, so contemporary, so logical, and so generic, promise to form a different kind.

---

[76] On the pseudo-Hippolytan pseudo-Roman pseudo-anaphora known as Eucharistic Prayer II, see John F. Baldovin, "Hippolytus and the *Apostolic Tradition*: Recent Research and Commentary," *Theological Studies* 64 (2003): 520–42. It should go without saying that I do not question the sacramental validity, *sensu stricto*, of any officially promulgated Eucharistic Prayer. But validity is not the only category in which we need to think about liturgy; it is the "low bar," so to speak, of the Church's public prayer. It is like asking whether a marriage is valid rather than looking at whether spouses have children and love them and each other, or whether a man has a job with a paycheck rather than asking whether his work is worthy of his human dignity and adequate to the needs of his family.

The attempted suppression and eventual marginalization of something as monumental and monolithic as the Roman Canon was the result not merely of poor aesthetic judgment or tendentious theories about liturgical history; it was the result of a growing impatience with the "medieval, scholastic, Tridentine" theology of the Mass and the Eucharistic Sacrifice, and a growing boldness about replacing its primary repository with just about anything else—not excluding a pastiche of texts finalized at a late-night café rendezvous.[77]

Since, moreover, the liturgy is the ultimate icon of Christ and His saints, and the Roman Canon is the central panel of this great ritual iconostasis— or perhaps we might compare it to the Pantocrator in the apse—it follows that the assault on a fixed canon was also a primordial act of iconoclasm, after which all other whitewashings, demolitions, and modernizations were mere afterthoughts.

A charming story about Pope Pius IX (1846–78) shows the extent to which the Canon was regarded as untouchable. When Pius IX was asked to add the name of Saint Joseph to the Canon, he replied: "This I cannot do; I am only the pope."[78] He had a keen appreciation of the weight of the

---

[77] Fr. Louis Bouyer, a member of the Consilium, recalls the scene: "You'll have some idea of the deplorable conditions in which this hasty reform was expedited when I recount how the second Eucharistic prayer was cobbled together. Between the indiscriminately archeologizing fanatics who wanted to banish the *Sanctus* and the intercessions from the Eucharistic prayer by taking Hippolytus's Eucharist as is, and those others who couldn't have cared less about his alleged *Apostolic Tradition* and wanted a slapdash Mass, Dom Botte and I were commissioned to patch up its text with a view to inserting these elements, which are certainly quite ancient—by the next morning! Luckily, I discovered, if not in a text by Hippolytus himself certainly in one in his style, a felicitous formula on the Holy Ghost that could provide a transition of the *Vere Sanctus* type to the short epiclesis. For his part Botte produced an intercession worthier of Paul Reboux's 'In the manner of . . .' than of his actual scholarship. Still, I cannot reread that improbable composition without recalling the Trastevere café terrace where we had to put the finishing touches to our assignment in order to show up with it at the Bronze Gate by the time our masters had set!" *The Memoirs of Louis Bouyer: From Youth and Conversion to Vatican II, the Liturgical Reform, and After*, trans. John Pepino (Kettering, OH: Angelico Press, 2015), 221–22. It must be pointed out that Bouyer never mentions the infamous "napkins" to which people often refer (which does not exclude the possibility that napkins were in fact employed).

[78] As Gregory DiPippo pointed out to me: while it may prove impossible to find a reliable primary source to back up this oft-repeated story, we may nevertheless safely treat it as a myth in the sense Tolkien famously expounded to Lewis—or, as a character in Barry Hughart's *Bridge of Birds* says: "fable has strong shoulders that carry far more truth than fact can." The point of the story is *not* that the Canon cannot be changed. We have always known

tradition and his role in passing along what the ages had deemed perfect. Pope John XXIII's decision in 1962 to insert the name of Saint Joseph into a Canon that had remained essentially unchanged from the death of Saint Gregory the Great in ca. 604 to 1962—that is, for close to 1,400 years—as innocent as that decision may have been *materially* speaking, was *formally* a declaration that the Church may now alter its most sacred inheritance.[79] Certainly Annibale Bugnini and others of his way of thinking saw this moment as a symbolic green light for their Promethean ambitions. Together with the bizarre reconfiguration of Holy Week, it is just one more reason why traditionalists should be skeptical of liturgical books issued after World War II, when the reformatory frenzy escalated.[80]

With over half a century of chaos behind us, we are well positioned to appreciate the astonishingly frank observation of the liturgist Bernard Botte, who wrote in 1953:

> We should be grateful to the people of the Middle Ages for having preserved the canon in its purity, and not having allowed their personal effusions or theological ideas to pass into it. One can imagine the complete sham we would have today if each generation had been permitted to remake the canon to the measure of their theological controversies or novel forms of piety. We can only hope for a continuing imitation of the good sense of these people, who had their own theological ideas but who understood that the canon was not their playground. To their eyes, it was the expression of

---

that the Canon has been subject to certain changes in the past. No less a personage than Benedict XIV, one of the greatest papal scholars of all time, wrote about the addition of the words "pro quibus tibi offerimus, vel," which are missing in the Old Gelasian Sacramentary and some other important ancient manuscripts. The point is rather than a properly formed Catholic mind has an instinctual horror at the idea of changing long-standing traditions for insufficient reasons, and at the potential consequences of doing so. And lo and behold!, after the Canon had stood untouched for many centuries (and had been subject to only very minor alterations even in the earliest phases of its use), John XXIII adds the name of Saint Joseph—and in less than ten years, Paul VI declares (on the most frivolous grounds possible) that it is perfectly licit for any priest of the Roman rite to never use it again.

See my article "On the Insertion of St. Joseph's Name into the Roman Canon," *NLM*, December 23, 2019.

See chapter 12.

a venerable tradition, and they felt that it could not be touched without opening the door to every sort of abuse.[81]

To this incisive and resoundingly true judgment, Catholics of the Latin rite today might reply in the melancholy words of the Psalmist: *Salvum me fac, Domine, quoniam defecit sanctus, quoniam diminutae sunt veritates a filiis hominum.* "Save me, O Lord, for there is now no saint: truths are decayed from among the children of men" (Ps 11:2).

Lovers of the classical Roman liturgy have the grave responsibility, joyful privilege, and truly evangelistic task of preserving the great Roman Canon in the public worship of the Catholic Church. In the face of freedom gone astray and authority abused, traditionalists hold that the only way forward to a liturgy that is one, holy, catholic, and apostolic, like the Church herself, is the recovery of our traditional rites, which are not only the canon or measure of the orthodox faith but also our spiritual fatherland and our foretaste of the world to come. By our clear-sighted love of the Latin liturgical tradition and our use of it in more and more places, we are demonstrating the continuity of the past, the present, and the future of Catholicism at a time when its internal coherence is threatened like never before.

---

[81] Bernard Botte, "Histoire des prières de l'ordinare de la messe," in *L'Ordinaire de la messe Texte critique, traduction et ètudes*, ed. B. Botte and C. Mohrmann, *Études liturgiques* 2 (Paris: Cerf, 1953), 27; trans. Zachary Thomas. And yet, having understood such a fundamental point, Botte went on to be a member of the Consilium and to draft, with Louis Bouyer, the second EP, the most frequently used neo-anaphora of the modern rite and the one most tainted by bad modern scholarship and most driven by modern rationalistic preferences (see Bouyer, *Memoirs*, 218–22). Such a lapsation as Botte's demonstrates the rapidity and completeness with which ideology can infect the human intellect and twist the will.

The elimination of the words *Mysterium Fidei* from the words of consecration can be considered a symbol of the demythologizing, and thus of the humanizing, of the central core of the Holy Mass.

—Roberto de Mattei

The reform of the Mass has fostered a profoundly anti-religious attitude among Catholics. Christian worship is no longer a gift of grace that is to be received on one's knees; instead it is a commodity that must be met with mistrust and ill-will, then tested, and often enough rejected. Holy Mass, which formerly was a hermetically closed mystery, had now to open itself up to the confusion of opinions. What previously had been venerated as a super-terrestrial phenomenon is now seen to be something manufactured, something arranged. And what can be arranged, can be rearranged. Now there can be no end of arranging! Anyone can come up with good ideas for changing the liturgy. It is strange, however: the more the Mass is re-shaped, the less enthusiasm one has for it.

—Martin Mosebach

9

The Displacement of
the *Mysterium Fidei*

The story of how the words of consecration spoken over the chalice were changed for the *Novus Ordo Missae* is a potent exhibition of many interrelated problems characteristic of the liturgical reform in general: false antiquarianism; a defective understanding of *participatio actuosa*; an infatuation with Eastern praxis coupled with a contempt for what is uniquely Western; disdain for medieval piety and doctrine; a lack of humility in the face of that which we cannot fully understand and a lack of reverence for that which is mysterious; a mechanistic reduction of liturgy to material that we can shape as it pleases us (as we try to do with the natural world using our modern technology); and an impatience to construct new forms due to boredom or discomfort with old ones. This example, therefore, serves as a crystal-clear illustration of the errors and vices that permeate the reform as a whole.

The traditional view

For centuries, going back into the mists of time, the priest has said the words "*Mysterium fidei*" in the midst of the words of consecration whispered over the chalice. These words powerfully evoke the irruption or inbreaking of God into our midst in this unfathomable Sacrament. The consecration of the wine completes the signification of the sacrifice of the Cross, the moment when our High Priest obtained for us eternal redemption (cf. Heb 9:12), the re-presentation of which, together with the application of its fruits, is the very purpose of the Mass. In the beautiful words of Mother Mectilde of the Blessed Sacrament (1614–1698):

The sacrifice of the cross is for all men and the one at the altar is for many. That is to say, Jesus died for all men on Calvary. He poured out His Blood and His life for the salvation of all mankind. It was His intention that all participate in it, St. Paul says. On the altar, there is a mystical shedding of blood, it is shed "for many," namely for all those who want to become worthy of it and receive it in a holy manner. For in communicating, the blood of Jesus is mystically poured out on our souls.[1]

On November 29, 1202, Pope Innocent III sent a letter *Cum Marthae circa* to Archbishop John of Lyon in which he wrote:

> You have asked who has added to the words of the formula used by Christ himself when he transubstantiated the bread and wine into his Body and Blood the words that are found in the Canon of the Mass generally used by the Church, but that none of the evangelists has recorded . . . [namely] the words "Mystery of faith" inserted into the words of Christ. . . . Surely there are many words and deeds of the Lord that have been omitted in the Gospels; of these we read that the apostles have supplemented them by their words and expressed them in their actions. . . . Yet, the expression "Mystery of faith" is used, because here what is believed differs from what is seen, and what is seen differs from what is believed. For what is seen is the appearance of bread and wine, and what is believed is the reality of the flesh and blood of Christ and the power of unity and love.[2]

The pope's answer amounts to this: there are many things Christ gave to the Apostles to hand down that are not recorded in Scripture, and this could well be one of them; or it could be an Apostle's own contribution. Writing only about seventy years later, Saint Thomas Aquinas turns the

---

[1] *The "Breviary of Fire": Letters by Mother Mectilde of the Blessed Sacrament, Chosen and Arranged by Marie de la Guesle, Countess of Châteauvieux*, trans. an Oblate of Silverstream Priory (Brooklyn, NY: Angelico Press, 2021), 234.

[2] This letter may be found in Heinrich Denzinger, *Enchiridion symbolorum definitionum et declarationum de rebus fidei et morum*, 43rd ed., ed. Peter Hünermann, Robert Fastiggi, and Englund Nash (San Francisco: Ignatius Press, 2012), at n. 782.

archbishop's question into the ninth objection against the fittingness of the words of consecration of the wine: "Further, the words whereby this sacrament is consecrated draw their efficacy from Christ's institution. But no Evangelist narrates that Christ spoke all these words. Therefore this is not an appropriate form for the consecration of the wine."[3] He responds to this objection:

> The Evangelists did not intend to hand down the forms of the sacraments, which in the primitive Church had to be kept concealed, as Dionysius observes at the close of his book *On the Ecclesiastical Hierarchy*; their object was to write the story of Christ. Nevertheless nearly all these words can be culled from various passages of the Scriptures. Because the words, "This is the chalice," are found in Luke 22:20, and 1 Corinthians 11:25, while Matthew says in 26:28: "This is My blood of the New Testament, which shall be shed for many unto the remission of sins." The words added, namely, "eternal" and "mystery of faith," were handed down to the Church by the apostles, who received them from Our Lord, according to 1 Corinthians 11:23: "I have received of the Lord that which also I delivered unto you."

Saint Thomas could have noted that the first Epistle to Saint Timothy includes the expression "holding the mystery of faith in a pure conscience" (1 Tim 3:9). Later, in his treatment of the exact wording of the formulas of consecration, Saint Thomas reiterates that such liturgical details were deliberately hidden in the early Church; Scripture does not have as its purpose the revelation of the precise manner in which sacramental mysteries are to be celebrated.[4]

The phrase's antiquity and obscurity

Even the great demythologizer among twentieth-century liturgical scholars, Fr. Josef Jungmann, SJ, does not attempt to dismiss or deconstruct what he calls "the enigmatic words":

---

[3] *ST* III, qu. 78, art. 3.
[4] See *ST* III, qu. 83, art. 4, ad 2.

The phrase is found inserted in the earliest texts of the sacramentaries, and mentioned even in the seventh century. It is missing
only in some later sources. Regarding the meaning of the words
mysterium fidei, there is absolutely no agreement. A distant parallel is to be found in the *Apostolic Constitutions*, where our Lord is
made to say at the consecration of the bread: "This is the mystery
of the New Testament, take of it, eat, it is My Body." Just as here
the *mysterium* is referred to the bread in the form of a predicate,
so in the canon of our Mass it is referred to the chalice in the
form of an apposition. . . . *Mysterium fidei* is an independent
expansion, superadded to the whole self-sufficient complex that
precedes.

What is meant by the words *mysterium fidei*? Christian antiquity
would not have referred them so much to the obscurity of what is
here hidden from the senses, but accessible (in part) only to (subjective) faith. Rather it would have taken them as a reference to the
grace-laden *sacramentum* in which the entire (objective) faith, the
whole divine order of salvation, is comprised. The chalice of the
New Testament is the life-giving symbol of truth, the sanctuary of
our belief. How or when this insertion was made, or what external
event occasioned it, cannot readily be ascertained.[5]

Several points are worth pondering. This phrase appears in all the oldest
sources of the Mass we have, which suggests a great antiquity for its origin.
The critical edition of the Canon of the Mass, published by Brepols in the
Corpus Orationum series, shows no variation whatsoever of the position
of the *mysterium fidei*.[6] The Roman text is cited in over fifty manuscripts
of various ages and origins, with no significant variations. The Ambrosian
text, which is the product of a Romanization of the Ambrosian rite effected

[5] Josef Jungmann, *The Mass of the Roman Rite: Its Origins and Development ("Missarum
Sollemnia")*, trans. Francis A. Brunner (Notre Dame, IN: Christian Classics, 2012), 2:199–
201.
[6] Tome X (1997), begun by Edmond Eugene Möller and continued by Jean-Marie Clément,
OSB, and Bertrandus Coppetiers 't Wallant. Within the body of the work, that part of the
Canon is Oratio 6265, with three major variants attested: 6265a is the Roman text, 6265b the
Ambrosian, and 6265c an anomalous Ambrosian text attested in a single manuscript.

in the Carolingian era, has only five manuscripts—but they have it in the same place as well.

The oddness (on the face of it) of such an insertion, and the fact that it would be so jealously guarded and passed on, implies that it was considered not an incidental feature of the rite but something that pertained to the essence of the rite of Rome. While we might disagree with his subtle dig at Innocent III's interpretation, Jungmann's notion that the "*mysterium fidei*" points to nothing less than "the entire objective faith" of the Church, "the whole divine order of salvation," as localized (so to speak) in the symbol of the chalice and its precious content, is an impressive one. The axis of reality runs through that vessel tilted on the altar.

Jungmann's account, together with the paleographical records, brings strongly to the fore the basic problem that faces liturgical historians when they cannot know with certainty the origin of a particular custom. In such circumstances, it is *impossible* to exclude the hypothesis that it is of apostolic or subapostolic institution. If even the most rigorous scholarship cannot detect a particular moment in history when the words *mysterium fidei* were added for the first time, and if we have a monolithic witness of extant manuscripts, is it not far better—indeed, is it not a solemn obligation of reverence for the most sacred things we have in our possession—to preserve the formula exactly as it has been handed down? Doing otherwise would surely risk profanation. This would have been both the hypothesis and the attitude of all Catholics until the twentieth century.

A campaign to remove the phrase

In an act of astonishing hubris, this phrase was removed from its immemorial place and turned into the prompt for a "memorial acclamation" that had never existed in the Roman rite before. What had been a secret and sublime acknowledgment of salvation—hidden, like the Christian, with Christ in God (cf. Col 3:3)—became an extroverted announcement to the public, for the sake of "participation" reductively understood as saying and doing things. How exactly did this take place, and why?

Around the time of the Second Vatican Council, liturgical surgeons had been itching to ply their scalpels on the Roman Canon, as soon as authority would permit them to remedy its "defects." In a book chapter pompously called "The Principal Merits and Defects of the Present Roman Canon," Cipriano Vagaggini, OSB, held forth in 1966: "The third important defect in the way it [the Canon] relates the instituting of the Eucharist is the insertion of the phrase *mysterium fidei* in the midst of the words said over the chalice. This has no parallel in any other liturgy, and within the Roman rite itself its origin in uncertain and its meaning debatable. However, it is obvious that in its present form at least the insertion *mysterium fidei* serves to break up and interrupt the words of institution."[7]

Bugnini tells us in his mighty tome *The Reform of the Liturgy* that Vagaggini, "in three months of intensive work in the library of the Abbey of Mont-César (Louvain) during the summer of 1966 . . . composed two models of new Eucharistic Prayers, which he presented to the group for discussion."[8] The experts concurred that something had to be done about that pesky *mysterium fidei*:

> The addition "the mystery of faith" in the formula for the conse-
> cration of the wine in the Roman Canon: is not biblical; occurs
> only in the Roman Canon; is of uncertain origin and meaning.
> The experts themselves disagree on the precise sense of the words.
> In fact, some of them assign the phrase a quite dangerous mean-
> ing, since they translate it as "a sign for our faith"; interrupts the
> sentence and makes difficult both its understanding and its trans-
> lation. The French, for example, have been forced to repeat the
> word "blood" three times: "This is the cup of my blood, the blood
> of the new covenant, mystery of faith, blood shed . . ." The same is
> true to a greater or lesser extent in the other languages. Once again,
> many bishops and pastors have asked that in the new anaphoras
> the addition "mystery of faith" be dropped. All this explains the

---

[7]   Cipriano Vagaggini, *The Canon of the Mass and Liturgical Reform*, trans. Peter Coughlan (Staten Island, NY: Alba House, 1967), 104.

[8]   Annibale Bugnini, *The Reform of the Liturgy 1948–1975*, trans. Matthew J. O'Connell (Collegeville, MN: The Liturgical Press, 1990), 450. The group was Coetus X, the one to which the *Ordo Missae* was entrusted.

course followed in the new anaphoras with regard to the words of consecration.[9]

Moreover, it was felt to be desirable that there be some "acclamation of the congregation after the consecration and elevation of the chalice"; and why? "The practice is native to the Eastern Churches, but it seems appropriate to accept it into the Roman tradition as a way of increasing the active participation of the congregation. Regarding the exact form of the acclamation, the rubric says that it can use 'these or similar words approved by the territorial authorities.' Since the acclamations are to be said, or even sung, by the congregation, it is necessary to leave enough freedom for them to be adapted to the requirements of the various languages and musical genres."[10]

At this point in the process, then, the idea was to remove the words "*mysterium fidei*" altogether and simply have an acclamation follow upon the elevation of the chalice.

On June 26, 1967, Cardinal Ottaviani, in his capacity as head of the Congregation for the Doctrine of the Faith, sent a letter to Annibale Bugnini, expressing the changes that the Congregation would prefer to see made to the four Eucharistic Prayers that had been submitted for doctrinal review.[11] Those who see Ottaviani as a hero for placing his name on the *Short Critical Study* two years later may be surprised and disappointed to see how readily he was rolling along with the Consilium's plan:

> About the omission of the parenthesis (*inciso*) "mysterium fidei": affirmative.
>
> With regard to the "acclamation" immediately after the elevation, "Mortem tuam . . . ," we would prefer a text that expresses more clearly an act of faith, and thus replaces the disappeared "mysterium fidei"—[a phrase] certainly inopportune for the position in

---

[9] Bugnini, 454. The assertion that "it is not biblical" is characteristically misleading: *no* historic Christian liturgy has ever used strictly and solely a formula of consecration recorded in the New Testament. These liturgical rites pre-date the biblical texts and reflect particular customs which have their own rationale.

[10] Bugnini, 455.

[11] Prot. N. 1028/67, found on p. 14 of http://www.prexeucharistica.org/_pdf/EPICLESI/PIO -Lp015-02.pdf.

which it found itself, but obviously indicated as a call to awaken faith at that solemn moment. The evangelical phrase "Deus meus et Dominus meus" has been suggested.

While Ottaviani consented to the removal of the formula, his suggestion that a text other than *Mortem tuam* be used as the acclamation was evidently disregarded.

At the Synod of Bishops in October 1967—whose participants were the first significant body of "outsiders" to be shown the *Missa normativa* or rough draft of that which Paul VI would later call the *Novus Ordo Missae*[12] and who were then asked to vote on it and contribute comments—the following question, among others, was put to the Synod Fathers, as reported by Bugnini: "*Should the words 'mysterium fidei' be removed from the formula for the consecration of the wine?* Of the 183 voting, 93 said yes, 48 no, and 42 yes with qualifications. In substance, the qualifications were these: 1) The words should also be omitted in the Roman Canon. 2) The words should not completely disappear from the liturgy but should be used as an acclamation after the consecration or in some other formula."[13] If we take the no votes and the qualified yes (*placet iuxta modum*) votes together, we see that the majority unqualifiedly in favor of removal was narrow: 93 to 90. Nevertheless, it seems that the attitude of most was like that of Ottaviani: why not take advantage of the general upheaval and turn this phrase into a vehicle of participation?

One cannot escape the impression of people "making things up as they go along," bereft of any real reverence for tradition or fear of the Lord.[14] The counsel of wisdom had been forgotten: "Pass not beyond the ancient bounds which thy fathers have set" (Prov 22:28).

---

[12] Consistory of Cardinals, May 24, 1976: "usus novi Ordinis Missae" and "Novus Ordo promulgatus est"—"the use of the new Order of Mass"; "the new Order has been promulgated."
[13] Bugnini, *Reform of the Liturgy*, 352.
[14] For an eye-witness account of the kind of reformatory madness to which Bugnini had surrendered himself at this time, see Archbishop Lefebvre's recounting of a meeting held in Rome with superiors general in the mid-1960s in *The Mass of All Time*, ed. Fr. Patrick Troadec, trans. Angelus Press (Kansas City, MO: Angelus Press, 2007), 183–84; cf. my article "What Bugnini Was Thinking When He Destroyed the Catholic Mass," *OnePeterFive*, February 5, 2019.

Paul VI insists on repurposing

The issue remained controversial within the Consilium. As Bugnini narrates, the topic came up again at the tenth general meeting (April 23–30, 1968), which met to discuss the six changes on which Paul VI had had the temerity (in the experts' view) to insist in regard to the *Missa normativa*. "The whole matter caused some dismay, since the pope seemed to be limiting the Consilium's freedom of research by using his authority to impose solutions."[15] The special subcommittee created to deal with the problem included, among others, Rembert Weakland, Joseph Gelineau, and Cipriano Vagaggini.

In regard to our present topic, Paul VI—who (as we saw in chapter 4) had chosen *Mysterium Fidei* as the title for his 1965 encyclical defending transubstantiation and condemning certain heretical tendencies in Eucharistic theology—disliked the idea of going straight from the elevation to the acclamation and had stipulated: "the words 'mysterium fidei' are [still] to be spoken by the priest before the acclamation of the congregation." Bugnini relates:

> What were the difficulties raised by the study group against the adoption of what the Pope wanted? . . . *Mystery of faith.* If the words were said by the celebrant before the acclamation of the congregation, (a) this would be an innovation not found in the liturgical tradition; (b) it would alter the structure of the Canon at an important moment; (c) it would change the meaning of the words in question, since they are no longer connected with the consecration of the chalice. If the words are to be kept, the report said, they should be connected either with the formula of consecration of the wine or with the acclamation.[16]

In the end, Paul VI prevailed. We are therefore not surprised to find this change and its pastoral "benefit" announced in the Apostolic Constitution *Missale Romanum* of April 3, 1969. The irony of its immediate context, however, deserves close attention:

Bugnini, *Reform of the Liturgy*, 370. What an ironic observation, when it is solely the pope's authority that will impose the Consilium's rite on the Church itself! The entire reform a gigantic papally-imposed "solution."

Bugnini, 371–72.

As to the words *Mysterium fidei*, removed from the context of the words of Christ our Lord and spoken by the Priest, these open the way, as it were, to the acclamation of the faithful.

Regarding the Order of Mass, "the rites have been simplified, due care being taken to preserve their substance." . . . Furthermore, "there have been restored . . . in accordance with the ancient norm of the holy Fathers, various elements which have suffered injury through accidents of history" (*SC* 50).

Unlike the justification for "restoring" the "responsorial psalm," which is based on false antiquarianism[17] and a reductive theory of participation,[18] here the pope offers no explanation *except* that it shall "open the way, as it were, to the acclamation of the faithful." Yet this change to the venerable Roman Canon (which was replicated in all the neo-anaphoras) *cannot* have been done with "due care" to "preserve [the] substance" of the rites. So far from "*restoring* elements that have suffered injury through accidents of history, in accordance with the ancient norm of the holy fathers,"[19] the ancient norm was expressly violated; the only injury inflicted was of the Consilium's design. It was rather through the accidents of the postconciliar liturgical reform that the Roman rite suffered injury.

Cardinals and theologians protest

Once the approved text of the Novus Ordo became available in 1969, Cardinal Ottaviani seems to have changed his mind sufficiently to be willing to sign his name, alongside Cardinal Bacci's, to the *Short Critical Study of the New Order of Mass*, in which we find the following critique by "a group

---

[17] See Peter Kwasniewski, *Reclaiming Our Roman Catholic Birthright: The Genius and Timeliness of the Traditional Latin Mass* (Brooklyn, NY: Angelico Press, 2020), 149–60.

[18] For a full treatment of "actual participation" (*participatio actuosa*) and errors concerning it, see Peter Kwasniewski, *Noble Beauty, Transcendent Holiness: Why the Modern Age Needs the Mass of Ages* (Kettering, OH: Angelico Press, 2017), 191–213; Kwasniewski, *Reclaiming Our Birthright*, 55–75; Peter Kwasniewski, *Ministers of Christ: Recovering the Roles of Clergy and Laity in an Age of Confusion* (Manchester, NH: Crisis Publications, 2021), 131–51.

[19] The theory propounded by some preconciliar scholars, to the effect that the *mysterium fidei* originated as something that the deacon said to the people at or just after the Consecration, was already dismissed in 1949 by Jungmann as "poetry, not history" (*Mass of the Roman Rite*, 199). This was a book *everyone* had read at the time.

of Roman theologians": "The old formula for the Consecration was a *sacramental* formula, properly speaking, and not merely *narrative*. . . . The Scripture text was not used word-for-word as the formula for the Consecration. St. Paul's expression *the mystery of faith* was inserted into the text as an immediate expression of the priest's faith in the mystery which the Church makes real through the hierarchical priesthood."[20]

I find this an excellent insight into the ascetical benefit for the priest: the *mysterium fidei* in the midst of the consecration of the Precious Blood is a "speed bump" that reminds him to be ever more aware of the awesome reality of what he is doing before God and for the people—no empty commemoration, but the making present of the objective Mystery "which hath been hidden from ages and generations, but now is manifested to his saints" (Col 1:26). The *Short Critical Study* continues:

> Furthermore, the people's Memorial Acclamation which immediately follows the Consecration—*We proclaim your death, O Lord . . . until you come again*—introduces the same ambiguity about the Real Presence under the guise of an allusion to the Last Judgment. Without so much as a pause, the people proclaim their expectation of Christ at the end of time just at the moment when He is *substantially present* on the altar—as if Christ's *real* coming will occur only at the end of time rather than there on the altar itself. The second optional Memorial Acclamation brings this out even more strongly: "When we eat this bread and drink this cup, we proclaim your death, O Lord, until you come again." The juxtaposition of entirely different realities—immolation and eating, the Real Presence and Christ's Second Coming—brings ambiguity to a new height.[21]

Even if the *Short Study* could have expressed this criticism more accurately (the language is too loose), it is unquestionably right to say that dislodging

---

[20] Alfredo Cardinal Ottaviani and Antonio Cardinal Bacci, *The Ottaviani Intervention: Short Critical Study of the New Order of Mass*, trans. Anthony Cekada (West Chester, OH: Philothea Press, 2010), 56.

[21] Ottaviani and Bacci, 58; text slightly modified to match the 2011 English text of the memorial acclamations.

a phrase of such antiquity, theological density, and priestly aid, and introducing acclamations that immediately shift attention to the eschatological
banquet and to the "assembly," cannot but modify the understanding of
the intended action.

A response printed in 1969 in *Notitiae*, the official journal of the Consilium (and later of the Congregation for Divine Worship), made it clear
that the transplantation of the *mysterium fidei* fundamentally altered its
character.

> Query: When no member of the faithful is present who can make
> the acclamation after the consecration, should the priest say "The
> mystery of faith"?
>
> Response: *In the negative.* The words *The mystery of faith*, which
> have been taken from the context of the words of the Lord and
> placed after the consecration, "serve as an introduction to the
> acclamation of the faithful" (cf. Const. *Missale Romanum*). When,
> however, in particular circumstances no one is able to respond, the
> priest omits these words, as is done in a Mass which, out of grave
> necessity, is celebrated without any minister, in which the greetings
> and the blessing at the end of Mass are omitted (*Inst. gen.*, n. 211).
> The same holds true for a concelebration of priests in which no
> member of the faithful is present.[22]

In other words, the phrase has been transformed from a theologically poly-
semous component of the formula of consecration with ascetical benefit for
the celebrant into a congregationally-directed prompt. Without the congregation, the *mysterium fidei*, in a sense, ceases to exist. This *Notitiae* response
testifies to the phrase's total severance from tradition.

Larger implications of the change

The removal of *mysterium fidei* from its hallowed position to a new position
with a new function had at least a quadruple effect.

---

[22] *Notitiae* 5 (1969): 324–25, n. 3. This translation of the original Latin is from http://notiti
ae.ipsissima-verba.org/.

First, it ratified once again, and in a rather dramatic way, the widespread tendency of modern liturgical scholars—not only Jungmann, who, as we have seen, is sound on the *mysterium fidei*, but even such eminent figures as Adrian Fortescue and Cardinal Schuster—to assume that long-standing parts of the text of the Canon and of many other parts of the liturgy are mere historical accidents, or more likely, mistakes introduced by ignoramuses. It slapped the Vagagginis of the world on the back and said: "Well done, thou critic of good and faithful servants!"

Second, it cancels out or at least brackets in suspicion the pious belief in the derivation of the formula from apostolic tradition and the medieval reception of the same tradition, a belief to which the exceptionless paleographical witness offers a support greater than any doubts scholarship can induce. In this way, it made its own contribution to that general undermining of piety toward inherited liturgical forms that was, perhaps, the most execrable fallout of the reform.

Third, by audaciously modifying the formula used at the most solemn moment of the Holy Sacrifice, the change sent the clear message—clearer even than the insertion of the name of Saint Joseph into the Canon in 1962, which was its precursor—that the liturgical changes undertaken in the sixties constitute a revolution, not a reform. Certain changes cannot plausibly be seen as refinements or adjustments that remain in continuity with tradition; they are, quite simply, ruptures. The sooner we recognize this, the sooner we can put aside the will-o'-the-wisp of "the Reform of the Reform" and resume lost continuity where it was broken off.[23]

Lastly, on a wholly practical level, there is the sheer banality of the fabricated "memorial acclamation" as carried out in practice in the plethora of vernacular versions into which the Roman rite has been balkanized.[24] When the Eucharistic Prayer is spoken aloud in the vernacular, the atmosphere—which a restrained *ars celebrandi* might even have rendered somewhat prayerful—is shattered at its most solemn point by the never quite unanimous muttering of one or another appointed text, led off by

---

See my article "Why the 'Reform of the Reform' Is Doomed," *OnePeterFive*, April 22, 2020.
In contrast to nearly every vernacular version I've ever heard, the Latin acclamation (*Mor-m tuam annuntiamus, Domine . . .*) is set to a beautiful chant melody. Nevertheless, the chant's aesthetic value cannot override the profound problems noted in this chapter.

the priest in his secondary role of schoolmarm. When the acclamation is sung, the results can be far worse: musicians malnourished on a diet of Haugen-Haas™ seem to fall beneath even their worst efforts when they set the memorial acclamations in treacly tunes with cartoon clichés. The immolation of the Bridegroom is mentally wiped out by a cheap imitation of Broadway.

From a ritual and theological point of view, this acclamation is nothing but an intrusion, an interruption, and an irrelevancy in the flow of the liturgical action, which at that moment centers on the holy Victim, the pure Victim, the spotless Victim, offered to the Father for the salvation of man. Our participation is to adore in silence, uniting ourselves to His sacrifice on the Cross and awaiting His abundant mercy. It is not the *mysterium fidei* that deserves to be denigrated as a "parenthesis," but the memorial acclamation, brainchild of Paul VI and the Consilium.[25]

As always, tradition is the way forward

The mystery of our faith is intimately and intrinsically bound up with *hunc praeclarum calicem*, "this precious chalice." The whispered words *mysterium fidei* stand at the *heart* of the consecration of the chalice. Their removal is emblematic of what was done to the liturgy as a whole, when the heart of so many rites was ripped out of them. Even if the words *mysterium fidei* are not necessary for signifying transubstantiation (and thus, the consecration can be "effective," and the Mass "valid," without them), the removal of the phrase from its age-old position exudes the attitude: nothing is sacred.

Psalm 15 uses the cup or chalice as a symbol of God's generous provision to His people: "The Lord is the portion of my inheritance and of my cup: it is thou that wilt restore my inheritance to me" (Ps 15:5). This

---

[25] As if the loss of *mysterium fidei* in the words of consecration were not bad enough, translations into many languages falsely rendered *pro multis* as "for all," causing consternation among Catholics educated enough to recognize that this verged on tampering with the very form of the sacrament. It was one of the main arguments used by those who wrongly, but understandably, denied the validity of the Novus Ordo. Pope Benedict XVI took steps to see that translations were corrected. This happened in the English-speaking world with the 201 edition of the *ritus modernus*, but the Germans stubbornly refused, even after the pope sent a letter *Pro Multis*, dated April 14, 2012, to the Episcopal Conference of Germany through its president, H. E. Robert Zollitsch.

verse—which is the form in the ceremony of tonsure and the vesting prayer for the cassock—reminds us of the nature of our *liturgical* inheritance. It is not the fallout of meandering chance and merely human intentions, subject to perpetual revision, but a living tradition that begins in the *Logos* of God and culminates in the *Logos*-made-flesh, our eternal High Priest who guides His Church by the gift of His Spirit. The attitude we are supposed to have toward our inheritance—that which "falls to our lot"—is captured in the next verse: "The lines are fallen unto me in goodly places: for my inheritance is goodly to me" (Ps 15:6).

These two words, *mysterium fidei* . . . That we do not know whence they came, or why they are where they are, imposes an insurmountable limit of humility to our scholarly pride; that we cannot comprehend the full scope of their meaning or sort them into Cartesian "clear and distinct" ideas thwarts the restless vanity of our ambitions, putting us in the place of beggars who look for whatever scraps of insight may fall from our master's heavenly table. That is what we truly are; this is where we truly belong. "Here is the patience and the faith of the saints. . . . Here is wisdom" (Rev 13:10, 18).

The unceasing celebration of the Church's liturgy in which the eternal truths are being constantly reasserted with ever increasing solemnity is the normal life of the people of God; yet it is a spiritual phenomenon so vast as to defy description, and therefore is not the object of the historiographer but a spectacle which the angels of God love to behold: it is truly eternal life on earth.

—Dom Ansgar Vonier

The spuriousness of the liturgical reform is not a matter of details. The overall truth is that the criticisms that were made of the old rite were pedantic trivia, while the faults of the modern liturgical practice are fundamental and go to the heart of the liturgy. They include the loss of the concept of sacrifice, of the true understanding of the altar, of the separateness of the sanctuary, of the liturgical principle of orientation, of hierarchical celebration, and above all of the sacramental and doctrinal realities without which liturgical science is mere flummery.

—Henry Sire

10

Byzantine, Tridentine, Montinian: Two Brothers and a Stranger

Most traditionalists believe, myself included, that the Byzantine Divine Liturgy and the traditional Roman Mass are spiritual close relations, while the Novus Ordo departs so far from the heritage they share in common that its kinship is remote and doubtful. But one sometimes encounters Catholics who, misled by superficial similarities between the Byzantine liturgy and the Novus Ordo (e.g., that they are often done in a vernacular language audibly pronounced) and by the obvious differences between the Byzantine liturgy and the traditional Roman rite (e.g., that there is much more silence in the latter than in the former, and that the people seem to play a more "active" role in the one than in the other), maintain that the Byzantine and Novus Ordo liturgies are more akin, and thus, when presented with a choice, will choose either the Byzantine or Novus Ordo over the Tridentine rite. Indeed, protagonists and apologists of the liturgical reform often profess to be admirers of the Eastern tradition and like to point out the many seemingly "Eastern" features of the neo-Roman liturgy.

The goal of the present chapter is to state *precisely* what the commonality between the Byzantine liturgy and the traditional Latin liturgy consists in, and how the Novus Ordo differs starkly from them both. We can see this commonality in the following principles:

1. Tradition

2. Mystery

3. Elevated mode

4. Ritual integrity or stability

5. Density

6. Adequate and repeated preparation

7. Truthfulness

8. Hierarchy

9. Parallelism

10. Separation

1. The Principle of Tradition

Both the Byzantine liturgy and the traditional Roman liturgy are the result of an organic development of an ancient apostolic core, transmitted through centuries of living faith; in spite of attributions of this or that liturgy to a famous saint such as Saint John Chrysostom or Saint Basil or Saint Gregory, in fact the rite is the work of many holy men, most of them anonymous. No Eastern liturgy or classic Western liturgy is the product of a committee of avant-garde experts out of touch with the people and captive to fashionable theories long since exploded. We may call this the principle of tradition, of receiving what is handed down. Put simply: *it is not the case that a liturgy is good because the authority of the Church deems it to be good; rather, the Church knows it to be good because she has received it.*

Here we strike at the root of that bizarre ultramontanism (or better, hyperpapalism) in the West that considers liturgy to be nothing other than what papal authority has decreed—as if liturgy is an infinitely malleable clay whose shape is left wholly to the sculptor's will.[1] I know a Catholic philosopher who maintains that the only reason a rite of Mass is legitimate

---

[1] See Geoffrey Hull, *The Banished Heart: Origins of Heteropraxis in the Catholic Church* (New York: T&T Clark, 2010). If Hull has a flaw, it would be his tendency to contrast Roman papal tyranny against a vision of enviable Byzantine stasis. To the extent that the East has been static, it may derive from a different kind of archaeologism—one made possible by the lack of centralized authority. It's not for nothing that in Vladimir Soloviev's *Short Story of Antichrist*, the Orthodox are offered a magnificent Museum of Christian Archaeology in exchange for their allegiance to a one-world government. Prior to World War II, it seemed general as if the popes knew how to enrich their own rite without destroying it.

is because the pope has declared it so, and that if the pope wanted to gut all the content of the rite and replace it with something totally different, it would be a true Catholic rite as long as it contained the words of consecration. Nothing more foreign to the spirit of apostolic, Patristic, historic, dogmatic Christianity could possibly be imagined.[2] If one might paraphrase Newman: "To be deep in history is to cease to be a hyperpapalist."

A palpable sign of tradition in East and West is the ever-accumulating sanctoral calendars that are only rarely simplified and never massively overhauled. The operative rule is to carry along beloved saints already devoutly honored for centuries while adding more saints as the Lord raises them up in His Church. In this department, it is no exaggeration to say "the more, the merrier." If there is a need to add another saint to a particular day, the ready solution is to commemorate both, rather than casting one of them into the outer darkness.[3]

2. The Principle of Mystery

Each of these liturgical traditions exhibits the principle of mystery: the liturgy, like the God it approaches, is a *mysterium tremendum et fascinans*, palpably sacred, a work and a wonder that God does in our midst, to which man is permitted to unite himself in fear and trembling, but also with intimate trust and hope of salvation from his sins. The prayers strongly emphasize the holiness of God, the primacy of His divine action, the awesomeness

---

[2] In 1958, Louis Bouyer said in a lecture in Strasbourg: "Recently in an English magazine, a Catholic writer with the assurance of an ultramontanist wrote that it is a waste of time to study the ancient liturgy in order to prepare for a liturgical revival. After all, said he, the supreme authority of the Church is not bound by anything and could freely give us an entirely new liturgy, answering to today's needs, without any further concern for the past. We need only, therefore, wait for this grant with confidence. A strange way, indeed, to exalt the authority of the Church, and one which strongly resembles, however little it might seem to at first sight, the apologetic approach of the modernists who said that the Church was above the Gospel, since it was her own fabrication. The logic of such a position exalting authority for its own sake, is the same as that of the cynical Anglican bishop of the eighteenth century who said that the Anglican Church did in fact teach the Trinity, but that only an act of Parliament would be needed to make it unitarian. Authority in the Catholic Church is very far from accepting such flatteries which, in reality, do it injury." *The Liturgy and the Word of God* (Collegeville, MN: The Liturgical Press, 1959), 65.

[3] See Peter Kwasniewski, "The Sanctoral Killing Fields: On the Removal of Saints from the General Roman Calendar," *NLM*, November 16, 2020.

of what is taking place, the unworthiness of the ministers, the need for continual purification as we dare to draw near.

Traditional liturgy is like the cloud on the mountain in which God is said to dwell and into which Moses disappears, "setting aside every earthly care." It has for its purpose "that we may receive the King of all, invisibly escorted by angelic hosts." There is no sense of a meeting with an agenda, conducted by company managers, characterized by a lot of reading of texts and sharing out of tasks. We lie prostrate on holy ground before the burning bush of divine self-revelation. At the conclusion, we are entitled to say: "We have seen the true light, we have received the heavenly Spirit, we have found the true faith, and we adore the undivided Trinity for having saved us." Every step of the way, the Tridentine liturgy, as austere as it is by comparison, prays in just the same spirit, and creates the same atmosphere, saturated with ineffable mystery.

3. The Principle of Elevated Mode

The prayers and lessons of traditional Eastern and Western liturgies are either chanted by cantors, deacons, subdeacons, and choirs, or whispered or proclaimed at the altar by the priest, but never merely recited like the daily news or a school lesson. Part of this elevation is the use of what we might call "high language." In the East, it takes the form of exquisite poetic compositions; in the West, of venerable Latin locutions. Latin is as truly, properly, and definitively the language of the Roman Catholic Church as certain elevated sacral vernaculars are the languages of Eastern rites.

One has to be careful about claiming that "use of the vernacular" is characteristic of Eastern rites *in the same way* in which it characterizes the Novus Ordo in the latter's vast number of translations into modern languages. The vernacular *can* be used, as when the Divine Liturgy is offered in English throughout the United States, yet a plurality of older customs will be found too. Greek-speaking churches/patriarchates use Byzantine liturgical Greek. The small Italian-Albanian Church in Calabria and Sicily continues to have most of its liturgy in Greek on Sundays and feasts. Slavic Orthodox churches were long accustomed to the use of Old Church Slavonic; Russians still use it predominantly or exclusively, and while Serbians, Bulgarians,

Macedonians, Belarusians, and Ukrainians use much vernacular, Slavonic is still in use. The Romanian Orthodox Church used Church Slavonic/liturgical Greek from the tenth to the seventeenth centuries, when it was replaced by Romanian (which was nevertheless influenced by Church Slavonic, making it quite non-vernacular in feel). The Georgian Orthodox Church uses old literary Georgian as a liturgical language. The Coptic Orthodox use the literary Coptic language, and although its use diminished during long Muslim rule, it is still alive and being reintroduced. The Ethiopian Orthodox use the "dead language" Ge'ez in their liturgy. The Melkite and Syrian liturgies of the Near East use classical Syrian and Arabic. The Armenians use a classical literary Armenian.[4]

The enduring use of Latin for over 1,600 years in the West is not a random accident but a constitutive principle, as none other than Pope John XXIII declared in his Apostolic Constitution *Veterum Sapientia*, signed sixty years ago, February 22, 1962, at the high altar of Saint Peter's Basilica, and never rescinded (albeit almost universally ignored). Those who attend the *usus antiquior* are well aware of the powerful effect on the faithful of the ceremonial use of an ancient language that has acquired a numinous force with the passage of time. The special setting-apart of this ancient language, consecrated as it were for the public worship of God, both objectively embodies and subjectively fosters awareness of that separation of sacred from profane that is at the heart of sacrificial religion.

4. The Principle of Ritual Integrity

Both the Divine Liturgy and the traditional Latin Mass pre-exist any given celebration as determinate, fully-articulated rites that clergy and people follow with humble obedience. The prayers, antiphons, readings, gestures, and chants are fixed and prescribed; above all, the most holy prayer, the anaphora, is either unchanging (in the West) or determined by

---

Moreover, what exactly is meant by "vernacular"? Old Church Slavonic, for example, was created so that the Slavs could understand the liturgy; yet it was also created to translate a poetic liturgical Greek, which meant it never sounded like a language spoken on the street, any more than did the rhetorical Latin of the fourth century into which the Roman rite was originally placed. In most cultures, moreover, there was a large gap between literary language and spoken language, much larger than is typical today, both because more people today are technically literate, and because high literary language has basically disappeared.

the liturgical calendar (in the East). In this way, the celebrant's personal preferences or choices are never driving the action. We may also call this the *principle of stability*, since the ritual integrity guarantees to the clergy and the people an immovable rock on which they may build their spiritual lives.

A writer for the progressivist blog *PrayTell*, Liborius Lumma, beautifully describes this benefit as he experiences it in the Eastern liturgy, while unwittingly offering a pointed critique of precisely that respect in which the modern "Roman" rite differs from the traditional Roman rite:

> I have never experienced Eastern liturgy as an arena for different theological tendencies. Western liturgy offers lots of creative options. Just one example: In a Roman [*sic*; he means modern] Mass you can (and have to) select one of several Eucharistic Prayers, a lot of hymns (if any—you can even omit them), write the Prayer of the Faithful completely by yourself, choose from different options for the Opening Rite, etc. All these options make it possible to adapt the liturgy to different communities and situations, but they can also turn [it] into an instrument of power. Those who arrange the liturgy exercise power over those who join the service without knowing what is going to happen. Western liturgical ministers are permanent decision-makers. There is no way to avoid this role, and it needs much theological knowledge and sense of responsibility to fulfill this role in a good manner.
>
> Eastern liturgical offices are much more regarded as roles in a sacred play. At first sight bishops, priests, deacons, and cantors are very dominant compared to the people. This gives Eastern liturgies a very hierarchical (and male-dominated) touch. But all these ministers make almost no decisions at all on single liturgical elements. Even when the cantors choose the melodies for several chants, the texts themselves remain undiscussed. They are given, not chosen. . . . This inflexibility can be a spiritual value: Liturgy is a treasure that is traded [delivered?] to us by our predecessors and it is meant to be passed to our successors. It is like a

flowing river that we get into and out of every now and then, but the river always stays the same.[5]

Everything Lumma says here about "Eastern liturgical offices" applies perfectly to the classical Roman rite. In traditional rites, Eastern or Western, at every moment throughout the action, it is clear what is to be done, said, or sung. Liturgy is a public, ecclesiastical action, not the province or prerogative of an individual celebrant who can play at being God, making the liturgy come into being at his own hands. God forbid! The ministers are only that: ministers. They receive what has been given to them and enact it according to the ritual of the Church, as her representatives and for the benefit of her children. Indeed, Saint Thomas goes so far as to call the priest an "animated tool" of Christ the High Priest, a rational instrument that places his mind and heart at the disposal of the Lord.[6]

5. The Principle of Density

The old Roman liturgy, and likewise the old Byzantine, is shot through with dogmatic, moral, ascetical-mystical content. The prayers are thick and rich and full of religion. They are a poetic tapestry of Scripture and other devout utterances. The Novus Ordo is patently exiguous by comparison. Think of the various troparia of the Byzantine tradition, or the wealth of proper antiphons in the Roman rite, and the Collects, Secrets, and Postcommunions, few of which survived intact the bowdlerizing scalpel of the Consilium. Carl Olson made this observation:

> Having now attended a Byzantine parish for nearly 20 years, it's interesting that while the Eastern Liturgies are not silent in the way

---

5 "Things I Like About Eastern Christianity, Part 3," *PrayTell*, June 21, 2018. For a perspective from even further East, see Joseph Shaw's review of Byung-Chul Han's *The Disappearance of Rituals*: "A Post-Modern Defence of Ritual," *The European Conservative*, March 3, 2022.
6 See Peter Kwasniewski, *Ministers of Christ: Recovering the Roles of Clergy and Laity in an Age of Confusion* (Manchester, NH: Crisis Publications, 2021), 13–30, esp. 24; *Resurgent in the Midst of Crisis: Sacred Liturgy, the Traditional Latin Mass, and Renewal in the Church* (Kettering, OH: Angelico Press, 2014), 71–78, 112; *Holy Bread of Eternal Life: Restoring Eucharistic Reverence in an Age of Impiety* (Manchester, NH: Sophia Institute Press, 2020), 95–96.

that the Latin Mass is—in fact, there is little silence in a Byzantine liturgy—the deeper similarities and convergences are found in reverence, transcendence, and theological richness. Frankly, listening to many of the prayers said at a Novus Ordo Mass about makes me lose my mind. Put another way, the Divine Liturgy and the Latin Mass both speak to the mind, the heart, and the senses in mysterious and deep ways that, while somewhat subjective to certain degrees, are at the service of objective truth and divine reality.[7]

Olson's point would apply to any of the "received" liturgical rites and uses, be it Sarum or Roman, Dominican or Premonstratensian, Ambrosian or Mozarabic, Slavic or Greek, Coptic or Armenian. Imagine if a liturgy professor were to give his students the following assignment (something quite possible to carry out in a big city like Washington, DC): "On six Sundays in succession, pick historic non-Western Christian liturgies to attend. On the seventh Sunday, attend a Solemn High Tridentine Mass, and on the eighth, attend a modern Catholic Mass. Then write up a report comparing and contrasting the experiences." But of course the professor would never do such a thing, as it would badly backfire. He is likely to be far more interested in how the liturgical reform opened up a new era of ecumenism with our separated (Protestant) brothers and sisters.

6. The Principle of Preparation

Closely connected with the foregoing is the principle of adequate and repeated preparation. In both East and West, the clergy and ministers prepare themselves thoroughly for their work at the altar, whether it be at a side table preparing the offerings with abundant prayers, or at the foot of the altar reciting Psalm 42, the Confiteor, and prayers of ascent. How could anyone who is possessed of the slightest consciousness of what the Holy Sacrifice of the Mass *is* saunter out of the sacristy and walk right up to the altar, as if it's no big deal? As if one were going up the steps of a post office, or visiting the salad bar at a restaurant? I have seen people at college commencements mount a platform or approach a podium with more decorum and consciousness of *gravitas*.

---

[7] Comment on Facebook.

As Catherine Pickstock noted so well, the repetition of prayers in all genuine liturgies is deliberate and of immense spiritual importance.[8] The Byzantine liturgy has the priest frequently praying secretly from start to finish as he prepares himself again and again for the next wondrous step that has to be taken into the mysteries of Christ. The authentic Roman liturgy is no different, with its ample Offertory, its three prayers of preparation for Communion, prayers of ablution, Placeat, and Last Gospel. We find much repetition in the Divine Liturgy and the Roman *usus antiquior*—in the former, cascading litanies of "Lord, have mercy" or "Grant it, O Lord"; in the latter, the ninefold Kyrie, the triple Confiteor, the triple "Domine, non sum dignus" (done twice to indicate the distinction between the priest's Communion and the faithful's). Another mode of repetition no less powerful in its formative and expressive value is the use of forefeasts, afterfeasts, and leavetaking (in the East) or vigils and octaves (in the West) to add special emphasis to particular celebrations and to linger over their mysteries.

We are well aware that these prayers were built up over time, and that (e.g.) the Last Gospel was a relatively late addition.[9] But the additions happened *for good reason*; they happened under the gentle influence of the Holy Spirit. It is one thing not to have known them in an earlier century; it is quite another to *remove* them after they had been appropriately and harmoniously added and had become a fixed part of the rite for centuries. The former is as pardonable as an Old Testament prophet's ignorance of exact circumstances in the life of Christ; the latter would be as unpardonable as a Christian's adoption of Judaism. As I argued in chapter 2, dropping what has been worthily added is nothing less than a repudiation of its theological content and liturgical function. The Constitution *Sacrosanctum Concilium* thus positively errs in claiming that the traditional liturgy contains "useless repetition" in need of purging. Anyone who enters prayerfully into the repetitions of the old liturgy understands their purpose, which has never

---

See Catherine Pickstock, *After Writing: On the Liturgical Consummation of Philosophy* (Oxford: Blackwell, 1998), esp. 169–252; see my lecture "Poets, Lovers, Children, Madmen—and Worshipers: Why We Repeat Ourselves in the Liturgy," *Rorate Caeli*, February 19, 2019.
    It entered the liturgy via the Dominicans in the thirteenth century and was made obligatory for the Church by the Dominican pope Saint Pius V.

presented any difficulty to Christians until the bad mental habits of rationalism and utilitarianism arose in modern times.

Moreover, the discipline of fasting and abstinence is best understood
not simply as a means of doing penance but as a way of ensuring a clear-
minded dedication to the worship of God and a pure reception of the holy
mysteries of Christ. The Byzantine calendar features four fasts during the
liturgical year: those of the Nativity, All Saints/Peter and Paul, the Dormi-
tion, and Great Lent. The traditional Roman liturgy retained for a long
time a greater Lenten fast and a lesser Advent fast, although the latter did
not survive modernity. Paul VI, as part of his campaign of relentless modernization, approved a liturgy that effectively abolished the sole fasting
season that was still left in the West.[10] If this counts as "looking to the
East" for inspiration, language has lost any meaning. In reality, the liturgical reformers' frequent appeal to Byzantine this or that should not blind
us to their willful selectivity. For example, some Westerners approve of the
Eastern custom of a married clergy; but are they willing to embrace the
age-old Byzantine discipline that a deacon or priest, from the day before
any Eucharistic liturgy, must abstain from marital relations? Of course not;
for the devil has induced in the West the strategy of praising anything Byzantine that chimes in with our modern or postmodern fancy, while totally
ignoring anything that runs against it, such as ascetical discipline or the
length and beauty of the liturgies.

7. The Principle of Truthfulness

The *whole* of the Gospel message is present in the traditional lectionaries—the so-called "difficult" parts, too, as well as the easier ones. In the
Novus Ordo, Scripture is edited to conform to modern prejudices, either
by suppressing passages that were always read in Roman Catholic worship
or by excising verses or offering abbreviated versions.[11] More broadly, th
traditional *lex orandi* contains and transmits with apostolic vigor the ful

---

[10] The days of fasting were reduced from forty to two (!); most of the prayers mentionin
fasting were eliminated; abstinence was minimized; and the pre-Lenten period of Septuage
ima, which has an exact parallel in the East, was abolished.
[11] For a list of articles critical of the new lectionary's principles and content, see Peter Kwa
niewski, "The Postconciliar Lectionary at 50: A Detailed Critique," *NLM*, May 25, 2019.

lex credendi of the Catholic Church, without any editing for contemporary sensibilities or sensitivities. Thus, to take one example from a thousand, the damnation of Judas, and the real possibility of hell for any of us, is taught unflinchingly, while the cursing psalms directed against our spiritual enemies are made use of plentifully. This kind of thing is excised from or heavily reduced in the Novus Ordo.[12] In this regard, it fails to pass on the fullness of the Faith as we find it in Scripture, the Fathers, the Councils, and the Doctors of the Church; it fails in its role as the *lex orandi* of the orthodox Church.

In fact, many doctrines of the faith are *seen and heard* in the old liturgies, whereas they have to be *studied* and blindly accepted in the context of the neo-Roman liturgy, because the rite itself does not make them evident. For example, consider the veneration that ought to be paid to the saints and the adoration of *latreia* that ought to be shown to the Blessed Sacrament. One who attends either the Byzantine or the traditional Roman liturgy will have a visceral experience of the venerability of the saints and the adorableness of the Eucharist. In contrast, the Novus Ordo has systematically pared down the focus on the saints[13] as well as the signs of reverence to be paid to the awesome mysteries of Christ.

8. The Principle of Hierarchy

Manifest in the clear division of roles for priest, deacon, subdeacon, acolyte, cantor, etc., is a profoundly hierarchical conception of the cosmos, the Church, and of the Church-at-prayer. This non-interchangeable diversity of roles is grossly confused and diluted in the Novus Ordo, with its loose regulations on laypeople functioning in the sanctuary.[14] Neither Byzantine nor authentic Roman liturgy allows unvested laymen to step right into the sanctuary during liturgy and perform works proper

---

[12] See my article "Damned Lies: On the Destiny of Judas Iscariot," *Rorate Caeli*, March 30, 2015; on the omission of psalms, see my article "The Omission of 'Difficult' Psalms and the Spreading-thin of the Psalter," *Rorate Caeli*, November 15, 2016.
[13] The Roman Canon, like the anaphora of the Divine Liturgy of Saint John Chrysostom, mentions many saints. The neo-anaphoras severely curtail this homage and appeal.
[14] For an extended treatment of this topic, see Kwasniewski, *Ministers of Christ*.

to the clergy, above all the handling of the Most Holy Eucharist. Rather, the identity of the cleric as one who offers or ministers to divine worship is thoroughly respected and demonstrated in action—and the identity of the layman as actively assisting at the sacrifice is likewise respected and demonstrated in action.

The liturgy bequeathed by tradition is a true embodiment of ecclesiology instead of an imaginary alternative to it. One would never be able to derive a coherent and consistent account of the hierarchical nature of the Mystical Body from the Novus Ordo, whereas it is easy to do so from either the Divine Liturgy or the traditional Roman Mass. Participation, therefore, is understood in a fundamentally different way in the traditional liturgies and in the neo-Roman rite. The correct view is that participation should befit the distinct roles of various parts of the Mystical Body, and that this differentiation should be *visible* to all in the dress, bearing, location, and tasks assigned—and *not* assigned—to participants.

In *Sacrosanctum Concilium*, participation becomes ideological because it is exalted above all other principles, which unavoidably causes distortion and corruption: "In the restoration and promotion of the sacred liturgy, this full and active participation by all the people is the aim to be considered *before all else*" (n. 14). Contrast this statement with Pope Pius X's in *Tra le Sollecitudini*: "We deem it necessary to provide before all else for the sanctity and dignity of the temple."[15] Perhaps a better term than participation would be *assistance*: every member of the body assists at the liturgy, each according to his place. Belonging is a more basic category than doing, just as our insertion into Christ at baptism is more basic to our identity than any particular act we perform.

9. The Principle of Parallelism

This principle is intimately connected with the preceding one of hierarchy. In any authentic Eastern or Western liturgy, we find that several things are often happening simultaneously (or to use the technical term, there is "parallel liturgy"). The deacon is leading a litany when the priest is reciting his

---

[15] On this contrast, see Kwasniewski, *Ministers of Christ*, 131–40.

own prayers; the people are singing the Sanctus while the priest has started the Canon.

> Often many things are going on simultaneously, with different ministers exercising different roles and following a line proper to them, as happens in the reality of the cosmos, with its hierarchies of angels and men, and its web of interconnected organisms, particles, forces, and systems. The chanted Introit soars while the priest and servers recite the prayers at the foot of the altar, and as the priest ascends the altar steps saying private prayers, the haunting melody of the Kyrie begins. . . .
>
> Such overlapping of words and actions takes place throughout the Mass. This is all to the good: the more we are surrounded by and immersed in prayer, the more our heart's aspirations are stirred up and given outlet. We are carried, in spite of the resisting gravity of fallen nature, into prayer, recollection, meditation, repentance, conversion. We stand mysteriously in the presence of the Holy Trinity, Our Lord Jesus Christ, the Virgin Mother, the angels and saints, in a massive density of fellowship and fervent love, to which the whole of God's creation ministers.[16]

Those who attend either Byzantine or traditional Latin liturgies come to see Christian worship as a multi-layered action made up of many individual actions converging on a common goal. It is most definitely *not* a logical sequence of discrete acts as in the Novus Ordo, a "sequential" or "modular" liturgy in which usually only one thing is allowed to take place at a time. There are a very few moments in the Novus Ordo when the priest can be doing something while the people and/or choir are doing something else: the prayer before the Gospel, said during the alleluia; the quasi-offertory prayers, if a chant is being sung; the fracture of the host while the Agnus Dei is being sung. But the number of such moments has been severely pared down, and their euchological content has been eviscerated.

Kwasniewski, *Reclaiming Our Birthright*, 37–38.

10. The Principle of Separation

All authentic Christian liturgies preserve and make ritual use of the theology inscribed in the architecture of the Old Covenant temple, which, as the Epistle to the Hebrews teaches, is recapitulated in Christ and therefore symbolized forever in our Eucharistic sacrifice. In the East, the separation of the sanctuary or holy of holies from the nave is more obvious due to the presence of an iconostasis through which only certain clergy may enter. In the West, curtains gave way to the rood screen, which in most places diminished into the Communion rail, but *always* the sanctuary remained distinct, elevated, and off limits to the laity. Additionally, we may say that in the Western sphere, the visual iconostasis yielded to a "sonic iconostasis" of Latin alternating with silence. Both the hieratic language and the enveloping absence of sound lower a veil over the holy of holies and shield the sacred mysteries from the profanation of casual treatment.[17] Thus, while Eastern and Western liturgies accomplish this "veiling of our faces to the Presence" in different ways, both are highly effective in achieving it, powerfully drawing the worshiper's attention to the hidden glory of God.[18]

Beyond these principles, which evidently point to the very nature of divine worship, there is a whole host of things that are not *necessarily* characteristic of the Novus Ordo, and yet accompany it in 99 percent of its instantiations, such as the *versus populum* stance, which departs from the common ancient tradition of East and West. After fifty years of clergy facing the people almost always and everywhere, with papal rebukes to those who dare to think differently, even the most optimistic proponent of the Reform of the Reform cannot maintain that *versus populum* does not typify the Novus Ordo in the minds of its architects, implementers, and end users.

The following chart summarizes our findings:

---

[17] The Eastern iconostasis can often be solid and extend high toward the ceiling, blocking the view entirely. An open plan permitting unobstructed vision of the sanctuary is an innovation that creeps into the West in the Counter-Reformation period, but the liturgy, as acting from a deep instinct for the holy, retained various ways of countering the deception of easy access. Under Latin influence, some Eastern iconostases, especially among Greek Catholics, make use of screens, slats, or bars to permit vision past the icons into the holy of holies, while the continued use of icons and ceremonial entry through the doors preserve the theological articulation of space.

[18] See Kwasniewski, *Reclaiming Our Birthright*, 28–42.

Principle of . . .	Byzantine	Traditional Roman	Modern "Roman"
Tradition	origins lost in time; handed down and received for centuries	origins lost in time; handed down and received for centuries	constructed by committee in the 1960s from reassembled bits of the Western and Eastern traditions
	attributed to great saints but mostly anonymous in authorship	attributed to great saints but mostly anonymous in authorship	authors/compilers known by name and most without reputations for sanctity (e.g., none of its architects has a cause open for canonization; Abp. Bugnini was later exiled for his schemings)
	has its authority from tradition	has its authority from tradition and papal legislation	has its authority from papal legislation alone
Mystery	redolent of mystery, which is emphasized by visual iconostasis	redolent of mystery, which is emphasized by sonic iconostasis of Latin, chant, and silence	only rarely escapes verbose horizontalism and familiarity, tends to disregard all barriers
	ad orientem—an apostolic tradition, followed of necessity	*ad orientem*—an apostolic tradition, followed of necessity	*versus populum*—practiced by nearly universal custom
Elevated Mode	liturgical texts are chanted or whispered, in a sacred language and/or poetic diction	liturgical texts are chanted, whispered, or uttered in hieratic Latin	liturgical texts are mostly spoken aloud in contemporary vernacular and in an everyday voice
Density	rich interweaving of ancient prayers, theologically dense	rich interweaving of ancient prayers, theologically dense	vastly reduced traditional textual and ceremonial content, with modern novelties added

Principle of . . .	Byzantine	Traditional Roman	Modern "Roman"
Ritual Integrity (Stability)	exhibits ritual integrity and fixity, such as appointed anaphoras	exhibits ritual integrity and fixity, such as daily use of Roman Canon	allows options, choices, and extemporaneous interjections
Adequate Preparation	repetition is a standard feature, lending to prayerfulness	repetition is a standard feature, lending to prayerfulness	repetitions largely removed as "useless" for our times; verbosity makes prayer difficult
Truthfulness	proclaims fullness of Christian message from Scripture and Tradition	proclaims fullness of Christian message from Scripture and Tradition	omits aspects of revelation and moral life deemed "difficult" for modern people
Hierarchy	church architecture articulates symbolic spaces with impermeable boundaries	church architecture articulates symbolic spaces with impermeable boundaries	church architecture lacks traditional symbolism and/ or the liturgy itself ignores it in practice
	sanctuary limited to vested ministers	sanctuary limited to vested ministers	sanctuary open to unvested laity
	sharply diverse roles for clergy and laity, and within the clergy, for different ranks	sharply diverse roles for clergy and laity, and within the clergy, for different ranks	shallow hierarchical model; leveling and confusion of clerical and lay roles (even according to official guidelines)
Parallelism	parallel liturgy: hierarchical and polyphonic	parallel liturgy: hierarchical and polyphonic	sequential liturgy (one thing at a time), horizontalized and rationalized
Separation	Blessed Sacrament handled only by ordained clergy	Blessed Sacrament handled only by ordained clergy	Blessed Sacrament handled by clergy and laypeople alike
	Communion received standing but on the tongue and from the priest only	Communion received kneeling, on the tongue, and from the priest or deacon only[19]	Communion is usually received standing and in the hand, from whomever is handing it out

[19] Can. 845 of the 1917 Code of Canon Law states that the ordinary minister of Holy Com-

Compared to the Novus Ordo, the Byzantine liturgy looks like a king next to a pauper, a Rembrandt next to a caricature, a feast after a famine. But the traditional Roman rite in all its intricate splendor and regimented solemnity is the equal of any Eastern rite seated at the table of tradition. We do an injustice to the Holy Spirit's work in the Western Church by speaking as if Byzantine liturgy is the "gold standard," when the Roman rite in its fullness—sadly, so rarely seen by Roman Catholics!—is fully its match. Instead, it is the Novus Ordo that should be shown the door, for it has no claim to be at the King's high table of authentic liturgical rites.

If someone objects at this point that the Novus Ordo can be celebrated in a way that is "in continuity" with the preceding Roman tradition (and therefore in a manner not dissimilar to the Divine Liturgy), my response is that this is not actually true. Several of the ten principles summarized above are not embodied *at all* by the Novus Ordo—and this *by design* (here, I would include at least 1, 4, 5, 6, 7, and 9); while the remaining principles (2, 3, 8, and 10) *might* be acted on—or then again, they might not, depending on who the "presider" is. In short, they are *possible* but not *necessary.* This fact, in and of itself, already demonstrates the profoundly anti-traditional character of the Novus Ordo, the Catholic quality of which depends largely on the decisions of its celebrant rather than its (and his) adherence to a fixed rule. Just as a chain is only as strong as its weakest link, so a liturgy filled with options is only as good as the worst of these options. It should be judged not by what it might be if many unlikely best choices were to be made, but by what it *usually* is when *customary* choices are made. Thus, whereas the Novus Ordo *could* be offered in a quasi-traditional way, the Byzantine and Tridentine liturgies *must* be offered in a traditional way—there is no choice in the matter.[20]

In that one difference alone, we can see the almost infinite gap that separates the modern Roman rite from *any* historic apostolic rite of Christianity, Eastern or Western. Its lack of doctrinal, moral, rubrical, and

---

munion is the priest but that a deacon may be authorized as an extraordinary minister. Annotations indicate that the use of the deacon in this capacity goes back to at least 1777.

This is not to say that either the Byzantine or the Tridentine rite will always be offered in a edifying or aesthetically appropriate manner—but that is not something that can be guaranteed in *any* rite, for we are still dealing with the frailties of fallen human beings. The claim ncerns rather the objective content and rubrics that belong to these rites.

ceremonial density, its modular-linear-rationalist structure, and its "optionitis" separate it *in essence* from the sphere of sacred culture that the Roman *usus antiquior* and the Byzantine Divine Liturgy inhabit in common. One might adapt to this situation the words of Abraham in the parable of Dives and Lazarus: "Between us and you, there is fixed a great chasm, so that they who would pass from hence to you, cannot, nor from thence come hither" (Lk 16:26). The *Short Critical Study* lays it out with refreshing frankness:

> The Apostolic Constitution [*Missale Romanum* of 1969] explicitly mentions the riches of piety and doctrine the Novus Ordo supposedly borrows from the Eastern Churches. But the result is so removed from, and indeed opposed to, the spirit of the Eastern liturgies that it can only leave the faithful in those rites revolted and horrified. What do these ecumenical borrowings amount to? Basically, to introducing multiple texts for the Eucharistic Prayer (the *anaphora*)—none of which approaches their Eastern counterparts' complexity or beauty—and to permitting Communion under both species and the use of deacons. Against this, the New Order of Mass appears to have been deliberately shorn of every element where the Roman liturgy came closest to the Eastern Rites. At the same time, by abandoning its unmistakable and immemorial Roman character, the Novus Ordo casts off what was spiritually precious of its own [heritage]. In place of this are elements which bring the new rite closer to certain Protestant liturgies, not even those closest to Catholicism. At the same time, these new elements degrade the Roman liturgy and further alienate it from the East, as did the reforms which preceded the Novus Ordo. In compensation, the new liturgy will delight all those groups hovering on the verge of apostasy who, during a spiritual crisis without precedent, now wreak havoc in the Church by poisoning her organism and by undermining her unity in doctrine, worship, morals, and discipline.[21]

---

[21] Alfredo Cardinal Ottaviani and Antonio Cardinal Bacci, *The Ottaviani Intervention: Short Critical Study of the New Order of Mass*, trans. Anthony Cekada (West Chester, OH: Philothea Press, 2010), ch. 7, pp. 69–71.

The same study then furnishes the parallels that are easiest to see—a description in which we will recognize many of the principles mentioned in the foregoing pages:

> Consider the following elements found in the Byzantine rite: lengthy and repeated penitential prayers; solemn vesting rites for the celebrant and deacon; the preparation of the offerings at the *proscomidia*, a complete rite in itself; repeated invocations, even in the prayers of offering, to the Blessed Virgin and the Saints; invocations of the choirs of Angels at the Gospel as "invisible concelebrants," while the choir identifies itself with the angelic choirs in the *Cherubicon*; the sanctuary screen (*iconostasis*) separating the sanctuary from the rest of the church and the clergy from the people; the hidden Consecration, symbolizing the divine mystery to which the entire liturgy alludes; the position of the priest who celebrates facing God, and never facing the people; Communion given always and only by the celebrant; the continual marks of adoration toward the Sacred Species; the essentially contemplative attitude of the people. The fact that these liturgies, even in their less solemn forms, last for over an hour and are constantly defined as "awe-inspiring, unutterable . . . heavenly, life-giving mysteries" speaks for itself. Finally, we note how in both the Divine Liturgy of St. John Chrysostom and the Liturgy of St. Basil, the concept of "supper" or "banquet" appears clearly subordinate to the concept of sacrifice—just as it was in the Roman Mass.[22]

What is truly surprising, given the foregoing, is how many Byzantine Catholics and "experts" in Eastern liturgy—the late Robert Taft, SJ, having been the most prominent—favor the "reformed" Roman liturgy, overlooking the monumental discrepancies, nay contradictions, between the principles according to which it was constructed and is enacted and the principles that are common, as I have shown, to Byzantine and traditional Latin liturgy. It is no exaggeration to say that the rite of Paul VI, both as a whole and in its particulars, is a deformation of Latin liturgy that cannot

---

[22] Ottaviani and Bacci, 70, n53.

be classified with authentic Catholic rites of history. Only thanks to a profound inconsistency could a Byzantine Catholic prefer the Novus Ordo on account of secondary or tertiary characteristics while overlooking, tolerating, or even seeming to approve of its deviations from fundamental principles of classical liturgy. Another writer for *PrayTell*, Teva Regule, provides a brilliant illustration:

> Some Catholics (usually of the more traditional variety), upon hearing that I am an Orthodox Christian, have made it a point to proclaim their love for the Orthodox liturgy and critique the changes to the Mass after Vatican II. Mainly, they lament the loss of beauty and reverence in their experience of the Novus Ordo and long for the Tridentine Mass. I smile, but, as a scholar of liturgy, know that the Mass of Paul VI has much more in common theologically (e.g., its stronger pneumatological dimension) and ecclesiologically with the Eastern Church than the Tridentine Mass. Still, having attended a few Masses (of the post-Vatican II style) that I found (in their words) overly "informal" and/or "dry," their concern resonates.
>
> Interestingly, the reform of the liturgy after Vatican II is also debated within some Orthodox circles. Some Orthodox Christians are critical of the reform of the Mass after Vatican II as well. In this case, they fail to distinguish between the greater theological and historical similarities of the Orthodox liturgy and the Mass after Vatican II while overemphasizing some of the phenomenological differences.[23]

If ever the world suffered a deficit of understatement, this quotation could make up the entire sum. The Mass of Paul VI has "more in common" with the Eastern Church only inasmuch as it was artificially Easternized by its architects, who had little or no respect for their own Latin tradition but endless enthusiasm for all things Byzantine. For example, it was all the rage to insist on the need or the desirability of an *epiclesis* for the anaphoras, because the scholars were too caught up in their theories to be able to

---

[23] "East Meets West in Liturgy," *PrayTell*, September 29, 2018.

admire the Roman Canon's antiquity that predates the Macedonian heresy in the East denying the divinity of the Holy Spirit, in response to which the *epiclesis* found its home in the liturgy of that half of the empire. The liturgical reformers evidently feasted on foods rich in antioccidents.

Then, the author—as if waking up to the idea for the first time—admits that some Eastern Orthodox have *problems* with the post-Vatican II liturgical reform. In reality, well-informed Orthodox Christians understand it to be a disaster of inconceivable magnitude, a thorough disembowelment of Western tradition that removes it still further from the common heritage of the first millennium. This is why the Moscow patriarchate hailed *Summorum Pontificum* with joy. As we have seen, the claim that there is greater theological and historical similarity between the Orthodox Divine Liturgy and the post-Vatican II Mass is blatantly false. The opposite is not only true but painfully true. The discrepancies between centuries-old Orthodox worship and the parvenu Novus Ordo are pushed aside as "phenomenological." Imagine describing the difference between a traditional Requiem and a modern funeral Mass as only "phenomenological." Yes, it is that, to be sure, and in spades, but it is first and foremost *theological* and *historical*, in the profoundest possible way. And to say that the *apparent* differences are overemphasized is quite simply pure rationalism—as if our experience of liturgy, of the right approach to and attitude toward the numinous, were not something that comes through our *senses* first, and only afterwards arrives in our intellects, in keeping with Aristotle's sane empiricism.[24]

This phrase in particular is incredibly condescending: "I smile, but, as a scholar of liturgy, know . . .": what a testimony to the lure of *gnosis*, abundantly on offer in the pseudo-scientific mystery cult of contemporary liturgiology! May the Lord in His mercy deliver us from professional liturgists.[25] The danger is not imaginary. Liturgists—presumably disturbed at

---

* Chapter 1 pursues this theme in full.

One recalls the famous exchange between Fr. Pierre-Marie Gy and Cardinal Ratzinger concerning the latter's book *The Spirit of the Liturgy*. Ratzinger had dared to criticize some of the untouchable "truths" of the liturgical reform, and Fr. Gy, whose life had been invested in this lame duck, was not amused: "How dare he write such a book—*he is not a liturgist!*" The same reaction greeted Pope Benedict's *Jesus of Nazareth* series, which the gurus of the historical-critical tribe could not abide. In reality, with *The Spirit of the Liturgy* Ratzinger was doing the work of a true theologian: he was writing liturgical *theology*, based on a solid grasp of the history and the texts, but going far beyond that limited scope into more fundamental

the stubbornly contrarian witness of Eastern Catholics in matters as basic as liturgical orientation, style of music, ascetical practices, and premodern dogmatism—have been talking for decades about how to undertake a "reform" of the Eastern rites to bring them into line with *Sacrosanctum Concilium* and Bugnini's Bauhaus blueprints.[26]

Coming at it from a different angle, Cardinals Cañizares and Koch pointed out that legitimate ecumenical relations with the Christian East must necessarily fail if Catholics cannot even agree among themselves to respect their own liturgical traditions, which overlap to a great extent with those of the East:

> Amidst the controversy [over *Summorum Pontificum*], it is often forgotten that the criticisms made against the rite received from the Roman Tradition also apply to the other traditions, first of all to the Orthodox: almost all liturgical aspects that those who have been opposed to the preservation of the ancient missal strongly attack are precisely the aspects that we had in common with the Eastern Tradition! A sign that confirms this, in contrast, are the enthusiastically positive expressions that arrived from the Orthodox world with the publication of the motu proprio.
>
> This document becomes in this way a key aspect for the "credibility" of ecumenism because, according to the expression of the president of the Pontifical Council for the Promotion of the Unity of Christians, Cardinal Kurt Koch, "it promotes in fact, if we may call it thus, an 'intra-Catholic ecumenism.'" We could consequently say that the premise *ut unum sint* presupposes the *ut unum maneant* [that they might be one . . . that they might abide], in

theological and philosophical considerations, as well as offering a more realistic assessmen of the actual cost, in souls and in sanity, of the postconciliar reforms, from the vantage of on who had benefited from extensive pastoral experience, which many of the white-smocke theoreticians lacked. It is, in truth, the specialists who are wearing blinders or suffering fror tunnel vision, and the non-specialists who can see deeper and farther, just as we notice tc day that it is often the youth who are instinctively and intuitively drawn to liturgical tr. dition while their elders, be they teachers or pastors, embarrassingly chase after the eve diminishing relevance of the latest whatever.

[26] Considerable damage has been done and is still being done among the Ruthenians and e pecially the Maronites. Fortunately, Catholics of other Eastern rites have pushed back agair what they call Latinization, which in many cases has far more to do with "Bugninification

such a way that, as the said Cardinal writes, "if the intra-Catholic ecumenism failed, the Catholic controversy on the liturgy would also extend to ecumenism."[27]

The combined force of a prejudice in favor of cultural pluralism, the inherent conservatism of the East, and the lack of a centralized authority capable of imposing gigantic liturgical changes has for now spared the Eastern rites of the worst excesses of the twentieth-century movement for liturgical reform. But this fragile peace may not last forever, especially if church leaders continue to display the twin traits of arrogance and myopia that have afflicted their kind for the past fifty years. It therefore behooves every Eastern Christian and every Roman sympathizer to understand the errors that led to the Pauline rites and are thickly embedded in them, and to oppose any reduction, compromise, or novelty in their own liturgical life.

If the reader is tempted to believe that I am exaggerating the arrogance of the mentality to be met with in "enlightened" postconciliar Catholic circles, I would offer as evidence the following evaluation of the East by Enzo Bianchi, founder of the so-called "Bose Monastic Community":

> The East has not experienced modernity, or Vatican Council II or Biblical or historical criticism. This says a lot. We cannot think they are like us at the end of this century and millennium. We do not understand them because of their different situation in time. They are much farther behind, and it is not their fault. . . . In a certain sense, the Catholic Church has had the grace of modernity. We should be at the service of the Orthodox and help them understand that a similar impact does not mean the end of faith. We should offer them help, at the university and theological level, so that they can regain lost ground. Today we are experiencing tremendous acceleration from the cultural point of view. Modern man has a religious capacity. This must also be perceived by the East, in the unfolding of the complex situation in which they live.[28]

27 Preface of Cardinals Cañizares to the Doctoral Thesis of Fr. Alberto Soria Jiménez, OSB, published at *Rorate Caeli* on July 16, 2014.
28 Zenit news dispatch dated May 9, 1999, now removed from Zenit's website. The divide Bianchi perceives between the Novus Ordo world he inhabits and that of the East is no different

To return to our point of departure: just as Latin-rite Catholics stand to benefit immensely from exposure to the riches of the East, so too do Eastern Orthodox and Greek Catholics who love their own liturgical tradition stand to benefit from exposure to the Western liturgical tradition preserved and handed down in the classical Roman rite. Precisely out of love for what is common to East and West, both Roman Catholics and Greek Catholics should avoid, at all costs, the neo-Roman liturgy of 1969, ruptured from Christian tradition by its inconsistent antiquarianism, modern novelties, and cognitive dissonances. It is nothing less than a *counter-sign* to the Greek and Latin traditions alike, working against the doxological expression of age-old dogmatic and moral truths that the liturgy has always shown forth and inculcated in the faithful. Roman and Byzantine Catholics know themselves to be safe, in good hands, when attending one another's authentic rites, but neither can feel safe attending the Novus Ordo. By all means, let us breathe with both lungs—but in their healthy condition, not their diseased condition!

Byzantine Catholics—and, for that matter, all Christians of non-Latin rites who are in communion with the pope of Rome—should recognize the authenticity of the traditional Latin Mass and reject the rupture of the *Novus Ordo Missae* for many reasons. Here are three.

1. If the pope of Rome has the authority to change radically the rite of his own Church—if, in other words, the one and only limit to what he can do in the realm of liturgy is the requirement of valid "form and matter"— then there is no theoretical limit to what he can do to *anyone's* rite. After all, as per Vatican I, he has *plenitudo potestatis*, supreme, universal, and immediate jurisdiction over everyone, with the keys of the kingdom in his hand. Either you swallow that in theory and perhaps (God forbid) in practice *or* you have to agree with traditional Roman Catholics that his role is to preserve the inheritance of apostolic Christianity and to pass it on faithfully, respecting each and every legitimate tradition. You can't have it both ways.

---

from the divide he would perceive between his world and that of Catholic traditionalists. In spite of his free commingling of Catholicism and Protestantism, Christianity and Judaism, and so forth, Bianchi has been honored by Benedict XVI, Francis, and others as a model "new evangelizer." This paragraph is chockablock with themes familiar from the Modernists as described by Pius X. Its liturgical implications are evident.

2. If you love and praise your own liturgy for being ancient, venerable, perennial, of all centuries, a fixed and stable reference point of ecclesial life, you should do your Western brethren the courtesy of loving and praising *their* ancient, venerable, perennial, of all centuries, fixed and stable liturgical rites (Tridentine, Ambrosian, Mozarabic, etc.). The Novus Ordo has little in common with any of these. As this chapter has argued, it is the "stranger" in the group: this no honest inquiry can sidestep.

3. If the reason Latins should respect Greeks is that the Holy Spirit raises up multiple complementary traditions, you should unhesitatingly recognize the Western liturgical tradition to be just as much the work of God's providence, just as much a fruit of the Spirit, as your tradition is. This appropriate humility rules out altogether the view of twentieth-century Western liturgists—a view chillingly akin to that of Protestants and Modernists[29]—that the Western liturgy had suffered such tremendous corruption in the Middle Ages and early modernity that it needed to be massively overhauled into a putatively "pure" original form that, oddly, also turned out to be sleekly modernist (how remarkable that the ancient *domus ecclesiae* anticipated concrete, steel, and glass!). If you would not allow your liturgy to be thus travestied, you should resist the same travesty in ours.

The ever-insightful Martin Mosebach observes:

> It is characteristic of this century that just as the axe was being applied to the green tree of liturgy, the most profound insights into liturgy were being formulated, albeit not in the Roman Church but in the Byzantine Church. On the one hand, a pope dared to interfere with the liturgy. On the other, Orthodoxy, separated from the pope by schism, preserved the liturgy and liturgical theology through the terrible trials of the century. For a Catholic who refuses to accept the cynic's easy conclusions, these facts produce a baffling riddle. One is tempted to speak of a tragic mystery, although the word tragic does not fit in a Christian context. The Mass of Saint Gregory the Great, the old Latin liturgy, now finds itself on the "lunatic fringe" of the Roman Church, whereas the Divine Liturgy of Saint John Chrysostom is alive in all its splendor in the very

See chapter 7.

heart of the Orthodox Church. The idea that we have something to learn from Orthodoxy is not a popular one. But we must accustom ourselves to studying—and studying thoroughly—what the Byzantine Church has to say about sacred images and the liturgy. This is equally relevant to the Latin Rite; in fact, it seems as though we can only get to know the Latin Rite in all its Spirit-filled reality if we view it from the Eastern perspective.[30]

And more succinctly still: "All the striving towards ecumenism, however necessary, must begin not with attention-grabbing meetings with Eastern hierarchs but with the restoration of the Latin liturgy, which represents the real connection between the Latin and Greek churches."[31] The following real letter exchange offers an illustration of how the dialogue between Christians of diverse rites, Eastern and Western, must be grounded in fidelity to our profoundly beautiful and very different—yet complementary—traditions.

Dear Dr. Kwasniewski,

I've asked versions of the following questions of many excellent Latins for years, and have never gotten a satisfying reply. I'm wondering if you can shed any light.

In human terms, there is a trade-off between optimization and flexibility. The human side of liturgy is the same. Generally, systems optimize for certain conditions until they crystallize, and if all of the flexibility has been optimized out, eventually the tiniest change in conditions knocks the whole thing over. Organizations and communities prepare for this through system redundancies (e.g., back-up plans), subsidiarity, and so on.

There is a *type* of flexibility in the Greek rite that I think works against "tinkeritis." Daily commemorations pile up, and patriarchates, eparchies and even parishes have latitude about which to celebrate. Certain canon and litanies find favor here or there, certain recensions and uses vary, even the logic of vestment colors. Decentralized and sometimes even competiti

---

[30] Martin Mosebach, *The Heresy of Formlessness: The Roman Liturgy and Its Enemy*, rev. (Brooklyn, NY: Angelico Press, 2018), 57.
[31] Mosebach, 187.

overlapping liturgical authorities have helped the Greek rite ecosystem stay very conservative—by and large, and certainly by comparison to the Roman rite.

When I listen to my Latin traditionalist (an honorable phrase in my mind) friends saying things like "You can't have a solemn Mass without a subdeacon," it just blows my mind. If the barriers of entry to progressive levels of liturgical excellence are too great at the local level, the traditioning process[32] is given over to specialists, and, what's worse, bishops.

On the contrary, when one of my children was initiated, my parish hadn't been using the rite of tonsure, probably ever. I asked my priest for the full ceremony, and so . . . he downloaded a perfectly excellent version from the internet. Similarly, we've had to have our people translate specific texts when need be from the original languages into English. I know that part of this is a *de facto* blessing of what you might call "the innocence of the rudeness" of the Eastern Church in the USA, and a lot of it is also the difference in how authority and tradition interplay in the Greek and Latin churches.

I can't help but wonder, doesn't a lot of the Roman rite's current liturgical crisis stem from a certain type of hyper-regulation, and then a preposterous reaction to it? Wouldn't the Roman rite benefit from a *certain type* of flexibility? Certainly not the one you got, unfortunately. Would the truly stupid ideas like *versus populum* have been heard of, if (for example) some dioceses could have "blown off steam" by using liturgical blue (or whatever)? I've never been able to penetrate the Latin Trad mindset in this regard, even though I am their biggest supporter otherwise. Small is beautiful. Big is always a temptation to mediocrity. Sameness is brittle. The strongest fabrics are cross-woven.

That is my personal and admittedly partial working theory of the human side of the Latin liturgical tragedy.

God bless,
A Greek Catholic

---

[2] My correspondent seems to be arguing that if it is too difficult for a local community to take hold of and implement the liturgical tradition, the community will not be able to live it or pass it on; it will become a domain of specialists only, or of people who don't understand or don't care.

Dear Greek Catholic,

I admire and love the Byzantine Divine Liturgy. I was blessed to be able to attend it several times a week while teaching at the International Theological Institute in Austria. I learned to cantor, which came in handy later on in Wyoming when we had weekly or monthly Divine Liturgies and I was the only one who knew how to chant the Troparion, Kontakion, Prokeimenon, etc. Even today, at every Roman Mass, I privately pray the great Byzantine prayer: "O Lord, I firmly believe and profess that you are truly the Christ, the Son of the living God, who came into the world to save sinners, of whom I am the first . . ." My son and my daughter both received the "holy mystery of penance" and Holy Communion in the Byzantine rite (for circumstantial and personal reasons). As a family we are traditionally Roman to the core, but precisely for that reason, we love our Eastern brethren and their rites.

What I think is so perplexing to people is how different the mentalities of East and West are. This difference has its roots in the contrast between the Western Roman empire (and the way it developed into Europe), and the Eastern Roman empire (and the way it developed into Byzantium, later moving into the Slavic realm). To speak in generalities, the Western mind is logical, linear, efficient, succinct, and focused; the Byzantine mind is circular, effusive, redundant, poetic, and diffuse. The strengths of each are also the source of their weaknesses, or at least of their temptations.

The liturgical reformers of the 1960s tore out their hair over this difference. In one sense, they wanted all liturgy to look the same, because, well, somehow there ought to be a "right liturgy" that everyone could subscribe to, like a sort of Esperanto. Ultimately, in a savage irony, the postconciliar liturgical reform created a set of rites that, so far from taking inspiration from the East or approaching more nearly to unity with it, amounted to an antithesis on almost every point of magnitude: respect for existing tradition; internal continuity in readings, prayers, antiphons, hymns; the orientation of the priest; reverence in receiving the holy mysteries; distinctions between clerical and lay, sanctuary and nave; and much else besides. As many have pointed out, the only ecumenism that mattered to the liturgical reformers was accommodation to Protestantism; in spite of lip service, the

Eastern Orthodox and the Eastern Catholics served a decorative function, adding a touch of irrelevant exoticism.

Pope Paul VI endorsed the Enlightenment rationalism represented by the Jansenist Synod of Pistoia, which had failed in the eighteenth century but triumphed in the twentieth with his aid. This reformist-constructivist mentality yielded rotten fruits at various moments in the last century, but its final and supreme fruit was the postconciliar reform, which stripped the Latin Church of all that was magnificent, orderly, and decorous and substituted in its place all that was industrial, modular, verbose, and hip. The East would never toy with liturgy this way, but neither would the West had it not fallen under the spell of Pistoia.

In place of the Protestantizing and rationalizing work of the Consilium, Catholics owe it to Our Lord and the providential guidance of His Spirit to respect rigorously the irreducible complexity and distinctness of the "two lungs" of the Church, and remain true to the originating genius, spirit, and traditions of each. The Western approach is good if, and only if, it remains true to itself. As long as we keep our inherited rituals—our concisely chiseled orations bristling with layers of meaning, our military but ravishing ceremonial, our unsurpassable Gregorian melodies, our special love of silence, our penchant for kneeling as a sign not so much of penance as of humble adoration—we will be healthy. We will be decisively *Roman*, not making a sorry embarrassment of ourselves by second- or third-rate imitations of the secular world, of Eastern Christianity, or of evangelical Protantism. We can be who we are, and do it brilliantly; that is all, and that is more than enough to keep us happily busy. We cannot be someone else and should not try, for failure waits at the door of rivalries and envies.

One of the obvious perfections of the East is the calmness, smoothness, and relaxedness (if that's a word) with which the clergy perform the services. They know what they are supposed to do, and they do it effortlessly, without fuss, and without rubrical elaborateness. Still, it is done reverently, ceremonially, not at all casually or randomly. In the West, centuries of rubrical development brought about a situation where every motion, posture, position, and interaction was carefully orchestrated and regulated. I happen to think this is a perfection peculiar to the Latin tradition, and again, if done well, it is magnificent to behold, like a sacred dance, like Japanese *Noh* theatre, like Her Majesty's guard on parade, like a flock of birds in geometric formation. It is a science and a study, a form of asceticism, an offering of the body in sacrifice. The moment one loses the meaning of it—that it is an outward expression and offering to God of a mind well-disciplined and subordinate to Him—it can become regimentation, formalism, rubricism. In other words, it becomes ripe for caricature, rejection, and replacement with a desperately bad attempt at naturalness.

The West cannot succeed except by being Western in the best possible way, just as the East cannot succeed except by being Eastern in the best possible way. One paradox in this regard is that the Roman rite is the most "catholic" of all the rites: retaining its original Roman traits, it has taken in so much from the universal Church: Gallican, Greek, and even Syrian (the Agnus Dei). The more elaborate settings of the Sanctus in Gregorian chant or in polyphony bring the Canon (insofar as the Canon really begins with the Preface) into an effusive mode of prayer that is more characteristic of the East than natively Roman—a continual thanksgiving and doxology, as in the Eastern anaphoras. A silent Canon with the priestly gestures overlaid with a Palestrina Sanctus combines the sober Roman "legalese" of the text, heard though it be only by the priest, with a "doxological" element that makes it a rather different total experience from the Canon as said by St. Leo the Great or in the early *Ordines Romani*. Maybe we could say that within the Roman rite, what is Greek or Gallican or Syrian should stay Greek, Gallican, or Syrian, and whatever is Roman should stay Roman!

For many centuries the Latin liturgy had the deacons, subdeacons, acolytes, and other ministers it needed, at least at the cathedrals and monasteries, and in smaller places on special occasions. It was all done according to local customs and expectations, which are good things to have in play. As Roman centralization asserted itself more and more, the local customs evaporated, and the age of legalism began. This, I would agree with you, has been a scourge on doing the liturgy well, because it places the same set of ideal standards on every locality, which rather discourages than encourages solemnity. Ultimately, the root of all of our woes is Roman centralization. Once the bishop of Rome thinks he is the absolute master of the Latin liturgy, it's all over. I would not say this of Pope Pius V, who codified an existing liturgy; but once we see Pius X radically changing the Divine Office, Pius XII radically changing Holy Week, and Paul VI radically changing everything, there is no longer any *paradosis* worthy of the name. It is, as Eastern Christians have rightly recognized (and as we should be humble enough to admit), the sacrifice of tradition by and for pastoral authoritarianism. I think more and more people are recognizing this deviation and seeking to do what they can about it—at least those who have an orthodox conception of what liturgy is and how it has always been handed down, not without development, of course, but never put on the chopping block of academic theory or pastoral expediency.

On the other hand, and I hope you won't mind my saying so, it seems to me that the Eastern tradition can be so loose that it is difficult to say what "ought" to be done. What ought to be done is what's fitting, yes; but who decides what's fitting? The local priest? The faithful? The eparchy? Why do certain customs vanish from whole territories, while variations creep in that may over time separate national churches from each other and work against mutual recognition? The Eastern flexibility with the tradition has allowed local uses to grow up to such an extent as to make concelebration or even mutual respect difficult at times for the Orientals. I've heard that Ukrainians sometimes look down their noses at Ruthenian usages. And a Greek Orthodox theologian told of an Orthodox meeting some years ago where two separate Divine Liturgies had to be celebrated in adjacent rooms because Greeks and Serbians (or maybe Romanians, or all three) couldn't agree enough to concelebrate! Local customization can be its own curse. Also: why are some Easterners so against development that they would wish to abolish devotions cherished and loved by the faithful, such as Eucharistic adoration and benediction, out of an archaic purism? Of course you are *far healthier* than we, in general; I am simply raising some questions.

Thank you again for writing to me. I very much enjoy this sort of dialogue.

Yours in Christ,
Dr. Kwasniewski

With my keen interest in all things liturgical, I have often lingered over the many obvious and subtle differences between the Divine Liturgy of Saint John Chrysostom, which I have had the privilege of attending regularly over the past few decades, and the Mass of the Roman rite that is my spiritual home. For my purposes here, I am assuming a Roman liturgy celebrated beautifully and reverently, "with all the stops pulled"; obviously the barren, perfunctory, verbose, and eclectic manner in which the Mass is often said nowadays does not allow for a fair comparison of the rites as they exist in their plenitude. A solemn High Mass in the *usus antiquior*, adorned with sacred music, can bring joy, solace, and wonder even to an Eastern Catholic, but alas, how rare is such a Mass today? Even in a major city, there might be only one or two on a Sunday, if at all. Still, the Latin liturgy at its fullest must be our point of reference for a fair and full comparison.

It is commonly said that the traditional Mass is more intent on reminding the worshiper of the death of Christ on the Cross and the believer's own sinfulness and unworthiness, whereas the Divine Liturgy brings to the forefront the eschatological victory of the risen Christ in whose triumph the Christian shares whenever he partakes of the Eucharist, the food of immortality.

It is easy, however, to exaggerate the difference between the "downward" symbolism of the Mass (Christ as the suffering redeemer of miserable Christian sinners) and the "upward" symbolism of the Divine Liturgy (Christ as eternal victor in whom Christians are already seated in the heavenly places). After all, both liturgies frequently recall the birth, life, passion, death, resurrection, and ascension of Our Lord. Even if the traditional Latin Mass emphasizes the advent of Christ as Redeemer and the re-presentation of the Sacrifice of Calvary, and in this way places the accent on man's sinfulness and God's infinite mercy, leading to purification and the forgiveness of sins, it could hardly be maintained that the Mass lacks an eschatological dimension. Similarly, if the Eastern liturgy tends to place worship in the context of the Eschaton—the kingdom of the Holy Spirit, in which the life of Christ figures as the exemplar of what all Christians are called to become anew, the image of the *Logos*—it is no less evident that the Eastern liturgy continually refers to the ongoing drama of redemption, centered on the sacrifice of the Lamb.

Perhaps the Western soul is more sharply conscious of the incompleteness of our present state, the need to work out our salvation "in fear and trembling" (Phil 2:12). The traditional Mass expresses the feeling of homesickness, the longing sinners have for the fatherland, and raises up before our eyes the Cross of Christ as our bridge, our path, to heaven. In the liturgy's solemnity, majesty, beauty, and silence, in its confessions of sin and hieratic distances, in its melismatic chants, we taste the glory of heaven while being reminded of the sins and limitations that bar us from the fullness of the kingdom. Thus there is both great joy and great sorrow. Are we not victors in Christ? Has He not risen from the dead and ascended to make intercession for us at the right hand of the Father? Is not the kingdom of God *here and now*, among those who are incorporated into Christ? Yes— and yet, this is not an unambiguous, final yes *on earth*, but a yes mixed with all the no's of humanity, the no of sin and spiritual death which reign in the kingdom of the prince of this world, the no of unconversion, the no of relapsing, the no of impenitence. Our joy is complete in its Source, but we are not completely His. Our Lord is risen; we are striving to rise. Our Lord is ascended into heaven, we are still torn between heaven and earth. Our Lord is in glory, but we are blinded by His glory, our eyes are not fully purged, our hearts not fully aflame with the love of God.

It is for this reason that the Catholic rejoices—and weeps; that the priest glorifies the God who is truly present in our midst—and, head bowed, beats his breast in silence; that the Church, sojourning in this vale of tears, waves the flag of victory even as she sounds the trumpet of battle.

In the traditional Roman liturgy, the word "glory," and the reality it signifies, is everywhere. One grows accustomed to hearing it, like a sweet song from afar: *gloria . . . gloria . . . gloria*. The whole purpose of the Christian life, and the goal toward which it moves, are expressed, evoked, fulfilled in this most serene of liturgies. The sparseness of the rite, in comparison with the Divine Liturgy, has its own loveliness: "To thee do we cry, poor banished children of Eve, to thee do we send up our sighs, mourning and weeping in this vale of tears." It is a liturgy of mourning, exile, and longing, suffused with peace and streaked with glory.

For he that rejecteth wisdom, and discipline, is unhappy: and their hope is vain, and their labours without fruit, and their works unprofitable. . . . For dreadful are the ends of a wicked race. . . . The multiplied brood of the wicked shall not thrive, and bastard slips shall not take deep root, nor any fast foundation. And if they flourish in branches for a time, yet standing not fast, they shall be shaken with the wind, and through the force of winds they shall be rooted out. For the branches not being perfect, shall be broken, and their fruits shall be unprofitable, and sour to eat, and fit for nothing.

—Wisdom of Solomon

Ye are forgers of lies; ye are all physicians of no value. Oh that ye would altogether hold your peace! And it would be your wisdom. . . . Will ye speak unrighteously for God, and talk deceitfully for him? . . . Shall not his majesty make you afraid, and his dread fall upon you? Your memorable sayings are proverbs of ashes, your defenses are defenses of clay.

—The Book of Job

But indeed for deceits thou hast put it to them:
when they were lifted up thou hast cast them down.
How are they brought to desolation?
they have suddenly ceased to be:
they have perished by reason of their iniquity.
As the dream of them that awake, O Lord;
so in thy city thou shalt bring their image to nothing.

—Psalm 7

Shall thy wonders be known in the dark; and thy justice in the land of fo getfulness?

—Psalm 8

11

Rescued from the
Memory Hole

It should strike us as exceedingly odd, at least *prima facie*, that liturgy committees, Vatican dicasteries, theology departments, chanceries, religious orders, and every other sort of postconciliar bureaucratic apparatus were not engaged in a huge song and dance in the month of April *or* the month of November of the year 2019. How could they miss the opportunity to commemorate the golden anniversary of the issuance of the new Mass by Pope Paul VI on April 3, 1969, or its effective start-date in most countries on the first Sunday of Advent of that year, November 30?[1]

Certainly (one might think), if there is *anything* postconciliar that deserves to be toasted, fêted, and proudly clapped on the back, it would be this monumental modern makeover. Yet the number of events, nay, the number of *mentions* on the part of the Pauline rite's friends and supporters could be counted on one hand. The total number of events celebrating *Summorum Pontificum*'s rather modest five-year and ten-year anniversaries, in contrast, went up into double digits. Perhaps the most high-profile piece—and it wasn't particularly high-profile—was an article in *L'Osservatore Romano* on April 6, 2019, by Fr. Corrado Maggioni, SMM, Under-Secretary of the Congregation for Divine Worship and the Discipline of the Sacraments, published in English at *PrayTell* on April 17.

On the lack of celebration of the fiftieth anniversary of the Novus Ordo, see also Clemens Victor Oldendorf, "Lessons from the Sixties: Selective Synodality and Princely Protests," *ILM*, October 24, 2019.

Can we understand this perplexing silence? The question led to an interesting exchange on Facebook, of which I will now reproduce the most valuable segments. It began this way:

> I have met plenty of people who call themselves Catholic who have never had the slightest idea there ever were any [liturgical] changes, and have no idea what the term "Novus Ordo" even means, the rewriting of history has been so complete.

Another fellow chimed in:

> When I was first at University I was vaguely aware that before Vatican II Mass was in Latin, but I thought it meant the liturgy exactly as we had it in the Steubenville chapel, but in Latin. Then I went to a TLM just out of curiosity and discovered just how wrong that idea was.

The first person replied:

> I assumed precisely the same thing. The idea that they would simply brazenly concoct something new by committee was something that I had to be forcibly convinced of. It wasn't until I had put the two texts side by side that I began to realize how we had been utterly swindled all our lives. Then I started reading Michael Davies and it was all over.

A third person volunteered:

> I converted from Anglicanism, having read my way to Catholicism. The Novus Ordo (though I didn't know it was called that at the time or for many years) was a bit of a shock, but I just thought that's how it was, and I had to get on with it. I never even knew the Latin Mass still existed. I lapsed, came back, and I will always believe it was no coincidence that the weekday Mass I happened to stay for after my confession was a TLM. Usual stuff after that— read Michael Davies, etc., went through the whole anger, "I've been cheated" thing—and out the other side. Praise God.

A question was raised: "Why among Catholics is there so much ignorance not just of history in general, but even of our *recent* history? Fifty
years ago isn't that much time. . . . You'd think that a Church 2,000 years
old would want its members to know how great it was that the bad old
dusty-musty liturgy was replaced by a shiny new model." And to it, there
came this reply:

> The answer to the puzzle is that there is no longer supposed to
> be any knowledge that the "Novus Ordo," as such, exists at all.
> It is supposed only to be "the Mass," full stop. The fact that there
> were ever any changes made to the liturgy is supposed to be sliding
> down the Memory Hole with each passing year. The people who
> remember the old Mass well, who would have known just how
> radically different the new is from the old, and who remember how
> violently the changes were made—these people are dying off. That
> is, the ones who didn't simply give up and leave long ago. Catholics
> who still practice the Faith are not supposed to know there ever was
> an "old rite" or that there is a "new rite" at all. The entire project of
> the Revolution at this stage is to deny there ever was such a thing
> as the Old Faith.
>
> Anyway, all this is why they are as furious as a bag of feral cats
> that there are still Traditionalists, and that the traddy movement
> is gaining ground. That lot was supposed to have died out or been
> driven out, and the fact that there are new ones, people like me
> who never knew the old rite in the wild, and the families now
> having twelve kids and going to the Missa Cantata, and all the
> homeschooling and whatnot. . . . Combine that with the internet's
> ability to let everyone know what's really happening, and plenty of
> beautiful pictures besides, and it must be making them absolutely
> apoplectic.

Apoplectic, perhaps; but also strangely silent. How many websites are
⟨th⟩ere that pursue a strongly *reformist* line? Not that many. Maybe just one:
⟨Pr⟩*ay Tell.* How many websites pursue a strongly traditionalist line? Quite a
⟨fe⟩w. It seems, in short, that the progressives have run out of steam, or run

out of confidence, or run out of on-board personnel, or think that talking about it involves too great a risk of introducing still more Catholics to the forbidden subjects—and thence, to possible defections. A reader of *OnePeterFive* wrote to the editor: "I was already looking for God when I went to school, but the fullness, reality, and beauty of the Church and her Tradition was unknown to me until I discovered 1P5. . . . I say my encounter with Tradition was a second conversion because my experience immediately following my baptism and confirmation within Francis' church was segregated from any knowledge that the Church before the 1960s had been different than it is today."

Exactly. The success of the "transformation of all forms" (about which I will speak below) ultimately depends on as many people in the Church *not knowing* what came before 1970 and not thinking that our worship and our life could, or should, be any different from that which the Vatican, the USCCB, the chancery, or [fill in the blank] would have us think it must be.

Michael Fiedrowicz's superb book *The Traditional Mass: History, Form, and Theology of the Classical Roman Rite* eloquently summarizes the points I have been making:

> The celebration of the liturgy in its traditional form thus constitutes an effective counterweight for all levelings, reductions, dilutions, and banalizations of the Faith. Many who are unfamiliar with the classical liturgy and are acquainted only with the re-created form believe that what they see and hear there is the entirety of the Faith. Scarcely anyone senses that central passages have been removed from biblical pericopes. Scarcely anyone notices if the Church's orations no longer expressly attack error, no longer pray for the return of those who have strayed, no longer give the heavenly clear priority over the earthly, make the saints into mere examples of morality, conceal the gravity of sin, and identify the Eucharist as only a meal. Scarcely anyone even knows what prayers the Church said over the course of centuries in place of the current "preparation of the gifts," and how these prayers demonstrated the Church's

understanding of the Mass as a sacrifice, offered through the hands
of the priest for the living and the dead.[2]

As I discovered the traditional Latin Mass in my late teens and early twen-
ties, I distinctly remember stumbling on important truths of the Faith—
truths taught by Sacred Scripture, the Church Fathers, the Councils, and,
of course, the Tridentine missal—that had become muted, invisible, or
even extinct in the Novus Ordo. And subsequent study has only confirmed
the extent of that systematic bias. This is why I like to say (admitting it's a
bit of an exaggeration): "My daily missal made me a traditionalist."

Catholics who do not give themselves trustingly to the two-thousand-year
tradition of the Church will *not be in contact* with the whole doctrine and
way of life of Catholicism. This is hard to hear, but so is much of the teaching
of Our Lord: "If any man will come after me, let him deny himself, and take
up his cross, and follow me" (Matt. 16, 24). The same is true, in a way, of tradition: we have to deny our modern prejudices, take up the blessed burden
of our tradition, and follow it, in order to be integrally Catholic.

Joseph Ratzinger famously and repeatedly said that forgetfulness of God
is *the* major problem of the West: "If the Liturgy appears first of all as the
workshop for our activity, then what is essential is being forgotten: God.
For the Liturgy is not about us, but about God. Forgetting about God is
the most imminent danger of our age. As against this, the Liturgy should
be setting up a sign of God's presence. Yet what happens if the habit of forgetting about God makes itself at home in the Liturgy itself, and if in the
Liturgy we are thinking only of ourselves?"[3]

Pope Benedict XVI wrote in his letter of March 10, 2009, concerning
the remission of the excommunications of the four bishops of the Priestly
Society of Saint Pius X:

> In our days, when in vast areas of the world the faith is in danger
> of dying out like a flame which no longer has fuel, the overriding
> priority is to make God present in this world and to show men and

Michael Fiedrowicz, *The Traditional Mass: History, Form, and Theology of the Classical Roman Rite*, trans. Rose Pfeifer (Brooklyn, NY: Angelico Press, 2020), 301–2.

Foreword to Alcuin Reid, *The Organic Development of the Liturgy*, 2nd ed. (San Francisco: Ignatius Press, 2005), 13.

women the way to God. Not just any god, but the God who spoke on Sinai; to that God whose face we recognize in a love which presses "to the end" (cf. Jn 13:1)—in Jesus Christ, crucified and risen. The real problem at this moment of our history is that God is disappearing from the human horizon, and, with the dimming of the light which comes from God, humanity is losing its bearings, with increasingly evident destructive effects.

It is still difficult for many in the Church today to realize—either because they are totally ignorant of the past (as the revolutionaries intended), or because, being aware of it, they are afraid to do their homework and connect the dots—that the changes in the liturgy have actually contributed, profoundly and lastingly, to the crisis of our forgetfulness of God, and that the primary cure for this amnesia will be the restoration of the classical Roman rite for Catholics of the Latin rite.

Friedrich Nietzsche spoke of the "transvaluation of all values": the inversion of our conceptions of good and evil in the post-Christian era. What had been regarded as good—humility, self-denial, obedience, love of the poor and of poverty, looking toward a world to come—was, in his system, to be seen as evil, and what had been regarded as evil—imposing one's will by domination, satisfying one's lusts, crushing the weak, dismissing thoughts of an afterlife, living for the moment—would now be virtues. The Übermensch or Superman would be the exact contrary of the Christian saint.

As the atrocity of abortion demonstrates, Nietzsche's view has prevailed in the secular society of the West. But has not a subtler form of this "transvaluation of all values" invaded Christianity as well—including the Catholic Church, which had seemed for so many centuries to be adamantly opposed to any compromise with modernity and its atheistic spirit? In the past thirty-five years of my life (that is, the years in which I have taken seriously the divine call to live according to the Faith), I have increasingly noticed a trend that certainly deserves to be called Nietzschean.

If, for example, one objects that a certain idea or practice is "Protestant," he is likely to be dismissed as "anti-ecumenical." In this way, a vague ecumenism has supplanted several *de fide* dogmas as the measure of being a Christian. "I don't believe in dogma, I believe in love," as a plainclothes nun once said to a priest tour-guide.

If one objects that a liturgical habit or opinion is contrary to the teaching of the Council of Trent or any other magisterial determination, he is likely to be shut down as "stuck in the past" or "not in line with the Council"— meaning, of course, the Second Vatican Super-Council in whose name all earlier councils can be ignored or negated. A new form of conciliarism has supplanted obedience to the deposit of faith in its integrity and adherence to ecclesiastical tradition in its received richness. "*That's pre-Vatican,*" as a difficult elderly nun used to bark at a certain priest whenever he stated the teaching of the Church.

In an article some time ago, I argued that lector praxis in the Novus Ordo is Protestant and Pelagian.[4] The reaction of today's progressives (that is, the mainstream Church) would undoubtedly be: "So what? We're chummy with the Protestants, and we don't care about obscure ancient heresies in these enlightened times. All that matters is active participation." With one badly-understood phrase, five, ten, fifteen centuries of Catholicism can be swept aside. Remarkably, even ecclesiastics who bring up the term Pelagianism seem incapable of seeing its most dynamic symbols and reinforcing practices right under their noses.[5]

Our Lord taught that divorcing and marrying another person was committing adultery, which is a mortal sin, but say this today and you are nearly put to death with verbal stones: "rigid, judgmental, unmerciful, unwelcoming, Pharisaical." Never mind that the Pharisees were the ones who approved divorce and bending big rules while imposing little ones; no one today cares about either history or logic. That, too, is essential to the "new paradigm": the banishment of history and the emasculation of logic.

See Peter Kwasniewski, "How Typical Lector Praxis Transmits a Pelagian and Protestant Message," *NLM*, January 15, 2018.

See Congregation for the Doctrine of the Faith, Letter *Placuit Deo* to the Bishops of the Catholic Church on Certain Aspects of Christian Salvation, February 22, 2018.

Such examples could be multiplied *ad nauseam*. They all point to one thing: what used to be orthodoxy is now viewed as heresy, and what used to be heresy is now viewed as orthodoxy. *The transvaluation of all values.*

We are standing at a juncture in the history of the Catholic Church. We might call it the nadir of *Pascendi Dominici Gregis*—the moment when an attempt is being made, in practice if not in theory, to substitute for the teaching of Saint Pius X its diametrical opposite. Saint Pius X had defined Modernism as "the collector of all heresies."[6] For many of today's church leaders and people in the pews, however, it is *orthodoxy* that is the collector of all heresies, and Modernism that is the Catholic Faith pure and simple. Indeed, it has become fashionable today, even in so-called conservative circles, to brand as "fundamentalists" Catholics who hold and teach what any historic catechism of the Church teaches, be it Trent's, Pius X's, or the *Baltimore Catechism* beloved to homeschooling families.

The transvaluation, or perhaps at times merely the devaluation, of all values can be seen if we survey popular theologians of our time. Hans Urs von Balthasar's downright bizarre Trinitarian theology is in no way reconcilable with the Church's orthodox Trinitarian theology.[7] Taking his cue from another of Balthasar's novelties, Bishop Robert Barron thinks that he can seriously claim that all men might be saved—a view utterly foreign to Our Lord in the Gospels, Our Lady of Fatima, and the entire tradition of orthodox Christianity prior to Vatican II. The standard watered-down version of Christology bears little resemblance to the Christology articulated and defended at such great cost by so many Fathers of the Church, such as Saint Athanasius and Saint Cyril of Alexandria. Compared to that of Saint

---

[6] The English translation of the encyclical says "synthesis of all heresies," but the Latin has *omnium haereseon conlectum*, which makes more sense: all heresies, even contrary ones, gather under the shade of Modernism, even if they cannot be harmonized.

[7] Fr. Bertrand de Margerie, SJ, published a short but scathing "Note on Balthasar's Trinitarian Theology" in *The Thomist* 64 (2000): 127–30, in which he quotes various heretical texts from Balthasar's work and comments: "We have here a paradox: some modern authors, evidently concerned with spirituality, have unwittingly fallen into a conception of the divine Being that is overly materialistic. . . . A kind of human psychologism risks drawing the readers of the Swiss theologian in the direction of tritheism. . . . Given the strong affirmations in the Gospels of the unity between the Father and the Son—affirmations reiterated by several ecumenical councils in underscoring their consubstantiality, we cannot accept the dialectical, obscure, and, above all, dangerous language of Balthasar, who appears to affirm and deny it at the same time."

Alphonsus Liguori or Saint Louis de Montfort, our Mariology is either non-existent, sentimental, or reductive. Catholic Social Teaching has been co-opted by the socialist Left and the capitalist Right, each for its own purposes, while the cardinal themes as we find them in Leo XIII—for example, the ontologically and institutionally necessary relationship of Church and State—are unknown or caricatured. As for our sacramental and liturgical theology, one may be pardoned for wondering if there is *any* orthodox theology left at the popular level, apart from a (simplistic) conception of validity and licitness.

How did we get here? The path is a long and winding one that leads back several centuries at least, with nominalism, voluntarism, Protestantism, rationalism, and liberalism each playing star roles. But in terms of how this Nietzscheanism came to find its home in almost every Catholic church and Catholic bosom, seeping into the nave, rising into the sanctuary, erasing or jackhammering the memories of our forefathers and the faces of saints and angels, I think the answer is more straightforward.

This transvaluation of all values follows necessarily from *the transformation of all forms.*

I refer to the way in which *nothing* of Catholic life was left untouched after Vatican II. Every bit of the Mass, every aspect of the Divine Office, every sacramental rite, every blessing, every piece of clerical and liturgical clothing, every page of Canon Law and the Catechism—*all* had to be revamped, reworked, revised, usually in the direction of diminution and softening: "the Word was made bland, and dwelt in the suburbs." The beauty and power of our tradition were muted at best, massacred at worst. No form was safe, stable, or deemed worthy of preservation as it stood, as it had been received.

The open or subliminal message wasn't hard to infer: the Catholic Church went off the rails many centuries ago and in all kinds of ways, and now had to play catch-up with the modern world. Everything was on the chopping block, ready for renegotiation. What measure to apply, what ideal to aspire to, what goal to reach before the changing stops—even these were left indeterminate, disputable, open-ended, like a badly written stream-of-consciousness story. Nothing was to be left intact in humble, grateful acknowledgment of its longevity and belovedness. We are done building on rock, for it is unchanging; shifting sand better suits the evolutionary flexibility and pluralism of Modern Man.

It was simply not possible for such an iconoclastic, vandalistic, self-doubting and self-creative process to occur without profoundly calling into question *all* Catholic beliefs and *all* Catholic practices. Ostensibly, the Church's liturgy was being reformed; in reality, Catholicism was being questioned from top to bottom, or shall we say, campanile to crypt. One crack in the dam is enough to lead to its entire collapse.

Hence, from the transformation of all forms came, as inevitably as exhaustion and dictatorship follow after revolution, the transvaluation of all values. One could almost approach it like a theorem in Euclid: "Assuming the *aggiornamento* of everything, demonstrate that orthodoxy will become the collector of all heresies." And so it happened as one might have predicted.

This larger context explains and, in fact, impels the dizzying events of the past decade under Pope Francis, such as the dismantling of the Franciscan Friars and Sisters of the Immaculate and the suppression of other traditional religious and priestly communities, the push for optionalizing clerical celibacy and the expansion of female ministries, the bitter hatred for the classical Roman rite and every traditional liturgical practice (e.g., *ad orientem* celebration) that has resurfaced in the wake of *Traditionis Custodes*, the antics of the Amorites who are working sleeplessly (in imitation of their master) to win acceptance in the Church for every sexual "expression,"[8] and so on and so forth.

It all falls into place the moment one sees that the new masters of the universe hold exactly the opposite of what you and I hold. We believe what Catholics have always believed; we want to live and pray as Catholics have always done;[9] and we are shocked to find ourselves the object of mockery,

---

[8] See Peter Kwasniewski, *Holy Bread of Eternal Life: Restoring Eucharistic Reverence in an Age of Impiety* (Manchester, NH: Sophia Institute Press, 2020), ch. 14: "Our Progressive Desensitization to the Most Holy Eucharist," 197–202. By "Amorites" I refer to the proponent of the errors of chapter 8 of *Amoris Laetitia*.

[9] The favorite comeback of progressives is that "the liturgy kept developing over time, so you can't say that Catholics 'always' worshiped this or that way." But that is a superficial response. The deeper truth is that Catholics have always worshiped according to the liturgy

hostility, and persecution. But we should not be shocked. We are living by the old paradigm, in which Modernism was the collector of all heresies. Our enemies follow a new paradigm—the paradigm, in fact, of systematic newness or novelty. The newer something is, the better, the more authentic, the more real, in the ever-evolving process of human maturation. For them, the so-called "orthodox Faith" defended by the likes of Saint Augustine, Saint John Damascene, Saint Thomas Aquinas, Saint Robert Bellarmine, and Saint Pius X, *this* is absolutely no longer "relevant" to Modern Man; it is a frozen relic of a dead past, an obstacle to the Progress that the ever-surprising Spirit of Newness wishes to bestow.[10]

The novelty-mongers will stop short, perhaps, at canonizing the more illustrious members of their house—Ockham, Descartes, Luther, Hegel, or Nietzsche—but they will do their best to canonize lesser factotums such as Giovanni Battista Montini, Annibale Bugnini, and Teilhard de Chardin. We should prepare ourselves spiritually to endure a season of sacrileges, blasphemies, and apostasies that Catholics have never dreamed of in the worst periods of pagan persecution or internal confusion.

We may take comfort in the certainty, as John Paul II reminded us in his last book *Memory and Identity*, that the Lord always puts a limit to evil, as He did with National Socialism and Soviet Communism. He will not tempt any man beyond what he can bear. And, sobering as the thought is, we may also draw some comfort from the certainty that Our Lord puts a

---

they have received, and any development occurred within this fundamental assumption of the continuity of rituals, chants, and texts. The work of the Consilium of the 1960s rejected his assumption (and thereby undermined the sense of tradition as such) in altering almost every aspect of the liturgy, adding and deleting material according to their own theories. Therefore, what they produced is not and can never be an expression of Catholic tradition; it will always remain a foreign body, just as a synthetic heart can never become a living member of the body in which it is implanted.

It is in keeping with this Darwinian-Hegelian evolutionism that we find today's "conservatives" so ready to embrace the view that whatever the current reigning pope says automatically trumps all that his predecessors have said on the same subject. In reality, a pope's teaching possesses authority precisely insofar as it contains and confirms the teaching of his predecessors, even if it expands on it in ways harmonious with what has already been taught. Moreover, elementary rules of magisterial interpretation tell us that a teaching given with greater level of authority, no matter how many decades or centuries old it may be, carries more weight than a recent teaching given with a lower level of authority. Level of authority is judged by the type of document in which, or the occasion on which, it is issued, the verbal formula employed, and other such signs.

limit to the evils each of us must endure by setting a boundary to our lives. For the faithful disciple who clings to Christ and His life-giving Gospel, death accepted in self-abandonment is, in addition to being a curse of the Fall, a blessing that liberates us from a world that is not and was never intended to be our lasting home (cf. Heb 13:14). This truth is not an invitation to quietism—work we must, and work we shall—but rather a call to preserve our peace of soul in the midst of earthly trials, which will never be lacking and which are meant to wean us, bit by bit, from our selfish attachments, as we prepare for the eternal wedding feast of the Lamb.

Meanwhile, during our pilgrimage in this life, it is ours to fight the good fight, to keep the true Faith, and to resist any and every deformity of it that raises its ugly head, as we pass on what we have received and enthrone Christ as King of our hearts, homes, parishes, countries, and all of creation.

Fr. Matthew Hood was a Detroit priest who discovered in early August 2020, thanks to watching an old video, that he had been invalidly baptized—that is, had not been baptized at all, and therefore had to receive all his sacraments over again (with the fallout that resulted for the many people who had received invalid sacraments from a non-priest). After having been quickly baptized, confirmed, and ordained, he published an article "Why the Words of Baptism Matter" at *First Things* on September 3. Several sentences in his article leapt out at me; I shall comment on them a few at a time, in light of what we have covered so far in this chapter.

> Throughout the world, with rare exceptions, the sacraments are celebrated validly. If we have clear and irrefutable evidence to the contrary, then we can act to correct the situation swiftly. But the faithful should not be anxious.

"Throughout the world, with rare exceptions, the sacraments are celebrated validly." To be able to say this in 2020 is indirectly to admit the colossal failure of the liturgical reform to live up to the vision of the original Liturgical Movement: a Church joyfully and knowledgeably drawing water from the sacramental springs of salvation handed down to us in o

Catholic tradition. The reformers felt themselves free to do nearly anything, with rare exceptions, because they had already in their minds equated the "essence" of sacraments with discrete formulas that guaranteed validity—and all else was up for grabs. This neoscholastic reductionism is incapable of seeing the beauty of the whole, the intangible life that animates the organic body; this reductionism murders to dissect, confident that it will find the golden egg once the goose is slaughtered.

This is the low bar to which we have been reduced: most sacraments are *valid*. I am reminded of C. S. Lewis's observation that if you seek the higher good, you'll get the lower good "thrown in," but if you seek the lower good apart from a higher good, you won't even securely obtain the lower one. In the case of the traditional Latin sacramental rites, in which every word and motion is scripted by the rubrics and a minister is like a train engine that stays inflexibly on its tracks as it makes for the station, we obtain not only the bare minimum, validity, but something more than that, opening like a flower: the likelihood of dignity, the preconditions of beauty, the reassurance of order. Fr. Hood continues:

> If anyone should be anxious, it should be the ministers of the Church, that they renew their efforts to celebrate the rites of the Church faithfully. . . . The beautiful, powerful gift of the sacraments is obscured when we replace the voice of Christ with our own voices. As "stewards of the mysteries of God" we are proven "trustworthy" when we faithfully administer the sacraments according to the law of Christ and his Church by allowing Christ to speak through us (cf. 1 Cor 4:2).

Were the liturgical reformers of the 1960s who had been ordained to celebrate the rites faithfully—were *they* faithful to the immense treasury conveyed to them by so many generations of believers? Were *they* worthy of their trust, letting Christ and His Church "speak through them"? Or did they dare to think themselves wiser than 500, 1,000, 1,500 years of Catholic tradition or even more, stretching back to the temple worship of the Jews—wiser not just on one or two minor points, which might perhaps have been possible, but on the *shape and substance* of the Church's rites from top to bottom, as the reformers systematically and thoroughly altered every sacrament and sacramental, every office of prayer and penance, everything connected with divine worship?

Then we reach Fr. Hood's poignant statement:

> We would not dare to change the words of Scripture to fit our own whims, so why would we change the words of the sacramental formula so that our own voices are heard?

Last time I checked, this kind of "daring" was par for the course in the liturgical reform. The reform, you might say, was *defined* by audacity on every level, riding the momentum of an ecumenical council and paid for by the slush fund of papal authority, accumulated over centuries and blown in a decade.

The liturgical reformers changed the sacramental formula for the consecration of the wine by displacing the *mysterium fidei*—not making the consecration invalid, but still tampering with something that had never been changed in the entire history of the Western Church. They removed from the Divine Office many verses of the Psalms that had always been prayed by the Church. They removed passages of Scripture that used to be read at Mass for as many centuries as we have records, and when they included more of Scripture, they navigated around particular verses they didn't want to have in there. The sacramental formulas of almost every sacrament were modified by Paul VI. Did they *have* to be so modified? Had anyone ever questioned their legitimacy or appropriateness before? Were the ranks of lower clergy and lay apostolates clamoring for urgent sacramental reform? No. Paul VI changed them so that (to use Fr. Hood's words) "*our own voices are heard*"—that is, modern scholarly up-to-date voices, not the voice of Catholic Tradition.

All of this background establishes the context for why Pope Francis felt free to contradict Scripture in *Amoris Laetitia* and the death penalty change, and why he could effectively dissent from the uniqueness and unicity of the Christian religion as a God-willed path of salvation. Neither sacraments nor Scripture are seen as inviolable anymore. That, in practice, is the legacy of Paul VI's liturgical reform, and until we confront the root of the problem head-on, we will be firefighting a conflagration with squirt guns.

The solution will not be as simple as "better seminary training." There will have to be, sooner or later, a wholesale restoration of what we were doing before, successfully, with organic continuity from the beginning of the Church to the mid-twentieth century—and down to the present wherever tradition still lives. It will not be, it cannot be, something cobbled together by a Vatican committee and atomized into as many varieties as there are "worshiping communities."

The thought process behind making up supposedly more meaningful or more inculturated rituals for local communities—which, when acted on, leads to invalid sacraments, illicit celebrations, and idiotic parodies of worship—is, to speak frankly, *identical* to the thought process behind the creation of the Novus Ordo, as one may see from reading the writings of its architects, so eager to adapt, adapt, adapt. The step from Annibale Bugnini to Deacon Mark Springer[11] is not as large as might be imagined. One was clever, the other foolish; one had plenty of training but no scruples, the other plenty of enthusiasm and no training. Yet they are two peas in a pod, and the pod is rotten.

In Book IV of his *Dialogues*, Pope Saint Gregory the Great, to whom the final redaction of the Roman Canon is attributed—after which it remained virtually unchanged until 1962, when Pope John XXIII had the name of Saint Joseph inserted into it—stirringly says: "For, who of the faithful can have any doubt that at the moment of the immolation, at the sound of the priest's voice, the heavens stand open and choirs of angels are present at the

---

This is the deacon who attempted to baptize Matthew Hood but failed—as he failed with pseudo-baptisms over a thirteen-year (!) period. See "Invalid Baptisms by Deacon Mark Springer," at St. Anastasia Parish website, www.stanastasia.org/news-events/invalid-baptisms-by-deacon-mark-springer-1986-1999. Several other such cases—some of them worse—have subsequently come to light. One wonders if we are looking at the tip of another iceberg like that of clerical sexual abuse. In the early phase of reportage, such abuse seemed like it might be a rare problem in this or that isolated situation. Later it turned out to be present in virtually every diocese on the face of the earth, like a cancer that had spread undetected and untreated.

mystery of Jesus Christ? There at the altar the lowliest is united with the most sublime, earth is joined to heaven, the visible and invisible somehow merge into one."[12] He asks if *any* of the faithful can have *any* doubt that an immolation is occurring; that, at the sound of the priest uttering the words of consecration, the heavens are opened and angels are present at a *mystery*; that the altar unites earth to heaven in the supreme atoning sacrifice. This is language redolent of the Roman Canon and the traditional Roman rite in its totality; it is language that equally describes all the authentic liturgies of East and West, in both theory and praxis.

As poll after poll has shown, it would seem that today, more than fifty years after the mandatory implementation of the reformed liturgy, one would have to rephrase this question: Who among the faithful any longer believes that any of this is happening? Who among them has ever heard of it? Who would catch a glimpse of it in the manner in which the "celebration" usually takes place? Rather, it is the faithful attached to the traditional Latin Mass, the rite that stretches all the way back to Saint Gregory the Great, who will experience the mystery he describes.

Earlier I posed the question of why we are hearing a deafening silence from the quarters and parties that would be most expected to blow the trumpet in the new moon for the golden anniversary of the Novus Ordo. November 30, 2019, exactly fifty years after the fateful First Sunday of Advent in the new rite, came and went. Ardent partisans of the postconciliar reform, represented in the United States by *Pray Tell*, remained stone silent. I think they know better than to expose themselves to ridicule and refutation. Defenders of the Catholic liturgical tradition, meanwhile, have been boisterous and ebullient.

More interestingly, perhaps, there were a few attempts by "conservatives" to defend a *via media*, reminiscent of Newman's prior to 1845; one has the impression that they, like him, are fighting a rearguard action, firing off few stray shots as they run for cover. Two such attempts were published back-to-back by the *National Catholic Register*: Fr. Roger Landry's "Celebrating the Novus Ordo as It Ought to Be" and Joseph O'Brien's "The Mass of Paul VI at 50: Marking the Golden Jubilee of the New Order."

---

[12] Gregory I, *Dialogi* 4,60,3 (*Sources Chrétiennes* 265:202); *Dialogues*, trans. by O. J. Zimmerman (New York, NY: Fathers of the Church, Inc., 1959), 273.

third, George Weigel's "The Reformed Liturgy, 50 Years Later," appeared at *First Things* online.[13]

Fr. Landry's article is a remarkable study in innocence. The very title of his article contains an insoluble conundrum, since there *is* no single way that the Novus Ordo *ought* to be celebrated; it is open to literally thousands of realizations based on the local choices of different combinations of its modules, musical options, and inculturated adaptations. Moreover, the author apparently does not realize that Pope Paul VI from 1965 to 1969 and beyond expressly *excluded* a traditional style of Novus Ordo Mass (in Latin, with chant, *ad orientem*, etc.) as foreign to the entire project and purpose of the reform, even as the Consilium had ignored the vote of no confidence in the *Missa normativa* at the 1967 Synod of Bishops. There never was any intention whatsoever to keep continuity with liturgical tradition in the actual content of the new liturgical books or in their roll-out and subsequent curial administration;[14] and even if so-called traditional options occasionally prevail, they remain neither more nor less than the particular realization chosen by this priest or this worshiping community.

---

[13] We might consider Rusty Reno's eloquent explanation of his preference for the TLM in his December 2019 editorial "Failed Leaders" as a kind of commemoration, though he doesn't bill it as such: see the section entitled "Et Cum Spiritu Tuo." Dr. Joseph Shaw has already gently refuted Reno's characterization of the strengths and weaknesses of the two "forms" in a pair of articles at Rorate: "Reply to Rusty Reno, Part 1: The TLM and Catechesis," December 3, 2019; "Reply to Rusty Reno, Part 2: The TLM and Community," December 4, 2019. Ken Wolfe published a short and sweet Op Ed in the *New York Daily News*; and at his blog, Fr. Zuhlsdorf shared a number of podcasts anent the anniversary. As latecomers, we might also add Christopher Carstens, "Silver and Gold," *Adoremus* Editorial, January 16, 2020, and Mary Healy, "The Gift of the Liturgical Reform," *Homiletic & Pastoral Review*, January 18, 2020, the latter of which elicited many rebuttals, including mine: see "The Gift of Liturgical Tradition" in Peter Kwasniewski, *Reclaiming Our Roman Catholic Birthright: The Genius and Timeliness of the Traditional Latin Mass* (Brooklyn, NY: Angelico Press, 2020), 161–79.

[14] Consider the responses published in *Notitiae* 14 (1978): 301–2, 534–37: "It must never be forgotten that the Missal of Pope Paul VI, from the year 1970, has taken the place of that which is improperly called 'the Missal of St. Pius V' and that it has done this totally, whether with regard to texts or rubrics. Where the rubrics of the Missal of Paul VI say nothing or say little in specifics in some places, it is not therefore to be inferred that the old rite must be followed. Accordingly, the many and complex gestures of incensation according to the prescriptions of the earlier Missal . . . are not to be repeated"; "the Missal formerly indicated at the *Agnus Dei* striking the breast three times, and in pronouncing the triple *Domine, non sum dignus*, striking the breast three times. . . . Since, however, the new Missal says nothing about this, there is no reason to suppose that any gesture should be added to these invocations"; and so forth.

Those who study the records closely can readily see the incoherence in attempting to defend an amorphous and voluntaristic missal as the basis of a stable, dignified, and truly unifying liturgical life, but we are up against a threefold obstacle: a profound ignorance compounded by five decades of distance; a tremendous atmosphere of indifference; and a well-intentioned but harmful indulgence in wishful thinking on the part of those who would reconnect severed limbs with adhesive bandages. Further rebuttal of Landry is hardly necessary, since, if one has the courage to open the *Register* comments section, one finds there a bloodbath of Napoleonic magnitude.

O'Brien's article is more even-handed, citing in good journalistic fashion various opinions about the motives and outcomes of the reform. It still suffers from an attempt to put a good face on a revolution in Catholic worship that remains profoundly troubling and troublesome. The very title of this article is more revealing than anything else in it: The Mass *of Paul VI.* Never before 1969 had it been possible to say, "The Mass *of (so-and-so)."* Not even Pius V contributed so much to the *Missale Romanum* that his 1570 edition could reasonably be called the Mass *of Pius V.* It was the Mass of the Roman Curia, the Mass of Saint Damasus, Saint Gelasius, Saint Gregory I, Hadrian, Saint Gregory VII, Innocent III, Gregory IX, and on and on—the Mass of *all* of them, and of *none* of them.[15]

Weigel's article is like much of his recent work: brief, insubstantial, and inconsequential, with an obligatory memorial of his latest book, and an optional memorial of his favorite Ordinary Form parish, where, thanks to the wonders of the internet, one can view, from thousands of miles away in the comfort of one's own home, one of the few places on planet Earth where the Novus Ordo is "done well"—that is, mostly not according to the wishes of Paul VI, but with a house blend of Tridentinisms and Anglicanisms.

What is perhaps most telling is that none of these authors is capable of yielding to unqualified praise for the Novus Ordo. Positive statements are hedged about with qualifications, if-onlys, regrets, and desiderata. One is

---

[15]   In point of fact, the Roman rite, although sometimes called "the rite of Saint Gregory the Great," is almost unique among major historical liturgies in that it did not traditionally circulate under the name of one of its creators—as did, for instance, the liturgies of Saint John Chrysostom, Saint Basil, Saint James, etc.—but solely on the authority of the Roman Church

left with the impression that we are celebrating an anniversary not so much of something that exists as of something that failed to exist, or exists only in embryonic form, blighted in its gestation. Meanwhile, the classical Roman rite lives on, in its fully-matured form, offered according to ironclad rubrics that protect it from diminution, arbitrariness, and groupthink.[16]

One wonders where we will be in another fifty years' time, at the centennial jubilee. The golden anniversary augurs a probable outcome: there will be still fewer articles from the ardent supporters of the reform, since, according to the sophisticated Vatican mathematics that gave us 2 + 2 = 5, zero is less than zero; and there may not even be any Reform-of-the-Reform-style articles, after the virtual schism between the neo-modernism of the conciliar epoch and the traditionalism of the preconciliar epoch will have become an outright parting of the ways, as it is bound to do—as, indeed, we see already happening.

Certainly, in comparison with the amorphousness of the Novus Ordo, which no one ~ems to be able to control, even the Roman rite as of 1962 looks mature, ironclad, and ·ll-protected by its own rubrics. But it is true that we will find the *fully-matured form* of the ~man rite only if we go back before the major "tinkeritis" of the twentieth century begins ~us X in regard to the *cursus psalmorum*, Pius XII in regard to Holy Week, vigils, octaves, ~ vestments). In order to recover it in its undiminished form, untouched by groupthink, ~ will need to settle in the future on the 1920 missal, with addenda through World War II, ~ reasons discussed in chapter 12.

The Mass—the testament of the Lord—is the Sun of our lives and our treasure. We love it due to the fact that it is substantially and principally of the Lord's institution. But we also love it as the Church, to whom Jesus entrusted its celebration, has handed it down to us through the centuries in the various liturgical traditions. For it is in order to explain and manifest to the eyes of the whole Church the unfathomable riches of the essential rite bequeathed by the Lord that the prayers and rites have developed over the centuries. . . . We can in no way renounce a heritage that was slowly built up by the faith of our fathers, their ardent devotion and theological reflection on the sacrament of the Lord's Passion. When we come into contact with the Mass of Saint Pius V—in which we also contemplate the purest masterpiece of Western civilization, at once hierarchical and sacral—our souls ascend and our hearts expand, while our minds taste the most authentic Eucharistic doctrine. This is why we want to understand and love the traditional Mass, our treasure, more and more, and why we will not stop defending and promoting it.

—Abbé Franck Quoëx

The reactionary does not yearn for the futile restoration of the past, but for the improbable rupture of the future with this sordid present.

—Nicolás Gómez Dávila

12

The Once and Future Roman Rite

Having explored in preceding chapters the most crucial differences between traditional liturgical rites (above all, that of the Church of Rome) and the committee-fabricated modern rite of Paul VI, it is now time to tackle a final ambitious topic: why the traditional movement should place a high priority on recovering the riches lost in the wave of reforms to the Mass of the Roman rite that took place in the *preconciliar* phase of liturgical reform—namely, from Pius XII's establishment in 1948 of the Pian Commission for Liturgical Reform that gave Annibale Bugnini his first Vatican job to John XXIII's 1962 modification of the Roman Canon and promulgation of a *Missale Romanum* with a new code of rubrics. More particularly, I will discuss, first, why the 1962 missal is an arbitrary and unsatisfactory resting-point.[1] Then I will delve into Palm Sunday, the Easter Triduum, the Vigil of Pentecost, Corpus Christi, and the feast of the Holy Innocents, followed by five general features of Mass and an excursus on First Vespers. Lastly, I will turn to practical and canonical issues, including the question of what kind of permission is necessary to recover the treasures of our Tridentine heritage.[2]

Although the problem of papal interference in liturgy goes back many centuries, an abyss separates anything done by popes prior to the twentieth

---

[1] On this period and the "radical subjectivism" by which liturgists increasingly sought to re-fashion liturgy in view of their theories about modern needs, see Dom Alcuin Reid, *The Organic Development of the Liturgy*, 2nd ed. (San Francisco: Ignatius Press, 2005), 145–301.

[2] I will not even consider the argument in favor of the missal of 1965, presented by a tiny band of enthusiasts as the ideal *via media* between 1962 and 1969. For explanation, see my article "*Sacrosanctum Concilium*: The Ultimate Trojan Horse," *Crisis Magazine*, June 21, 2021 and the references given there.

century from that which was done by Pius X to the breviary in 1911, Pius XII to Holy Week and the calendar in the 1950s, and Paul VI to absolutely everything connected with worship in the years 1965–1975. Compared to earlier centuries, we are dealing here with a difference in kind, not just a difference in degree. Moreover, we could say each of those papal steps was exponentially graver than the preceding. Pius X reordered part of the Roman rite's prayer; Pius XII refashioned the heart of the Roman rite's year; Paul VI replaced the entire Roman rite with a modern rite.

To explain more fully: Pius X moved about the pieces of the traditional breviary while retaining its material content; it would be as if a pope took the *usus antiquior* and moved the orations, Epistles, and Gospels to different places in the missal, while keeping the same texts: materially the same, formally different.[3] Pius XII's reforms to the calendar and the rubrics were equally severe; yet it was his alteration of Holy Week that moved from structure to substance: the new ceremonies were a mutation of the old ones, not merely a reorganization of content, done on the specious double pretext of removing "corruptions" and promoting "active participation" (without explaining how one will increase participation by offering the faithful less to participate *in*, as we will see further on in this chapter). We may add here that John XXIII's 1962 missal not only includes the defective material of his predecessor but also a problematic code of rubrics from 1960 that, if it solves certain problems left by Pacelli, also introduces novelties foreshadowing the Novus Ordo. Finally, Paul VI created a new set of liturgical rites that bear only a generic resemblance to what came before; his work is both materially and formally different.

In short: Pius X dared to reorder the Roman rite, Pius XII dared to refashion it, Paul VI dared to replace it. It is therefore less problematic to pray the Pius X breviary than to follow the Pius XII Holy Week; and

---

[3]   To be perfectly accurate, one should note he also added new antiphons because of the new distribution and division of psalms. Pius X's motivations were worthy of respect: to restore the praying of the entire psalter each week to the extent possible and to ensure due primacy to the Sunday office. Traditionalists today regard his new breviary as an extreme and imperfec solution to a nearly intractable real problem. A solution has yet to be found that would retai the traditional *ordo psallendi* while maintaining Pius X's valid *desiderata*. It would seem tha just as the monastic office borrowed historically from the Roman, so today the Roman offic may wish to look to the monastic for a model, as well as the pastoral realism of the Byzantine who require only some, but not all, daily hours to be said by clergy in active ministry.

the 1962 missal, though defective, is altogether less problematic than the
Novus Ordo.

The *lex orandi* comes first

Thus we can see that major tinkering with the liturgy was already happening before Vatican II was even a twinkle in Roncalli's eye, before Montini
ever darkened a papal throne. The Novus Ordo did not emerge out of thin
air like the apparition of Mephistopheles in Goethe's *Faust*. The ground
was painstakingly prepared by decades of scholarly utopianism and pastoral
experimentation. The period after World War II, in particular, was a period
of restlessness for the Church, of "experts" itching to modify or abandon
old liturgical forms and introduce new ones.

In the dictum *lex orandi, lex credendi*, one must take seriously that *lex
orandi* comes first: doctrine is expressed principally in and through our
inherited worship. Yes, we know that doctrine can indirectly flow into liturgy, as when a new doctrinal emphasis leads to new feasts or votive Masses;
we know that, in addition to liturgy, there are other channels by which doctrine reaches us, such as conciliar canons, papal encyclicals, and catechisms.
Nevertheless, the liturgy is the "home" of the Faith. It is the primary canon
that measures all canons, the most authoritative utterance of revelation, the
primordial catechism that contains and passes on our holy religion. In the
words of Dom Guéranger: "Just as the virtue of religion contains all the
acts of divine worship, so too the Liturgy, which is the social form of this
virtue, equally contains them all. It may even be said that the Liturgy is the
highest and most holy expression of the Church's thought and intelligence,
because it is exercised by the Church in direct communication with God
in confession, prayer, and praise. . . . God owed His Church a language
worthy of serving such high thoughts, such ardent desires."[4]

In the twentieth century, however, the saying was flipped around by none
other than Pius XII,[5] who in *Mediator Dei* famously made the *lex credendi*

Institutions liturgiques, vol. I, 2nd ed. (Paris: Sociéte générale de librairie catholique,
78), Pt. I, ch. 1, pp. 2, 4. Translation mine.

See Fr. Christopher Smith, "Liturgical Formation and Catholic Identity," in *Liturgy in the
enty-First Century: Contemporary Issues and Perspectives*, ed. Alcuin Reid (New York:
omsbury, 2016), 260–86.

govern the *lex orandi*. Whether he intended it or not, this inversion allowed the theories of liturgists—theories based on questionable interpretations of historical data[6] and an engineering mentality that views liturgy as raw material for exploitation and construction—to reshape the liturgical rites of the Church. John W. O'Malley credits Pope Pius XII for "two decrees, in 1951 and 1955, in which he completely reorganized the liturgies for the last three days of Holy Week to bring them in line with liturgists' recommendations," thereby preparing the way for Vatican II's liturgical reforms.[7] Prior to the unhindered reign of Bugnini from 1963 to 1975, there were lots of "little Bugninis" already toying with the liturgy, for purportedly "pastoral" reasons reminiscent of French "workerism," or for antiquarian reasons that served as cover for novelty, even as *ressourcement* theologians advanced their *avant-garde* ideas behind a patristic front. In the Eastern Christian world, too, one could (and still can) find such agitators, who want to cut away the long litanies, remove the iconostasis, abbreviate this or that penitential rite, insist that all the priestly prayers be said out loud, etc. Fortunately, the East is so disorganized that almost nothing ever comes of it.

The Western Church is characterized by the blessing and the curse of centralized authority: once an idea grips the mind of a curial official and he can bend the pope's ear to it, *voila!*, one billion people are suddenly committed to a new path. It's the kind of power a dictator would not even dare to dream of, and which, therefore, ought to be used with a sparingness bordering on catalepsy. Sadly, popes in the twentieth century have repeatedly thrown the weight of their office behind massive renovation and construction projects, which is not really the point of the Petrine office.

This was the fundamental problem all along. Paul VI's Novus Ordo and Liturgy of the Hours are an extreme (admittedly, very extreme) version c

---

[6]   Such as the argument for *versus populum*—which even Jungmann held in suspicion. Se his book (outdated in many ways) *The Early Liturgy to the Time of Gregory the Great*, tran Francis A. Brunner (Notre Dame, IN: University of Notre Dame Press, 1959), 133–39.

[7]   John W. O'Malley, *When Bishops Meet: An Essay Comparing Trent, Vatican I, and Vatic II* (Cambridge, MA: The Belknap Press of Harvard University Press, 2019), 49. Pius XII i complex figure and there is reason to believe that some, at least, of the liturgical damage do under his reign was orchestrated by operators who took advantage of his declining hea and increasing withdrawal. See my article "Lights and Shadows in the Pontificate of Pius X *OnePeterFive*, September 22, 2021; cf. "Coincidences During the Reign of Pius XII? Polit Background to Vatican II and Liturgical Changes," *LifeSiteNews*, May 25, 2021.

the same papal tinkeritis that had been driving the liturgical reforms of John XXIII, Pius XII, and Pius X.[8] That is unquestionably how Montini himself regarded the matter: "It was felt necessary," he writes in his Apostolic Constitution *Missale Romanum* of April 3, 1969, "to revise and enrich the formulae of the Roman Missal. The first stage of such a reform was the work of Our Predecessor Pius XII with the reform of the Easter Vigil and the rites of Holy Week, which constituted the first step in the adaptation of the Roman Missal to the modern mentality" (*qui proinde primum quasi gradum posuit ad Missale Romanum novis huius temporis animi sensibus accommodandum*).

In reality, what is prior to everything is the liturgical heritage we receive from the centuries that come before us. The "Orthodox" attitude toward liturgy is simply the "orthodox" attitude toward it. The pope is not the master and possessor of the liturgical rites, in the way that Descartes wanted modern man to be the master and possessor of nature.

The limitations of Lefebvre

A defense of the 1962 missal (including its 1955 Holy Week) must base itself on a belief that all was theologically sound in the Vatican until the stroke of midnight on October 10, 1962, and therefore, that everything promulgated before then ought to be accepted. Yet several of the most cringeworthy things about the Novus Ordo—e.g., prayers *versus populum*, the corporate recitation of the Pater Noster (which had never been a part of the Roman tradition), the use of the vernacular (in the fabricated renewal of baptismal vows), suppression of the prayers at the foot of the altar—were first introduced in connection with the 1955 Holy Week, in a "trial balloon" approach. Father Carlo Braga, member of the Liturgical Commission and right-hand man of Annibale Bugnini, described the Pacellian Holy Saturday of 1951 as "the head of the battering ram that penetrated the

---

Wikipedia (believe it or not) has a good factual overview of the "Liturgical reforms of Pope Pius XII." A similar comparison between the missal of Pius X and the missal of John XIII may be found at http://www.traditionalmass.org/articles/article.php?id=18. Such links are for the purpose of access to information and do not constitute any kind of endorsement of positions expressed. Overviews and studies of the differences between the old Holy Week and the Pacellian reworking of it are conveniently gathered at two websites: www.pre15holyweek.com and www.restorethe54.com.

fortress of our hitherto static liturgy."[9] By the time Pius XII died in 1958, the Roman rite was laid out on the operating table, the doctors' scalpels glinting. Isn't it more likely—if we consider the way in which momentous historical changes usually unfold in stages, not happening like a *Deus* (or *diabolus*) *ex machina*—that the dismemberment of the Roman rite and its substitution by another rite in 1969 was prepared gradually over many years rather than suddenly happening "because of Vatican II" or "because of the dynamic duo of Bugnini and Montini"?

A passage from Annibale Bugnini's *magnum opus* tells us what it was like to work at the Vatican in the years 1948 to 1960:

> In the twelve years of its existence (June 28, 1948, to July 8, 1960) the [Pian liturgical] commission held eighty-two meetings and worked in absolute secrecy. So secret, in fact, was their work that the publication of the *Ordo Sabbati Sancti instaurati* at the beginning of March 1951 caught even the officials of the Congregation of Rites by surprise. The commission enjoyed the full confidence of the Pope, who was kept abreast of its work by Monsignor Montini and even more, on a weekly basis, by Father Bea, confessor of Pius XII. Thanks to them, the commission was able to achieve important results even during periods when the Pope's illness kept everyone else from approaching him. It must be honestly acknowledged that the work accomplished despite the limitations of personnel and business was enormous. Almost all the liturgical books were revised, including the Ritual. . . . It [the "restored" Easter Vigil] was a signal that the liturgy was at last launched decisively on a pastoral course. The same reforming principles were applied in 1955 to the whole of Holy Week and in 1960, with the Code of Rubrics, to the remainder of the liturgy, especially the Divine Office.[10]

---

9   Carlo Braga, "*Maxima Redemptionis Nostrae Mysteria*: 50 Anni Dopo (1955–2005)," *Ecclesia Orans* 23 (2006): 11–36, at 33; see the English translation published in installments a NLM on June 1–4, 2022.

10 Bugnini, *Reform of the Liturgy*, 9–10. Note that this comes at the beginning of his almo 1,000-page tome: what he has just described is only the warm-up exercises for the Olymp contest to follow!

Another argument made by proponents of the 1955 Holy Week is that no bishops (e.g., Lefebvre) opposed it at the time, whereas later some opposed the 1969 missal; therefore it must have been the case that they discerned a serious problem in the latter that was not present in the former. Are we better judges than these men, who were equipped with the charism of apostolic succession and were "right there" in the midst of these experiences?

This argument self-destructs. The vast majority of bishops who lived through this period made no objections to *either* the earlier liturgical changes *or* the Novus Ordo of 1969. Are we really supposed to believe that it took only fourteen years (from 1955 to 1969) for the worldwide episcopate to be transformed from fearless paladins of the Catholic religion who would have opposed any liturgical reform that was not a suitable expression of the Faith, to the supine, complacent, indifferent lot who coughed and looked elsewhere when Paul VI betrayed what they themselves had signed on to and asked for in *Sacrosanctum Concilium*?

For a law to be binding, it must have the character of stability: "*lex dubia non obligat.*" Bugnini states in his commentary on the simplified rubrics of 1955 that the said reform was but a "bridge to the liturgy of the future" and, as mentioned, Braga praised the new Easter Vigil as a battering ram. So, if, on the one hand, the theological backbone of *Summorum Pontificum* is that the old rite, having *droit de cité* or full rights of citizenship, had never been and cannot be abolished; and if, on the other hand, the old rite was being progressively reformed from 1948 to 1968 before the full-blown Novus Ordo was rolled out in 1969, *why* would the permitted form of the inabolishable Roman rite be a random year from the middle of twenty years' worth of increasingly audacious reforms? The reason, as it happens, is purely accidental: it was a policy decision made for the Priestly Society of St. Pius X by Archbishop Marcel Lefebvre.

Sedevacantism?

Some say that questioning the liturgical reforms of popes boils down to sedevacantism. If the pope's the pope, everyone should rigorously follow what he promulgates. If one refuses to do so, or doubts the legitimacy of what he has dictated, or continues to celebrate a rite in its earlier form, one is (at least implicitly, if not explicitly) calling into question his incumbency of office; that is, one thinks either that there is no pope, or that the pope is someone else, or perhaps (as in sedeprivationism) that there is a pope *materialiter* but not *formaliter*.

But there is no reason to draw this melodramatic conclusion. The question of whether certain revisions to liturgy are good or bad, deserving of acceptance or rejection, in continuity with tradition or opposed to it, is simply not the same question as whether a certain pope is pope—unless, in the ultramontanist vein of William George Ward, one believes that the pope's office guarantees him unerring good judgment and freedom from error in *all* regards. In the absence of this pious overbelief, one could very well think that a valid pope had made bad liturgical law, and that a certain lazy conservatism combined with theological fuzziness might prevent his successors from cleaning up the mess.[11] One could have eminently sound reasons (that is what this entire book seeks to show) for continuing to use a traditional rite and refusing to use its intended replacement—all the while remembering the pope in the Canon.[12]

Special feasts or times of year

Holy Week

The Holy Week liturgies, with their exquisite Gregorian chants, rich prayers, dense symbolism, and elaborate rituals, developed in the Roman rite over a lengthy period of time, from antiquity to the Middle Ages. The core elements came from both the ancient Roman tradition and the ancient Gallican or Frankish tradition north of the Alps. These two streams were combined in the later Middle Ages to form the mature Roman rite that culminated in the Missal of Pius V in 1570. As with every other histori-

[11] Thus, in point of fact, liturgical practice among sedevacantists varies. Some follow a of the Pius XII reforms (not the John XXIII ones, obviously), such as the group called th CMRI. Others, like Father Cekada's group, do not follow these reforms. Sedevacantism *such* does not dictate a liturgical policy. Likewise, many non-sede trads follow the more less "pure" 1962 form, especially the SSPX, while more and more "approved" trads are op to, or even following, the pre-Pacellianized liturgy, albeit usually in piecemeal fashion; a in this regard, diocesan priests or single monasteries have more freedom than the form Ecclesia Dei institutes with hundreds of priests and loads of parishes to take into account
[12] For a thought-provoking treatment of these issues, see John Lamont, "Is the Mass of P VI Licit?," *Dialogos Institute*, March 20, 2022, http://dialogos-institute.org/blog/wordpr /disputation-on-the-1970-missal-part-1-dr-john-lamont/.

Christian liturgy of apostolic descent, the Tridentine rite reached a state of perfection, a beauty of form and fullness of content that allowed for no further substantial improvement.[13] As with the mature Byzantine Divine Liturgy of Saint John Chrysostom, so with the traditional Roman rite: nothing essential needed to be added or removed; from that point on, change would concern only matters of detail, such as adding new saints to the calendar while perhaps reducing others to commemorations.

Tragically, Pius XII allowed himself in the early 1950s to be talked into the project of "revising" Holy Week, which had not been changed in any notable way for over five hundred years. Under cover of the excuse that the Triduum liturgies needed to be "restored to their original times of day," Holy Week was brought before the Pian Commission—a sort of dry run for the later Consilium—and Palm Sunday, Good Friday, and the Easter Vigil underwent alterations on a scale unprecedented in Western ecclesiastical history.[14] It was not so much a retouching as a reconstruction—as when builders dismantle a building and recycle its materials into a new construction. On February 9, 1951, Pius XII launched an experimental Easter Vigil, and in 1955 he promulgated new liturgical rites for the remainder of Holy Week. That is why people often call the *old* Holy Week (by which I mean the Tridentine one) the "pre-55."

I still remember clearly the first time I attended a pre-55 Holy Week in full. Expecting to be impressed, I was blown away; expecting to be bewildered, I was dazzled and provoked. The next few pages will draw attention to some of the major features of the Tridentine Holy Week that were done away with by Pius XII.

---

[13] For a detailed comparison between the venerable Roman Holy Week and the Pacellian Holy Week, see the nine-part series by Gregory DiPippo at *NLM*, under the heading "Compendium of the 1955 Holy Week Revisions of Pius XII," running from March 26, 2009 to May 11, 2009; Fr. Stefano Carusi, "The Reform of Holy Week in the Years 1951–1956," *Rorate Caeli*, July 25, 2010; Philip J. Goddard, *Festa Paschalia: A History of the Holy Week Liturgy in the Roman Rite* (Leominster: Gracewing, 2011).

[14] Prior to Pius XII's changes, all the Holy Week liturgies were celebrated early in the day, a position they had occupied for some centuries after the Middle Ages. The liturgists, rightly or not, wanted to change their times: an evening Mass for Holy Thursday, a mid-afternoon liturgy for Good Friday, and a nighttime liturgy for the Easter Vigil. Whatever the merits or demerits of these time changes, it is clear that they did not require *any change whatsoever* in the actual content of the liturgical rites. Today, when the pre-1955 rites are utilized, they are generally done at the later times of day.

Palm Sunday

The old Palm Sunday liturgy begins with a *Missa sicca* or "dry Mass" at the beginning,[15] with an Epistle, Gradual, and Gospel, then a Preface leading into the blessing of the palms—all of this, mind you, *prior* to the procession with palms, the entrance after knocking at the doors, and the Mass of the day, with the chanting of the Passion according to Saint Matthew. This *Missa sicca* may well be the most perfect exemplification of the Catholic principle of "sacramentality" in the old missal. By this I mean the principle that God, having created a world for us, then reveals Himself to us using the things He has created as His language or vocabulary: plants, animals, people, events, become signs or symbols; and in turn, Holy Mother Church, having received this language from her Lord, communicates with Him (and with us) in the same language. Here is how the Preface of the Palm Sunday *Missa sicca* conveys this truth:

> It is truly meet and just, right and availing unto salvation, that we should always and in all places give thanks unto Thee, O Lord, Father almighty, everlasting God, Who dost glory in the assembly of Thy Saints. For Thy creatures serve Thee, because they acknowledge Thee as their only Creator and God; and Thy whole creation praiseth Thee, and Thy Saints bless Thee. For with free voice they confess that great Name of Thine only-begotten Son before the kings and powers of this world. Around whom the Angels and Archangels, the Thrones and Dominions stand; and with all the host of the heavenly army, sing the hymn of Thy glory, saying without ceasing: Holy, holy, holy Lord God of hosts . . .

The first prayer of blessing after the Preface has an astonishing kinship with Eucharistic consecration:

> We beseech Thee, O holy Lord, almighty Father, everlasting God, that Thou wouldst vouchsafe to bless ✠ and hallow ✠ this creature of the olive tree, which Thou didst cause to shoot out of the substance of the wood, and which the dove when returning to the ark

---

[15] A "dry Mass" is a liturgical rite that follows the basic structure of the Mass but culminate in a consecration of something other than the bread and wine of the Holy Eucharist.

brought in its mouth: that whosoever shall receive it may find protection of soul and body; and that it may be to us, O Lord, a saving remedy and a sacrament of Thy grace [*tuae gratiae sacramentum*].[16]

Authors like Alexander Schmemann, Aidan Kavanaugh, and David Fagerberg like to talk about "the sacramental cosmos," but there are no texts anywhere in the Roman tradition that convey the idea of sanctified creation better than the ones in the old Palm Sunday liturgy.[17] The third prayer of blessing underlines the mystical significance of what the ancient Hebrews did and what we are now doing:

O God, who, by the wonderful order of Thy disposition, hast been pleased to manifest the dispensation of our salvation even from things insensible: grant, we beseech Thee, that the devout hearts of Thy faithful may understand to their benefit what is mystically signified by the fact that on this day the multitude, taught by a heavenly illumination, went forth to meet their Redeemer, and strewed branches of palms and olive at His feet. The branches of palms, therefore, represent His triumphs over the prince of death; and the branches of olive proclaim, in a manner, the coming of a spiritual unction. For that pious multitude understood that these things were then prefigured; that our Redeemer, compassionating human miseries, was about to fight with the prince of death for the life of the whole world, and, by dying, to triumph. For which cause they dutifully ministered such things as signified in Him the triumphs of victory and the richness of mercy. And we also, with full faith, retaining this as done and signified, humbly beseech Thee, O holy Lord, Father almighty, everlasting God, through the same Jesus Christ our Lord, that in Him and through Him, whose members Thou hast been pleased to make us, we may become victorious

---

One might add that this prayer—which is typical of the entire liturgy of the day—is the ʒimate response to traditionalists who get hung up on any use of the word "sacrament" that ᴎot limited to the seven sacred signs we customarily call by that word. Saint Thomas Aquiː would simply say we need to understand that the word "sacrament" is used analogously ʒifferent kinds of things, with the basic meaning of "a sign that conveys grace."
For more thoughts along these lines, see Claudio Salvucci, "'Palm' Sunday and the Sanctition of Creation," *Liturgical Arts Journal*, April 17, 2019.

over the empire of death, and may deserve to be partakers of His glorious Resurrection. Who liveth and reigneth . . .

The fact that such texts were suppressed in the 1950s, precisely when liturgists were waxing eloquent on this theme, is more than a little perverse, but it fits into a larger pattern, where we see actual reforms undermining the goals put forward as their justification. A great example is the constant talk about active participation: the more the liturgy was changed to accommodate the action of the people, the more the people drifted away from church—because they could sense that the greatness of the mystery of faith, which is the magnet that draws us into spiritual activity, was vanishing. As Joseph Ratzinger says, once the liturgy becomes a place where we seem to be celebrating ourselves as a community and the works of our hands, it ceases to have any transcendent meaning that carries us out of ourselves into the presence of God. As a result, it quickly becomes boring and inferior to the entertainments and distractions offered by the world.

Another poignant element in the Tridentine Palm Sunday liturgy is when the subdeacon strikes the base of the closed church door with the processional cross, as the procession wends its way back to the church. It is the King of Glory knocking; he has come to Jerusalem's gates to make His triumphant entrance, accompanied by the people's "Hosannas"—all the while fully aware that only days later they will turn against Him. That the people singing on the outside of the church are answered by a few singers who remain inside symbolizes fallen man's separation from the heavenly Jerusalem of the angels, a separation that only the passion of Christ—begun with His entry into the Holy City—was capable of overcoming, as it threw open to us the doors to the city of paradise.

Holy Thursday

With the pre-55 Holy Thursday, one thing that was quite new to me was the omission of the Mandatum, or ceremonial washing of the feet—a ceremony that migrated into the Mass only in the mid-twentieth century and has caused all manner of debate and distraction. Which men should have their feet washed? The parish council's, or a random selection, or half poor people and half benefactors? Should women be included? How about

Protestants, or even non-Christians? In other words, the foot-washing, like so much else in modern liturgies, quickly turned into a political battle. What was forgotten was the actual origin of this ceremony in monasteries where the abbot washed the feet of younger brethren or where a monk washed the feet of poor men brought in from outside.

In the pre-55 rite, the Mandatum is done as a paraliturgy (that is, something modeled off of the liturgy) *after* Mass. It might be done, for example, in the church basement. A temporary altar is set up with candles. Once the altars upstairs have been stripped of their altar cloths in imitation of the humiliating treatment of Christ in His passion, everyone proceeds to where the Mandatum ceremony will take place. Thirteen men sit in chairs or on a bench (this number thirteen goes back to a vision of Saint Gregory the Great). The priest, deacon, and subdeacon enter, with acolytes.

The ceremony begins with the solemn chanting of the Gospel, after which the priest dons an apron and washes the men's feet while the choir sings the *Ubi caritas*. The priest returns to the altar, chants a number of versicles, and sings a Collect; all bow and depart. Doing the Mandatum on its own after Mass gives it a special place or dignity; one can focus more directly on the lesson of the high serving the low. It also matches better the idea that first we worship God for love of Him, and then, with His grace, we go out into the world to love others made in His image.

Good Friday

The solemn pre-55 Good Friday opens with two chanted lessons and two chanted tracts, which allow the faithful to slow down and *ease into* the enormous mystery of the day. The chanting of the Passion according to Saint John by the three designated deacons (or, in lieu of them, the three ministers of the Mass as long as none is inferior to a deacon in rank) follows, with the confident, commanding bass melody for Christ; the skipping-along, matter-of-fact narrator; and the eerie high-pitched "ring tone" of the one who speaks for Peter, Pilate, the Jews, the crowd, and every other shady character. When the Passion is finished, the readers split up, and the deacon of the Mass chants the "proper" Gospel of the day in a special tone, recounting the burial of Christ. The silence after the Passion and the special treatment paid to the burial are highly fitting. (Saint Matthew's Passion is sung in the same manner on Palm Sunday, Saint Mark's on Holy Tuesday, and Saint Luke's on Holy Wednesday.)[18]

After the great intercessions, the veneration of the Cross begins with a procession of discalced or barefoot ministers who genuflect three times on their way to It. In some churches, the first genuflection takes place at the back, the second in the middle of the aisle, and the third right before the Cross, which is lying on a cushion, as if a royal personage on his divan. The chanting of the Reproaches and the *Crux fidelis* accompanies the slow procession of many people. It is well for us that it takes so much time: it burns our time like incense.

The strangest aspect of the venerable Good Friday liturgy is the treatment of the Most Holy Eucharist. Only one large Host has been reserved from the night before, placed in a chalice (not a ciborium) with a paten and pall, all of which are covered with a white silk veil and tied with a white silk ribbon. The Host is carried by the celebrant in procession, accompanied by the mighty hymn *Vexilla Regis*. The first two verses set the tone:

> The royal banners forward go
> The Cross shines forth in mystic glow,
> Where Life Himself our death endured,
> And by His death our life procured.
>
> Where deep for us the spear was dyed,
> Life's torrent rushing from His side,
> To wash us in that precious flood,
> Where mingled water flowed, and blood.

---

[18] The old practice was to assign the singing to three dedicated deacons who had no other role in the liturgy except to chant the Passion (see Pio Martinucci II, 27, 90). Moreover, certain readings were to be sung only if there were ordained lectors. Under the influence of the Liturgical Movement, the 1950 *Memoriale Rituum* allows ministers of the Mass to double as deacons of the Passion, since outside of cathedrals and monasteries it is not likely one would be able to find so large a host of ministers. It is beyond the scope of this book to enter into the pros and cons of such accommodations for promoting sung liturgy in the absence of customary ministers, but I am sympathetic to efforts to rebuild a culture of solemn sung liturgy after the musical-ritual desolation of the past half-century.

The priest incenses the Blessed Sacrament, places the Host on the corporal; prepares the chalice with wine and water; incenses the oblation and the altar; washes his hands; and says "Pray, brethren, that my sacrifice and yours may be acceptable to God the Father Almighty"—but receives no response. He chants the Lord's Prayer in the ferial tone, elevates the Host with one hand for all to see and adore, fractures It, mixes a particle into the unconsecrated wine, and then receives the Host with the usual prayer, and the wine in the chalice without the usual prayer.

The Good Friday liturgy symbolizes the states of the Passion. As Christ was taken into captivity and then hauled into court, the Host is brought forth from its place of reservation; as Christ was lifted up on Calvary, so the Host is lifted up on high; and as Christ was taken down and placed inside the earth, so the Host is consumed. Abruptly, the liturgy is ended with the priest bowing before the altar and departing in silence. The Real Presence of Christ in the Blessed Sacrament is no more to be found in the church, in the tabernacle, on the altar, even in the congregation: *He is gone.* The desolation of Good Friday reaches its peak; the total surrender of the Son has been enacted, and we await the Resurrection and the renewal of the glorious sacrifice of the Mass.

On this day, the priest alone receives Communion; for everyone else, it is the *Adoration of the Cross* that takes center stage. The acolytes, the deacon and subdeacon, the faithful—all come forward to commune, as it were, with the *Cross.* This is what "replaces" Holy Communion on Good Friday. Of course, we encounter the mystery of the Cross every time we receive the Eucharist, but the veils of bread and wine may, in a sense, distract us from our union with the death of Christ. Once a year, Good Friday makes the Cross stand out visibly; the Cross is the sacred sign we touch and kiss.[19]

Gregory DiPippo: "It is true that Communion was given to the faithful on Good Friday once upon a time, and in this sense *alone,* the 1955 mutilation of Good Friday does indeed turn to an ancient practice. There is a legitimate debate to be held over this particular question. I will simply point out, in that regard, that every *other* historical rite in Christendom ended up at the same conclusion as the one the Roman rite ended up at by the fourteenth century: there is no Communion ritual on Good Friday *at all* in any historical Christian rite. (In point of fact, the *Consilium ad exsequendam,* realizing how far the Roman rite had been divorced in this regard in 1955 both from its own tradition and the broader Christian liturgical tradition, seriously considered just removing the Communion altogether when they created the Novus Ordo.) However, this specific question also fully demonstrates the

In its medieval elaboration as codified in the Tridentine rite, Good Friday is the one day of the year when are made to taste the desolation that the Virgin Mary and the Apostles lived through. The Church could hardly have come up with a better way of doing this than by depriving us of sacramental Communion on this day. The one who has died and been laid in the tomb is away from us. Instead, the liturgy focuses our adoration on the life-giving Cross by which He won our salvation, and bids us pray for the needs of the Church and the entire world.

This pre-55 Good Friday liturgy is far more like a Mass than the Communion service of Pius XII or its subsequent replacement in the Novus Ordo—yet it feels like a tragically incomplete Mass, one could even say a hollow Mass. This uncomfortable strangeness was accentuated by the combination of great solemnity and stark simplicity, made possible by the level of ceremonial detail contained in this pre-1955 rite, much of which was later jettisoned. At the start, the lessons and lengthy tracts are chanted without anything preceding them; at the end, the priest silently receives the Host—and then the liturgy just stops, as if it's been beheaded, or like a play interrupted in mid-act, before the actors are done with their lines, and with the plot at loose ends. Although Christ says, "It is finished" in the Gospel, the liturgy transmits the strong feeling "it is not finished." I see this as a typically marvelous liturgical paradox: on the day that confronts us with the historical event by which our Redemption was objectively accomplished, the liturgy itself, through which we subjectively commune with Christ, is allowed to be the most incomplete in feel. All the changes from the 1950s onward greatly diminished how strikingly different this day was meant to feel, as the living representation (*"vivax repraesentatio"*) of that day when the maximum disorder redounded to the restoration of order.

---

incompetence and duplicity of the creators of the 1955 Holy Week, because literally eve single Ordo of the Roman rite that says anything about how the Good Friday ritual was do says that there was a fraction rite (as Andrieu documented in a series of articles in *Revue* Sciences Religieuses in 1922–24), and yet in 1955 they removed it. This is because it was ne their intention to restore the historical traditions of the Roman rite in their integrity. It always their procedure to decide ahead of time what they were going to change, and th fish around in the older liturgical books of the Roman rite, or of other rites, for a puta justification for the change they had previously decided to make. In short: no different a from the procedure by which the Novus Ordo was created" (comment to me on Faceboo

Pius XII's Holy Week abridges the Passions of Saint Matthew, Saint Mark, and Saint Luke by removing their accounts of the Institution of the Eucharist. As a result, the Synoptic accounts of the Institution do not occur anywhere in the liturgical year in the 1962 missal.[20] Coupled with the radical redesign of the Good Friday ceremony, which deliberately excises or minimizes all that imitates the rite of Mass, how does this *not* communicate a radical divorce between the Institution of the Eucharist and the Sacrifice of the Cross?

Scripture commentors draw attention to how Christ at the Last Supper drank from only three of the four cups of wine—the fourth being the wine He tasted on the Cross just before He said, "It is finished." The Passover from the night before is now brought to completion with the fourth drink of wine, showing forth the unity of the unbloody Sacrifice of Thursday and the bloody Sacrifice of Friday. Under the guidance of the Holy Spirit, the ancient Good Friday ritual has a cup of wine that is drunk, which, combined with the Host consecrated the night before, links the two liturgies in the same way.

Easter Vigil

The pre-55 Easter Vigil is sublime. The '55 and '69 rites come across, in comparison, as arbitrary collections of rituals. In the Tridentine Easter Vigil, these rituals all coalesce in a single act of worship that has the unity of a man's walking, step by step, toward a goal. A mighty recapitulation of *all* the mysteries of Christianity—from God's inner nature to the revelation of the Trinity to the Incarnation of the Word to the bloody Redemption to the glorious Resurrection to our incorporation into the Son of God—the old Vigil has a majesty to it, a mounting series of mingled but unconfused symbols, which the orations and lessons and ceremonies bring forth at a stately, leisurely pace: fire, candle, water, all *directly* addressed in words of power. The Church takes command of the rudiments of creation and liter-ally *orders* them to serve Christ and the salvation of souls.

Implanted in the liturgy are two ceremonies that resemble a "*missa icca*," or dry Mass: first, the Preface, preceded by the usual dialogue, lead-ng up to the consecration of the candle; second, the same structure for the

---

A piece of Luke's (Lk 22:14–20) is in the missal in one Votive Mass, that of Our Lord Jesus hrist, Supreme and Eternal High Priest.

consecration of the water. In both cases, we start with worldly elements and set them apart for God, asking Him to make them in some sense Himself: to make them sacraments or sacred signs of His grace.

The liturgy begins outside the church with the blessing of the fire—not of the candle, but just the fire itself, symbol of the eternal divine nature.[21] From this fire is lit the trikirion, or three-branched candlestick, that carries multiple symbolisms: it represents the Trinity, or the progressive revelation of the Trinity in salvation history, as one by one the candles of the trikirion are lit in procession to the sanctuary; or the three days in the tomb, and the three Marys approaching the tomb on Easter morn. The staff represents the bronze serpent which Moses fashioned on a rod to heal the Israelites in the desert. This procession culminates in the *Exsultet*, the text of which makes sense *only* in the pre-55 context, when the actions described in the *Exsultet* are actually performed on the candle then and there. The deacon places the five incense nails into the candle, symbol of "the Lamb slain before the foundation of the world" (Rev 13:8), and then lights it from one of the three candles of the trikirion: the second Person taking flesh to save us. From this point onward, all flames in the church are taken from the Paschal candle.

The twelve prophecies have a compelling directionality to them. They are preoccupied with water, light, fire, and sacrifice, with an underlying theme of resisting and overcoming the devil, which is made explicit in the prayers surrounding the blessing of the font.[22] The first half or so hinges on major figures: Adam, Noah, Abraham, Moses, with David touched on. The second half shifts to the calling of Israel, old and new. The final reading is the tale from Daniel 3 of Shadrach, Meshach, and Abednego refusing to worship the giant idol and being thrown into the fiery furnace. It may be sung to the prophecy tone or to a special tone that is surprisingly lyrical and joyous.

The antiphon *Sicut cervus* then makes perfect sense as the accompaniment to the procession that moves from the sanctuary to the baptistery or a font at the back of the church: "As the deer panteth for streams of living

---

[21] See my article "God as Fire," *NLM*, March 14, 2016.

[22] In pre-55 missals, one finds a rubric stating that, during the Prophecies, those preparing for baptism should receive their exorcisms and other preparatory ceremonies.

water, so hath my soul longed for Thee, O my God." Having heard all these prophecies, it is time to make their promises really and truly present in the regenerating water, so that new Christians can be buried and raised with Christ. The formal procession to the font with the Paschal candle at its head makes it clear that the candle is the column of fire at the Red Sea, and that Israel is about to be delivered from Egyptian captivity through the death-dealing and life-giving waters. (In Pius XII's ceremony, on the other hand, the water to be blessed is bizarrely placed up front at the sanctuary so that everyone may see what's going on, and afterwards the newly consecrated baptismal water is carried in procession to the font while the *Sicut cervus* is sung. This shreds the ancient symbolism of the procession to the baptistery described above.)

The liturgy as a whole is set off by many delightful "irregularities," such as the triple Alleluia chant followed by a verse and a Tract,[23] no Offertory antiphon, no Agnus Dei, and, instead of a Communion antiphon, a truncated Vespers with Magnificat. Just as with Good Friday's irregularities, such features drive home the truth that this liturgy is *different* from all others. The strangeness of it is an incentive to a deeper interior participation. Might it be confusing to the faithful? Yes, for sure—and that is all to the good. The mortal conflict of Life and Death is not a tea party.

The old Easter Vigil is one vast hymn of praise to the might of God revealed in the creation of the world, the creation of the old Israel, and the creation of the new Israel, possessing a cosmic sweep, historical narrative, and immersion into mystery that are found nowhere else in the liturgical year. All of its parts are seamlessly interconnected, without those awkward modular joints or ceremonial disconnects typical of the work of Vatican committees after 1948.

The pre-55 Easter Vigil may, indeed, be called the crown jewel of the Tridentine rite. As with Palm Sunday and Good Friday, I am astonished that any reformers would have dared to lay hands on such perfect marriages of art and theology. Nearly everything that I have just described—nearly everything!—was reduced to rubble or reconfigured in a new way in Pius

___

The Tract is a penitential chant, so it is most unusual to have it following an Alleluia: more the chiaroscuro of the Easter Vigil, in which we are no longer confined in the darkness of th but not yet emerged into the full light of day.

XII's "restoration." A priest friend of mine who has celebrated both forms of the preconciliar Holy Week (the pre-55 and the 55/62) told me: "The old liturgies are coherent in what they contain and when they present it; the new versions are piecemeal and chaotic."[24] Within the movement to restore tradition in the Catholic Church, recovering the old Holy Week and giving it once again its due prominence is an urgent task.

The Vigil of Pentecost

Another casualty of the 1950s was the Vigil of Pentecost. As early as the days of Tertullian, who died in the middle of the third century, the Vigil of Pentecost was the second most common day for initiating the faithful, if for some reason they could not be initiated at Easter (e.g., they had fallen sick), or if there were more converts wishing to enter the Church.

The holding of a liturgy the day before Pentecost that heavily reflects, almost parallels, that of the Easter Vigil was well-established by the fifth century. By serving as a kind of "last echo" of the great Easter Vigil, this Pentecost Vigil served as an admirable "hinge" for swinging to the great feast of the Holy Spirit and the long green season afterwards. It was also, as typical for all vigils, a day of fasting and abstinence to prepare well for the solemnity to follow. The orations after the six (instead of twelve) prophecies—very rich in doctrine and sweet in savor—"focus, each in its own manner, on the continuity between the two Testaments."[25] To take two examples, the prayers after the second and fourth prophecies read as follows:

> O God, who by the light of the New Testament hast expounded
> the miracles wrought in the first ages of the world, so that the
> Red Sea was a figure of the sacred font, and the deliverance of

---

[24] He continued: "The old liturgical rites drive home the integral and essential connecti between the sacrifice of the Cross and the Eucharistic sacrifice. The new [Pacellian] versic systematically downplay this. . . . In fact, some of the same people who worked on the ' newed' Holy Week later worked on the Novus Ordo, and when they got around to fix some of the problems they themselves had introduced, they blamed the problems not their own bungling of the work, but on the 'old liturgy'! How's that for mendacious?"

[25] Gregory DiPippo, "The Suppression of the Ancient Baptismal Vigil of Pentecost," N May 18, 2018.

the people out of the bondage of Egypt did represent the Christian sacraments: grant that all nations who have now obtained the birthright of Israel by the merit of faith may be born again by the participation of Thy Spirit.

O almighty and eternal God, who by Thy only Son hast shown Thyself the husbandman of Thy Church, mercifully cultivating every branch which bringeth forth fruit in that same Christ, who is the true vine, that it may be more fruitful; let not the thorns of sin prevail against Thy faithful, whom Thou hast transplanted like a vineyard out of Egypt by the baptismal font; but protect them by Thy Holy Spirit, that they may be enriched by everlasting fruits. Through the same Lord . . . in the unity of the same Holy Ghost . . .

We see in these beautiful orations the tight link between being baptized into Christ and being born again by receiving the Holy Spirit, and the no less tight link between incorporation into Christ, the true vine, and the spiritual fruitfulness of the branch. The loss of such prayers in Pius XII's severe abridgement of the Vigil (they are thereby lost to the missal as a whole) is nothing short of tragic.

Pius XII's slimmed-down 1955 version of the Vigil lops off all the Prophecies, Tracts, Orations, Blessing of the Font, and Litany of the Saints, and turns the day into a regular Mass like any other (with minor variations), casting into the shade the strong connection the old liturgy made between baptism and confirmation. The Pacellian version has an abrupt, pinched, "low-fat" feel to it—not the weight, the density, one would expect of the ceremonies that bring Easter to an end and inaugurate the feast, octave, and season of Pentecost. Think about it: Easter Sunday receives its due preparation by means of the Easter Vigil, the Triduum, and Holy Week as a whole; Christmas too receives its due preparation by means of a Vigil opening on to three distinct Masses, like a bud opening into full flower (Midnight, Dawn, and Day). Pentecost deserves no less amplitude and magnificence. If Paschaltide is supposed to be like one great feast (as the liturgical reformers parroted, without showing much understanding of what they were saying), then it makes even more sense to close off the period of rejoicing in the resurrection of Christ by an echo of the great Easter Vigil, like the opening and closing of great doors, before the next "chapter" of salvation history opens upon us in the solemn feast of Pentecost with its octave and the long line of green Sundays numbered according to it. Just as the pre-55 Easter Vigil joins the darkness of Holy Saturday to the full light of Easter Sunday, so the pre-55 Pentecost Vigil profoundly unites the Easter mystery to the outpouring of the Holy Ghost.

The pre-55 Pentecost Vigil is the form of the rite that was celebrated over the course of at least a millennium, from well before the time of the Council of Trent until the proto-revolutionary pontificate of Pius XII. Pacelli's version, in contrast, had the inglorious lifespan of about fourteen years before it was bulldozed by Bugnini & Co. in the 1969 missal. The Vigil from 1955 to 1969 is a blip, a speck of dust, in the timespan of Roman Catholic worship (as is the Novus Ordo, which is a slightly larger and more irritating speck of dust). Like the Tridentine inheritance of which it is a part, the traditional Vigil boasts an ancient lineage; it has all the force of immemorial tradition on its side. This glorious liturgy just *is* the Roman rite's Pentecost Vigil, and it is time to claim it back. We have the books; we have the know-how; we have the clergy and laity. *Tolle, et lege; lege, et ora; ora, et laetare.* Take, and read; read, and pray; pray, and rejoice.

Two further examples from the calendar

In response to Our Lord's request to Saint Juliana of Liège early in the thirteenth century, the feast of Corpus Christi was instituted in 1264 by Pope Urban IV, who established it with an octave. The point of an octave is to bask in the light of a great mystery for eight days, a symbol of eternal life; the octave allows due honor to be paid to the Lord or His Mother or an especially important saint. It was inconceivable that a feast to thank Our Lord for the gift of Himself in the Holy Eucharist and to offer Him a special annual homage would be celebrated for one day only. About 500 years later, on June 16, 1675, Our Lord appeared to Saint Margaret Mar Alacoque and said: "I ask of you that the Friday after the Octave of Corpu Christi be set apart for a special Feast to honor My Heart, by communica ing on that day, and making reparation to It by a solemn act, in order make amends for the indignities which It has received during the time It has been exposed on the altars. I promise you that My Heart shall expand Itself to shed in abundance the influence of Its divine love upon those who shall thus honor It, and cause It to be honored." Thus was born the feast of the Most Sacred Heart. I would draw attention to the fact that Jesus specifically asked for it to be on "the Friday after the Octave of Corpus Christi." How absurd, then, that Pius XII in 1955 suppressed *all* octaves—all of them, except for Christmas, Easter, and Pentecost![26]

Prior to 1956, there were a minimum of twenty-three octaves observed in any diocese. These octaves came in three basic forms: privileged, common, and simple, which affected whether other feasts could take precedence and which Office was said for the day. At their highest level, every day in the octave was treated as the feast day. At the lowest level, only the eighth day (or octave day) would be observed with a proper Mass. All this made the calendar considerably richer, more interwoven with the mysteries of Christ and the memory of His saints. The loss of the octaves is connected with a larger problem: the loss or thinning-out of the notion of *sacred time*, which increasingly gave way to a secular, linear, work-oriented approach to time. The continual pressure to "shorten the liturgy," eliminate holy days, and transfer feasts to Sundays has to be understood from this vantage. Modern people think they have so many more important things to do than worship God. The inability to see and to feel that worship is our highest, best, most human, and most divinizing activity is arguably our gravest spiritual sickness.

My last example from the liturgical calendar is the feast of the Holy Innocents. Prior to 1956, there was a most beautiful custom whereby this feast on December 28, in recognition of the mournful character of the slaughter of infants, was celebrated in violet vestments, without a Gloria, with a Tract instead of an Alleluia, and with a Benedicamus Domino, whereas on their octave day (which, remember, signifies eternal life) the same Mass was celebrated in red vestments, with a Gloria, an Alleluia, and

The feast of the Sacred Heart remains on the Friday of the week after Corpus Christi, but the absence of the octave that gave it its place, it seems like an isolated devotional moment rather than the completion of an arc.

an *Ite missa est*, announcing their heavenly triumph as martyrs.[27] This, to my mind, is a perfect example of the theological and psychological subtlety of the old liturgy. Again, this was dropped in 1955.

General features of Mass

It was not only the temporal and sanctoral cycles that suffered tinkeritis, but also general features of the Mass. I will describe five of these features that were changed or discarded in the period prior to 1962, all of which deserve to be recovered: folded chasubles and broad stoles; multiple orations; repetition of the readings by the priest; more frequent recitation of the Credo; and the use of "Benedicamus Domino" in place of "Ite, missa est" on days without the Gloria.

Folded chasubles and broad stoles

Among the unusual things Catholics will see in celebrations of the pre-55 Holy Week and on other penitential days are the so-called "folded chasuble" and "broad stole."[28] It's worth understanding how these vestments originated.

The early Christians in the Roman Empire did not have distinctive liturgical vestments, but simply wore what they were accustomed to wear at the time—their "Sunday best," you might say. The full outer garment was called the chasuble. The deacon and subdeacon who sang the lessons would either take off their chasubles or fold them up and wrap them over one shoulder for convenience so that they could move about more freely and hold the lectionaries (and let's not forget how hot vestments can become especially in a crowded Mediterranean church, lit by many candles!). A

---

[27] If the twenty-eighth fell on a Sunday, however, the vestments for the feast would be re the Alleluia would be sung, etc.

[28] "In modern usage, the basic rubric is that folded chasubles are worn in place of dalma and tunicle on days of fasting and penance when violet is worn. This includes the Sund: and weekdays of Advent and Lent—with the obvious exception of the 'rose' Sundays—as w as Ember days (except those in Whitsun) and during the Candlemas blessing of candles a procession. Folded chasubles in the liturgical color black were also used on Good Friday. course, whatever is said of the folded chasuble also applies to the broad stole, which is re just another form of the folded chasuble." Shawn Tribe, "History and Designs of the Fol Chasuble," *Liturgical Arts Journal*, December 4, 2017.

secular fashions changed, the Church, ever conservative in her mentality, preserved the original Roman garments, which in time came to be seen as clerical garments for liturgical services. Later, in the fifth century, the more convenient as well as more sumptuous dalmatic for the deacon and tunicle for the subdeacon were introduced. Initially they were white and adorned with the purple vertical bands of senatorial garb; they were viewed as "vestments of joy and innocence, which made them entirely inappropriate for penitential seasons."[29] This is conveyed also by the prayer the deacon says when putting on the dalmatic ("Clothe me, O Lord, with the garment of salvation and the vestment of joy, and ever encompass me with the dalmatic of justice") and the subdeacon when putting on the tunicle ("May the Lord clothe me in the tunicle of delight and the garment of rejoicing").

Consequently, in the penitential seasons—which in Rome have always been characterized by the persistence of older customs—the folded chasuble continued to be used, all the way through the Middle Ages and the Baroque right up to the time of Pius XII. In the pre-55 customs, both the deacon and the subdeacon wear a chasuble folded in front rather than wearing the dalmatic and tunicle. The subdeacon removes this chasuble for the Epistle and resumes it once he finishes. The deacon takes off the folded chasuble and replaces it with the broad stole before the singing of the Gospel; after the ablutions he removes it, resuming the folded chasuble. (In some cases, the folded chasuble itself may be wrapped around to make a broad stole, which is the historical origin of the latter.) In 1955, Pius XII legislated that the deacon and subdeacon would henceforth incongruously wear their vestments of joy and innocence during Holy Week. Four years later, in 1960, John XXIII's code of rubrics abolished the folded chasuble and broad stole altogether. In this way, one of the most striking signs of fasting days or seasons—Advent, Lent, and Ember Days—was put down the memory hole, and popes once again demonstrated that their pens could do more damage to liturgical custom than any number of barbarian invasions, wars, plagues, famines, or political revolutions.

See Henri de Villiers, "The History of the Folded Chasuble, Part 1," *Canticum Salomonis*, March 23, 2018. This is why the deacon wears a white dalmatic for the *Praeconium Paschale* or *Exsultet*. Cf. Shawn Tribe, "Use, History and Development of the 'Planeta Plicata' or Folded Chasuble," *NLM*, March 8, 2009.

Multiple orations

In each Mass, there are three very important prayers called "orations": the Collect, which comes near the beginning; the Secret, said silently at the end of the Offertory; and the Postcommunion, said after the ablutions. For centuries, it was the custom for priests to say or to sing more than one set of orations at Mass.[30] The rubrics told the priest which additional prayers to use. For example, in Advent, from the first Sunday, the Missal prescribed the addition of a second Collect of the Blessed Virgin Mary and a third Collect either for the Church or for the pope, although if there were saints to be commemorated, *their* prayers would be used instead. To give you a sense of the power of these prayers, here is the Collect for the Living and the Dead, which would be said daily from Ash Wednesday to Passion Sunday:

> O almighty and eternal God, who hast dominion over both the living and the dead, and hast mercy on all whom Thou foreknowest shall be Thine by faith and good works: we humbly beseech Thee that all for whom we have resolved to make supplication, whether the present world still holds them in the flesh or the world to come has already received them out of the body, may, through the intercession of all Thy saints, obtain of Thy goodness and clemency pardon for all their sins.

This was being prayed daily for a month each year. All of the recurring prayers are comparably potent.

On Sundays, too, saints would be commemorated instead of simply ignored. Just to give you a sense of how this would work in practice, let's take Sunday, June 30, 2019. I choose this day because it was a typical "constellation" of Roman feast days: the Third Sunday after Pentecost, in the Octave of the Sacred Heart and of the birth of Saint John the Baptist, but also the commemoration of Saint Paul, who is always accompanied by his fellow Apostle Saint Peter. So the priest at Mass would say or sing five Collects: Sunday's, followed by Saint Paul, Saint Peter, the Sacred Heart

---

[30] This carried over into Lauds and Vespers as well. See, for more detail, my article "In Defense of Multiple Orations," *NLM*, February 8, 2021.

and Saint John the Baptist. Such a confluence was rather rare; most of the time there would be three orations.

On other days, it was possible for the priest, especially at private Masses, to add votive orations or orations for community needs, drawing from the magnificent Roman treasury of prayers, such as:

- To implore the intercession of the saints
- For people in authority and those under their charge
- Against persecutors and evildoers
- In time of earthquake
- For rain
- For fine weather
- To avert storms
- For the gift of tears
- For those in temptation and in tribulation
- Against evil thoughts

I imagine some readers are thinking: Wait a minute, this almost sounds like the General Intercessions or Prayer of the Faithful! In a way, that's correct. The Roman rite *already had within itself* a way of praying for the celebrant's own needs, and for those of the local community, the larger world, or certain categories of people. It was already all there.

Prior to 1955, the maximum number of Orations at a low Mass on simple days was five or seven (depending on circumstances). In 1955, this number was reduced to three, and mandatory prayers of the season were abolished. In 1960, the possibility of additional orations was reduced still further, and, for most Sundays of the year, done away with altogether. All this was done in pursuit of streamlined rational simplicity, seemingly on the assumption that we can or should never have more than one "theme" for a given "service," which insults our intelligence and stifles our devotion. The end game was the Novus Ordo, which never has more than one set of orations per Mass.

Repetition of the readings by the priest

Prior to 1956, the priest at the altar in a Solemn Mass would read quietly to himself all of the antiphons, prayers, and readings of the Mass, even while other ministers were singing them according to their roles in the liturgy. This custom developed out of the Low Mass, where the priest had become accustomed to saying everything. In 1955, the priest was instructed no longer to do the readings during Holy Week; and in 1960, he was instructed never to do the readings if someone else was doing them. In 1969, with the Novus Ordo, he was told not to say the Kyrie, Gloria, Creed, Sanctus, or Agnus Dei if a choir or the people were also singing it; but instead, to sing it with them, or to listen.

This trend was a mistake, for two reasons. On the practical side, there is a subjective or personal devotional value in reading, with one's own eyes and lips, the Epistle and the Gospel, and the Ordinary of the Mass. It allows for maximum textual and ceremonial continuity from day to day, regardless of the greater or smaller scope of the liturgy offered. On the theological level, we know that the priest stands at the altar *in persona Christi*. Just as most prayers (and the Prefaces) are said *per Dominum nostrum*, so too do all the actions of worship go from the Church's ministers, through Christ (represented by the priest), to God the Father. This Patricentric orientation includes the readings too, which are not merely didactic but latreutic. Thus the priest is either acting as himself, as a member of the Church (prayers at the foot, prayers before Communion, parts of the Offertory); acting *in persona Christi* at the consecration, and, in a different way, when doubling what others are doing; and acting *in persona Ecclesiae* for everything else. Here the deep theological rationale for the lack of concelebration in the old rite shines through: apart from a quasi-concelebration during the Mass of a priest's ordination, in the old rite there is only ever *one* priest-celebrant through whom the entire liturgy "passes," in an unbroken line of mediation and representation of the one Eternal High Priest.

When the priest recites the Introit, he is standing in the person of Christ the prophet, announcing some mystery to be accomplished. When recites the threefold Kyrie, he is beseeching the mercy of almighty God again acting visibly in the person of the High Priest who offers sacri on behalf of sinners. When he reads the Gospel, it is as the living image of Christ that he reads it. None of this downplays or dilutes the roles that belong to other ministers or to the people; instead, it merely draws into maximal unity the liturgical action by having it flow from and return to the same Alpha and Omega, Christ Himself, whose unity of being and operation is sensibly represented by the celebrant.

The recitation of the Credo

The Niceno-Constantinopolitan Creed was not originally included in the Roman rite of Mass; it was imported from north of the Alps, like many other features. However, once it found its place, the usual process began by which it was assigned for more and more occasions, for reasons of fittingness. In the Tridentine rite, it is said on all Sundays and high-ranking feasts of Our Lady and the Apostles and their octave days, but also on the feasts of the Angels (because their creation is mentioned in the Creed), the Doctors of the Church (because the Creed embodies the Catholic doctrine of which they are the most exalted expounders and defenders), and on the feast of Saint Mary Magdalene, because she was "the Apostle to the Apostles," honored with the first appearance of the resurrected Lord.

All of this seems perfectly reasonable and fitting. No one could complain. An opportunity to sing one of the beautiful Gregorian settings of the Creed is always welcome; and as for reciting it at Low Mass, it takes a little over one minute, and gives us the opportunity to honor the Blessed Trinity with three bows of the head and to honor the Incarnation with a genuflection.[31] In 1956, the restless liturgical reformers abolished the Creed for the Angels, Saint Mary Magdalene, octave days, and a few others; in 1960, it was abolished for Doctors of the Church and solemn Votive Masses.

Benedicamus Domino

In the Tridentine rite, whenever a Mass contains the Gloria (which always occurs when the *Te Deum* is present in the Office), the priest (or deacon)

The head is bowed at the start, for the Father; at the name of Jesus; and at the *simul adoratur et conglorificatur* for the Holy Ghost: a perfect Trinitarian confession with the body. The genuflection, of course, takes place at the *Et incarnatus est.*

concludes with *Ite, missa est*; but if there is no Gloria, the phrase used instead is *Benedicamus Domino*. (The response to either is the same: *Deo gratias*.) This is just one of the many subtle ways in which feast days are distinguished from ferial days and penitential days. According to the 1960 rubrics in the 1962 missal, every Mass is concluded *Ite, Missa est*, with *Benedicamus Domino* to be used only when a procession or other function follows. This is a small detail, to be sure, but a lot of small details add up to general impressions. There was, and is, a certain unity of spirit to the Tridentine rubrics. This unity was increasingly lost in the reforms of the 1950s and early 1960s, before being simply chucked out the window from the mid-sixties forward.

First Vespers

Although this chapter, like the rest of the book, focuses on the Mass, I wish to include one important point concerning the Divine Office. For an authentic *vita liturgica*, the primacy of First Vespers must be reestablished. The earliest extant liturgical records of the Roman rite indicate First Vespers of feasts; the same holds true of all historic liturgies. The Byzantine rite, for instance, has *only* First Vespers. It would be no exaggeration to say that this is part of our inheritance from the synagogue. The abolition of First Vespers for most feasts was carried out in Pius XII's 1955 simplification of the rubrics, *De Rubricis ad Simpliciorem Formam Redigendis*, which was driven by concern for clerics' convenience: "Since in this age of ours priests, and especially those who have the care of souls, are burdened by new and various duties of the apostolate every day, so that they can hardly attend to the recitation of the Divine Office with the necessary tranquility of mind . . ." Yet it is impossible to see how the abrogation of First Vespers was a necessary step or in any way compatible with the genius of the Roman rite.[32]

The normative cancellation of First Vespers (as opposed to its exceptional overriding) was recognized to be a mistake by the time of the revisio-

---

[32] This is why 1955 is the real watershed for liturgical destruction: it was the first time th- texts and ceremonies were changed for the sake of simplifying rubrics rather than rubri- being changed for the sake of governing texts and ceremonies.

of the Ambrosian Office, which retains First Vespers for all feasts and adds Second Vespers for solemnities. There is, accordingly, an urgent need for the reprinting of pre-55 breviaries, both Roman and monastic, to match the recovery of the pre-55 missal; and, eventually, a time will come for intelligently recovering "the Breviary of All Ages," that is, a breviary with the ancient and constant Roman *ordo psallendi* that was shattered in Pius X's radical reordering of the Divine Office in 1911. Many clergy today are taking up some version of the preconciliar Office, and this is all to the good: praying the Office is an *essential* part of assimilating the wisdom and piety of the traditional liturgy, in which the Mass does not stand alone. It is the summit but not the entire mountain. The readings at Matins, for example, and the Martyrology at Prime are vitally important for clergy who wish to come to a full understanding of the sacrificial nature of the priesthood and how it has been lived through the centuries. Moreover, chanting some of the Office—at least Sunday Terce and Vespers—is indispensable for any serious attempt to restore Catholic culture.

Instances of disregard of 1960

Having looked at elements of the classical Roman rite that were lost or maimed from 1951 onwards, I will now address some practical and canonical issues.

It is important to note that certain changes made in the 1960 *Code of Rubrics*, which is included in the 1962 missal, are almost never observed in celebrations of the traditional Mass today.[33] These discrepancies are not only tolerated but practiced by high-ranking prelates, at least some of whom know perfectly well that in so doing they are following older rubrics. The most obvious is the retention of the Confiteor immediately before Communion,[34] which was abolished in 1960, but has survived with tenacity and nowadays far more common than its omission. Another example is the priest bowing toward the crucifix when he says "Oremus," when, according to the 1960 rubrics, he should be bowing toward the book instead.

See "*Summorum Pontificum* & the Rite of Écone" at *The Rad Trad* weblog, July 7, 2014.
See my article "Why the Confiteor Before Communion Should Be Retained (or Reintroduced)," *NLM*, May 27, 2019.

In the rubrics that govern the 1962 missal, the Mass can in fact be truncated, very much as it is in the Novus Ordo. When a ceremony is held before Mass, like a Candlemas or Rogation procession, the prayers at the foot of the altar are supposed to be cut—which means it is possible to have an "EF Mass" with no Confiteor whatsoever;[35] and when a ceremony follows Mass, such as Absolution of the Dead or a Corpus Christi procession, the Last Gospel is supposed to be cut. Many traditional priests don't follow these foolish and arbitrary rules that mutilate the Mass, but that is nonetheless what the 1962 missal's rubrics require.

Moreover, the Pontifical Council Ecclesia Dei, before it was folded into the Congregation for the Doctrine of the Faith and then abolished in the *Traditionis Custodes* purge, had been giving indications that approaches to the rubrics could be a little more, shall we say, flexible. In typically Roman fashion, instead of issuing an instruction, they simply issued a liturgical Ordo that had two noteworthy features. First, it said, for the Masses *de tempore* of Advent, Septuagesima, and Lent (i.e., without Gloria), *Benedicamus Domino* may be used instead of *Ite missa est*. Second, it made a reference *en passant* to the "octave of Corpus Christi," as if hinting that indeed an octave of this feast can be observed. I am aware of several Benedictine monasteries that celebrate full Corpus Christi octaves, with the festal Mass and Office every day, together with processions, adoration, and Benediction.

More importantly, while it still existed, the Ecclesia Dei Commission granted permission to the Institute of Christ the King and the Fraternity of St. Peter to utilize the authentic Tridentine Holy Week for three year (2018, 2019, and 2020), with a decision to be made thereafter about making the permission permanent. Official permission had also been granted for the old Pentecost Vigil. Instead of the anticipated permission being given, however, the entire Vatican old rite apparatus was shut down and a terrifying campaign to annihilate the Roman liturgical tradition from the face of the earth was announced in 2021.[36] We can therefore say wi

---

[35] That is, if the prayers at the foot are cut and the Confiteor at communion is omitted (a is "supposed" to be).

[36] See Peter Kwasniewski, ed., *From Benedict's Peace to Francis's War: Catholics Respon the Motu Proprio* Traditionis Custodes *on the Latin Mass* (Brooklyn, NY: Angelico Pr 2021) for a full analysis.

certainty that the question has been fundamentally altered. It is no longer about fine points like "do we get to use folded chasubles and broad stoles?" It is about life or death, survival or extinction. Since the hatred of the modernists currently in power is directed against any and all Catholic tradition, whatever it may look like (consider the wild thrashing against *ad orientem* in the Novus Ordo, in spite of liturgical law standing in its favor!), the question of what may or may not be done in the realm of tradition has been both simplified and blown wide open, with legal niceties thrown to the winds of war. We may and we *must* do all that is required to save the Roman tradition, in its entirety and purity, as one of the greatest treasures of the Catholic Church, and eminently pertinent to her common good.[37]

The inherent permissibility of the pre-55 liturgy

The fundamental principle is this: a liturgical rite possesses authority *from itself*, from its long use and reception by the Church, and not primarily from the decree of any authority. The inherent weight of immemorial tradition is such that no pope can abolish or abrogate it. We could call it the "sacred and great" principle, as expressed in Benedict XVI's *Letter to Bishops* of July 7, 2007: "What earlier generations held as sacred, remains sacred and great for us too, and it cannot be all of a sudden entirely forbidden or even considered harmful. It behooves all of us to preserve the riches which have developed in the Church's faith and prayer, and to give them their proper place."

Benedict XVI consistently testified that he considered *Summorum Pontificum* to be the expression of a properly theological and ecclesiological stance—that is, not merely a disciplinary one. For example, in response to the claim that his purpose in issuing it was primarily the reconciliation of the SSPX, he replied: "That is just absolutely false! It was important for me that the Church is one with herself inwardly, with her own past; that what was previously holy to her is not somehow wrong now. . . . But as I said, my intentions were not of a tactical nature, they were about the substance of the matter itself."[38]

My tract *True Obedience in the Church* makes the case for radical decisions and actions.
Benedict XVI, *Last Testament: In His Own Words*, trans. Jacob Phillips (New York: oomsbury, 2016), 202.

The argument by which *Summorum Pontificum* bears witness to the continuing licitness of the 1962 missal and other rites establishes exactly the same for the Tridentine inheritance in general—including the old Holy Week, the Vigil of Pentecost, the Corpus Christi octave, the differentiation between the feast of the Holy Innocents and its octave, folded chasubles and broad stoles, multiple orations, doubling of readings, the recitation of the Creed, and the use of *Benedicamus Domino*. The traditional liturgy has more inherent ecclesiastical authority than any decision of a pope or curial office. In the words of Martin Mosebach: "The liturgy IS the Church—every Mass celebrated in the traditional spirit is immeasurably more important than every word of every pope. It is the red thread that must be drawn through the glory and misery of Church history; where it continues, phases of arbitrary papal rule will become footnotes of history."[39] Fr. John Hunwicke gives expression to the same Catholic sensibility: "The great Apostolic liturgical traditions are part of the Apostolic *datum*; the *Depositum fidei*; the *Tradition which comes through the Apostles*; they sit beside the Canon of Scripture, the Creeds, and the Ministry. The *Lex orandi* which takes pride of place over the *Lex credendi* ranks beside—perhaps even above—the doctrinal Decrees of the great, dogmatic, Ecumenical Councils. It lies far beyond the whimsies, prejudices, and personal antipathies of each pope."[40]

Once upon a time, official permission from Ecclesia Dei or the fourth Section of the CDF was helpful for reassuring delicate consciences and avoiding arbitrariness (especially when crafting policy for institutes with priests who are spread across the world, for whom a serene unanimity of approach would be desirable), but seeking and obtaining explicit permission is by no means necessary. During the years of *Summorum Pontificum*, more and more diocesan churches were doing the old Holy Week; the authorities knew about it and took no steps to block it. This is a very Italian way of signifying "go ahead, just don't make fools of yourselves." Tacit, non-verbal approval is an approach that the Anglo-Saxon mentality does not always understand; we would rather have it in writing on

[39] Martin Mosebach, *The Heresy of Formlessness: The Roman Liturgy and Its Enemy*, rev. ed. (Brooklyn, NY: Angelico Press, 2018), 188.
[40] "Popes, Liturgy, and Authority (2): A Single (*unicus*) Form of the Roman Rite?" *Fr Hunwicke's Mutual Enrichment*, March 28, 2022.

piece of paper, in legal language. But we have to remember that, given the atmosphere at the Vatican, it is much more difficult and dangerous for officials to put something into writing than merely to let it be understood or inferred. My earlier example of the Vatican Ordo for the *usus antiquior* illustrates the Italian method: there is no document that says "You may use *Benedicamus Domino* or observe a Corpus Christi octave"; the Ordo simply mentions them in Latin (the ultimate code language!), without comment, so that only the *cognoscenti* will notice.

It is true that, over the centuries, certain rites or rubrics are promulgated by the hierarchy, but that is not what bestows legitimacy on the rites and rubrics; it merely identifies a certain book as the correct printing or standard of its kind. The fact of promulgation is a *necessary* but not a *sufficient* condition for the book's reception by the Church. Prior to the invention of printing and the centralization of the Roman Missal, the equivalent to promulgation would be simply tacit approval; that is, any Catholic liturgy that had long been celebrated without demur from ecclesiastical authority could be considered to stand "approved" precisely by not standing condemned. This is the attitude we need to recover today. It was not Saint Pius V who fashioned the Tridentine rite and bestowed authenticity upon it; this it already had *of itself,* before he even existed. The missal of 1570 is, in all important respects, the same as the Roman Curia's missal of 1474, which in turn transmits the rite as it was found in earlier centuries, in a continuous organic sequence. At most, Pius V was responsible for specifying that a certain *edition* of a book—a book containing the texts and rubrics of a rite that was valid, legitimate, and fitting *in itself*—is to be used at the altar, for prudential reasons. In this prudential arena, moreover, mistakes are possible.[41]

For example, Pius V, over-compensating perhaps in an era of Protestant emphasis on biblical foundations, suppressed the feasts of Saint Joachim, Saint Anne, and the Presentation of the Blessed Virgin Mary because they were derived from an apocryphal source. All three feasts were swiftly restored by Pius V's successors: Saint Anne by Gregory XIII in 1584, the Presentation by Sixtus V in 1585, and Saint Joachim by Gregory XV in 1622. Can we truly believe that if a priest had continued to celebrate those feasts between 1570 and 1584, 1585, 1622, he would have been guilty of wrongdoing? See Gregory DiPippo, "Liturgical Notes the Presentation of the Virgin Mary," *NLM,* November 21, 2021.

It does no harm for a pope to issue an indult—that is, an act of positive law directed to individuals or groups—such as John Paul II's indults in 1984 and 1988 for the use of the 1962 liturgical books, if that pope is under the impression that he needs to do so, or that it will assist the beneficiaries. But if Benedict XVI is correct to state that no permission is needed for the old rite because it was never abrogated and could not be abrogated, then logically the indults of 1984 and 1988 were never necessary. Moreover, the rite that was never abrogated would have to be *either* the last iteration of the Roman rite before its replacement by the Novus Ordo—which would mean the semi-solidified lava of 1967—*or*, in view of the instability of the Roman rite from the latter part of Pacelli's pontificate onward, the *status quo ante* prior to 1951/55. Permission to celebrate the Roman rite as of 1948 would thus be universal *not* by virtue of positive law but by virtue of custom and tradition—in other words, the very basis of *Summorum Pontificum*'s argument that the *usus antiquior* was never abrogated. This, it seems to me, is the rock-solid basis for the gradual restoration of the Tridentine Roman rite, even in situations where no explicit permission has been requested or obtained. Can anyone take seriously the idea that a remodeled Holy Week that officially lasted for only about fourteen years (1955–1969) could have a greater right to exist or to be used, could enjoy more binding force or canonical authority, than ceremonies that endured continuously for five hundred or a thousand years or more?

Priests and faithful all over the world have gloried in the richness and splendor of the pre-55 Holy Week ceremonies in larger numbers than ever and we can certainly expect that those who have experienced it will never wish to turn back. Those who are hesitating because of scruples about "permission" should reflect on the sad fortunes of the liturgy for the past several decades. One bad decision after another has been handed down, to the great detriment of the faithful, and often in the teeth of unbroken tradition (e.g., Paul VI's subversion of minor orders and the subdiaconate, or John Paul II's caving-in on altar girls, or the easy granting of rescripts for Communion in the hand, which was extorted by disobedience and tolerated by cowardice and lukewarm faith). One could give too many examples where permission for abuse has been granted, while that which is "sacred a great" has been forbidden.[42] The admission of Benedict XVI that the *usus antiquior* had never been abrogated, contrary to the *modus operandi* of all of its opponents for decades, should be enough to make us genial skeptics about the "official" line.

No Catholic may rightly believe that immemorial and venerable tradition has to "justify itself" in a court of law. It bears within itself its own justification for existing because it is given to us by the generosity of Divine Providence, through the outpouring of the Holy Ghost, and has been received and celebrated by countless Catholics for centuries, even millennia. Yes, the hierarchy of the Church has a certain responsibility for regulating these things, but the whole point of regulating the liturgy is to ensure that it reaches us intact in its splendor, not to strangle it or butcher it. Authority is given for the common good, not for the private good of its wielders, or for the promotion of strange philosophies. In short: one who thinks explicit permission is required for the pre-55 Holy Week has not yet grasped the inherent rights of immemorial tradition or the limits of papal and curial authority.

The principal argument used to defend adherence to 1962 is that "we should do what the Church asks us to do." But who, or what, is "the Church" here? In this period of chaos, it is no longer self-evident that "the Church" refers to an authority that is handing down laws for the common good of the people of God. From at least 1948 on, "the Church" in the liturgical sphere has meant radicals struggling to loosen the bonds of tradition, pushing their own agenda of simplification, abbreviation, Protestantization, modernization, and pastoral utilitarianism on the Church, and sealing it with papal approval—that is, by the abuse of papal power. These things are not rightful commands to be obeyed but aberrations to be resisted. Of course, they should be resisted patiently, intelligently, and in a principled manner, but nevertheless with a firm intention to restore over time the integrity and fullness of the Roman rite.

It is, moreover, simply illogical to hold on to the 1962 missal when it is just a random "freeze-frame" in the middle of a roughly twenty-five-year

---

See Peter M. J. Stravinskas, "Disobey and You'll Get Your Way," *Catholic World Report*, January 26, 2022. Naturally I do not think that either permission for abuse or forbiddance of tradition carries any legal weight whatsoever, much less morally binding force.

process of liturgical reform stretching from 1948 to 1975. The 1962 rite, although not theologically problematic in the way the Novus Ordo is, is nevertheless deficient *as liturgy*. It is much "flatter" than the real, full Roman rite—especially in the calendar and the Divine Office: suffrages, preces, non-doubling of antiphons, octaves, commemorations, etc. Most lay people take note only of the *Ordo Missae*, but clergy and religious, and those laymen who dive deeper, know how much the calendar affects one's daily experience of the liturgy. For example, are the four days after January 1 the octaves of the *Comites Christi* and then the Vigil of Epiphany, or are they a made-up "Time of the Nativity"? Was September 19, 2020 the feast of Saint Januarius (*basta!*), or was it the Ember Saturday of autumn, the feast of Saint Januarius *and* the (anticipated) Vigil of Saint Matthew (with proper Last Gospel)?, etc. In short, the 1962 missal is a hack job, as is the breviary that accompanies it; and while both are a far sight better than what came later, they fall short of our inheritance.

Traddy antiquarianism?

"Now wait a minute," an interlocutor might say. "Aren't you guilty of doing the same thing you blame your opponents for doing—namely, reaching back to earlier forms while holding later developments in contempt?" No, none of what we are proposing amounts to "traddy antiquarianism." What is clear is that the Liturgical Movement after World War II went off the rails. Changes to the liturgical books from that point on were motivated by global theories about "what is best for the modern Church," which led to the abundant contradictions and ambiguities of *Sacrosanctum Concilium*, the Montini-Bugnini reign of terror, and the crowning disgrace of the 1969 *Ordo Missae* and other rites of that period.

The point is not to go back indefinitely but to take up a missal that i essentially the one codified by Trent and Pius V, with the kind of smal additions or emendations that characterize the slow progress of liturg through the ages. Since 1570, it has been possible for many centuries no to take up an old missal, put it on the altar, and offer Mass. The change are so minor that the missal is virtually the same from *Quo Primum* to tl twentieth century.[43] Saints go on and saints come off, but even the calendar is remarkably stable. After Pius XII's reign, however, it is much harder for an "old" missal and a "new" (i.e., 1955 Pacellian, 1962 Roncallian, 1965/67 Montinian) missal to share the same ecclesial space; they cannot be swapped one for the other, including at some very important moments in the Church year. This already shows, in a rough and ready way, that a rupture has occurred; and all this, *prior* to the Novus Ordo of 1969.

Pius V's condition that only rites older than two hundred years could continue to be used after his promulgation of the Tridentine Missal is another way to see that our argument is backed by common sense. A rite younger than two hundred years old could seem like a recent invention, but a rite that's existed for two centuries or more has acquired a hefty weight of custom—something not to be disturbed or replaced. This, indeed, is the crux of the problem with the Mass of Paul VI: that which it was made to replace was not something older than a mere two hundred years, but something with a two-thousand-year history of continual unfolding that shows no momentous ruptures prior to the deformations of the Liturgical Movement, but only assimilation, expansion, and consolidation. The rule of Pius V also suggests that something *less* than two hundred years old would hardly count as antique. For example, if certain octaves and vigils were abolished only a few decades ago, and if the rationale for this change deserves to be rejected, their recovery could not be considered, by any stretch of the imagination, an example of antiquarianism. It would imply be either an intelligent recovery of something that had been lost by mischance, error in transmission, or bad policy, or the appropriate rejection of an innovation. After all, as Joseph Shaw points out, the Old Testament gives us examples of liturgical restoration far more dramatic than the recovery of pre-Pacellian rites would be for us.[44]

One does see more dramatic change in the explicitation of rubrics. Pope Clement VIII did major "reboot" of the Missal of Pius V aimed at clarifying the rubrics. Any edition of the sal from Pius X onwards includes an enormous bloc of rubrics added at the front, which isn't there before. Nevertheless, the broad point that one could use any edition of the missal disputable; it would apply to the majority of feasts and the temporal cycle.

oseph Shaw, ed., *The Case for Liturgical Restoration: Una Voce Studies on the Traditional n Mass* (Brooklyn, NY: Angelico Press, 2019), 11–17.

Antiquarianism or archaeologism—often qualified with the adjective "false"—is the attempt to leap over medieval and Counter-Reformation developments to reach a putatively "original, authentic" early Christian liturgy. The term does not correctly apply to setting aside modernist, progressive, or utilitarian deformations. How ironic if a move *against* false antiquarianism were now to be targeted as being itself an example of the same! Let us put it this way: Catholics have always been intelligently antiquarian in that they care greatly for and wish to preserve their past heritage and seek to restore it when it has been plundered or damaged. The Liturgical Movement, on the other hand, presented us with the spectacle of an arbitrary, violent, and agenda-driven antiquarianism. The two phenomena are as different as patriotism and nationalism. It is supremely ironic that the Tridentine rite contains vastly more unadulterated first-millennium content than does the modern rite of Paul VI.

Our situation in the Latin Church has achieved the clarity of a silver-point drawing: (1) the modern rite of Paul VI, risibly declared by Pope Francis and Arthur Roche to be "the sole expression of the *lex orandi* of the Roman rite," has established itself as a pseudo-tradition of vernacularity, versus-populism, informality, banality, and horizontality, as William Riccio described with gut-wrenching accuracy;[45] (2) the "Reform of the Reform," on which hopeful conservatives during the reign of Benedict XVI had gambled away their last pennies, is not only dead but six feet under; (3) the traditional Latin liturgy, though by no means readily available to all who desire it, is firmly rooted in the younger generations on all continents and in nearly every country, and shows no sign of budging. Many traditionalist clergy already prefer to use a missal from the first half of the twentieth century, and of those who remain, there are plenty who, at least in the company of trustworthy friends, will admit they find the ersatz Holy Week and the John XXIII missal irksome. As C. S. Lewis says: "If you have taken a wrong turning, then to go forward does not get you any nearer. If you are on the wrong road, progress means doing an about-turn and walking back to the right road. . . . Going back is the quickest way on."[46]

---

[45] See "An Experience of Horror: 'My car broke down, and I went to the nearest Novus Ordo . . .'," *Rorate Caeli*, August 5, 2019.

[46] C. S. Lewis, *Mere Christianity* (New York: HarperCollins, 2001), 28–29.

Returning from exile

Sometimes one will hear people complain that the old rite is "frozen in time." That is not my impression. In the "wild West," organic development *is* happening—only it is not moving toward the unreachable utopia of modernization dreamt of by Paul VI, but rather, toward recovering, piece by piece, noble, idiomatic, and highly expressive elements of the Roman liturgy that were pared away or transmogrified during the twentieth century. While the greatest example is, of course, the return of the pre-55 Holy Week, one sees here and there the recovery of vigils, octaves, multiple Collects, doubled readings, and many features that were suppressed by positive law. When old customs are tried anew, clergy and faithful find that they *make sense*: they work beautifully. It was a strange bout of madness that led to their suppression in the first place.

Perhaps for the first time since Vatican I's *Pastor Aeternus*, and certainly for the first time since Vatican II's *Sacrosanctum Concilium*, we are privileged to be living at a moment when it is possible for the laity and lower clergy to be taking the steps needed to recover our glorious inheritance. We are the ones who must do it, or it will not happen. The febrile atmosphere of the pontificate of Francis has greatly facilitated the reexamination of liturgical questions. The Lord wants us to see, very clearly, that we must find sounder principles than the autocratic will of whoever happens to be seated on the papal throne or the parsimonious permissions of his curial mandarins. If the pope will not honor tradition and pass it down without meddling and messing with it, we, for our part—compelled by love of our predecessors in the Faith and of the treasures we have received from them as well as by our dignity as sons of God and heirs to His kingdom—will defend Catholic tradition, uphold it, live it, and hand it on intact. For those of us who believe that the Tridentine rite represents, as a whole and in its parts, the pinnacle of the Roman rite as it gradually unfolded by the synergy of the Church and the Holy Spirit, an altar Missal from circa 948 or even the *editio typica* of Benedict XV from 1920 gives us the stable ground we need.

I have heard the opinion expressed, and I am inclined to agree with it, that it was by a special mercy of Providence that, after a certain point in time, the postconciliar liturgical reformers in their overweening pride simply put aside the old liturgical tradition, as if into a tomb or deep freeze, or like an unwelcome saint exiled to a distant province, and started over more or less from scratch with blank notepads. Had they kept tinkering with the Tridentine liturgical rites in endless updates and revisions, we would have ended up with a messy hybrid of old and new—something far more incoherent and schizophrenic than the Pauline liturgical books, which display a fairly consistent Bauhaus aesthetic. The reformers took a more audacious route, one inconceivable to a believing Catholic, and thereby set themselves up for total failure; meanwhile, the traditional liturgy had been left more or less intact for rediscovery. "O happy fault that preserved for us so great a liturgy!" Of course, as we have seen, some serious damage had already been done to Holy Week, vigils, octaves, vestments, and so forth, but in the larger scheme of things, these Pacellian missteps are easy to correct. At this point, the organic development of the Roman rite takes the form of casting off the iconoclasm of the mid-twentieth century and restoring the beauty of the rite in its Tridentine plenitude.

With the wisdom of hindsight, we can identify the unholy spirit behind the changes from 1948 to the eve of the Second Vatican Council and beyond: the spirit of Pistoian rationalism, pastoral utilitarianism, neoscholastic reductionism, false antiquarianism, and, most of all, "presentism," the view that everything should be judged by modern-day notions and adjusted to them. Were *any* of the post-World War II changes good? Yes: it is only to be expected that a few ideas will be on the right track. The prioritizing of the Lenten ferias, with their extremely ancient proper Station Masses, is one example of a good step.[47]

In 586 BC, the Jews of old were violently removed from the Temple in Jerusalem and its sacrificial cultus and led off to exile where they had only

---

[47] Of course the Roman Rite always commemorates the saints whose feasts are not celebrated due to the Lenten ferias, because there is no prejudice in tradition against multiple orations. The CDF decree issued on March 25, 2020, *Cum Sanctissima*, provides for occasions when saints' feasts may once again take precedence over certain Lenten ferias (e.g., Saint Thomas Aquinas on March 7, Saint Gregory the Great on March 12, and Saint Patrick on March 17). It was a gentle correction to a perhaps excessive privileging of every seasonal feria. How ironic that this legislation, which fulfilled one of the desiderata stated in *Summorum Pontificum*, was effectively snubbed by *Traditionis Custodes* less than a year and a half later.

memories of their traditional divine worship. Seventy years later, in 516 BC, they began to return to the land of their fathers—those who, listening to Ezra, longed for true worship and were willing to make a new life in the old land. In our day, the same grace is being given, thanks be to God: at the end of seventy years of liturgical captivity, beginning around 1948 with Pius XII's fateful creation of a liturgical reform commission, not only is the *usus antiquior* coming back to our churches, but the more authentic rites of the *usus antiquior* are returning as well. We are in a position to say with the Hebrew psalmist: *Quis dabit ex Sion salutare Israel? Cum averterit Dominus captivitatem plebis suae, exsultabit Jacob, et laetabitur Israel.* "Who shall give out of Sion the salvation of Israel? When the Lord shall have turned away the captivity of his people, Jacob shall rejoice and Israel shall be glad" (Ps 13:7).

Le CELEBRANT distribué les CIERGES le jour de la CHANDELEUR.   PROCESSION de la CHANDELEUR.

Les TENEBRES.   On porte le St SACREMENT dans le TOMBEAU.

Le FEU nouveau le jour du SAMEDI SAINT.   BENEDICTION du CIERGE PASCAL.

Epilogue

Oppositions

ὁ μὲν οὖν πιστός, ὡς χρή, καὶ ἐρρωμένος οὐδὲ δεῖται λόγου καὶ αἰτίας, ὑπὲρ ὧν ἂν ἐπιταχθῇ, ἀλλ᾽ ἀρκεῖται τῇ παραδόσει μονῇ.

Ho men oun pistos, hōs chrē, kai errhōmenos oude deitai logou kai aitias, huper ōn an epitachthēi, all᾽ arkeitai tēi paradosei monēi.

The faithful man, duly strengthened, requires neither argument nor cause for what has been enjoined, but is satisfied with the tradition alone.

—Saint John Chrysostom

To the cult of man who has made himself God, the Church opposes the cult of God-made-man.

To the absence of God in the world, the Church opposes His Real Presence on the altar.

To the banality and sterility of evil, the Church opposes the wondrous life-giving Cross.

To the sacrificial machinery of liberalism, the Church opposes the one liberating Sacrifice of Calvary.

To the empire of the Prince of this world, the Church opposes the inbreaking of the kingdom of heaven.

To ineffectual laments and humanistic dreams, the Church opposes her potent Sacraments of life and death.

To the hollow monotony of materialism, the Church opposes the adoration and vigilance of hosts of angels, each its own species with its own voice of praise.

To navel-gazing nihilism, the Church opposes the only human beings who are fully real: the saints.

To the worship of free will, the Church opposes the service of charity.

To the obsession with activity, the Church opposes the inscrutable power of resting at the feet of Christ.

To instant communication, the Church opposes timeless communion.

To the pursuit of novelty and relevance, the Church opposes her perpetual newness and essential rightness.

To the stifling self-limitations of modern art, the Church opposes the grandeur and creativity of the arts nurtured in her bosom.

To the noise of the modern world, the Church opposes the still, small voice of God.

To the cacophony of amplified sound, the Church opposes the imperturbable silence of her prayer.

To the enervating clichés of worldly music, the Church opposes the elevating freshness of her chant.

To inundation with empty words and shifting images, the Church opposes one Word of infinite density and one stable set of signs.

To suffocating pleasures of the flesh that end in worms, the Church opposes the flight of contemplation and the glory of resurrection.

To the deathly ennui of life without God, the Church opposes being lost in Christ and found by Him.

To the idolatry of Progress and mindless modernization, the Church opposes the inexhaustible fruitfulness of immemorial Tradition.

If there were ever a body of people that called itself "the Church" but did *not* oppose the world in all these ways, we would know that it is not and cannot be the immaculate Bride of Christ, permanently united to Him, imitating Him, faithful to Him; it is not and cannot be the Mystical Body founded and sustained by Jesus Christ, its Head and Master. This, in turn may prompt the realization that the Church is smaller, more scattered more of a remnant than we had been accustomed to thinking before.

It may also prompt the realization of the unshakeable centrality of traditional religious life, in which all characteristics of the true Church a concentrated and crystallized, enfleshed and exalted.

Acknowledgments

A s mentioned in the preface, this book has had a long gestation. That it has reached a stage where it can be safely entrusted to the publisher—in spite of its remaining imperfections, of which I am only too conscious—owes much to innumerable friends who have freely given of their time discussing our common love of liturgical history and theology, and some of whom offered comments and corrections on the manuscript in full or in part. Deserving of special thanks in this regard are Gregory DiPippo, Stan Metheny, Matthew Roth, Fr. Thomas Crean, and an expert rubrician who must go unnamed. I am also grateful for those who have invited me to give lectures that subsequently became some of the chapters herein: Stuart Chessman, Ronan Reilly, Alex Begin, Frank Bruno, Fr. Richard Cipolla, Fr. Gerald Saguto, and Canon William Avis, among others. Earlier versions of several chapters were published online, at *Rorate Caeli* (chapters 2, 3, 4, 5, and 8), *New Liturgical Movement* (chapter 7 and parts of chapter 6, 10, 11, and 12), *The Remnant* (chapter 9), *OnePeterFive* (parts of chapters 6 and 11), *LifeSiteNews* (part of chapter 11), and *Views from the Choir Loft* (part of chapter 10). The better part of chapters 1 and 12 is published here for the first time. Lastly, I thank Stuart Chessman for his superb translation of Martin Mosebach's Foreword.

Florida Medical Clinic Orlando Health
13602 N 46TH ST
Tampa, FL 33613
813-284-2255

7/9/2024 9:56 AM

PATIENT
James Connolly

BILLED TO
Payment Method: Cash
Reference # 11491863
Type: Sale

ITEM	TOTAL
Copayment amount for today's visit	$30.00
TOTAL	$30.00

Pope Paul VI on the Liturgical Reform

Confusion and Annoyance

Address to a General Audience

March 17, 1965[1]

Our family conversation, in an audience such as this, cannot fail to return to the theme of the day: the application of the liturgical reform to the celebration of Holy Mass. Our desire, if the public nature of this meeting did not prevent it, would be to ask you—as we do in other meetings of a private nature—what your impressions are of this great novelty. It certainly merits everyone's attention. In any case, we believe that your answer to our question would not be dissimilar to others we have been receiving these days.

What do people think about the liturgical reform? The replies can be reduced to two categories. The first category is that of responses that note a certain confusion, and therefore a certain annoyance. Before, these observers say, it was quiet, everyone could pray as he wished, everything was known about the course of the rite; now everything is novelty, surprise, change; even the ringing of the bell at the Sanctus has been abolished; and then those prayers that no one can find any longer [in a daily missal], and standing to receive Communion; and the end of the Mass cut off abruptly after the blessing; everyone making the responses, much moving about, prayers and readings are spoken out loud. . . . In short, there is no more peace and things are understood less than before, and so on.

Translated freshly from the Italian text at the Vatican website. For another translation, see *OL* n. 27. It should be noted that shortly before this (on March 7, 1965), a rite of concelebration and a rite of communion under both kinds were introduced.

We will not criticize these remarks, because we would have to show how they reveal a poor penetration of the meaning of religious ceremonial and allow us to glimpse not a true devotion and a true appreciation of the meaning and worth of the Holy Mass, but rather a certain spiritual laziness, which is not prepared to expend some personal effort of intelligence and participation directed to a better understanding and better fulfillment of this, the most sacred of religious acts, in which we are invited, or rather obliged, to participate.

We will repeat what is being repeated these days by all priests who are pastors of souls and by all good teachers of religion. First, it is inevitable that some confusion and annoyance will arise at the beginning. A practical and spiritual reform of deeply-rooted and piously observed religious habits will naturally produce a little upheaval, which is not always pleasant to everyone. But, secondly, some explanation, some preparation, some thoughtful assistance will soon remove uncertainties and immediately give the sense and taste of a new order. Because, thirdly, one must not believe that after some time one will return to being quiet and devout or lazy, as before. No, the new order must be different, and must prevent and shake the passivity of the faithful present at Holy Mass. Before it was enough to attend; now, it is necessary to participate. Before, presence was enough; now, attention and action are needed. Before, one could doze off and perhaps have a chat; now, however, he must listen and pray.

We hope that celebrants and faithful will very soon be able to obtain the new liturgical books[2] and that, in their new form, whether literary or typographical, these books will reflect the dignity of the old ones.

The assembly will become alive and active—to participate means to let the soul enter into activity, the activity of attention, conversation, song, gesture. The harmony of a communal act, performed not only with external gestures but with the inner movement of the sentiment of faith and piety, gives the rite

---

[2] Note that Paul VI is using the phrase "new liturgical books" in 1965: it was believed by many, including high-ranking figures at the Vatican, that the 1965 changes were the end of the liturgical reform, since it had (more or less) done what could be deduced from a progressive reading of SC. In retrospect, we see that this was only an interim phase to detach the faithful from good custom and to destabilize their piety in ways that would allow the more radical steps that had already been decided on by Bugnini and his associates prior to the Council.

a particular strength and beauty: it becomes a chorus, a concert, the rhythm of an immense wing flying toward the heights of mystery and divine joy.

The second category of comments that reach us about the first celebrations of the new liturgy is, instead, that of enthusiasm and praise. They say: now, at last, we can understand and follow the complicated and mysterious ceremony; at last we are enjoying it; at last, the priest speaks to the faithful, and we see that he acts with them and for them. We have moving testimonies, from ordinary people, from children and youths, from critics and observers, from pious people earnest in fervor and prayer, from men of wide and serious experience and high culture. These are positive testimonies. An old and distinguished gentleman, a great-souled man of the finest discrimination and therefore never spiritually fully satisfied, felt obliged, at the end of the first celebration of the new liturgy, to go up to the celebrant to tell him candidly his happiness at having finally, perhaps for the first time in his life, participated to the full spiritual measure in the holy sacrifice.

It may be that this admiration and this sort of holy excitement will soon subside and settle down into a new and peaceful habit. What is there that man will not grow accustomed to? But it is to be expected that the awareness of the religious intensity demanded by the new form of the rite will not diminish; and with it the consciousness of the obligation to perform two spiritual acts simultaneously: one of true and personal participation in the rite, with all that is essentially religious that this may entail; the other, of communion with the assembly of the faithful, with the "*ecclesia*"—the first of which tends to the love of God, the second to the love of our neighbor. This is the Gospel of charity realizing itself in the souls of our time: it truly something beautiful, new, great, full of light and hope.

But you will have understood, dear sons and daughters, that this liturgical innovation, this spiritual rebirth, cannot take place without your willing and serious participation. We so desire your cooperation that, as you have seen, we have made it the subject of our talk; and in the confidence that you will indeed give your cooperation, we promise you many, many graces from the Lord, of which Our Apostolic Blessing wishes to assure each of you from now on.

The Mass is the Same

Address to a General Audience
November 19, 1969[3]

Our Dear Sons and Daughters:

1. We wish to draw your attention to an event about to occur in the Latin Catholic Church: the introduction of the liturgy of the new rite of the Mass. It will become obligatory in Italian dioceses from the First Sunday of Advent, which this year falls on November 30. The Mass will be celebrated in a rather different manner from that in which we have been accustomed to celebrate it in the last four centuries, from the reign of St. Pius V, after the Council of Trent, down to the present.

2. This change has something astonishing about it, something extraordinary. This is because the Mass is regarded as the traditional and untouchable expression of our religious worship and the authenticity of our faith. We ask ourselves, how could such a change be made? What effect will it have on those who attend Holy Mass? Answers will be given to these questions, and to others like them, arising from this innovation. You will hear the answers in all the churches. They will be amply repeated there and in all religious publications, in all schools where Christian doctrine is taught. We exhort you to pay attention to them. In that way you will be able to get a clearer and deeper idea of the stupendous and mysterious notion of the Mass.

3. But in this brief and simple discourse We will try only to relieve your minds of the first, spontaneous difficulties which this change arouses. We will do so in relation to the first three questions which immediately come to mind because of it.

4. How could such a change be made? Answer: It is due to the will expressed by the Ecumenical Council held not long ago. The Council decreed: "The rite of the Mass is to be revised in such a way that the intrinsic nature and purpose of its several parts, as also the connection between them, can be more clearly manifested, and that devout and active participation by the faithful can be more easily accomplished.

---

[3]　Translation from *L'Osservatore Romano*, English edition, November 27, 1969. For an alternative translation, see *DOL* n. 211.

5. "For this purpose the rites are to be simplified, while due care is taken to preserve their substance. Elements which, with the passage of time, came to be duplicated, or were added with but little advantage, are now to be discarded. Where opportunity allows or necessity demands, other elements which have suffered injury through accidents of history are now to be restored to the earlier norm of the Holy Fathers" (*Sacrosanctum Concilium* 50).

6. The reform which is about to be brought into being is therefore a response to an authoritative mandate from the Church. It is an act of obedience. It is an act of coherence of the Church with herself. It is a step forward for her authentic tradition. It is a demonstration of fidelity and vitality, to which we all must give prompt assent.

7. It is not an arbitrary act. It is not a transitory or optional experiment. It is not some dilettante's improvisation. It is a law. It has been thought out by authoritative experts of sacred Liturgy; it has been discussed and meditated upon for a long time. We shall do well to accept it with joyful interest and put it into practice punctually, unanimously, and carefully.

8. This reform puts an end to uncertainties, to discussions, to arbitrary abuses. It calls us back to that uniformity of rites and feeling proper to the Catholic Church, the heir and continuation of that first Christian community, which was all "one single heart and a single soul" (Acts 4:32). The choral character of the Church's prayer is one of the strengths of her unity and her catholicity. The change about to be made must not break up that choral character or disturb it. It ought to confirm it and make it resound with a new spirit, the spirit of her youth.

9. The second question is: What exactly are the changes?

10. You will see for yourselves that they consist of many new directions for celebrating the rites. Especially at the beginning, these will call for a certain amount of attention and care. Personal devotion and community sense will make it easy and pleasant to observe these new rules. But keep this clearly in mind: Nothing has been changed of the substance of our traditional Mass. Perhaps some may allow themselves to be carried away by the impression made by some particular ceremony or additional rubric, and thus think that they conceal some alteration or diminution of truths which were acquired by the Catholic faith for ever, and are sanctioned by

it. They might come to believe that the equation between the law of prayer, *lex orandi*, and the law of faith, *lex credendi*, is compromised as a result.

11. It is not so. Absolutely not. Above all, because the rite and the relative rubric are not in themselves a dogmatic definition. Their theological qualification may vary in different degrees according to the liturgical context to which they refer. They are gestures and terms relating to a religious action—experienced and living—of an indescribable mystery of divine presence, not always expressed in a universal way. Only theological criticism can analyze this action and express it in logically satisfying doctrinal formulas. The Mass of the new rite is and remains the same Mass we have always had. If anything, its sameness has been brought out more clearly in some respects.

12. The unity of the Lord's Supper, of the Sacrifice on the cross, of the re-presentation and the renewal of both in the Mass, is inviolably affirmed and celebrated in the new rite just as they were in the old. The Mass is and remains the memorial of Christ's Last Supper. At that Supper the Lord changed the bread and wine into His Body and His Blood, and instituted the Sacrifice of the New Testament. He willed that the Sacrifice should be identically renewed by the power of His Priesthood, conferred on the Apostles. Only the manner of offering is different, namely, an unbloody and sacramental manner; and it is offered in perennial memory of Himself, until His final return (cf. De la Taille, *Mysterium Fidei*, Eluc. IX).

13. In the new rite you will find the relationship between the Liturgy of the Word and the Liturgy of the Eucharist, strictly so called, brought out more clearly, as if the latter were the practical response to the former (cf. Bouyer). You will find how much the assembly of the faithful is called upon to participate in the celebration of the Eucharistic sacrifice, and how in the Mass they are and fully feel themselves "the Church." You will also see other marvelous features of our Mass. But do not think that these things are aimed at altering its genuine and traditional essence.

14. Rather try to see how the Church desires to give greater efficacy to her liturgical message through this new and more expansive liturgical language, how she wishes to bring home the message to each of her faithful, and to the whole body of the People of God, in a more direct and pastoral way.

15. In like manner We reply to the third question: What will be the results of this innovation? The results expected, or rather desired, are that the faithful will participate in the liturgical mystery with more understanding, in a more practical, a more enjoyable, and a more sanctifying way. That is, they will hear the Word of God, which lives and echoes down the centuries and in our individual souls; and they will likewise share in the mystical reality of Christ's sacramental and propitiatory sacrifice.

16. So do not let us talk about "the new Mass." Let us rather speak of the new epoch in the Church's life.

With Our Apostolic Benediction.

Changes in Mass for Greater Apostolate

Address to a General Audience
November 26, 1969[4]

Our Dear Sons and Daughters:

1. We ask you to turn your minds once more to the liturgical innovation of the new rite of the Mass. This new rite will be introduced into our celebration of the holy Sacrifice starting from Sunday next which is the first of Advent, November 30.

2. A new rite of the Mass: a change in a venerable tradition that has gone on for centuries. This is something that affects our hereditary religious patrimony, which seemed to enjoy the privilege of being untouchable and settled. It seemed to bring the prayer of our forefathers and our saints to our lips and to give us the comfort of feeling faithful to our spiritual past, which we kept alive to pass it on to the generations ahead.

3. It is at such a moment as this that we get a better understanding of the value of historical tradition and the communion of the saints. This change will affect the ceremonies of the Mass. We shall become aware, perhaps with some feeling of annoyance, that the ceremonies at the altar are no longer being carried out with the same words and gestures to which we are accustomed—perhaps so much accustomed that we no longer took notice of them. This change also touches the faithful. It is intended to

Translation from *L'Osservatore Romano*, English edition, December 4, 1969. For an alternative translation, see *DOL* n. 212.

interest each one of those present, to draw them out of their customary personal devotions or their usual torpor.

4. We must prepare for this many-sided inconvenience. It is the kind of upset caused by every novelty that breaks in on our habits. We shall notice that pious persons are disturbed most, because they have their own respectable way of hearing Mass, and they will feel shaken out of their usual thoughts and obliged to follow those of others. Even priests may feel some annoyance in this respect.

5. So what is to be done on this special and historical occasion? First of all, we must prepare ourselves. This novelty is no small thing. We should not let ourselves be surprised by the nature, or even the nuisance, of its exterior forms. As intelligent persons and conscientious faithful we should find out as much as we can about this innovation. It will not be hard to do so, because of the many fine efforts being made by the Church and by publishers. As We said on another occasion, we shall do well to take into account the motives for this grave change. The first is obedience to the Council. That obedience now implies obedience to the bishops, who interpret the Council's prescriptions and put them into practice.

6. This first reason is not simply canonical—relating to an external precept. It is connected with the charism of the liturgical act. In other words, it is linked with the power and efficacy of the Church's prayer, the most authoritative utterance of which comes from the bishop. This is also true of priests, who help the bishop in his ministry, and like him act *in persone Christi* (cf. St. Ignatius, *ad Eph.* I, V). It is Christ's will, it is the breath o the Holy Spirit which calls the Church to make this change. A propheti moment is occurring in the Mystical Body of Christ, which is the Churcl This moment is shaking the Church, arousing it, obliging it to renew th mysterious art of its prayer.

7. The other reason for the reform is this renewal of prayer. It is aim at associating the assembly of the faithful more closely and more effectiv with the official rite, that of the Word and that of the Eucharistic Sacrifi that constitutes the Mass. For the faithful are also invested with the "ro priesthood"; that is, they are qualified to have supernatural conversat with God.

8. It is here that the greatest newness is going to be noticed, the newness of language. No longer Latin, but the spoken language will be the principal language of the Mass. The introduction of the vernacular will certainly be a great sacrifice for those who know the beauty, the power, and the expressive sacrality of Latin. We are parting with the speech of the Christian centuries; we are becoming like profane intruders in the literary preserve of sacred utterance. We will lose a great part of that stupendous and incomparable artistic and spiritual thing, the Gregorian chant.

9. We have reason indeed for regret, reason almost for bewilderment. What can we put in the place of that language of the angels? We are giving up something of priceless worth. But why? What is more precious than these loftiest of our Church's values?

10. The answer will seem banal, prosaic. Yet it is a good answer, because it is human, because it is apostolic.

11. Understanding of prayer is worth more than the silken garments in which it is royally dressed. Participation by the people is worth more—particularly participation by modern people, so fond of plain language which is easily understood and converted into everyday speech.

12. If the divine Latin language kept us apart from the children, from youth, from the world of labor and of affairs, if it were a dark screen, not a clear window, would it be right for us fishers of souls to maintain it as the exclusive language of prayer and religious intercourse? What did St. Paul have to say about that? Read chapter 14 of the first letter to the Corinthians: "In Church I would rather speak five words with my mind, in order to instruct others, than ten thousand words in a tongue" (I Corinthians 14:19).

13. St. Augustine seems to be commenting on this when he says, "Have no fear of teachers, so long as all are instructed" (PL 38, 228, *Serm.* 37; cf. also *Serm.* 229, p. 1371). But, in any case, the new rite of the Mass provides that the faithful "should be able to sing together, in Latin, at least the parts of the Ordinary of the Mass, especially the Creed and the Lord's Prayer, the Our Father" (*Sacrosanctum Concilium* 19).

14. But, let us bear this well in mind, for our counsel and our comfort: the Latin language will not thereby disappear. It will continue to be the noble language of the Holy See's official acts; it will remain as the means of teaching

in ecclesiastical studies and as the key to the patrimony of our religious, historical, and human culture. If possible, it will reflourish in splendor.

15. Finally, if we look at the matter properly we shall see that the fundamental outline of the Mass is still the traditional one, not only theologically but also spiritually. Indeed, if the rite is carried out as it ought to be, the spiritual aspect will be found to have greater richness. The greater simplicity of the ceremonies, the variety and abundance of scriptural texts, the joint acts of the ministers, the silences which will mark various deeper moments in the rite, will all help to bring this out.

16. But two indispensable requirements above all will make that richness clear: a profound participation by every single one present, and an outpouring of spirit in community charity. These requirements will help to make the Mass more than ever a school of spiritual depth and a peaceful but demanding school of Christian sociology. The soul's relationship with Christ and with the brethren thus attains new and vital intensity. Christ, the victim and the priest, renews and offers up his redeeming sacrifice through the ministry of the Church in the symbolic rite of his last supper. He leaves us his body and blood under the appearances of bread and wine, for our personal and spiritual nourishment, for our fusion in the unity of his redeeming love and his immortal life.

17. But there is still a practical difficulty, which the excellence of the sacred renders not a little important. How can we celebrate this new rite when we have not yet got a complete missal, and there are still so many uncertainties about what to do?

18. To conclude, it will be helpful to read to you some directions from the competent office, namely the Sacred Congregation for Divine Worship. Here they are:

"As regards the obligation of the rite: 1) For the Latin text: Priests who celebrate in Latin, in private or also in public, in cases provided for by the legislation, may use either the Roman Missal or the new rite until November 28, 1971. If they use the Roman Missal, they may nevertheless make use of the three new anaphoras and the Roman Canon, having regard to the provisions respecting the last text (omission of some saints, conclusions, etc.). They may moreover recite the readings and the prayer of the faithful in the vernacular. If they use the new rite, they must follow the official text, with the concessions as regards the vernacular indicated above.

"2) For the vernacular text. In Italy, all those who celebrate in the presence of the people from November 30 next, must use the *Rito della Messa* published by the Italian Episcopal Conference or by another National Conference. On feast days readings shall be taken: either from the Lectionary published by the Italian Center for Liturgical Action, or from the Roman Missal for feast days, as in use heretofore. On ferial days the ferial Lectionary published three years ago shall continue to be used. No problem arises for those who celebrate in private, because they must celebrate in Latin. If a priest celebrates in the vernacular by special indult, as regards the texts, he shall follow what was said above for the Mass with the people; but for the rite he shall follow the Ordo published by the Italian Episcopal Conference."

19. In every case, and at all times, let us remember that "the Mass is a Mystery to be lived in a death of Love. Its divine reality surpasses all words. . . . It is the Action *par excellence*, the very act of our Redemption, in the Memorial which makes it present" (Zundel).

With Our Apostolic Benediction.

I have offered detailed commentary on the foregoing texts in chapter 4. As it happens, Paul VI frequently felt the need to address the "naysayers" who were complaining about the stream of changes to the Roman liturgy in the decade from ca. 1964 to 1974. Pope Paul had a curious way of talking as though a rapturous majority of laity and clergy were rushing to embrace the new form of the Mass with zeal for active participation, like happy citizens of a Communist Workers' Paradise. Evidence both published and anecdotal, together with an ever-more precipitous decline in church attendance throughout the 1960s and 1970s, suggest that no more than a tiny minority felt the "good vibrations" of the Bugnini Boys.[5]

Paul VI's tirades, therefore, were directed not only at the majority of his religionists, which would have been unsaintly enough; in reality they

---

[The] Beach Boys' hit "Good Vibrations" appeared in 1966, the year in between the provisional 1965 missal and the *Missa normativa* of 1967.

THE ONCE AND FUTURE ROMAN RITE

were directed against centuries of traditional Catholic practice that, in spite of whatever faults or room for improvement it may have had, kept large numbers of the baptized attached to the Church and to their Faith with a seriousness of commitment that could rarely be found, and was never surpassed, in religious practice outside of Catholicism.[6]

Courtesy of that mammoth doorstopper called *Documents on the Liturgy 1963–1979*—a book that would enjoy a more accurate acronym if its title were *Documents Undermining Liturgical Life 1963–1979*—I offer additional quotations from Paul VI that reveal the full amplitude (or better, narrowness) of the pontiff's mind as to the meaning of *participatio actuosa* and the flagitious behavior of those who were stubbornly resisting the march of progress.

Address to Italian Bishops, April 14, 1964 (*DOL* 21)

The liturgical reform opens up to us a way to reeducate our people in their religion, to purify and revitalize their forms of worship and devotion, to restore dignity, beauty, simplicity, and good taste to our religious ceremonies. Without such inward and outward renewal there can be little hope for any widespread survival of religious living in today's changed conditions. . . . Promote sacred song, the religious, congregational singing of the people. Remember, if the faithful sing they do not leave the Church; if they do not leave the Church, they keep the faith and live as Christians.

General Audience, January 13, 1965 (*DOL* 24)

Through your [*sc.*, laity's] own endeavor to put the Constitution on the Liturgy into exact and vital effect you show yourselves to have that understanding of the times which Christ recommended to his first disciples (see Mt 16:4) and which the Church today is in the process of awakening and recognizing in adult Catholics. . . . You show that you understand the new way of religion which the current liturgical reform intends to restore. . . . The Church's solicitude now broadens; today it is changing certain aspects of ritual discipline

---

[6] See my article "Could the Traditional Latin Mass Be Improved—And Should It Eve. Attempted?," *NLM*, May 26, 2015.

that are now inadequate and is seeking boldly but thoughtfully to plumb their ecclesial meaning, the demands of community, and the supernatural value of ecclesial worship. To understand this religious program and to enjoy its hoped-for results we must all change our settled way of thinking regarding sacred ceremonies and religious practices as calling for no more than a passive, distracted assistance. We must be fully cognizant of the fact that with the Council a new spiritual pedagogy has been born. That is what is new about the Council and we must not hang back from making ourselves first the pupils and then the masters in this school of prayer now at its inception. It may well happen that the reforms will affect practices both dear to us and still worthy of respect; that the reforms will demand efforts that, at the outset, are a strain. But we must be devout and trusting: the religious and spiritual vista that the Constitution opens up before us is stupendous in its doctrinal profundity and authenticity, in the cogency of its Christian logic, in the purity and richness of its cultural and aesthetic elements, in its response to the character and needs of modern man.

Address to Pastors and Lenten Preachers, March 1, 1965 (*DOL* 25)

Here are some of the issues: to change so many attitudes that in a number of respects are themselves worthy of honor and dearly held; to upset devout and good people by presenting new ways of prayer that they are not going to understand right away; to win over to a personal involvement in communal prayer the many people used to praying—or not praying—in church as they please; to intensify training in prayer and worship in every congregation, that is, to introduce the faithful to new viewpoints, gestures, practices, formularies, and attitudes, amounting to an active part in religion than many are unused to. In a word, the issue is engaging the people of God in the priestly liturgical life. Again, we say that it is a difficult and delicate matter, but adding that it is necessary, obligatory, providential, and renewing. We hope that it will also be satisfying.

Homily at Parish in Rome, March 27, 1966 (*DOL* 33)

The Council has taken the fundamental position that the faithful
have to understand what the priest is saying[7] and to share in the
liturgy; to be not just passive spectators at Mass but souls alive.
. . . Look at the altar, placed now for dialogue with the assembly;
consider the remarkable sacrifice of Latin, the priceless repository
of the Church's treasure. The repository has been opened up, as the
people's own spoken language now becomes part of their prayer.
Lips that have often been still, sealed as it were, now at last begin
to move, as the whole assembly can speak its part in the colloquy.
. . . No longer do we have the sad phenomenon of people being
conversant and vocal about every human subject yet silent and apathetic in the house of God. How sublime it is to hear during Mass
the communal recitation of the Our Father! In this way the Sunday
Mass is not just an obligation but a pleasure, not just fulfilled as a
duty, but claimed as a right.

Paul VI may have been prophetic about contraception, but he was no
prophet when it came to liturgy, as the next passage shows.

General Audience at Castel Gandolfo,
August 13, 1969 (*DOL* 45)

Through an intense and prolonged religious movement, the liturgy, crowned, and, as it were, canonized by Vatican II, has gained
a new importance, dignity, accessibility, and participation in the
consciousness and the spiritual life of the people of God and, we
predict, this will continue even more in the future.

---

[7] This claim is, of course, a bald lie on Paul VI's part, since the Council took no such positio
and in fact took a different one. It was a lie he repeated on dozens of occasions, and one th
men like Pope Francis and Archbishop Roche have been contented to perpetuate. See "T
Council Fathers in Support of Latin: Correcting a Narrative Bias," *NLM*, September 13, 20
See also "Christ's Universal Dominion and the Modern Tower of Babel," in *The Road fr
Hyperpapalism to Catholicism: Rethinking the Papacy in a Time of Ecclesial Disintegration* (V
terloo, ON: Arouca Press, 2022), vol. 2, ch. 58.

General Audience at Castel Gandolfo, August 20, 1969 (*DOL* 46)

A second category, whose ranks have swelled with troubled people after the conciliar reform of the liturgy, includes the suspicious, the criticizers, the malcontents. Disturbed in their devotional practices, these spirits grudgingly resign themselves to the new ways, but make no attempt to understand the reasons for them. They find the new expressions of divine worship unpleasing. They take refuge in their moaning, which takes away their ancient flavor from texts of the past and blocks any taste for what the Church, in this second spring of the liturgy, offers to spirits that are open to the meaning and language of the new rites sanctioned by the wisdom and authority of the postconciliar reform. A not very difficult effort at acceptance and understanding would bring the experience of dignity, simplicity, and newfound antiquity in the new liturgies and would also bring to the sanctuary of each person's self the consolation and life-giving force of community celebrations. The interior life would yield a greater fullness.

General Audience, April 22, 1970 (*DOL* 49)

To go right to the point: community and liturgical prayer is in the process of becoming widespread again, of being shared in and understood; this is indeed a blessing for our people and our era. We also must take notice of the prescriptions of the liturgical reform as they are at work; they represent the will of the Council, have been studied with wise and patient care by foremost liturgists in the Church, and have been counseled by experts in pastoral ministry. It will be the liturgical life, carefully nurtured and fully assimilated into the minds and practice of the Christian people, that will keep awake and alive the religious sense in these secular, desacralized times, and that will give to the Church a new springtime in its spiritual, Christian life.

General Audience, November 3, 1971 (*DOL* 53)

The Church praying (*Ecclesia orans*) has received at the Council its most splendid idealization. We must not forget that regarding the stirring reality of liturgical reform. Great weight, even regarding the spiritual conditions of today's world, is due to that reform because of its originating, pastoral intent to reawaken prayer among the people of God. This is to be a pure and shared prayer, that is, interior and personal, yet at the same time public and communal. Its meaning is not simply a matter of ritual, pertaining to the sacristy or an arcane and merely liturgical erudition. Prayer is to be a religious affirmation, full of faith and life: an apostolic school for all seekers of the life-giving truth; a spiritual challenge thrown down before an atheistic, pagan, and secularized world.

General Audience, August 6, 1975 (*DOL* 57)

The people of God must be made up of believers who know, who participate, and up to a point concelebrate with the priest, the *alter Christus* who speaks for God to the people and for the people to God. The liturgy is a communion of minds, prayers, voices, *agape* or charity. Passive presence is not enough; participation is required. The people must see in the liturgy a school for listening and learning, a sacred celebration presented and guided by the priest, but in which, as a gathering of hearts and voices, they join by their response, their offerings, their prayer, and their song. If the Council and the Holy Year will have strengthened the people in their obligation to participate and sing in the liturgy, they will have succeeded in an achievement of immense value for religion and community. Whoever sings participates and whoever participates is not bored but full of joy. Whoever finds joy in prayer remains and develops as a Christian. Whoever is a Christian is saved.

From our vantage more than fifty years later, as we watch the liturgical reform either imploding on itself or being slowly left behind by an ever-stronger traditionalist movement, we enjoy the hard-won benefit of knowing what must never be done to one's precious inheritance, accompanied by an unshakeable resolve to continue rediscovering and promoting this inheritance for the good of souls. For the great irony is that it is not, and was never, the "new" liturgy that serves as "an apostolic school for all seekers of the life-giving truth; a spiritual challenge thrown down before an atheistic, pagan, and secularized world." Instead, more and more, we see how aptly this description suits the classical Roman rite, which has risen as a phoenix from its ashes.

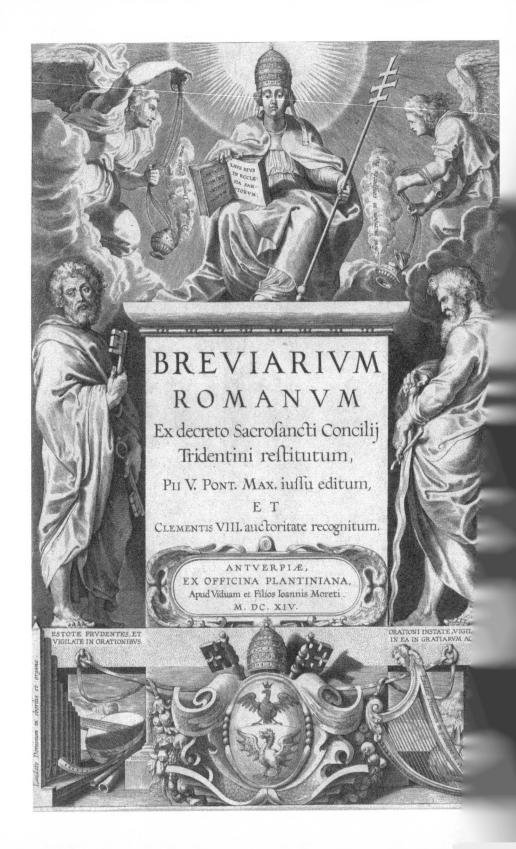

BREVIARIVM
ROMANVM

Ex decreto Sacrosancti Concilij
Tridentini restitutum,

PII V. PONT. MAX. iussu editum,

ET

CLEMENTIS VIII. auctoritate recognitum.

ANTVERPIÆ,
EX OFFICINA PLANTINIANA,
Apud Viduam et Filios Ioannis Moreti.
M. DC. XIV.

ESTOTE PRVDENTES, ET
VIGILATE IN ORATIONIBVS.

ORATIONI INSTATE , VIGIL
IN EA IN GRATIARVM AC

Sources of Epigraphs

FRONT MATTER. Psalm 10:4. Joseph Ratzinger, Foreword to Dom Alcuin Reid's *The Organic Development of the Liturgy*, 2nd ed. (San Francisco: Ignatius Press, 2005), 10–11.

CHAPTER I. Dom Prosper Guéranger, *Institutions liturgiques*, vol. I, 2nd ed. (Paris: Société générale de librairie catholique, 1878), Pt. I, ch. 1, pp. 4–5. Translation mine. / John Henry Newman, *Loss and Gain: The Story of a Convert* [1848] (London: Longmans, Green, and Co., 1906), Part I, chapter 7, p. 44. / H. J. A. [Henry] Sire, *Phoenix from the Ashes: The Making, Unmaking, and Restoration of Catholic Tradition* (Kettering, OH: Angelico Press, 2015), 226.

CHAPTER 2. Guéranger, *Institutions Liturgiques*, vol. I, Pt. I, ch. 1, p. 3. / Herman Schmidt, "The Structure of Mass and Its Restoration, as Reflected in the New Holy Week Ordo," in *Studies in Pastoral Liturgy*, ed. Placid Murray (Maynooth: Furrow Trust, 1961), 25–46, cited in Reid, *Organic Development*, 308. / Radulph of Rivo, *De canonum observantia* (1397), 6, prop. VI, trans. Aelredus Rievallensis, published at *Canticum Salomonis*, December 26, 2021.

CHAPTER 3. Joseph Ratzinger, commentary in *Simandron—Der Wachkopfer. Gedenkschrift für Klaus Gamber (1919–1989)*, ed. Wilhelm Nyssen (Cologne: Luthe-Verlag, 1989), 13–15, cited in *Theologisches*, 20.2 (Feb. 1990), 103–4; translation mine. / Sire, *Phoenix*, 270–71; 274.

CHAPTER 4. Interview with Fr. Philippe Laguérie, "The Battle for the Mass Is Won," interview granted to Anne Le Pape for the daily *Présent*, on January 18, 2022, trans. Jerome Stridon, published at *Rorate Caeli*, January 2022. / Nicolás Gómez Dávila, Aphorism n. 2200, translation from *Don Colacho's Aphorisms*, http://don-colacho.blogspot.com.

Chapter 5. Joseph Ratzinger, letter to Wolfgang Waldstein, original German text in "Zum motu proprio *Summorum Pontificum*," *Una Voce Korrespondenz* 38/3 (2008), 201–14; translation mine. / Sire, *Phoenix*, 451.

Chapter 6. Roberto de Mattei, *Love for the Papacy and Filial Resistance to the Pope in the History of the Church* (Brooklyn, NY: Angelico Press, 2019), 84. / *Catechism of the Catholic Church*, nn. 1124 (in part) and 1125 (*in toto*).

Chapter 7. St. Thomas Aquinas, *Summa theologiae* II-II, qu. 93, art. 1; ibid., ad 3. / Sire, *Phoenix*, 205.

Chapter 8. Nicholas Gihr, *The Holy Sacrifice of the Mass, Dogmatically, Liturgically, and Ascetically Explained* (St. Louis: B. Herder, 1949), 581. / Michael Moreton, quoted by Fr. John Hunwicke, "A Pontifical Act Lacking *Auctoritas*," in *From Benedict's Peace to Francis's War: Catholics Respond to the Motu Proprio* Traditionis Custodes *on the Latin Mass*, ed. Peter Kwasniewski (Brooklyn, NY: Angelico Press, 2021), 31. / Guéranger, *Institutions liturgiques 1840–1851: Extraits* (Vouillé: Éditions de Chiré, 1977), 107; translation from http://catholicapologetics.info/modernproblems/newmass/antigy.htm.

Chapter 9. Martin Mosebach, *Subversive Catholicism: Papacy, Liturgy, Church*, trans. Sebastian Condon and Graham Harrison (Brooklyn: Angelico Press, 2019), 66–67. / Roberto de Mattei, "Reflections on the Liturgical Reform," in *Looking Again at the Question of the Liturgy with Cardinal Ratzinger: Proceedings of the July 2001 Fontgombault Liturgical Conference*, ed. Alcuin Reid (Farnborough, UK: St. Michael's Abbey Press 2003), 136.

Chapter 10. Dom Ansgar Vonier, *The Collected Works of Abbot Vonier* (London: Burns Oates, 1952), vol. 2, p. 82. / Sire, *Phoenix*, 276.

Chapter 11. Wisdom 3:11, 19; 4:3–5. / Job 13:4–5, 7, 11–12. / Psalm 72:18–20. / Psalm 87:13.

Chapter 12. Abbé Franck Quoëx, "Le Messe, notre trésor," Revue *Baptistère*, n. 1 (March 2003), http://salve-regina.com/index.php?tit La_Messe,_notre_trésor; translation mine. / Nicolás Gómez Dávila, Aphorism n. 1297, translation from *Don Colacho's Aphorisms*, http://don-co ho.blogspot.com.

Sources of Artwork

All the artworks in this book (including that on the cover) are public domain copyright-free images made available by the Rijksmuseum of Amsterdam. Descriptions are courtesy of the museum. The page on which the work appears is given in the left column.

Select Bibliography

This bibliography does not list all the works cited throughout this book. Its purpose, rather, is to recommend books that the author has found helpful in furnishing the background to, offering illustrations of, or developing further the topics taken up in these pages. There is no attempt at being comprehensive, since additional books could be listed in each category. Readers looking for more extensive bibliographies will find them in my other works on the liturgy as well as in Michael Fiedrowicz's *The Traditional Mass*. The categories below overlap to some degree.

The Classical Roman Rite and the Tridentine Mass

Hebdomada Sancta. The Rites and Ceremonies for Use by the Laity. Holy Week Pre-1955 Liturgy, Latin and English. N.p.: Roman Seraphic Books, 2021.

Beaubien, Richer-Marie. *Your Mass and Your Life.* Translated by Ella-Marie Cooper. Five volumes. Saint Marys, KS: Angelus Press, 2020.

Bellarmine, St. Robert. *On the Most Holy Sacrifice of the Mass.* Translated by Ryan Grant. Post Falls, ID: Mediatrix Press, 2020.

Bergman, Lisa. *Treasure and Tradition: The Ultimate Guide to the Latin Mass.* Homer Glen, IL: St. Augustine Academy Press, 2014.

de Chivré, Bernard-Marie. *The Mass of Saint Pius V: Spiritual and Theological Commentaries.* Translated by Ann Marie Temple. Winona, MN: STAS Editions, 2007.

Dulac, Raymond. *In Defence of the Roman Mass.* Translated by Peadar Walsh. N.p.: Te Deum Press, 2020.

Fiedrowicz, Michael. *The Traditional Mass: History, Form, and Theology of the Classical Roman Rite.* Translated by Rose Pfeifer. Brooklyn, NY: Angelico Press, 2020.

Gihr, Nicholas. *The Holy Sacrifice of the Mass Dogmatically, Liturgically, and Ascetically Explained*. St. Louis: B. Herder, 1949.

Guéranger, Dom Prosper. *The Traditional Latin Mass Explained*. Translated by Dom Laurence Shepherd. Brooklyn, NY: Angelico Press, 2017.

Lefebvre, Archbishop Marcel. *The Mass of All Time*. Edited by Fr. Patrick Troadec. Translated by Angelus Press. Kansas City, MO: Angelus Press, 2007.

Lefebvre, Dom Gaspar. *St. Andrew Daily Missal*. Great Falls, MT: St. Bonaventure Publications, 1999. [This missal features the pre-55 liturgical calendar and contains the traditional Holy Week.]

Leonard of Port Maurice, St. *The Hidden Treasure: Holy Mass*. Charlotte, NC: TAN Books, 2012.

Ross Williamson, Hugh. *The Great Prayer: Concerning the Canon of the Mass*. Leominster: Gracewing, 2009.

Spataro, Roberto. *In Praise of the Tridentine Mass and of Latin, Language of the Church*. Translated by Zachary Thomas. Brooklyn, NY: Angelico Press, 2019.

von Cochem, Martin. *The Incredible Catholic Mass*. Originally published in English as *Cochem's Explanation of the Holy Sacrifice of the Mass*. Charlotte, NC: TAN Books, 2012.

Walsh, Milton. *In Memory of Me: A Meditation on the Roman Canon*. San Francisco: Ignatius Press, 2011.

Comparative or Critical Studies

(Anon.) *The Problem of the Liturgical Reform: A Theological and Liturgical Study*. Kansas City, MO: Angelus Press, 2001.

Belleza, Jose Isidro. *"Lex Loquendi, Lex Orandi": On the Reform of the Roman Offertoria*. Berkeley, CA: T.S.O. Publishing, 2019.

Byrne, Carol. *Born of Revolution: A Misconceived Liturgical Movement*. Volume 1: "Active Participation." N.p.: Holyrood Press, 2020.

Casini, Tito. *The Torn Tunic. Letter of a Catholic on the "Liturgical Reform.* Originally published by Fidelity Books in 1967; repr. Brooklyn, NY: Angelico Press, 2020.

Cekada, Anthony. *Work of Human Hands: A Theological Critique of the Mass of Paul VI*. West Chester, OH: Philothea Press, 2010.

Coomaraswamy, Rama P. *The Problems with the Other Sacraments Apart from the New Mass*. San Rafael, CA: Reviviscimus, 2010.

Davies, Michael. *Liturgical Time Bombs in Vatican II. The Destruction of Catholic Faith Through Changes in Catholic Worship*. Rockford, IL: TAN Books, 2003.

———. *Pope Paul's New Mass*. Kansas City, MO: Angelus Press, 2009.

Dobszay, László. *The Restoration and Organic Development of the Roman Rite*. Edited by Laurence Paul Hemming. London/New York: T&T Clark, 2010.

Farret d'Astiès, Cyril. *Un heureux anniversaire? Essai sur les cinquante ans du missel de Paul VI*. Paris: Presses des Déliverance, 2020.

Gamber, Klaus. *The Reform of the Roman Liturgy: Its Problems and Background*. Translated by Klaus D. Grimm. San Juan Capistrano, CA: Una Voce Press and Harrison, NY: The Foundation for Catholic Reform, 1993.

Goddard, Philip J. *Festa Paschalia: A History of the Holy Week Liturgy in the Roman Rite*. Leominster: Gracewing, 2011.

Graham, Daniel. *"Lex Orandi": Comparing the Traditional and Novus Ordo Rites of the Seven Sacraments*. N.p.: Preview Press, 2015.

Hazell, Matthew, ed. *Index Lectionum: A Comparative Table of Readings for the Ordinary and Extraordinary Forms of the Roman Rite*. N.p.: Lectionary Study Aids, 2016.

Kwasniewski, Peter A., ed. *From Benedict's Peace to Francis's War: Catholics Respond to the Motu Proprio* Traditionis Custodes *on the Latin Mass*. Brooklyn, NY: Angelico Press, 2021.

———. *Ministers of Christ: Recovering the Roles of Clergy and Laity in an Age of Confusion*. Manchester, NH: Crisis Publications, 2021.

———. *Noble Beauty, Transcendent Holiness: Why the Modern Age Needs the Mass of Ages*. Kettering, OH: Angelico Press, 2017.

———. *Resurgent in the Midst of Crisis: Sacred Liturgy, the Traditional Latin Mass, and Renewal in the Church*. Kettering, OH: Angelico Press, 2014.

———. *Reclaiming Our Roman Catholic Birthright: The Genius and Timeliness of the Traditional Latin Mass*. Brooklyn, NY: Angelico Press, 2020.

———. *Tradition and Sanity: Conversations and Dialogues of a Postconciliar Exile*. Brooklyn, NY: Angelico Press, 2018.

Lamont, John. "Is the Mass of Paul VI Licit?" *Dialogos Institute*, March 20, 2022. http://dialogos-institute.org/blog/wordpress/disputation-on-the-1970-missal-part-1-dr-john-lamont/.

Leone, Don Pietro. *The Destruction of the Roman Rite*. Fitzwilliam, NH: Loreto Publications, 2017.

Mole, John W. *Whither the Roman Rite?* Ottawa: Word of God Hour, 2000.

Mosebach, Martin. *The Heresy of Formlessness: The Roman Liturgy and Its Enemy*. Revised and expanded edition. Translated by Graham Harrison. Brooklyn, NY: Angelico Press, 2018.

———. *Subversive Catholicism: Papacy, Liturgy, Church*. Translated by Sebastian Condon and Graham Harrison. Brooklyn: Angelico Press, 2019.

Nichols, Aidan. *Looking at the Liturgy: A Critical View of Its Contemporary Form*. San Francisco: Ignatius Press, 1996.

Ottaviani, Alfredo Cardinal, Antonio Cardinal Bacci, and a Group of Roman Theologians. *The Ottaviani Intervention: Short Critical Study of the New Order of Mass*. Translated by Anthony Cekada. West Chester, OH: Philothea Press, 2010.

Pristas, Lauren. *The Collects of the Roman Missals: A Comparative Study of the Sundays in Proper Seasons Before and After the Second Vatican Council*. London/New York: Bloomsbury T&T Clark, 2013.

Ross Williamson, Hugh. *The Great Betrayal: Thoughts on the Destruction of the Mass*. Waterloo, ON: Arouca Press, 2021.

Schneider, Athanasius. *The Catholic Mass: Steps to Restore the Centrality of God in the Liturgy*. Manchester, NH: Sophia Institute Press, 2022.

Shaw, Joseph, ed. *The Case for Liturgical Restoration*. Brooklyn, NY: Angelico Press, 2019.

Wetherell, John. *"Lex Orandi, Lex Credendi": An Examination of the Ethos the Tridentine Mass and That of the Novus Ordo of Paul VI*. Cambridge: The Saint Joan Press, 2005.

Various Liturgical Subjects

Batiffol, Pierre. *History of the Roman Breviary*. Translated by Atwell M. Y. Baylay. London: Longmans, Green and Co., 1912; repr. N.p.: Forgotten Books, n.d.

Calvet, Dom Gérard. ["A Benedictine monk."] *Discovering the Mass*. Translated by Jean Pierre Pilon. London: The Saint Austin Press, 1999.

————. *The Sacred Liturgy*. London: The Saint Austin Press, 1999.

Dix, Gregory. *The Shape of the Liturgy*. London/New York: Continuum, 2005.

Duffy, Eamon. *The Stripping of the Altars: Traditional Religion in England 1400–1580*. Second edition. New Haven/London: Yale University Press, 2005.

Journet, Charles Cardinal. *The Mass, The Presence of the Sacrifice of the Cross*. Translated by Victor Szczurek, O.Praem. South Bend, IN: St. Augustine's Press, 2008.

Kwasniewski, Peter A. *Holy Bread of Eternal Life: Restoring Eucharistic Reverence in an Age of Impiety*. Manchester, NH: Sophia Institute Press, 2020.

————, ed. *John Henry Newman on Worship, Reverence, and Ritual: A Selection of Texts*. N.p.: Os Justi Press, 2019.

Lang, Uwe Michael. *Signs of the Holy One: Liturgy, Ritual, and Expression of the Sacred*. San Francisco: Ignatius Press, 2015.

————. *Turning Towards the Lord: Orientation in Liturgical Prayer*. San Francisco: Ignatius Press, 2004.

————. *The Voice of the Church at Prayer: Reflections on Liturgy and Language*. San Francisco: Ignatius Press, 2012.

Martin, Marie-Madeleine. *Immortal Latin*. Translated by Brian Welter. Waterloo, OH: Arouca Press, 2022.

Monti, James. *A Sense of the Sacred: Roman Catholic Worship in the Middle Ages*. San Francisco: Ignatius Press, 2012.

Parsch, Pius. *The Breviary Explained*. Translated by William Nayden and Carl Hoegerl. St. Louis: B. Herder Book Co., 1952; repr. N.p.: Os Justi Press, n.d.

Ratzinger, Cardinal Joseph. *The Spirit of the Liturgy*. Translated by John Saward. Commemorative edition, with Romano Guardini's work of the same name. San Francisco: Ignatius Press, 2018.

——. *Theology of the Liturgy: The Sacramental Foundation of Christian Existence. Collected Works of Joseph Ratzinger*, volume 11. Edited by Michael J. Miller. San Francisco: Ignatius Press, 2014.

Reid, Alcuin, ed. *Liturgy in the Twenty-First Century: Contemporary Issues and Perspectives*. London/New York: Bloomsbury T&T Clark, 2016.

——, ed. *T&T Clark Companion to Liturgy*. London/New York: Bloomsbury T&T Clark, 2016.

Tück, Jan-Heiner. *A Gift of Presence: The Theology and Poetry of the Eucharist in Thomas Aquinas*. Translated by Scott G. Hefelfinger. Washington, DC: Catholic University of America Press, 2018.

von Hildebrand, Dietrich. *Liturgy and Personality*. Steubenville, OH: Hildebrand Project, 2016.

Historical and Biographical

Amerio, Romano. *Iota Unum: A Study of Changes in the Catholic Church in the XXth Century*. Translated by John P. Parsons. Kansas City: Sarto House, 1996.

Blanchard, Shaun. *The Synod of Pistoia and Vatican II: Jansenism and the Struggle for Catholic Reform*. New York: Oxford University Press, 2020.

Bolton, Charles A. *Church Reform in 18th-Century Italy (The Synod of Pistoia, 1786)*. The Hague: Martinus Nijhoff, 1969.

Bullivant, Stephen. *Mass Exodus: Catholic Disaffiliation in Britain and America since Vatican II*. Oxford: Oxford University Press, 2019.

Chiron, Yves. *Annibale Bugnini, Reformer of the Liturgy*. Translated by John Pepino. Brooklyn, NY: Angelico Press, 2018.

——. *Paul VI: The Divided Pope*. Translated by James Walther. Brooklyn, NY: Angelico Press, 2022.

Davies, Michael. *Cranmer's Godly Order: The Destruction of Catholic through Liturgical Change*. Fort Collins, CO: Roman Catholic Books, 1995.

————. *Modernism: Developed from a lecture delivered to Pro Ecclesia et Pontifice*. N.p.: Pro Ecclesia et Pontifice, n.d.

de Mattei, Roberto. *Love for the Papacy and Filial Resistance to the Pope in the History of the Church*. Brooklyn, NY: Angelico Press, 2019.

————. *Saint Pius V*. Translated by Giuseppe Pellegrino. Manchester, NH: Sophia Institute Press, 2021.

————. *The Second Vatican Council: An Unwritten Story*. Translated by Patrick T. Brannan, Michael J. Miller, and Kenneth D. Whitehead. Edited by Michael J. Miller. Fitzwilliam, NH: Loreto Publications, 2012.

Dwyer, Robert J. *Ecclesiastes: The Book of Archbishop Robert Dwyer. A Selection of His Writings*. Edited by Albert J. Steiss. Second ed. Waterloo, ON: Arouca Press, 2021.

Fanous, Daniel. *A Silent Patriarch. Kyrillos VI (1902–1971): Life and Legacy*. Yonkers, NY: St. Vladimir's Seminary Press, 2019.

Gnocchi, Alessandro and Mario Palmaro. *The Last Mass of Padre Pio*. Translated by Marianna Gattozzi. Kansas City, MO: Angelus Press, 2019.

Graber, Bishop Rudolf. *Athanasius and the Church of Our Time*. Translated by Susan Johnson. Palmdale, CA: Omni Publications, n.d.

Hull, Geoffrey. *The Banished Heart: Origins of Heteropraxis in the Catholic Church*. London/New York: T&T Clark, 2010.

Meloni, Julia. *The St. Gallen Mafia: Exposing the Secret Reform Group within the Church*. Gastonia, NC: TAN Books, 2021.

Muggeridge, Anne Roche. *The Desolate City: Revolution in the Catholic Church*. Revised and expanded. New York: HarperCollins, 1990.

Murr, Charles Theodore. *The Godmother: Madre Pascalina, A Feminine Tour de Force*. N.p.: Independently published, 2017.

Murr, Charles Theodore. *Murder in the 33rd Degree: The Gagnon Investigation into Vatican Freemasonry*. N.p.: Independently published, 2022.

Reid, Alcuin, ed. *A Bitter Trial: Evelyn Waugh and John Carmel Cardinal Heenan on the Liturgical Changes*. San Francisco: Ignatius Press, 2011.

————. *The Organic Development of the Liturgy. The Principles of Liturgical Reform and Their Relation to the Twentieth-Century Liturgical*

Movement Prior to the Second Vatican Council. Second edition. San
Francisco: Ignatius Press, 2005.

Sire, H. J. A. [Henry]. *Phoenix from the Ashes: The Making, Unmaking,
and Restoration of Catholic Tradition.* Kettering, OH: Angelico Press,
2015.

The Traditionalist Movement

*Eleven Surveys for the History: The Ancient Liturgy and the Motu Proprio
Summorum Pontificum as Seen by the Catholic Faithful of Nine Coun-
tries in the World.* Les Dossiers d'Oremus/Paix Liturgique. Croissy:
Oremus, 2017.

*Priest, Where Is Thy Mass? Mass, Where Is Thy Priest? Seventeen Priests Tell
Why They Celebrate the Latin Mass.* Second edition. Kansas City, MO:
Angelus Press, 2004.

Chessman, Stuart. *Faith of Our Fathers: A Brief History of Catholic Traditionalism in the United States, from Triumph to* Traditionis Custodes.
Brooklyn, NY: Angelico Press, 2022.

Dashiell, David, ed. *Ever Ancient, Ever New: Why Younger Generations Are
Embracing Traditional Catholicism.* Gastonia, NC: TAN Books, 2022.

Houghton, Bryan. *Judith's Marriage.* Originally published by Credo House,
1987; repr. Brooklyn, NY: Angelico Press, 2020.

———. *Mitre and Crook.* Originally published by Arlington House Books,
1979; repr. Brooklyn, NY: Angelico Press, 2019.

———. *Unwanted Priest: The Autobiography of a Latin Mass Exile.* Brooklyn, NY: Angelico Press, 2022.

Kwasniewski, Peter A. *True Obedience in the Church: A Guide to Discernment in Challenging Times.* Manchester, NH: Sophia Institute Press,
2021.

Larson, Anne M., ed. *Love in the Ruins: Modern Catholics in Search of th*
Ancient Faith. Kansas City: Angelus Press, 2009.

Mohrmann, Christine. *Liturgical Latin: Its Origins and Character.* Washington, DC: Catholic University of America Press, 1957. [Repri
available from Lulu.]

Normandin, Yves. *Pastor Out in the Cold. The Story of Fr. Normandin's Fight for the Latin Mass in Canada*. St. Marys, KS: Angelus Press, 2021.

Studies on Tradition

Agius, George. *Tradition and the Church*. Rockford, IL: TAN Books, 2005.

Dekert, Tomasz. "Tradition, the Pope, and Liturgical Reform: A Problematization of Tradition in the Catholic Church and Catholic–Orthodox Rapprochement." *Nova et Vetera* (English ed.) 20.1 (2022): 101–31.

de Mattei, Roberto. *Apologia for Tradition. A Defense of Tradition Grounded in the Historical Context of the Faith*. Translated by Michael J. Miller. Kansas City, MO: Angelus Press, 2019.

Kwasniewski, Peter A. "The Pope's Boundedness to Tradition as a Legislative Limit." In Kwasniewski, ed., *From Benedict's Peace to Francis's War: Catholics Respond to the Motu Proprio* Traditionis Custodes *on the Latin Mass*, 222–47. Brooklyn, NY: Angelico Press, 2021.

McClay, Wilfred M. "The Claims of Memory." *First Things*, January 2022. Available online.

Pieper, Josef. *Tradition as Challenge. Essays and Speeches*. Translated by Dan Farrelly. South Bend, IN: St. Augustine's Press, 2015.

———. *Tradition: Concept and Claim*. Translated by E. Christian Kopff. South Bend, IN: St. Augustine's Press, 2010.

Ripperger, Chad. *Topics on Tradition*. N.p.: Sensus Traditionis Press, 2013.

Stanley, Tim. *Whatever Happened to Tradition? History, Belonging, and the Future of the West*. New York: Bloomsbury Continuum, 2021.

Miscellaneous

Calderón, Álvaro. *Prometheus: The Religion of Man. An Essay on the Hermeneutics of the Second Vatican Council*. Translated by Inés de Erausquin. Saint Marys, MS: Angelus Press, 2021.

Silveira, Arnaldo Vidigal Xavier. *Can Documents of the Magisterium of the Church Contain Errors? Can the Catholic Faithful Resist Them?* Translated by John R. Spann and José Aloisio A. Schelini. Spring Grove, PA: The American Society for the Defense of Tradition, Family and Property, 2015.

————. *Can a Pope Be…a Heretic? The Theological Hypothesis of a Heretical Pope.* Translated by John Spann. Porto: Caminhos Romanos, 2018.

Kwasniewski, Peter A., ed. *Are Canonizations Infallible? Revisiting a Disputed Question.* Waterloo, ON: Arouca Press, 2021.

————. *The Road from Hyperpapalism to Catholicism: Rethinking the Papacy in a Time of Ecclesial Disintegration.* 2 volumes. Arouca Press, 2022.

Lamont, John R. T. and Claudio Pierantoni, eds. *Defending the Faith against Present Heresies.* Waterloo, ON: Arouca Press, 2020.

Martin, Malachi. *Windswept House: A Vatican Novel.* New York: Doubleday, 1996.

Schneider, Athanasius, and Diane Montagna. *Christus Vincit. Christ's Triumph Over the Darkness of the Age.* Brooklyn, NY: Angelico Press, 2019.

Index

In this index, as in the book, certain Vatican "dicasteries" (as they are known since Pentecost Sunday 2022) are referred to by their former names, to retain historical accuracy, e.g., "Congregation for Divine Worship [and the Discipline of the Sacraments]."

About the Author

Peter A. Kwasniewski holds a BA in Liberal Arts from Thomas Aquinas College and an MA and PhD in Philosophy from the Catholic University of America, with a specialization in the thought of Saint Thomas Aquinas. After teaching at the International Theological Institute in Austria, he joined the founding team of Wyoming Catholic College, where he taught theology, philosophy, music, and art history and directed the choir and schola until 2018. Today, he is a full-time writer and public speaker whose work is seen at websites and in periodicals such as *New Liturgical Movement, OnePeterFive, Rorate Caeli, The Remnant, Catholic Family News,* and *Latin Mass Magazine.* Dr. Kwasniewski has published extensively in academic and popular venues on sacramental and liturgical theology, the history and aesthetics of music, Catholic Social Teaching, and issues in the contemporary Church. He has written or edited many books, including most recently *True Obedience in the Church: A Guide to Discernment in Challenging Times* (Sophia Institute Press, 2021) and *The Road from Hyperpapalism to Catholicism: Rethinking the Papacy in a Time of Ecclesial Disintegration* (Arouca Press, 2022). His work has been translated into at least eighteen languages. For more information, visit his website: www.peterkwasniewski.com.